CAREER DEVELOPMENT AND PLANNING

M000107020

CAREER DEVELOPMENT AND PLANNING
A COMPREHENSIVE APPROACH

Third Edition

Robert C. Reardon, Ph.D.
Florida State University

Janet G. Lenz, Ph.D.
Florida State University

James P. Sampson, Jr., Ph.D.
Florida State University

Gary W. Peterson, Ph.D.
Florida State University

CENGAGE
Learning™

Australia • Brazil • Japan • Korea • Mexico • Singapore • Spain • United Kingdom • United States

**Career Development and Planning:
A Comprehensive Approach, 3e**
Robert C. Reardon, PhD,
Janet G. Lenz, PhD
James P. Sampson, Jr., PhD,
Gary W. Peterson, PhD

V.P Product Development: Dreis Van Landuyt

Developmental Editor: Sarah Blasco

Technology Project Manager: Angela Makowski

Marketing Coordinator: Lydia Lestar

Custom Production Editor: Kim Fry

Permissions Specialist: Kalina Ingham Hintz

Manufacturing Manager: Donna M. Brown

Sr. Production Coordinator: Robin Richie

Cover Image: Getty Images

Compositor: Integra Software Services Pvt. Ltd.

© 2009, 2006 Cengage Learning

ALL RIGHTS RESERVED. No part of this work covered by the copyright herein may be reproduced, transmitted, stored or used in any form or by any means graphic, electronic, or mechanical, including but not limited to photocopying, recording, scanning, digitizing, taping, Web distribution, information networks, or information storage and retrieval systems, except as permitted under Section 107 or 108 of the 1976 United States Copyright Act, without the prior written permission of the publisher.

For product information and technology assistance, contact us at
Cengage Learning Customer & Sales Support, 1-800-354-9706

For permission to use material from this text or product,
submit all requests online at **cengage.com/permissions**
Further permissions questions can be emailed to
permissionrequest@cengage.com

Library of Congress Control Number: 2005906357

Book ISBN-13: 978-1-426-63135-1

Book ISBN-10: 1-426-63135-9

Cengage Learning
5191 Natorp Blvd.
Mason, OH 45040
USA

Cengage Learning is a leading provider of customized learning solutions with office locations around the globe, including Singapore, the United Kingdom, Australia, Mexico, Brazil, and Japan. Locate your local office at:
international.cengage.com/region

Cengage Learning products are represented in Canada by Nelson Education, Ltd.

Visit our corporate website at **cengage.com**

Printed in the United States of America
3 4 5 6 7 8 12 11 10

DEDICATION

To over two hundred and fifty team-teaching members who have feely shared their time, ideas, and talents since 1973 to make this course and text a better learning experience for students and instructors throughout the world.

CONTENTS

PREFACE TO THE FIRST EDITION

The aim of *Career Development and Planning: A Comprehensive Approach* is to provide instructors and students with a knowledge base drawn from cognitive psychology that can be used to solve career problems and make career decisions. This text and related teaching materials provide a comprehensive, integrated system of career learning activities intended to improve instruction and increase learner outcomes.

In order to meet college level general education requirements, the knowledge base of a textbook is of crucial importance. The three knowledge domains of this text are (1) cognitive and social foundations, (2) the occupational world and work behavior, and (3) career choice and development in individuals and organizations. In this Preface, we discuss learner outcomes, text design, approach, and validation.

LEARNER OUTCOMES

As a result of using this text in a course, students will be able to:

1. Understand the multidisciplinary nature of information in the career and work behavior area and how individuals differ in the use of that information;
2. Understand the acquisition of semantic and personal knowledge;
3. Understand how memory and cognitive information processing relate to human problem solving in general and career decision making more specifically;
4. Understand how the cognitive approach, including the Pyramid of Information-Processing Domains and the CASVE Cycle, are applied to individual career decision making and problem solving;
5. Identify unique, personal information, including self-knowledge, occupational knowledge, decision-making skills, and metacognitions, affecting career development;
6. Understand how interdisciplinary social and behavioral sciences inform persons about the job acquisition and employment process;
7. Formulate personal goals and action plans designed to proactively enhance one's career; and
8. Develop personal, employment-related skills and information.

TEXT DESIGN

The text includes theoretical work in cognitive psychology and relevant knowledge from the applied behavioral sciences.

- Part One (chapters 1–5) focuses on the theory base in cognitive information processing, with detailed, practical examples of the application of the theory in typical career situations, including self-knowledge, occupational knowledge, and decision making.

- Part Two (chapters 6–10) provides a multidisciplinary overlay of issues that affect career decisions, such as economic trends, organizational culture, and dual careers.
- Part Three (chapters 11–15) focuses on concrete steps for executing a strategic career plan and seeking employment, including an examination of familiar topics such as interviewing, resume writing, negotiating, and work adjustment, from a cognitive and multidisciplinary perspective.

We believe *Career Development and Planning: A Comprehensive Approach* is unique among undergraduate career texts. The core of this difference is in the focus on a knowledge base external to the student and on the instructional approach. Viewed as a *figure-ground* relationship, this text focuses on the *ground* or knowledge base in cognitive psychology and applied behavioral science, and the *figure* or student learner who acquires and personalizes this knowledge. Many other texts focus almost exclusively on the *figure* or student, with less attention to the *ground* or knowledge base. Moreover, this text presents material from a Piagetian perspective (Peterson, Sampson, & Reardon, 1991), i.e., moving from more concrete cognitive operations in Part One of the book to more formal operations in Part Two.

In addition:

1. This text draws upon Cognitive Information Processing Theory (CIP; Peterson, Sampson & Reardon, 1991; Peterson, Sampson, Reardon, & Lenz, 1996) and the applied behavioral sciences which can assist faculty in obtaining approvals for offering an undergraduate career course at the university level that merits credit for liberal studies or general education. The text could be adopted by a faculty member in psychology, counselor education, social sciences, or business.
2. This text is written from a specific theoretical perspective (CIP), which provides a coherent organizing schema for the assorted ideas, issues, exercises, materials, and learning activities typically included in career development.
3. This text uses a learning theory model rather than a counseling practice model to guide the organization and presentation of material. This means that each student will be expected to acquire cumulative knowledge about career development, in addition to learning strategies for solving specific individual career problems.
4. This text has been forged in practice, specifically a variable credit, three semester hour, repeatable career course offered in a university setting since 1974.
5. This text provides an interdisciplinary view of career-related topics, including knowledge from the areas of the sociology of work, labor market economics, organizational behavior, family systems, and multicultural views of work and leisure.

The structure and design of this text and related materials are intended to provide a flexible format for variations in academic calendar, scope and level of campus career services, teaching styles, learning styles, and grading practices. Instructors in other settings can readily adapt this text to different course management procedures.

APPROACH

In addition to the text, two additional monographs are designed to enhance instructional effectiveness. The learning activities incorporated into these materials are primarily exploratory and experiential in nature. The *Student Manual* includes questionnaires and other worksheets designed to provide students with an opportunity to develop personal reactions to and interpretations of the text. The *Instructor's Manual and Test Blank* (over 200 pages) completely integrates material from the text and the *Student Manual*.

Career Development and Planning: A Comprehensive Approach is in reality an integration of career resources, interventions, and materials that are typically scattered over a college campus. The effective use of this text is based on the premise that many of those resources can be organized, coordinated, and managed as instructional resources. For example, it is assumed that multimedia library resources on occupations and work organizations are available in the main library or career center library; that computer-based career guidance systems and/or career assessment inventories are available to students somewhere on the campus; that business and professional directories and company profiles are available to students; and that books and media materials on job hunting are available for integration into comprehensive course learning activities.

VALIDATION

The undergraduate career course at Florida State University has undergone peer review in four journal articles (Gerken, Reardon, & Bash, 1988; Lee & Anthony, 1974; Reardon & Regan, 1981; Reardon & Wright, 1999), and has been reported in detail in Gimmestad (1984) and Peterson, Sampson and Reardon (1991). This level of professional review for a career course is unique in the field. This same basic course has been offered since 1974, has been taken by an estimated 6,200 students, has been taught by more than 180 different teaching team members, and has been continually evaluated using the student instructional rating system used at the university. In addition, CIP Theory and related materials have also undergone peer review, and client versions of the theory-based materials used in the text appeared in the *Career Development Quarterly* (Sampson, Peterson, Lenz, & Reardon, 1992) and *Improving Your Career Thoughts: A Workbook for the Career Thoughts Inventory* (Sampson, Peterson, Lenz, Reardon, & Saunders, 1996).

The four authors involved in this course project have successfully collaborated in the past in professional writing and research. On more than 40 occasions, varied combinations of two of the four authors have joined to write a referred journal article or monograph. The authors have more than 90 years of combined professional experience in career theory and practice at the university level. The first author of this text has taught this course more than 45 times.

Finally, we are indebted to many past and present career and academic advisors at Florida State University who provided special assistance in completing this project. These include Kathy Barrett, Byron Folsom, Gerry Frost, Jeff Garis, Jill Lumsden, Linda Mahler, Jeff O'Dell, Debbie Osborn, Lenora Pridgen, Corey Reed, Denise Saunders, Scott Strausberger, Jodi Thiel, Myrna Unger, and Laura Wright. We thank these colleagues for their contributions.

Robert C. Reardon, Ph.D.
Janet G. Lenz, Ph.D.
James P. Sampson, Jr., Ph.D.
Gary W. Peterson, Ph.D.

June 1999
Tallahassee, Florida

REFERENCES

Gerken, D., Reardon, R., & Bash, R. (1988). Revitalizing a career course: The gender roles infusion. *Journal of Career Development, 14*, 269–278.

Gimmestad, M. (1984). Career planning through instruction. In H. Burck & R. Reardon (Eds.), *Career development interventions* (pp. 212–232). Springfield, IL: Charles Thomas.

Johnston, J., Reardon, R., Kramer, G., Lenz, J., Maduros, A., & Sampson, J. (1991). The demand side of general education: Attending to student attitudes and understandings. *Journal of General Education, 40,* 180–200.

Lee, J., & Anthony, W. (1974). An innovative university career planning course. *Journal of College Placement, 35,* 59–60.

Peterson, G., Sampson, J., & Reardon, R. (1991). *Career development and services: A cognitive approach.* Pacific Grove, CA: Brooks/Cole.

Peterson, G., Sampson, J., Reardon, R., & Lenz, J. (1996). A Cognitive Information Processing approach. In D. Brown & L. Brooks (Eds.), *Career choice and development* (3rd, pp. 423-475). San Francisco: Jossey-Bass.

Reardon, R., & Regan, K. (1981). Process evaluation of a career planning course. *Vocational Guidance Quarterly, 29,* 265–269.

Reardon, R., & Wright, L. (1999). The case of Mandy: Applying Holland's Theory and Cognitive Information Processing Theory. *Career Development Quarterly, 47,* 195–203.

Sampson, J., Peterson, G., Lenz, J., & Reardon, R. (1992). A cognitive approach to career services: Translating theory into practice. *Career Development Quarterly, 41,* 67–74.

Sampson, J., Peterson, G., Lenz, J., Reardon, R., & Saunders, D. (1996). *Improving your career thoughts: A workbook for the Career Thoughts Inventory.* Odessa, FL: Psychological Assessment Resources, Inc.

Preface to the Second Edition

After considering (1) the experience gained teaching over 1,500 students in 60 course sections, (2) the use of the first edition at scores of other institutions, and (3) the invitation from Thomson Learning to produce a second edition through their Custom Publishing Division, we introduce this new book.

This second edition draws even more upon Cognitive Information Processing Theory as an organizer for improved understanding of career problem solving and decision making. As before, this is a comprehensive undergraduate career text based on theory and research about career development and vocational behavior. Articles by Folsom, Peterson, Reardon, and Mand (2005, in press); Reed, Reardon, and Leierer, (2001); and Vernick, Reardon, and Sampson (2004) add to the extensive documentation regarding the goals and outcomes of this course intervention.

Goals of the Second Edition

We had six goals in producing this second edition. First, we wanted to update sources and provide new information about occupations and employment. Several chapters were extensively revised by describing new systems for the delivery of occupational information (3), research about employment (7), work arrangements (9), work/life balance (10), and developments with the Internet (12). Other chapter references and links were updated as appropriate.

Second, we removed material from several chapters because the book was simply too dense in some places—there was just too much content for students to learn or instructors to teach in a three-hour semester class. So, we removed some content about theories in chapter 1; reduced the classification systems covered in chapter 3; and condensed chapters 6, 8, 9, 10, and 15.

Third, we took the *Student Manual*, which was a separate book with the first edition of the text, downsized it, and inserted it as appendices A–L to this second edition. Key worksheets, assignments, and other instructional and learning tools can be found in these materials.

Fourth, the *Instructor's Manual* which was produced as separate book with the first edition has been revised and updated. This 200 page document includes alternative teaching activities for 28 classes, over 500 PowerPoint slides, and other teaching tools.

Fifth, and most important, this second edition is printed as a paperback text, which means it is available to students at a cost about 25 percent below the first edition.

Acknowledgements

Finally, many of our Career Center colleagues worked very hard to help us get this second edition ready for the fall 2005. Special thanks to Christin Shumaker and Darrin Carr who assisted with production. Adam Marsh, our Cengage Learning Custom Editor, was most supportive throughout.

We look forward to producing timely, revised editions of this text in the future, and welcome the comments of instructors and students to that end.

Robert C. Reardon, Ph.D.
Janet G. Lenz, Ph.D.
James P. Sampson, Jr., Ph.D.
Gary W. Peterson, Ph.D.

July 2005
Tallahassee, Florida

REFERENCES

Folsom, B., Peterson, G., Reardon, R., & Mann, B. (2005, in press). Impact of a career-planning course on academic performance and graduation. *Journal of College Retention*, 6(4).

Reed, C., Reardon, R., Lenz, J., & Leierer, S. (2001). Reducing negative career thoughts with a career course. *Career Development Quarterly*, 50, 158–167.

Vernick, S., Reardon, R., & Sampson, J. (2004). Process evaluation of a career course: A replication and extension. *Journal of Career Development*, 30, 201–213.

PREFACE TO THE THIRD EDITION

We welcomed the opportunity to create a third edition of our text and related instructional materials for several reasons.

It enabled us to choose a new cover design that shows a pathway or *course* through an ancient forest. We did this because "career" in the *Oxford English Dictionary* is defined as the general *course* or progression of one's working life and professional achievements. Carrière in Old French suggested a *road* for carts or wagons moving people and things. This book is about constructing a unique life *course* through space and time when considering your options, which we believe this cover suggests. Career development and planning involves seeing the forest as well as the trees.

It also enabled us to further draw upon cognitive information processing (CIP) theory as an organizer for improved understanding of career problem solving and decision making. The book continues to be a comprehensive undergraduate career text based on published theory and research about career development and vocational behavior. Recent articles by Folsom, Peterson, Reardon, and Mann (2005), Reardon, Leierer, and Lee (2007), and Vernick, Reardon, and Sampson (2004) add to the extensive documentation regarding the effectiveness of this curricular intervention.

GOALS OF THE THIRD EDITION

We had several goals in producing this third edition. First, we wanted to update sources and provide new information about occupations and employment. Several chapters were revised by describing new systems for the delivery of occupational information (3), research about employment (7), ways to work (8), work arrangements (9), work/life balance (10), and developments with the Internet (12). All chapter references and links were updated as needed.

Second, we continued to remove material from some chapters because the book was simply too conceptually dense in places—there was just too much content for students to learn or instructors to teach in a three-hour semester class. So, we pruned content in chapters 5, 6, 8, 10, 11, 14, and 15.

Third, we updated the *Instructor's Manual* with more strategies based on principles of "active learning." Worksheets, assignments, and other learning tools for students can be found in the appendices of the text. This 270-page manual includes alternative teaching activities for 28 classes, over 370 PowerPoint slides, and other teaching materials.

Fourth, this edition continues to be printed as a paperback text making it available to students at a lower cost. It is a complete package of information and learning activities that is designed to become a "handbook" for lifetime use in career planning and job hunting.

ACKNOWLEDGEMENTS

Finally, many of our colleagues have provided ideas to help us produce this third edition. We are especially appreciative of the work of Adam Marsh, our Cengage Learning Custom Editor for the second edition, and Sarah Blasco, our Developmental Editor with Cengage Learning. We look forward to producing timely, revised editions of this text in the future, and welcome the comments of instructors and students to that end.

Robert C. Reardon, Ph.D.
Janet G. Lenz, Ph.D.
James P. Sampson, Jr., Ph.D.
Gary W. Peterson, Ph.D.

April 2008
Tallahassee, Florida

REFERENCES

Folsom, B., Peterson, G., Reardon, R., & Mann, B. (2004–2005). Impact of a career-planning course on academic performance and graduation. *Journal of College Retention, 6*, 461–473.

Reardon, R., Leierer, S., & Lee, D. (2007). Using grades over 26 years to evaluate a career course. *Journal of Career Assessment, 15*, 483–498.

Vernick, S., Reardon, R., & Sampson, J. (2004). Process evaluation of a career course: A replication and extension. *Journal of Career Development, 30*, 201–213.

LIST OF TABLES

LIST OF FIGURES

CAREER
CONCEPTS AND
APPLICATIONS

INTRODUCTION TO CAREER PLANNING

Most of us who have grown up in the United States of America take for granted the idea of having a career. It is almost like a birthright. As the jingle goes, "It's as American as the 4th of July, baseball, apple pie, and Chevrolet." Parents, teachers, and friends *expect* us to have a career. Our success in life and our identities are measured by our careers. We go to school and choose a field of study to prepare for our career. The "right" career, we are told, will lead to happy, successful, fulfilling lives.

These are some common ideas about career, and they are shared by important people in society who shape our attitudes and values. These beliefs are instilled by teachers, parents, TV broadcasters, preachers, and politicians. These expectations put a lot of pressure on us to pick the right occupation and on society to ensure there are good jobs available to us.

This book departs from some of these common attitudes, so you must be prepared to rethink many of the prevailing ideas about career.

These "uncommon" ways of looking at career and the career-planning process are based on the latest research and theory, and they have been proven effective in helping students solve practical career problems and make career decisions.

A HISTORICAL PERSPECTIVE

Before we explore this new approach to career problem solving and decision making, it is useful and appropriate to take a brief look at the past. Where did this career idea come from anyway? Has it always been there? What forces out there have contributed to our current thinking about career?

The whole concept of career is pretty new, at least in historical terms. Indeed, the practice of choosing an occupation was not the norm for most people until the beginning of the twentieth century. In other words, the principle of "having a career" is only about 100 years old. Before that, most people automatically adopted the occupations of their parents. If you were a male and your father was a farmer, a shopkeeper, or a carpenter, then you would follow in his footsteps. If you were a female, then you did whatever your mother did, on the farm or in town. Career *choice* was almost nonexistent. Your career was what you were born into. There was no need to plan and finally make a decision yourself; you just followed the path laid down by your family's circumstances.

There were some exceptions. For example, if your family was very wealthy, of a privileged class, or willing to spend extraordinary family resources, you could prepare for one of the professions. You could pursue positions like priest, diplomat, physician, teacher, artist, or government official. This was especially true if you were male. Of course, all of these required college training, and at that time, college was generally restricted to white men.

Why did things change? Most of the changes were brought about by an external force—the industrial revolution—which in turn brought about other changes. In the United States, the development of new, big industries such as oil, railroads, textiles, meat packing, shipping, automobiles, utilities, construction, timber, banking, and steel transformed the economy. The jobs created by these industries attracted workers from farms and rural areas who were eager to accumulate wealth and enjoy a higher standard of living. These positions were totally new; they had not been available to older generations. An enormous number of options were available.

There were also changes due to the freedom and the nature of the economic system in America. In the early 1900s, hundreds of thousands of Europeans uprooted their families, left their native homes, and emigrated to America, the land of opportunity. America wasn't only a place, it was an ideal, and a chance for a person to start over and be anything he or she wanted to be. A newcomer could go into a new trade, start a business, develop new skills, and become rich and successful in the process. Of course, there were risks. One might fail, but the opportunity to be free of old ways of thinking and living was a powerful attraction. All of this newfound freedom was bound up in career choice and the responsibility to make a good career plan.

There were some problems. In the early 1900s, many of these new jobs were dangerous. Some employers in the factories exploited children and recently arrived immigrants. Young people would leave school and get a factory job to help support their family. In some Eastern cities, the school dropout rate was 90 percent. Eventually, laws were passed by the federal government that protected the safety and education of children, enabled workers to organize into unions, and mandated safe working conditions. Many new immigrants did not speak English or know how to be citizens in this American democracy, and they were sometimes used and abused by dishonest politicians and businesspeople. In many ways, this all sounds like the United States now in the early 21st century.

ENTER VOCATIONAL GUIDANCE

To help both young people and adults sort out this increasingly complex process of choosing an occupation, a man named Frank Parsons created the Vocations Bureau in 1908 in a neighborhood settlement house in Boston. This new program guided job seekers (especially new immigrants) in examining their personal characteristics and local employment options and then selecting the best job available. This was the beginning of the career counseling process as we know it today.

Parsons' ideas were very popular, and his book, *Choosing a Vocation* (Parsons, 1909), explained his program to those interested in developing one in another city. Parsons' program defined three steps for making a wise vocational choice:

1. careful self-assessment of one's interests, skills, values, goals, background, and resources,

2. study of all of the available options for school, additional training, employment, and occupations, and

3. a careful reasoning of which choice was best in light of information uncovered in the first two steps.

Parsons' three-step model may strike you as a very logical, rational approach to solving career problems and making career decisions. Perhaps it reflects Parsons' early training as a lawyer, engineer, and professor. At any rate, Parsons' ideas are still useful today, a major breakthrough in the way we think about career choice.

Since the early 1950s, career theorists have increasingly promoted the idea that career is not only an occupation or a job, but also a lifelong process of deciding how one wants to live his or her life. In other words, Parsons' three-step process is used over and over again as a person makes adjustments in his or her life roles. These life roles include worker, student, parent, and citizen. In this more recent view, vocational guidance is seen to involve more than just choosing and entering an occupation. We will explore these newer ideas later in this chapter.

CAREERS IN THE PRESENT DAY

This brings us to the present. How is career planning different now from 100 years ago? First, the atmosphere of rapid change that controls our lives today strikes at the heart of the career development process. The dramatic transformations that affect us all influence when, how, where, and why we work. This, in turn, affects how we plan and pursue our careers.

The basic nature of work is changing, just as it did a century ago. Gone are the days when one began his or her career at a company or organization and remained there as a loyal employee until retirement. That idea just does not fit the reality of life for most working people. In addition, work and organizations have become international in scope, not simply bound to one country. Companies are now multinational, rather than American or Canadian, and workers are viewed as a commodity, like fuel or electricity. An American worker is viewed in terms of costs and returns in comparison with a worker in countries like Mexico or China. Chapters 6 and 7 examine these ideas in more detail.

In addition to 40-hour workweeks with benefits, many employees' work schedules are part-time, flextime, temporary, on contingency, involve telecommuting or other work arrangements, often without benefits. These new, flexible work schedules provide increased complexities for career building. Chapters 7 and 8 will examine these ideas.

Diversity in the workplace has impacted work and careers in dramatic ways. Organizations in America are now composed of a workforce that dramatically reflects the recent wave of immigrants from Central and South America and from Asia and Southeast Asia, surpassing the multitude that came ashore in the early 1900s.

The balance between gender and work is changing. This phenomenon is certainly related to current ideas about family life, but the fact that women are increasingly taking jobs outside the home has led to dramatic shifts in work organizations and in daily family life. Women's entry into the workforce has led to many changes in the way organizations now define job duties and make work-related decisions. This trend has also created pressures for more egalitarian views of male and female roles in the home. Dad is expected to do his share of the cooking, housework, childcare, and running the household now that Mom works outside the home.

Finally, the career materials and resources available to help people make career and job choices have expanded dramatically. Career professionals call these things career interventions, meaning the computer systems, inventories, books, multimedia and print materials, and professional and paraprofessional staff that can be used to help people in their career development. The array of potential interventions is much larger now than ever before, and it can be difficult for consumers to know which is best to use in any particular situation.

In summary, career planning has become a much more challenging task as the result of dramatic, rapid changes in our social and economic life. However, even with all the changes and new complexities, we believe that it is possible for you to learn how to formulate and execute a career plan.

CAREER PROBLEMS

Individuals often experience great trauma as a result of job loss, a change of career direction, or family-work conflicts. Organizations, however, also suffer great difficulties because of the career problems of workers. One of the most critical issues for any organization is to get the right person into the right position because this greatly impacts the organization's performance. Even nations are aware of the importance of career development. Both new, emerging nations and older, industrialized nations seek to develop educational and economic programs that will enable citizens to be engaged in meaningful career activities wherever possible.

Full employment is the goal of just about every nation in the world today. A nation's health and strength is often judged in terms of whether its people are working and whether it can produce more than it needs for itself. Nations get into trouble when people are unemployed or underemployed, because as citizens become restless, fearful, and angry at the nation's leaders there is increased likelihood of revolution and strikes. Sometimes a nation will try to use international trade policies as a way to help keep its own citizens employed. Many international conflicts have involved one nation's efforts to keep jobs "at home." In this way, individual career development is directly tied to national and global political and economic forces that stimulate job growth.

The quality of career life is important because increases in unemployment have been directly related to increases in individual health problems, domestic violence, and crime. For individuals, the loss of a job is sometimes a trigger for cardiovascular problems, stomach ulcers, emotional stress, and other health problems. Job loss is also associated with increases in child and spouse abuse, robbery, assault, and other forms of personal injury and loss of property. All of this means that when the quality of work life in a nation declines, the social and economic costs to the nation spiral upwards.

In recent years, giant organizations such as Enron, AT&T, Exxon IBM, General Motors, the CIA, and the City of New York have experienced significant changes. Some of them have laid off thousands of employees, dramatically revamped jobs and positions, or have even gone out of business. The trauma of the collapse or failure of such organizations has far-reaching effects on both individuals and communities. Your individual career development may be directly tied to the success and stability of an industry or an organization.

Career problems are important because of their magnitude. Every day millions of people move in and out of employment or move from one job to another; there is great instability in the job market. Sometimes these shifts can even be thought of as "careerquakes" (Bolles, 2008). Given the importance of full employment for individuals and nations, cataclysmic events such as an economic recession, where millions become unemployed in a short period of time, are profoundly important. To make matters worse, the system for getting people back into the workforce is very inefficient. The quality of your career will likely be affected by the economic health of your country, industry, and organization, as well as the methods you use to find jobs.

CAREER DEVELOPMENT TERMS

Thinking back to your social science courses (economics, sociology, psychology), you may remember that common words took on new or special meanings. **Career development**, as a field of study in the social sciences, follows a similar pattern. There is a special professional jargon or language in this field, and it is important for you to know it in order to be an effective career problem solver and decision maker.

Familiar words like *career, vocation, work, employment, job, occupation, position,* and *industry* deserve special attention in this book because in the career development field they have different meanings from their ordinary, common usage in the news media or casual conversation. We will give other words such as *interest, value, skill, ability,* and *goal* special treatment in terms of definitions.

Why are these special definitions needed? One reason is because this is the way knowledge and facts in the career development field are organized and communicated. It is important for you in your personal career problem solving and decision making to know the difference between *occupational information, employment information,* and *career information,* because the facts and data for each of the three are different. When you seek assistance in solving a career problem, you need to ask for the right kind of information in order to get it. Using the correct terms helps you more quickly get the right answers.

Another reason is that the tools of career development services, such as inventories and computer information systems, use this special terminology. In order to be an informed consumer of career services, you need to know and effectively use the terminology of this field. In using career services at a school or library, or those provided by an employer or a private consultant, the old adage of "let the buyer beware" is your best insurance. **Becoming informed is your way of becoming powerful in making career decisions and in shaping your career path.**

Definitions

Here are several of the most important definitions in the career field. We will focus on other important terms that you need to know throughout the book. The following definitions are taken from an article by Susan Sears (1982) in the *Vocational Guidance Quarterly*.

> ***Career Development.*** The total constellation of economic, sociological, psychological, educational, physical, and chance factors that combine to shape one's career.

Career development is a big concept, as this definition indicates. It is affected by money and financial resources, group membership and social class, mental health and personality, educational level and record, physical abilities and traits, and chance factors. All of these factors, both within and outside the individual, combine to influence how one's career path unfolds. It is important to note that no single one of them determines a person's career, but they combine in complex ways to shape it. Later on, we will look more closely at how one expert, Anne Roe, thought these factors might combine to shape a person's career.

> ***Career.*** Time extended working out of a purposeful life pattern through work undertaken by the person.

This definition was developed by the National Career Development Association and is the one most widely used in the career field. There are some important ideas contained in this definition of career that have practical importance for persons engaged in career planning.

Time extended indicates that career is not something that happens as the result of one event or choice. A career is not time limited or tied to one particular job or occupation. Rather, a career is a process that is lifelong in nature, and it is affected by forces within and outside a person. Some experts in the field even use the term "life/career" as a way to connect life processes to the idea of career.

Working out indicates that career is the result of compromises and tradeoffs between what a person might want and what is possible, between the ideal and real. A career develops as a result of a continuing series of choices that the person makes when considering the costs and risks of particular options in light of the rewards. There is no "perfect" career path for a person, but there may be one that is optimal.

Purposeful means that a career has meaning and purpose for the person. A career doesn't just happen by accident or luck; it is planned, contemplated, worked on, and executed. A career develops because of the motivation, aspirations, and goals of the person. It reflects the person's values and beliefs.

Life pattern means that a career is more than one's employment or job. Career encompasses all the adult life roles: parent, spouse, homemaker, student, and the ways in which the person blends and arranges those roles.

Work is probably one of the most misunderstood words in the career field. We all have an idea what it means, but among career professionals *work is an activity that produces something of value for oneself or others.*

Work, then, is not limited to activity for which we get paid. It can include unpaid, volunteer activity if it produces something valuable for us or another person, such as coaching youth baseball, leading the church choir, painting landscapes, or mastering a computer program. Leisure activities, then, can be part of one's career, and sometimes a very important part. Work, not employment, is the way in which the concept of career is operationally defined.

Cawsey, Deszca, and Mazerolle (1995, p. 44) cited Handy's (1989) description of five types of work to underscore this point.

1. *Wage work*, where payment is for time and effort.

2. *Fee work*, where payment is for results.

3. *Home work* is done in the home—child raising or lawn care.

4. *Gift work* is voluntary or charitable work.

5. *Learning work* is studying and learning new skills.

Finally, *"undertaken by the person"* underscores the idea that a career is unique to the person. In reality, no two people have the same "career" because the career is based on an individual's particular history and situation. While people may have similar interests or skills and be employed in the same occupation and work for the same organization, their careers are different.

In summary, this definition of the word career changes the focus from "finding a career out there that's right for me" to "developing the *career* that is me." The good news for some people is that the focus of career planning shifts to one's self. For others, the responsibility of developing one's career is frightening. The purpose of this book is to help you acquire tools to make good career choices and to take responsibility for them.

Those involved in solving career problems and making career decisions often confuse the terms *career, occupation, position,* and *job*. In a nutshell, careers are defined and have meaning in terms of people, and they are all ultimately unique to each individual. Occupations, positions, and jobs, on the other hand, exist in organizations and industries, separate from what people bring to them. We can use our research skills to find out about them because the information exists "out there."

> **Occupation.** A group of similar positions found in different industries or organizations.

An occupation, which might be a trade or a profession, exists apart from a person. It is found in an industry or an organization. Accountant, for example, is an occupation, and it might exist in the pharmaceutical industry or the FBI (an organization).

> **Position.** A group of tasks performed by one person in an organization; a unit of work with a recurring or continuous set of tasks. A task is a unit of job behavior with a beginning point and an ending point performed in a matter of hours rather than days.

Positions are formed when an organization identifies an area of knowledge or a set of skills—tasks—that will enable the organization to function better if the tasks are completed. For example, the X-Y-Z Company decides it needs someone to improve the information flow among employees, customers, and investors. The company writes a new position description for a "communication specialist" and then seeks to hire a person to do the job.

A position exists whether it is vacant or filled, though when one is "looking for a job," he or she typically applies for a vacant position. A person may work in many different positions over the course of lifelong employment, even if it is in the same organization or occupation. Ordinarily, positions are filled by paid employees, but some organizations have identified unpaid, volunteer positions.

Job. A paid position held by a person requiring some similar traits or attributes.

A job may consist of one or a group of similar paid positions held by persons, traditionally performed within a 40-hour week. A person may work in numerous different jobs over the course of a lifetime. Jobs may involve self-employment or have special meaning if employment is in a particular organization. Jobs are filled by people, and they are task-, outcome-, and organization-centered. To help you compare and contrast the terms *position* and *job,* think of them this way: People lose or gain *jobs;* organizations lose or gain *positions.*

In conclusion, let's remember that only career is unique to each person as he or she makes life choices over the years. A career may or may not include one's occupational activities, which means that all of us are already in our career. A career isn't really something we prepare for—that's an occupation or a job—but it's something that we live, experience, and are already in the process of becoming. Ultimately, our career is a vital aspect of our lives.

We told you that this book would present some new ideas about the whole career idea, and these concepts and their definitions, which will be used throughout the book, will help you understand exactly what we are talking about.

FACTORS INVOLVED IN CAREER DECISIONS

Thus far, we have outlined some of the current ways of thinking about careers from individual, organizational, and national perspectives to help you expand your perception of the scope of the career field beyond that of simply an individual making a single career choice. Successful career planning in today's world requires considerable knowledge and skill.

One career theorist, Dr. Anne Roe, devoted a major part of her life to unraveling some of the complexities associated with career decisions and shedding some light on what leads a person to choose a particular occupation. She began to study career behavior of scientists and artists in the 1940s. She theorized that there were 12 different factors that could be grouped into four different categories that explain a person's occupational choice (Roe & Lunneborg, 1990). She arranged these factors into an algebraic formula, shown in Table 1.1, which looks a bit scary but really helps us understand more fully the complexity of career choices. Let's take this formula apart piece by piece. Roe used the lower-case letter to show how each of the 12 general factors, shown in upper case, can be affected by the unique characteristics of a person at a particular point in time, given a person's unique circumstances. Each person's formula would be unique. It is interesting to note that only S (sex) has no modifier before the factor, but it is a general modifier that impacts all 11 other factors. Do you think gender is that important in occupational choice?

TABLE 1.1   ROE'S FORMULA

Occupational Choice = S[(eE + bB + cC) + (fF, mM)) + (lL + aA) + (pP x gG x tT x il)]

S = sex	L = general learning and education
E = the general state of the economy	A = special acquired skills
B = family background, ethnicity	P = physical characteristics
C = chance	G = cognitive or special natural abilities
F = friends, peer group	T = temperament and personality
M = marital situation	I = interests and values

Roe, Anne and Lunneborg, Patricia W. "Personality Development and Career Choice," formula on p. 88. In D. Brown, L. Brooks, and Associates, *Career Choice and Development: Applying Contemporary Theories to Practice,* 2nd ed. Copyright 1990 Jossey-Bass Inc., Publishers. Reprinted with permission.

Finally, Roe grouped the factors (other than sex) into four groups, each within parentheses. In general, the first group includes factors over which a person has little control, whereas the factors in the last three groups include those that are based on both inheritance and experience. We assume that a person can to some degree choose his or her experiences or interests. Roe's analysis helps us understand why career development and occupational choice are sometimes so difficult. Solving career problems and making career decisions is a complex task but with time, motivation, and effort, we can develop skills and learn how to take control of our career. That is the philosophy of this book.

THEORIES OF CAREER CHOICE AND DEVELOPMENT

What is the best current thinking about career development? What do career experts tell us that might be helpful? Since Parsons began his work in the early 1900s, psychologists, sociologists, economists, and educators have sought to improve our understanding of how people make career choices and solve career problems. The knowledge they have accumulated can be thought of as a discipline or a body of knowledge. This scholarly field of work is multidisciplinary and includes vocational psychology, occupational sociology, labor market economics, vocational behavior, and career development. There are special sections of scholarly books and journals in libraries under these headings.

The research and theory presented in this book support the practical suggestions on how you can increase the likelihood of career satisfaction. You are likely to make better career decisions if you use information based on scholarship and approach the task systematically.

There is another practical reason to learn about career theories. Simply stated, we intuitively use our "Personal Career Theory," or PCT (Holland, 1997), in solving career problems and making career decisions. For example, you might say, "I'm an outdoor kind of person, and I like the water and my biology classes. I think I'll be a marine biologist." People who know you well might say, "I think you'd be a great elementary school teacher." In both instances, both knowledge of yourself and educational and occupational options were used to create a match and specify an occupation. Some career theorists (Holland is one example) have been studying these kinds of matches for 40 years. Learning more about Holland's theory might help you improve your PCT.

When your PCT breaks down and no longer is effective in helping you solve career problems and make career decisions, then you might consult a professional career counselor or obtain special assistance to improve your PCT. The purpose of this book, in a real sense, is to help you improve the quality of your PCT and to enable you to become a more effective career decision maker.

In this book, we draw upon the work of several career theorists whose ideas have taken shape in many of the inventories, computer systems, and materials used in this course as career interventions. We will begin with the work of Frank Parsons and John Holland and conclude with the work of Donald Super and the group at Florida State University.

Parsons. Frank Parsons is considered a structured theorist. Why? He focused on each occupational or career choice separately and independently, and he wanted to examine all the factors associated with both the individual and the occupational alternatives. Parsons emphasized the need for good information in career decision making, both for the person and his or her options. For Parsons, the final step was for the person to carefully use logical, reasoning skills to decide which option was best. A person with poor information about self or occupations and jobs and/or a person with poor reasoning skills would be in danger of making a poor occupational choice. Parsons viewed high-quality self-assessment and occupational and employment information combined with a skilled counselor as essential to helping persons solve career problems.

Holland. Dr. John Holland (1997) developed a "typological" theory about personality types and matching environmental groups. We will examine more closely Holland's RIASEC theory later, because his work since 1950 has led to the creation of the most widely used tools and materials in the career field. Holland's theory continues to produce a great amount of research—more than 1,000 published studies—on how persons choose occupations. His interest inventory, the *Self-Directed Search,* has sold over 27 million copies and been translated into 25 languages since it was introduced in 1970. Holland's approach can also be used to study various social and work environments, including occupations, positions, organizations, schools, and interpersonal relationships.

Super. One of the most important "process" theorists was Dr. Donald Super. Super (1990) began to introduce new ways of thinking about career development in the early 1950s. For example, he noted that an occupational choice is based partly on a person's *self-concept*; that is, a person seeks to implement his or her self-concept through the choice of occupation(s). This idea bound together the concepts of personality and occupation, resulting in the idea of career.

Super introduced the *life/career rainbow* because he believed that nine life roles were a good way for us to understand the concept of career. Each person occupies one or more of these roles at different times throughout his or her lifetime. In addition, the intensity or strength of each role varies over time for each person. The combination and intensity of life roles are the basis of the person's career. Some roles are defined in terms of biology and inheritance, and some are chosen by the individual (this is similar to what Roe observed). As you can see in Figure 1.1, the nine roles are (1) child (son or daughter), (2) student, (3) leisurite, (4) citizen, (5) worker, (6) annuitant/pensioner, (7) spouse or partner, (8) homemaker, and (9) parent or grandparent. Which roles do you anticipate having in your life/career? How strong or intensely will you be involved in those roles? At what age or ages will those roles be active? How is your participation in these roles determined? Which forces are internal and which are external?

By focusing on career development in terms of a person's self-concept, age, and life roles, Super has helped us more clearly understand what is involved in career development and decision making. Clearly, career planning involves more than selecting a college major, an occupation, or a place of employment. It involves a thorough examination of oneself and all of the roles we play in life.

Now that we have examined these scholars' thoughtful contributions to our understandings of career behavior, we can now venture forth in our efforts to further engage the process of career problem solving and decision making and take a look at the Cognitive Information Processing (CIP) approach to understanding career development.

COGNITIVE INFORMATION PROCESSING

In 1991, Drs. Gary Peterson, James Sampson, and Robert Reardon wrote *Career Development and Services: A Cognitive Approach.* This book presented a new way of thinking about career development. This Cognitive Information Processing, or CIP, approach was based on eight assumptions. The essence of these assumptions is as follows:

1. Career choices are based on how we think and feel.

2. Making career choices is a problem-solving activity.

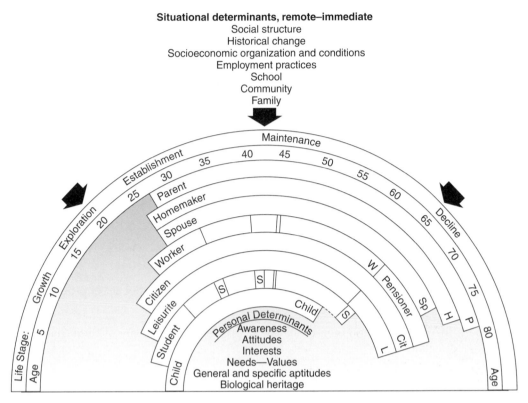

Situational determinants, remote–immediate
Social structure
Historical change
Socioeconomic organization and conditions
Employment practices
School
Community
Family

FIGURE 1.1

Super's Life/Career Rainbow

Reprinted by permission of Academic Press Inc. and Charles M. Super from D. Super. *Journal of Vocational Behaviour*, *16*, p. 289. Copyright 1980 Academic Press Inc.

3. Our ability as career problem solvers is based on what we know and how we think.

4. Career decisions require a good memory.

5. Career decisions require motivation.

6. Career development continues as part of our lifelong learning and growth.

7. Our career depends largely on what and how we think about it.

8. The quality of our career depends on how well we learn to make career decisions and solve career problems.

What do we mean by cognition? Basically, it is the way we think or how we process information in our heads. Psychologists believe that we maintain several different kinds of knowledge structures or components in our long-term memories that are important in career decision making. The first deals with facts and concepts about occupations, majors, and so forth. Second, we maintain memories about experiences and past events in our lives. Third, we have sets of rules and guidelines that we use in finding solutions to problems. Fourth, we have more general strategies or rules of thumb that we use in problem solving.

The CIP approach has been refined and improved since 1991 (Peterson, Sampson, Lenz, & Reardon, 2002; Sampson, Reardon, Peterson, & Lenz, 2004). CIP as used in this book is ultimately based on ideas about how our brain takes in, codes, stores, and uses information and knowledge in career problem solving and decision making. This can get rather complicated in a hurry, so we will move on to how CIP works in practice.

WHAT IS INVOLVED IN CAREER CHOICE

We believe that career problems have some common characteristics.

1. They can be defined in terms of a gap between what exists and what we want. It's the difference between what's happening and what, ideally, we want to happen.

2. Career problems are often complex and involve feelings; they present ambiguous cues or signals. The complexity comes from conflicting desires and motives, pressures from others, and feelings such as worry and embarrassment.

3. The solution to career problems often involve multiple options, not just a single correct choice. Each option seems to affect others, interdependently, so the best solution is typically a combination of options.

4. There is almost always some uncertainty about the outcome of the choice. No chosen solution to a career problem comes with a guarantee for success and satisfaction.

5. A decision about a major career problem almost always leads to another set of problems that are not fully known beforehand.

We think these five things are common to all career problems. How many of these relate to your present career situation?

AN INFORMATION-PROCESSING PYRAMID

Figure 1.2 shows a pyramid with the components involved in making a career choice. The bottom two parts of the pyramid are called the *knowledge domain*, and they include knowing about myself (*self-knowledge*) and knowing about my options (*occupational knowledge*). Self-knowledge includes knowing about my values, my interests, my skills, and related personal characteristics. Occupational knowledge includes understanding about specific occupations, college majors, and/or jobs and how they can be organized.

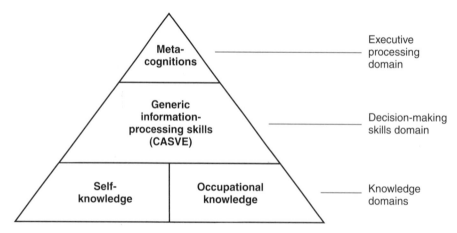

FIGURE **1.2**

Pyramid of Information-Processing Domains in Career Decision Making

Reprinted, by permission, from Gray W. Peterson, James P. Sampson, and Robert C. Reardon, *Career Development and Services: A Cognitive Approach.* Copyright 1991 by Brooks/Cole Publishing Company, a division of International Thomson Publishing Inc. All right reserved.

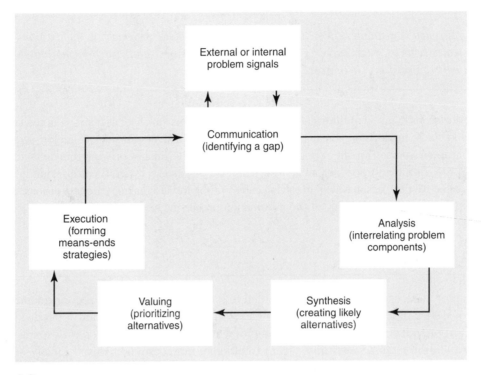

FIGURE 1.3

CASVE Cycle of Information-Processing Skills

Reprinted, by permission, from Gray W. Peterson, James P. Sampson, and Robert C. Reardon, *Career Development and Services: A Cognitive Approach*. Copyright 1991 by Brooks/Cole Publishing Company, a division of International Thomson Publishing Inc. All right reserved.

The bottom of the pyramid, the knowledge domain, can be likened to the data files stored in the memory of a computer. The bits of information are stored as schemata, or a dynamic piece of information. These schema (the plural of schemata) enable us to work with and process information in career problem solving and decision making. In the occupational knowledge domain, for example, as we learn more about accountants, we develop better, more detailed schema about an accountant's job, skills, interests, and so forth. Likewise, in the self-knowledge domain, when we take an interest inventory, we may grasp a clearer picture of our interest patterns.

The second level of the pyramid, knowing how I make decisions (*decision skills domain*), includes the five-step guide to good decision making (see Figure 1.3). This level can be likened to the computer programs that use facts and data stored in the memory and files of the computer. Career problem solving uses a lot of the memory space and requires a lot of information-processing capacity in our brains. In order to do it well, we have to be focused and concentrate, just like an athlete preparing for a race. This leads us to the top of the pyramid.

Thinking about my decision making (*executive processing domain*) is the top of the pyramid. This part of the pyramid is like the job-control function that tells the computer in what order the programs in the second level of the pyramid are to be run. For example, you might work on solving the problem of choosing a major before you focus on occupations and organizations to work for, or you might focus on your preferred lifestyle (e.g., frequent travel) and then work on occupational choices. These thoughts govern when and how we decide to work on our goals or the way in which we will solve career problems. And these kinds of thoughts help us figure out when we have reached our goals.

This CIP approach is a simple, effective way to help you learn how to solve career problems and make career decisions. It improves career development because it focuses on how to locate, store, and use information in decision making.

What does your Pyramid of Information-Processing Domains look like? Is it strong in the knowledge domains and weak in decision making, (e.g., CASVE Cycle)? Does it change as you acquire new information about yourself or the world of work? What is the quality of your thinking (negative or positive) in the executive processing area? The nature of a person's Pyramid can provide information about how effective that person will be in solving career problems and making career decisions. This book should help you improve the quality of the information-processing in your Personal Career Theory.

Summary

In this chapter, we looked at social forces that led to the beginnings of the career development field in the early 1900s. Examples of why and how career problems are important for individuals and nations were provided. We also reviewed some of the highlights of how modern experts view the career area and how those views differ from traditional, more common views. Finally, we briefly introduced the Cognitive Information-Processing approach and the Pyramid of Information-Processing Domains, which are explored in more detail later in the book.

References

Bolles, R. (2008). *A practical manual for job hunters and career changers: What color is your parachute?* Berkeley, CA: Ten Speed Press.

Cawsey, T. F., Deszca, G., & Mazerolle, M. (1995, Fall). The portfolio career as a response to a changing job market. *Journal of Career Planning and Employment*, pp. 41–46.

Handy, C. (1989). *The age of unreason*. Boston: Harvard Business School Press.

Holland, J. (1997). *Making vocational choices* (3rd ed.). Odessa, FL: Psychological Assessment Resources.

Parsons, F. (1909). *Choosing a vocation*. Tulsa, OK: National Career Development Association.

Peterson, G., Sampson, J., & Reardon, R. (1991). *Career development and services: A cognitive approach*. Pacific Grove, CA: Brooks/Cole.

Peterson, G. W., Sampson, J. P., Jr., Lenz, J. L., & Reardon, R. C. (2002). A cognitive information processing approach in career problem solving and decision making. In D. Brown (Ed.), *Career choice and development* (4th ed., pp. 312–369). San Francisco: Jossey-Bass.

Roe, A., & Lunneborg, P. (1990). Personality development and career choice. In D. Brown & L. Brooks (Eds.), *Career choice and development* (2nd ed., pp. 68–101). San Francisco: Jossey-Bass.

Sampson, J. P., Jr., Reardon, R. C., Peterson, G. W., & Lenz, J. L. (2004). *Career counseling and services: A cognitive information processing approach*. Pacific Grove, CA: Wadsworth-Brooks/Cole.

Sears, S. (1982). A definition of career guidance terms: A National Vocational Guidance Association perspective, *Vocational Guidance Quarterly, 31*, 137–143.

Super, D. (1990). A life-span, life-space approach to career development. In D. Brown & L. Brooks (Eds.), *Career choice and development* (2nd ed., pp. 197–261). San Francisco: Jossey-Bass.

KNOWING ABOUT MYSELF

Students come to the career center needing to decide on their major field of study and their first question is "What major will guarantee that I get a job when I graduate?" Others sometimes ask "What are the best paying jobs available to me after I graduate?" In both cases, the students are looking for information about things "out there" in order to make a career decision.

These students are focusing on the part of the Pyramid of Information-Processing Domains that involves "knowing about my options." As we explained in Chapter 1, this is one part of the knowledge domain where facts and information are stored. In solving career problems and making career decisions, this is the place where some people want to begin the process.

However, we think it is better to start with the part of the knowledge domain that involves "knowing about myself " (see Figure 2.1). Starting with this area puts the initial focus on you, the decision maker. Ultimately, you will be the one who must take the final responsibility for making your career choices. Also, it is easier and less confusing to begin the career-planning process by looking at yourself. This information is already available to you in your life experiences, the episodes that have shaped your life thus far.

The facts and data about occupations, employers, and fields of study can be overwhelming; the *Dictionary of Occupational Titles* (U. S. Department of Labor, 1991) described over 12,000 different occupations, and new ones are created every day. We believe you know yourself well enough to specify some things you like and don't like, and this should narrow the options "out there" that you need to get more information about. This can help you avoid wasting time and energy learning about occupations that aren't important to you, may not exist tomorrow, and don't match your interests and skills.

Self-knowledge will be the cornerstone of your career planning. We will examine some ways that you can improve your self-knowledge for career decision making and provide some methods for you to use in that process. You should use this information to improve the quality of your *Personal Career Theory*, especially with respect to the Pyramid of Information-Processing Domains and CASVE Cycle.

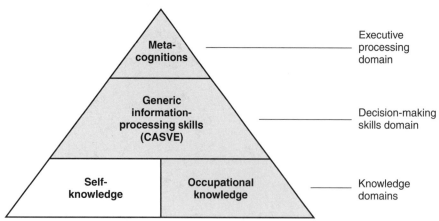

FIGURE **2.1**

Self-Knowledge

Reprinted, by permission, from Gary W. Peterson, James P. Sampson, and Robert C. Reardon, *Career Development and Services: A Cognitive Approach.* Copyright 1991 by Brooks/Cole Publishing Company, a division of International Thomson Publishing Inc. All rights reserved.

In Chapter 1, we reviewed the work of some of the more important career theorists. We noted that Dr. Anne Roe had identified 12 different factors that were important in choosing an occupation. Other psychologists have identified even more personal characteristics that they believe are involved in career decisions. While more detailed lists of self-knowledge factors are sometimes useful in special cases, we believe that three factors, values, interests, and skills, are the most essential parts of self-knowledge in career decisions made by college students. We will examine how each of these three contributes to improved self-knowledge and career planning.

VALUES

Beginning in the 1950s, Dr. Donald Super, Dr. Martin Katz, and other psychologists began to study how values, or more specifically work values, might be involved in career choices. The results of this research have shown that values are indeed a factor in career decision making, and they are also related to levels of later job satisfaction. A person's well-being and self-esteem are highest when that person lives according to his or her values.

The concept of values, however, can be somewhat difficult to define. One useful way of defining a value is "something that is important or desirable to you." There may even be an element of "should" associated with a value, "something you *should* do." Values are sometimes confused with interests, which are more likely thought of as "things you *like* to do for fun or enjoyment." Both values and interests are important parts of self-knowledge in career decisions.

Values are learned, and even very young children are able to identify and rate the relative importance of their values. Our work values seem to develop separately from how much we know about occupations. A host of factors are involved in shaping our values, including the values of our family and community, our ethnic and cultural traditions, our teachers and educational experiences, our religious experiences and beliefs, and our friends and peers. Studies show that men and women have somewhat different career-related values, which have not changed greatly over time (Jurgensen, 1978, in Herr & Cramer, 1993, p. 162). For example, men considered the values of job security, advancement, type of work, the company, and salary important to a good job. For women, it was type of work, the company, security, coworkers, and advancement. You will note that men and women share four of the top five values, although the order is different. What do you think about the fact that salary is important to men but women are concerned about coworker relations? Research indicates that making effective career decisions is associated with how clearly a person is able to specify his or her values; the clearer our values, the easier the career-planning process. This finding suggests the importance of clarifying the relative importance of our individual values as a part of effective career planning.

Work Values

Super and others (Nevill & Super, 1986) studied the idea of work importance, sometimes called **work salience**, from the standpoint of values. They discovered that some people don't place very much value on work, which is why they may have difficulty in career decision making. They may place more importance on parenting and family life, spouse or partner relationships, leisure and play, or learning and being a student. We will examine this idea more in Chapter 10 when we explore changing work and family roles.

However, another psychologist, Martin Katz, identified work-related values that might help a person clarify the rewards and satisfactions available in an occupation. In the late 1960s, Katz (1993) conducted an exhaustive study of about 250 occupations in order to determine how they might be rated on 10 career values. Table 2.1 shows the 8 currently being used values and Katz's definitions for each. Katz eventually developed a values-clarification exercise for use in a computer-based career guidance system called System for Interactive Guidance Information (SIGI is pronounced "Siggy"). The current version is called SIGI[3] (Valpar International Corp., 2007).

One aspect of Katz's exercise was the idea that one must prioritize values because it is not always possible to have all of one's important values implemented in an occupational choice.

TABLE 2.1 SIGI Values

1. **HIGH INCOME**: Some minimum income (enough for survival) is essential for everyone. People have different ideas about how much income is "high." Therefore, HIGH INCOME is defined here as a specific amount. It means more than enough to live on. It means money to use as you wish after you have paid your basic living expenses. You can buy luxuries and travel first-class.

2. **PRESTIGE**: If people respect you, look up to you, listen to your opinions or seek your help in community affairs, you are a person with PRESTIGE. Of course, PRESTIGE can be gained in several ways. But in the present-day, occupation is often the key to PRESTIGE. Rightly or wrongly, we respect some occupations more than others.

3. **INDEPENDENCE**: Some occupations give you more freedom than others to make your own decisions, to work without supervision or direction from others. At one extreme might be talented freelance artists or writers who may work without supervision. At the other extreme might be military service or some big business organizations with chains of command, which severely limit the decisions that each person can make.

4. **HELPING OTHERS**: Most people are willing to help others, and show it every day outside of their work. They put themselves out to do favors, make gifts, donate to charities, and so on. THIS DOES NOT COUNT HERE. The question here is, do you want HELPING OTHERS to be a main part of your occupation? To what extent do you want to devote your life work directly to helping people improve their health, education, or welfare?

5. **SECURITY**: In the most SECURE occupations, you will be free from fear of losing your job and income. You will have tenure—you cannot be fired very easily. Employment will tend to remain high in spite of recessions, and there will be no seasonal ups and downs. Your income will generally remain stable and predictable; it will not vanish with hard times. Your occupation is not likely to be wiped out by automation or other technological changes.

6. **VARIETY**: Occupations with the greatest VARIETY offer many different kinds of activities and problems, frequent changes in locations, new people to meet. VARIETY is the opposite of routine, predictability, or repetition. If you value VARIETY high, you probably like novelty and surprise, and enjoy facing new problems, events, places, and people.

7. **LEADERSHIP**: Do you want to guide others, tell them what to do, be responsible for their performance? People who weight LEADERSHIP high usually want power to control events. They want to influence people to work together effectively. If they are mature, they know that RESPONSIBILITY goes with LEADERSHIP. They are willing to accept the blame when things go wrong, even though they were not at fault.

8. **LEISURE**: How important is the amount of time your occupation will allow you to spend away from work? LEISURE may include short hours, long vacations, or the chance to choose your own time off. To give a high weight to LEISURE is like saying, "The satisfactions I get off the job are so important to me that work must not interfere with them."

Reprinted by permission of Valpar International Corporation, the copyright owner of SIGI and SIGI PLUS. SIGI is a registered trademark of Valpar International Corporation.

Occupations and jobs have not been created for the purpose of fulfilling all of our important values. Another idea from Katz was that a person's system of values—that is, how compatible or harmonious several top values were with one another—was as important in career decisions as the person's most important value. For example, the values of "high income" and "security" are often not very compatible. Katz believed values were more important than interests in career decision making, but as we shall see, other psychologists disagree on this point.

Values Clarification

People who have a clear sense of their values have less difficulty in career planning. Some experts (Raths, Simon & Harmin, 1966) have suggested that it is the process of clarifying one's values that is most important, not the actual content of the values themselves. They have identified seven steps in the valuing or values clarification process, grouped into three phases. The first phase in the valuing process is *choosing a value*, in which you (1) select a value freely and without pressure from other persons, (2) from among other alternative values, and (3) after thinking about the results from each choice. The second phase, *prizing your values*, involves (4) cherishing or being pleased with your values choices and (5) being willing to state your choice publicly to others when appropriate. The third phase in the valuing process, *acting on your values*, involves (6) doing something behavioral in relation to your choice (such as voting) and (7) acting in a pattern that is consistent and repetitive with your values choices. Think about one of your important work values. See if you can "clarify" it by going through the seven steps identified above.

INTERESTS

From the earliest days of Frank Parsons, career development experts have zeroed in on interests as an important part of occupational choice. Before psychological tests and inventories were developed, career counselors would ask persons to list their hobbies, identify people they admired, or describe their likes and dislikes in an autobiography. Even today, these are good ways to identify a person's interests. Identification of a person's interests was seen by early career counselors as a way to identify possible future occupations.

We defined interests as "those things a person does for fun or enjoys." Interest inventories and tests were developed by Dr. Frederick Kuder, Dr. E. K. Strong, and other psychologists in the 1940s that were geared to helping people sort out their likes and dislikes. These psychologists had discovered that people working in various occupations had distinctive patterns of interests. For example, the interests of accountants were different from those of engineers, nurses, and so forth. Thus, if interests could be quickly and reliably measured, it would simplify the career planning process.

The development and extensive use of these interest inventories were highly successful. The Strong Interest Inventory (Strong, 1994), the Kuder Career Search with Person Match™ (Zytowski & Kuder, 1999), and many other such tests are still widely used today. The essence of these interest inventories is that they measure a person's responses to several hundred items about personal likes and dislikes, and then the inventories compare the person's profile with the profiles of others already in occupations to see if there are any matches.

Holland's Typology

In the early 1970s, another psychologist, Dr. John Holland, began to introduce some new ways of thinking about interests and interest measurement (Holland, 1997). Holland suggested that interests were simply another way of describing personality characteristics and that it was really the broader concept of personality that was most important in occupational choice. Personality was seen as a combination of interests, values, needs, skills, beliefs, attitudes, and learning styles. With respect to occupational choice, however, interests were the most important part of personality on which to match people with occupations.

Holland also discovered that interests could be quickly and reliably measured by asking a person to list in order the occupations they would most like to enter. He called this "expressed" interest measurement. Whereas some psychologists used longer inventories with many test items to measure interests, sometimes called "assessed" interest measurement, Holland focused on expressed interest measurement. Holland's approach took some of the mystery out of interest measurement and occupational choice, and placed in the hands of ordinary people, the tools to search for occupations compatible with their personalities.

How does Holland's idea work? The reason for the success of this new matching approach was based on Holland's development of a hexagon model for examining how interests in one area compared with interests in another area and ultimately for matching people and occupations. In a nutshell, the theory is based on four ideas (see Tables 2.2 and 2.3).

1. Most people can be categorized as one of six RIASEC types: **R**ealistic, **I**nvestigative, **A**rtistic, **S**ocial, **E**nterprising, or **C**onventional.

2. There are also six kinds of RIASEC environments: **R**ealistic, **I**nvestigative, **A**rtistic, **S**ocial, **E**nterprising, or **C**onventional.

3. People search for environments that will let them exercise their skills and abilities, express their attitudes and values, and take on agreeable problems and roles.

4. A person's behavior is determined by an interaction between his or her personality and characteristics of an environment.

Let's examine these four basic assumptions or ideas behind Holland's theory in more detail. First, the idea that people can be categorized into types is a familiar one in psychology. People, or more precisely, their personalities are sometimes grouped in terms of friendliness, competitiveness, creativity, and other characteristics. Holland's idea of using six different categories for sorting personality is based on this familiar idea. However, the six RIASEC types that Holland identified have been shown, through extensive research since the late 1950s, to be useful, reliable ways to categorize personalities. More importantly, this research demonstrated that interests can be reliably measured in terms of these six different types and that our personality is basically composed of combinations of these six types. A person's interests and personality for the most part become more stable and less likely to change beginning about age 21. It may be helpful to think of personality as a pie with six slices, some of which may be much larger than others. Each person's pie is a unique combination of these six interests, but usually one of the six types is the largest piece.

Second, what about the idea of six environments like the six types? For Holland, an environment could be an occupation, a job, a leisure activity, an educational program or field of study, a college, or even the culture of an organization. Environments can be thought of as dominated by a given type of personalities, that is, the **R**ealistic environment is dominated by or has the largest percentage of **R**ealistic types. An environment can even be thought of as a social relationship with another person. For example, your "realistic" friend creates a realistic environment for you because of her interests, hobbies, skills, and so forth.

Third, persons seek out environments where their personality characteristics will be respected, valued, rewarded, and used. Think of this as the "birds of a feather flock together" saying. For example, **A**rtistic persons will seek out **A**rtistic environments—jobs, leisure, clubs, friends—where their creativity, independence, and idealism will be valued and prized.

TABLE
2.2 **RIASEC Personality Typology**

Attribute	Realistic	Investigative	Artistic	Personality Type Social	Enterprising	Conventional
Preferences for activities and occupations	Manipulation of machines, tools and things	Exploration, understanding and prediction or control of natural and social phenomena	Literary, musical, or artistic activities	Helping, teaching, treating, counseling, or serving others through personal interaction	Persuading, manipulating, or directing others	Establishing or maintaining orderly routines, application of standards
Values	Material rewards for tangible accomplishments	Development or acquisition of knowledge	Creative expression of ideas, emotions, or sentiments	Fostering the welfare of others, social service	Material accomplishment and social status	Material or financial accomplishment and power in social, business, or Political arenas
Sees self as	Practical, conservative, and having manual and mechanical skills—lacking social skills	Analytical, intelligent, skeptical, and having academic talent—lacking interpersonal skills	Open to experience, innovative, intellectual—lacking clerical or office skills	Empathic, patient, and having interpersonal skills—lacking mechanical ability	Having sales and persuasive ability—lacking scientific ability	Having technical skills in business or production—lacking artistic competencies
Others see as	Normal, frank	Asocial, intellectual	Unconventional, disorderly, creative	Nurturing, agreeable, extroverted	Energetic, gregarious	Careful, conforming
Avoids	Interaction with people	Persuasion or sales activities	Routines and conformity to established rules	Mechanical and technical activity	Scientific, intellectual, or abstruse topics	Ambiguous or unstructured undertakings

Reproduced by special permission of the publisher, Psychological Assessment Resources, Inc., 16204 North Florida Avenue, Lutz, Florida 33549, from the *Dictionary of Holland Occupational Codes—Revised* by Gary D. Gottfredson, Ph.D. and John L. Holland, Ph.D. Copyright 1992, 1996.

TABLE
2.3 **RIASEC Environmental Typology**

			Environmental Type			
Attribute	**Realistic**	**Investigative**	**Artistic**	**Social**	**Enterprising**	**Conventional**
Requires	Manual and mechanical competencies, interaction with machines, tools, and objects	Analytical, technical, scientific, and verbal competencies	Innovation, or creative ability, emotionally expressive interaction with others	Interpersonal competencies, skill in mentoring, treating, healing, or teaching others	Skills in persuasion and manipulation of others	Clerical skills, skills in meeting precise standards for performance
Demands and rewards the display of	Conforming behavior, practical accomplishment	Skepticism and persistence in problem solving, documentation of new knowledge, understanding or solution of problems	Imagination in literary, artistic, or musical accomplishment	Empathy, humanitarianism, sociability, friendliness	Initiative in the pursuit of financial or material accomplishment; dominance; self-confidence	Organizational ability, conformity, dependability
Values or personal styles allowed expression	Practical, productive and concrete values; robust, risky, adventurous styles	Acquisition of knowledge through scholarship or investigation	Unconventional ideas or manners, aesthetic values	Concern for the welfare of others	Acquisitive or power-oriented styles, responsibility	Conventional outlook and concern for orderliness and routines
Occupations or other environments involve	Concrete, practical activity; use of machines, tools, materials	Analytical or intellectual activity aimed at troubleshooting or creation and use of knowledge	Creative work in music, writing, performance, sculpture, or unstructured intellectual endeavors	Working with others in a helpful or facilitating way	Selling, leading, manipulating others to attain personal or organizational goals	Working with things, numbers, or machines to meet predictable organizational demands or specified standards
Sample occupations	Carpenter, truck operator	Psychologist, microbiologist	Musician, interior designer	Counselor, clergy member	Lawyer, retail store manager	Production editor, bookkeeper

Reproduced by special permission of the publisher, Psychological Assessment Resources, Inc., 16204 North Florida Avenue, Lutz, Florida 33549, from the *Dictionary of Holland Occupational Codes—Revised* by Gary D. Gottfredson, Ph.D. and John L. Holland, Ph.D. Copyright 1992, 1996.

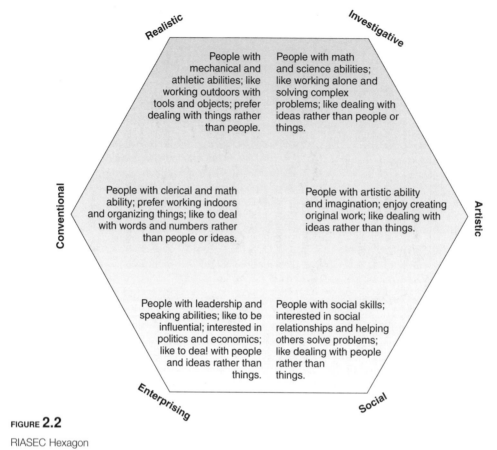

Realistic

Investigative

People with mechanical and athletic abilities; like working outdoors with tools and objects; prefer dealing with things rather than people.

People with math and science abilities; like working alone and solving complex problems; like dealing with ideas rather than people or things.

Conventional

Artistic

People with clerical and math ability; prefer working indoors and organizing things; like to deal with words and numbers rather than people or ideas.

People with artistic ability and imagination; enjoy creating original work; like dealing with ideas rather than things.

People with leadership and speaking abilities; like to be influential; interested in politics and economics; like to dea! with people and ideas rather than things.

People with social skills; interested in social relationships and helping others solve problems; like dealing with people rather than things.

Enterprising

Social

FIGURE 2.2

RIASEC Hexagon

Reproduced by special permission of the publisher, Psychological Assessment Resources, Inc., from *Making Vocational Choices*. Copyright 1973, 1985, 1992, 1997 by Psychological Assessment Resources, Inc. All rights reserved.

Fourth, a person's behavior is the result of the interaction between personality and environmental characteristics. If a **R**ealistic person ends up in a **S**ocial environment, he or she may be unhappy, tense, stressed, alienated, perform poorly, and will soon take steps to get out of that **S**ocial environment.

Inspection of the hexagon in Figure 2.2 provides some additional insight into Holland's typology theory. First, you will notice that the types that are adjacent or closest on the hexagon have relatively more in common, for example, **E** and **S**. Second, notice that the types farthest apart on the hexagon have the least in common: **R** and **S** or **C** and **A**. One of Holland's colleagues discovered that the six types relate to one another in ways that resemble this hexagon figure. One of the practical results of this finding is that people and occupations typically include types that are adjacent or alternate on the hexagon.

Holland developed a number of practical devices for helping people identify their type and compatible environments. For example, the Self-Directed Search (SDS) (Holland, 1994) is widely used to help people identify their interests or personality type in relation to career planning. When persons complete the SDS inventory, they obtain a three-letter "summary code," because the results are reported in the three-letter combination that best describes their personality characteristics. For example, a person might obtain a code of **IAS**, which would indicate the three letters associated with this interest type. These could be thought of as a pie graph, with the "**I**" having the largest slice, the "**A**" the next largest, and so on. Regarding environments, Holland developed the *Occupations Finder* (Holland, 1999) and the *Dictionary of Holland Occupational*

Codes (Gottfredson & Holland, 1996) to identify Holland codes for 1,335 and 7,500 occupations, respectively. Other instruments were created to identify Holland codes for leisure activities and fields of study.

Other Classifications of Interests

Besides Holland's scheme, there are several other classifications of interests, personal characteristics, and related occupations that are sometimes used in various career services settings. These include the ACT World-of-Work Map (ACT, 2001) and the Myers-Briggs Type Indicator® (MBTI; McCaulley, 1990). Each of these includes an interest or personality assessment and a matching classification of occupations thought to be compatible with the personal characteristics.

The ACT World-of-Work (WOW) Map. This system is included in the Career Planning Program developed by the ACT (ACT, 2001). You may have used this program when you were taking the ACT as a part of college entrance examinations. The UNIACT Interest Inventory and WOW Map are also included in the DISCOVER computer-based career guidance system, which is similar to the SIGI PLUS program mentioned earlier. The UNIACT Interest Inventory enables a person to develop a profile of interests and personality characteristics related to six types that are almost exactly the same as those developed by John Holland. (The major difference between the UNIACT and the SDS is that the former uses norms to determine scores, while the latter uses raw scores only.) In addition to the six types, the profile provides information related to four quadrants divided by data-ideas and people-things (see Figure 2.3).

The WOW arranges 26 career areas (groups of similar jobs) into 12 regions. Together these regions cover almost all U.S. jobs. The location of each career area on the WOW Map is arranged according to four job clusters: (1) DATA, facts, numbers, files, accounts, business procedures; (2) IDEAS, insights, theories, new ways of saying or doing something, possibly with words, equations, or music; (3) PEOPLE, people you can help, serve, inform, care for, or sell things to; and (4) THINGS, machines, tools, living things, and materials such as food, wood, or metal.

Table 2.4 shows how approximately 500 occupations can be grouped into six job clusters and 26 career areas. Note that the six clusters are very similar to Holland's six RIASEC types.

Myers-Briggs Type Indicator® (MBTI). The MBTI® is one of the most widely used personality inventories (McCaulley, 1990). Like the Self-Directed Search, it is based on a typological theory of personality. The theory is based on four dimensions of personality (see Table 2.5), and related instruments produce scores that identify the person as one of 16 types (all possible combinations of the eight letters). As with Holland codes, people sometimes characterize themselves by their code letters—for example," I'm an ESTJ." Table 2.5 shows the 16 major categories of information included in the MBTI® typology. The MBTI® is widely used in solving career problems, especially in organizational settings involving worker supervision and team building.

However, interests are probably the most important aspect of self-knowledge related to career decision making and occupational exploration. They are like a beacon that points the direction a person will probably move in his or her career development. Understanding the different ways that interests and personality are classified and measured is important in improving self-knowledge for improved career planning.

In summary, John Holland's theory and instruments have dominated the career development field for over 50 years and it is the reason we emphasize RIASEC theory in this book. More than 1,600 publications (Ruff, Reardon, & Bertoch, 2008, in press) have explored the theory and have shown the usefulness of the practical devices he has created to help people identify occupations that would be compatible with both their interests and personality.

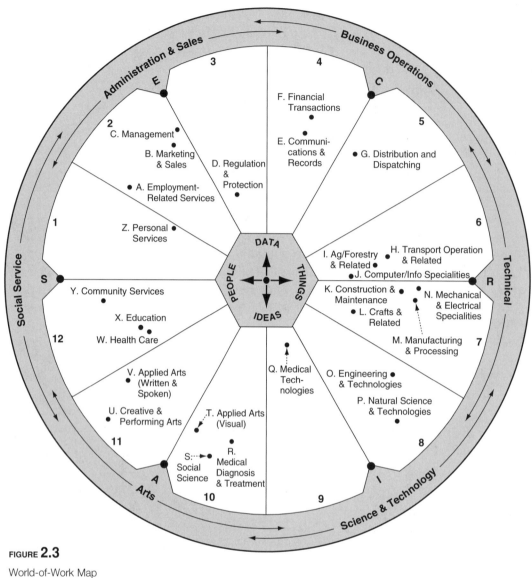

FIGURE 2.3

World-of-Work Map

Copyright 2001 by ACT, Inc. All rights reserved. Reproduced with permission.

SKILLS

Besides values and interests, we believe that skills are a third important part of self-knowledge. The area of skills is one that is of special interest to employers and boils down to the question "What can you do?" Like values and interests, skills are an important part of our personality. They distinguish us in terms of the things we can do well (or poorly), the behaviors we have learned or acquired along the way, and the special talents and abilities that we have. In this regard, skills are different from *aptitudes*, another term often used in career assessment. Skills involve knowledge and physical behaviors that are developed and learned, whereas aptitudes refer to our inherited capacity or untapped capabilities to learn or develop skills. For our purposes, we want to focus primarily on the notion of skills. It is also important to note that we are not distinguishing between the terms *abilities* and skills—for our purposes in this text they mean the same thing.

TABLE 2.4   CAREER CLUSTERS AND AREAS

The 26 career areas listed below are arranged within the six career clusters. For each career area, examples of occupations are provided.

Administration and Sales Career Cluster

1. Employment-Related Services
   Managers (Human Resources, Training/Education, Employee Benefits, etc.); Recruiter; Interviewer; Job Analyst.

2. Marketing & Sales
   Agents (Insurance, Real Estate, Travel, etc.); Buyer; Sales/Manufacturers' Representatives; Retail Sales worker; Telemarketer.

3. Management
   Executive; Executive Secretary; Purchaser; General Managers (Financial, Office, Property, etc.); Specialty Managers (Retail Store, Hotel/Motel, Food Service, etc.).

4. Regulation & Protection
   Inspectors (Customs, Food/Drug, etc.); Police Officer, Detective; Park Ranger; Security Manager; Guard.

Business Operations Career Cluster

5. Communications & Records
   Receptionist; Secretary (including Legal and Medical); Court Reporter; Clerks (Order, Billing, Hotel, etc.).

6. Financial Transactions
   Accountant/Auditor; Cashier; Bank Teller; Budget/Credit Analysts; Tax Preparer; Ticket Agent.

7. Distribution & Dispatching
   Shipping/Receiving Clerk; Warehouse Supv.; Mail Carrier; Dispatchers (Flight, Cab, etc.); Air Traffic Controller.

Technical Career Cluster

8. Transport Operation & Related
   Truck/Bus/Cab Drivers; Locomotive Engineer; Ship Captain; Aircraft Pilot; Sailor; Chauffeur.

9. Agriculture, Forestry, & Related
   Farmer; Nursery Manager; Pest Controller; Forester; Logger; Groundskeeper; Animal Caretaker.

10. Computer & Information Specialties
    Programmer; Systems Analyst; Info. Systems Manager; Computer Repairer; Desktop Publisher; Actuary.

11. Construction & Maintenance
    Carpenter; Electrician; Bricklayer; Tile Setter; Painter; Plumber; Roofer; Firefighter; Custodian.

12. Crafts & Related
    Cabinetmaker; Tailor; Chef/Cook; Baker; Butcher; Jeweler; Silversmith; Hand Crafter.

13. Manufacturing & Processing
    Tool & Die Maker; Machinist; Welder; Bookbinder; Printing Press Operator; Photo Process Worker; Dry Cleaner.

14. Mechanical & Electrical Specialists
    Mechanics/Technicians (Auto, Aircraft, Heating & AC, Electronics, Dental Lab, etc.); Repairers (Office Machine, Appliance, TV/VCR, CD Player, etc.).

Science and Technology Career Cluster

15. Engineering & Technologies
    Engineers (Aerospace, Ag, Nuclear, Civil, Computer, etc.); Technicians (Electronics, Mechanical, Laser, etc.); Surveyor; Drafter; Architect; Technical Illustrator.

16. Natural Science & Technologies
    Physicist; Astronomer; Biologist; Statistician; Soil Conservationist; Food Technologist; Crime Lab Analyst.

17. Medical Technologies
    Pharmacist; Optician; Prosthetist; Technologists (Surgical, Medical Lab, EEG, etc.); Dietitian.

18. Medical Diagnosis & Treatment
    Physician; Psychiatrist; Pathologist; Dentist; Optometrist; Veterinarian; Nurse Anesthetist; Audiologist; Physician Assistant.

19. Social Science
    Sociologist; Experimental Psychologist; Political Scientist; Economist; Criminologist; Urban Planner.

Arts Career Cluster

20. Applied Arts (Visual)
    Artist; Graphic Artist; Photographer; Illustrator; Floral/Fashion/Interior Designers; Merchandise Displayer.

21. Creative & Performing Arts
    Writer/Author; Musician; Singer; Dancer; Music Composer; Movie/TV Directors; Fashion Model.

22. Applied Arts (Written & Spoken)
    Reporter; Columnist; Editor; Advertising Copywriter; Public Relations Specialist; TV Announcer; Librarian; Interpreter.

Social Service Career Cluster

23. Health Care
    Administrator; Recreational Therapist; Psychiatric Technician; Dental Hygienist/Assistant; Geriatric Aide.

24. Education
    Administrator; Teachers & Aides (Preschool, Elementary & Secondary, Special Education, PE, etc.).

25. Community Services
    Social Service Director; Social Worker; Lawyer; Paralegal; Home Economist; Career Counselor; Clergy.

26. Personal Services
    Waiter/Waitress; Barber; Cosmetologist; Flight Attendant; Household Worker; Home Health Aide; Travel Guide.

Copyright 2001 by ACT, Inc. All rights reserved. Reproduced with permission.

TABLE
2.5

MBTI Types

Characteristics Frequently Associated with Each Type

	Sensing Types	Intuitive Types
Introverts		

ISTJ
Quiet, serious, earn success by thoroughness and dependability. Practical, matter-of-fact, realistic, and responsible. Decide logically what should be done and work toward it steadily, regardless of distractions. Take pleasure in making everything orderly and organized—their work, their home, their life. Value traditions and loyalty.

ISTP
Tolerant and flexible, quiet observers until a problem appears, then act quickly to find workable solutions. Analyze what makes things work and readily get through large amounts of data to isolate the core of practical problems. Interested in cause and effect, organize facts using logical principles, value efficiency.

ISFJ
Quiet, friendly, responsible, and conscientious. Committed and steady in meeting their obligations. Thorough, painstaking, and accurate. Loyal, considerate, notice and remember specifics about people who are important to them, concerned with how others feel. Strive to create an orderly and harmonious environment at work and at home.

ISFP
Quiet, friendly, sensitive, and kind. Enjoy the present moment, what's going on around them. Loyal and committed to their values and to people who are important to them. Dislike disagreements and conflicts, do not force their opinions or values on others.

INFJ
Seek meaning and connection in ideas, relationships, and material possessions. Want to understand what motivates people and are insightful about others. Conscientious and committed to their firm values. Develop a clear vision about how best to serve the common good. Organized and decisive in implementing their vision.

INFP
Idealistic, loyal to their values and to people who are important to them. Want an external life that is congruent with their values. Curious, quick to see possibilities, can be catalysts for implementing ideas. Seek to understand people and to help them fulfill their potential. Adaptable, flexible, and accepting unless a value is threatened.

INTJ
Have original minds and great drive for implementing their ideas and achieving their goals. Quickly see patterns in external events and develop long-range explanatory perspectives. When committed, organize a job and carry it through. Skeptical and independent, have high standards of competence and performance—for themselves and others.

INTP
Seek to develop logical explanations for everything that interests them. Theoretical and abstract, interested more in ideas than in social interaction. Quiet, contained, flexible, and adaptable. Have unusual ability to focus in depth to solve problems in their area of interest. Skeptical, sometimes critical, always analytical.

TABLE
2.5 **MBTI TYPES (CONTINUED)**

Characteristics Frequently Associated with Each Type

Sensing Types		Intuitive Types
Extraverts		

ESTP

Flexible and tolerant, they take a pragmatic approach focused on immediate results. Theories and conceptual explanations bore them—they want to act energetically to solve the problem. Focus on the here-and-now, spontaneous, enjoy each moment that they can be active with others. Enjoy material comforts and style. Learn best through doing.

ESFP

Outgoing, friendly, and accepting. Exuberant lovers of life, people, and material comforts. Enjoy working with others to make things happen. Bring common sense and a realistic approach to their work, and make work fun. Flexible and spontaneous, adapt readily to new people and environments. Learn best by trying a new skill with other people.

ENFP

Warmly enthusiastic and imaginative. See life as full of possibilities. Make connections between events and information very quickly, and confidently proceed based on the patterns they see. Want a lot of affirmation from others, and readily give appreciation and support. Spontaneous and flexible, often rely on their ability to improvise and their verbal fluency.

ENTP

Quick, ingenious, stimulating, alert, and outspoken. Resourceful in solving new and challenging problems. Adept at generating conceptual possibilities and then analyzing them strategically. Good at reading other people. Bored by routine, will seldom do the same thing the same way, apt to turn to one new interest after another.

ESTJ

Practical, realistic, matter-of-fact. Decisive, quickly move to implement decisions. Organize projects and people to get things done, focus on getting results in the most efficient way possible. Take care of routine details. Have a clear set of logical standards, systematically follow them and want others to also. Forceful in implementing their plans.

ESFJ

Warmhearted, conscientious, and cooperative. Want harmony in their environment, work with determination to establish it. Like to work with others to complete tasks accurately and on time. Loyal, follow through even in small matters. Notice what others need in their day-by-day lives and try to provide it. Want to be appreciated for who they are and for what they contribute.

ENFJ

Warm, empathetic, responsive, and responsible. Highly attuned to the emotions, needs, and motivations of others. Find potential in everyone, want to help others fulfill their potential. May act as catalysts for individual and group growth. Loyal, responsive to praise and criticism. Sociable, facilitate others in a group, and provide inspiring leadership.

ENTJ

Frank, decisive, assume leadership readily. Quickly see illogical and inefficient procedures and policies, develop and implement comprehensive systems to solve organizational problems. Enjoy long-term planning and goal setting. Usually well informed, well read, enjoy expanding their knowledge and passing it on to others. Forceful in presenting their ideas.

Modified and reproduced by special permission of the publisher, Consulting Psychologists Press, Inc., Palo Alto, CA 94303 from *Introduction to Type*, 5th ed. by Isabel Briggs Myers. Copyright 1993 by Consulting Psychologists Press, Inc. All rights reserved. Further reproduction is prohibited without the publisher's written consent.

Skills Identification

Over the years, numerous psychological tests have been developed to measure skills thought to be related to particular jobs and occupations. The most widely used tests include the Differential Aptitude Test (DAT) and the General Aptitude Test Battery (GATB). Both of these tests were developed for use with persons having a high school education or less and are not as useful with college students. These tests measure abilities such as vocabulary, computational skills, hand-eye coordination, clerical speed and accuracy, and mechanical reasoning.

Some employers, professional groups, and industries have developed highly specialized aptitude tests to measure traits that predict the ability to learn specific job skills, for example, sorting, dentistry, welding. However, these tests are used mostly to admit applicants to training programs or to qualify them for particular positions in organizations. In the performing arts, auditions and portfolio work samples are used, rather than paper-and-pencil tests, to assess skills in dance, music performance, and graphic arts.

For most college-level and professional jobs, tests do not typically provide useful results that will tell persons what their skills are and whether they will be successful in a professional-level occupation or job. Scholastic aptitude tests such as the SAT, MAT, ACT, LSAT, and MCAT are used to predict the ability to acquire high-level verbal and quantitative skills necessary to process technical information. Thus, we have to rely on expressed measurements rather than assessed measurements to identify skills related to self-knowledge for career decisions.

Perhaps the most common and widely used ideas about skills and career decision making are included in a best-selling book by Richard Bolles, *What Color Is Your Parachute?* Bolles' (2008) basic idea is that people who want to solve career problems or make career decisions need to identify their skill competencies, which have been developed in various life activities such as school, leisure activities, volunteer work, or prior jobs. Once they have completed a thorough inventory of their skills, people can then begin to prioritize their skills in terms of those that are important or satisfying to them, those that might be related to employment, or those that need to be further developed. Bolles believes that many people underestimate and overlook their skills, which handicaps them in solving career problems. Bolles' *Parachute* book provides numerous exercises for identifying and developing job-related skills.

Another method of skills identification can be illustrated using the Florida State University Career Portfolio system (Lumsden, Garis, Reardon, Unger & Arkin, 2001). This program lists nine basic, general skills that transcend any specific job—they are transferable from one job to another, or one life role to another. These nine skills were identified by a consensus of career center staff, faculty, and employers associated with the university. They are broad skills, not unique to any specific major field of study such as engineering or nursing, which may train a person in a more specialized skill area.

These are also the kinds of skills that often appear on one's resume and are discussed in employment interviews. Managers and leaders use most of these general skills. What are they?

1. communication

2. creativity

3. critical thinking

4. leadership

5. personal management

6. social responsibility

7. teamwork

8. technical/scientific

9. research/project development

A detailed description of these nine basic skills is provided in Table 2.6. A portfolio of accomplishments is a good device for documenting these skills because they are not readily measured with a paper-pencil test.

TABLE
2.6 **NINE GENERAL PORTFOLIO SKILLS**

The nine descriptions below provide information about the meaning of selected career/life skills. Think about examples where you could develop, use, or have used these skills.

CRITICAL THINKING

Critical thinking involves things such as identifying problems in a situation or organization, thinking about the complexity of problems, gathering evidence through research, evaluating options to solve the problem, and deriving a conclusion or solution. In developing options to solve a problem, you may need to think about what are both possible and likely solutions. To compare these options you need some type of measurement criteria or standard, and this may be drawn from various sources. Coming to a position, taking a stand, and making a recommendation to solve a problem are the culmination of critical thinking. Think about situations in classes or working on projects where you have exercised critical thinking in the past. Think about situations where you could develop this skill in the future.

TEAMWORK

Teamwork may include initiating ideas within a team or having team members cooperate and negotiate with each other. Effective teamwork behaviors involve a commitment to join with others to achieve a goal (cooperation). Teamwork involves recognizing your and others' strengths and weakness, and encouraging team assignments that draw on strengths and minimize weaknesses. Think about situations where you have been (or could be) a team member in a class group project, campus organization (officer, committee chair, etc.), community, or church group and you used teamwork skills.

LEADERSHIP

Leadership is the ability to set goals and point out directions for the group to take. You have been a "formal" leader when you suggested a plan or a way to achieve a group goal. This might have involved "making a motion" to move a group to take action on an issue. Leadership also involves the ability to delegate responsibility or authority to someone else. It involves the skill of motivating others. An example of this might be asking clarifying questions about the team's goals or presenting a proposal to your group, as a way to solve a specific problem. Think about where you might have held or would want to hold a leadership role in a class group project, campus organization (officer, committee chair, etc.), community or church group.

LIFE MANAGEMENT

Life management includes such things as managing time, both for long-term projects and activities, as well as day-to-day time management (e.g., finishing class projects, effectively managing work and school demands on a weekly basis). This includes being on time and being prepared to act. Life management can also include the ability to adapt to change. Your personal life management skills may also include the ability to manage finances (e.g., writing budgets, assessing expenses and income, and keeping accurate records). Think about where you have demonstrated life management skills in the past, or how you could demonstrate these skills in the future.

COMMUNICATION SKILLS

Communication skills include reading, speaking, writing, editing, listening, making presentations, and interpersonal relations. These skills are critically important in the workplace because they involve the transmission of information among people. Think about projects in and out of class that have emphasized communications, or that might be available to you in the future. This could include working on the school yearbook, writing up a research project, or authoring an essay for a class; personal courses and skill training; or other experiences that are related to communication skills.

CREATIVITY

Creativity may include skills in the many different areas, e.g., artistic, literary, mechanical, and social areas. Think about a time that you came up with an innovative solution to a problem and what made it so unique. What experiences could you seek in the future to develop skills in creativity?

TECHNICAL/SCIENTIFIC

Technical/scientific skills relate to experiences in the social, biological, and physical sciences. The most popular current application of technical/scientific skills involves the applications of computers. Think about a time where you used a software program for a particular project or activity. Technical skills may include system management (e.g., managing data warehouses or web services) and using the Internet for research and related activities. What experiences could you seek that would enhance skills in this area?

TABLE 2.6	NINE GENERAL PORTFOLIO SKILLS (CONTINUED)

SOCIAL RESPONSIBILITY

Social responsibility involves respecting individual and cultural differences. Finding admirable qualities in others, especially those who appear to be quite different physically, mentally, or in personality style, are acts of being a responsible person. Social responsibility relates to good citizenship. Individuals with skills in this area actively take part in community building projects on a regular basis. Think about instances when you were involved in your community, e.g., being a member of a community service group, a church group, a recreation group, as well as providing some community service.

RESEARCH/PROJECT DEVELOPMENT

Research and/or project development involves finding and using information for problem solving and decision making. In researching an issue or problem, individuals read and evaluate reports of prior work or collect new data that can be summarized in a written or oral presentation in order to provide new information. In addition to investigating a problem, individuals may develop plans for projects that provide a logical series of activities for eliminating the problem. This includes planning for the direction and coordination of a project to ensure that the goals and objectives are met in a cost-effective way and within budget. Think about research papers assigned in classes by your professors, work projects given by your job supervisors, and service projects for clubs and organizations, e.g., orienting new members, fundraising.

In summarizing our description of the three areas of self-knowledge important in career decision making—values, interests, and skills—we repeatedly noted that external, objective measures are often not completely helpful in improving our self-knowledge. Objective measures, such as those that might be provided by psychological tests or expert career counselors, may be less useful than our own self-examination and reflection. We noted that *expressed* measures, together with *assessed* measures, could be useful in improving self-knowledge about values, interests, and skills. Together, they enable us to form schema about who we are and what kind of work we might pursue.

IMPROVING OUR SELF-KNOWLEDGE

In the process of getting to know ourselves better in order to solve career problems and make career decisions, there are several things we can do. First, we can make sure that we keep a positive attitude about ourselves and that we don't let negative thoughts mess up our thinking about our values, interests, or skills. We need to make sure we are thinking "better" about ourselves and as clearly and accurately as we possibly can. Second, we need to know how to improve the quality of the information about ourselves that we use in solving career problems and making career decisions.

Thinking "Better" About Myself

What kinds of things can we do to improve the quality of our self-knowledge? First, we need to be careful about over generalizing from past experiences. Perhaps you once had a bad experience solving math problems or dealing with bugs on a camping trip, and as a result you decided to exclude all occupations involving math or outdoors from your career explorations. Such over generalizing can severely limit your ability to successfully explore all of the possible occupations that could bring you satisfaction. We can over generalize on the basis of positive experiences, too. Doing really well in one math class might not mean that you should pursue advanced education in a top flight engineering school. There are many other important pieces of information to consider in effective career decision making.

Second, we need to be careful about relying too much on another person's opinions about what our values, interests, and skills might be in relation to our career choice. This is especially true in the case of people with greater prestige or social power, such as family members, teachers, supervisors, and even career counselors. While you might seek feedback and suggestions from others about your skills and interests, you may want to choose or avoid choosing an occupation just because members of two prior generations in your family have entered it (for example, both your grandfather and your mother were lawyers).

Third, we need to avoid making career decisions if we are in some kind of emotional crisis. We sometimes see students who have just failed a chemistry course and then decided to forget about all occupations in the health care field. Other students may have received a letter from their parents informing them that further college costs would not be paid unless the major was in business. When you are in a highly emotional state, it is almost impossible to consider all the relevant information about your values, interests, and skills that is important in making a good career decision.

Finally, it is important to make full and thoughtful use of the tools that are included in state-of-the-art career interventions. Many of us can use some of these materials with little outside assistance, but professional career counselors can provide expert assistance in selecting and interpreting the results of inventories, psychological tests, computer-based career guidance systems, and other devices.

Approaches to Improving Self-Knowledge

It is important to understand that our storehouse of self-knowledge information is based on our experiences, on events that have happened in our lives that we can recall. While the events themselves are important, it is our recollection of them that is particularly important in building up our store of career-related self-knowledge. Therefore, it is important for us to seek out and acquire as many different career/life experiences as we possibly can. Even if they turn out to be experiences we don't like and are unhappy about, the experiences will improve our self-knowledge store. It is also important to process and talk about our experiences, to reflect on the feelings related to the experiences, because they are the building blocks of self-knowledge that clarify our values, interests, and skills. Ultimately, it is our feelings about these things that are important in career problem solving and decision making.

We should also connect and relate these life events and experiences to each other. What are the relationships between your values, interests, and skills. Do they connect in meaningful ways? Are they related? For example, a person who likes being with children (interests) and has experience developed in babysitting and teaching church school (skills) determines that childhood education is a career to pursue because the future of the nation is connected to the quality education of children (value). However, another person with a very good academic record in math (skills) and wanting to make a lot of money (value) may not choose to become an actuary or accountant because of liking the outdoors (interests). It is important to understand not only your skills but also the values and interests related to your skills. In other words, it is important to develop more complex ways of thinking about self-knowledge by linking groups of values, interests, and skills together in relationships that *make sense to you*.

The clearer, sharper, and stronger our self-knowledge regarding our values, interests, and skills, the more likely we will be able to solve career problems and career decisions. How is this done? We can develop stronger images of ourselves by getting varied experiences in many different work settings and by paying attention to our feelings and reactions to these experiences. As the old saying goes, "If you follow your own nose, you'll never get lost." This can mean that even a part-time, volunteer experience may help you sharpen and clarify your values, interests, and skills related to occupations and work. Teaching six-year-olds may help you realize how happy or frustrated you become when working with children. "Watch your feet" to see how you're really thinking and feeling, because we talk with our mouths but "vote" with our feet.

Finally, you must realize that improving self-knowledge related to career decision making is a lifelong process; it is never finished. Every new life event and experience adds to our storehouse of information about values, interests, and skills. Moreover, no life experiences are wasted—important lessons come from experiences that are sometimes initially considered failures. Sometimes, students say that they have gotten into the wrong major or that they took the wrong job. That's usually the short-term evaluation. In the longer term, those experiences can be used to sharpen and clarify one's career journey. One of the most distinguished clinical psychologists at our university once noted that he had majored in chemistry as an undergraduate, and had later come to realize that his knowledge of chemistry had enabled him to more fully appreciate the importance of physiology and brain chemistry in explaining human behavior. Perhaps there is indeed a "seamless web of knowledge" at work in the world that we sometimes fail to appreciate in our career decision making as we try to understand our options and opportunities.

SUMMARY

We have examined the area of self-knowledge, "knowing about myself," as a beginning point in career problem solving and decision making. Three areas—values, interests, and skills—were highlighted as important parts of self-knowledge. The differences in assessed and expressed measurement approaches were outlined, and strategies for developing and improving self-knowledge in the areas of values, interests, and skills were presented. This should help you improve the quality of information in the self-knowledge domain of your Personal Career Theory.

REFERENCES

ACT. (2001). *Career Planning Survey technical manual*. Iowa City, IA: Author.

Bolles, R. (2008). *A practical manual for job hunters and career changers: What color is your parachute?* Berkeley, CA: Ten Speed Press.

Gottfredson, G., & Holland, J. (1996). *Dictionary of Holland Occupation Codes* (3rd ed.). Odessa, FL: Psychological Assessment Resources, Inc.

Herr, E., & Cramer, S. (1993). *Career guidance and counseling through the lifespan* (4th ed.). Glenview, IL: Scott, Foresman/Little, Brown.

Holland, J. (1997). *Making vocational choices* (3rd ed.). Odessa, FL: Psychological Assessment Resources.

Holland, J. (1999). *Occupations finder*. Odessa, FL: Psychological Assessment Resources, Inc.

Holland, J. (1994). Self-Directed Search. Odessa, FL: Psychological Assessment Resources, Inc.

Jurgensen, C. E. (1978). Job preferences (What makes a job good or bad?) *Journal of Applied Psychology, 63,* 267–276.

Katz, M. (1993). *Computer-assisted career decision making: The guide in the machine.* Hillsdale, NJ: Lawrence Erlbaum.

Lumsden, J., Garis, J., Reardon, R., Unger, M., & Arkin, S. (2001). Developing an on-line career portfolio. *Journal of Career Planning & Employment, 62*(1), 33–38.

McCaulley, M. H. (1990). The Myers-Briggs Type Indicator: A measure for individuals and groups. *Measurement & Evaluation in Counseling & Development, 22,* 181–195.

Nevill, D., & Super, D. E. (1986). Salience Inventory. Palo Alto, CA: Consulting Psychologists Press.

Raths, L., Simon, S., & Harmin, M. (1966). *Values and teaching: Working with values in the classroom*. Columbus, OH: Merrill.

Ruff, L. A., Reardon, R. C., & Bertoch, S. C. (2008, in press). Holland's RIASEC theory and applications: Exploring a comprehensive bibliography. *Career Convergence*.

Strong, E. (1994). Strong Interest Inventory. Palo Alto, CA: Consulting Psychologists Press.

Super, D. E. (1970). Work Values Inventory. Boston: Houghton Mifflin.

Super, D. E., & Nevill, D. (1986). Values Scale. Palo Alto, CA: Consulting Psychologists Press.

U.S. Department of Labor. (1991). *Dictionary of occupational titles* (4th ed., revised 1991). Washington, DC: U.S. Government Printing Office.

Valpar International Corp. (2007). SIGI[3]. [computer software]. Tucson, AZ: Author.

Zytowski, D. G., & Kuder, F. (1999). Kuder Career Search with Person Match. Adel, IA: National Career Assessment Services, Inc.

KNOWING ABOUT
MY OPTIONS

Career problems and career decisions require learning about oneself, but they also involve exploring fields of study, occupations, and leisure activities. Knowledge about self and career options are the information base, the foundation stones, for career decision making.

In our world, the number of options to work, learn, and play is very great and can even be overwhelming at times. However, living and working effectively and responsibly in today's complex global economy means digging into information about options and understanding how options are organized and connected to one another. As we noted in Chapter 2, it is better to begin this process of exploring options by first developing and understanding information about yourself.

This chapter focuses on the second part of the knowledge base of the Pyramid of Information-Processing Domains. This includes what we know about options in occupations, fields of study, and leisure activities. We will examine labor market and occupational information, how it's organized, and how to find it and evaluate it; we will learn about education and training options, including sources of financial support; and we will explore leisure and avocational options. Finally, we will review how you can improve your knowledge about occupational, educational, and leisure options.

Option knowledge is the second cornerstone of your career planning. We will examine some ways that people can improve their option knowledge and provide some materials for you to use in that process. This information will help you improve the quality of *your* Personal Career Theory, especially the Pyramid of Information-Processing Domains and the CASVE Cycle (see Figure 3.1).

CONNECTING OCCUPATIONS, EDUCATION, AND LEISURE

Besides *What Color is Your Parachute?* Richard Bolles (2008) wrote another book, *Three Boxes of Life* (Bolles, 1981), which analyzed the connections between education, work, and retirement.

Bolles suggested that many of us believe that education, work, and retirement (or play) occur during three separate periods, or boxes, of life. Earlier generations viewed these three periods as very distinct and divided, and a person sought to prepare for and live effectively in each time period as if it were unrelated to the others. Bolles suggested it is more important to view education (learning), work (working), and play (retirement) as three interconnected aspects of life/career. The three areas are blended throughout our lives, not separated into distinct "boxes" according to age. Perhaps you can think about how you blend learning, working, and playing into your life right now; how you did this in the past; and how you will do it 20 years from now. Given Bolles' observations, it

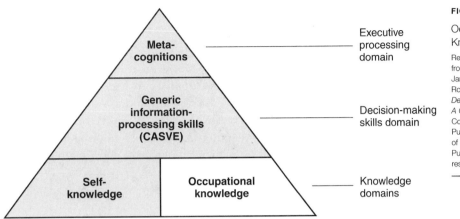

FIGURE **3.1**

Occupational
Knowledge

Reprinted, by permission,
from Gary W. Peterson,
James P. Sampson, and
Robert C. Reardon, *Career
Development and Services:
A Cognitive Approach.*
Copyright 1991 by Brooks/Cole
Publishing Company, a division
of International Thomson
Publishing Inc. All rights
reserved.

is appropriate to view education, work, and leisure as related options to be explored in career problem solving.

Educational, work, and leisure options exist "out there," and much information can be obtained from publications or from talking with people who are already there. Some information about options is in the form of tables that detail salaries, training requirements, costs, and other characteristics. In this way, our knowledge and information about options is very different from knowledge and information about ourselves, which is stored mostly in memories of our experiences. For example, occupational knowledge is broadly shared in government documents, written reports, biographies, computer files, films, and other media sources. These are concrete, objective sources of information, and they exist apart from our direct, subjective experience of them. Information about options can be stored on library shelves, in book chapters, and in various multimedia formats.

OCCUPATIONS

First we should review the definitions of *work, career, occupation, job,* and *position* that were introduced in Chapter 1. We defined *occupation* as a group of similar jobs found in different industries or organizations. This chapter presents the essential elements of occupational information, changes in knowledge about occupations, common schemes for classifying occupations, and major sources of information about occupations. (It is worth noting that some sources use these terms interchangeably and imprecisely.)

Number of Occupations

We noted in Chapter 1 that the *Dictionary of Occupational Titles* (U.S. Department of Labor, 1991) defined over 12,700 different occupational titles, with as many as 17,000 titles cross-referenced. How do we make sense out of all that? Well, the first step is to figure out meaningful ways to combine, group, and categorize them into smaller units. This could be by educational level, by income, by similarities of work activities, or by any way that would help simplify learning about them. Over the past 60 years, many different schemes have been used to group similar occupations, and we will look at some of them.

The fact that there are over 12,700 different occupations is only part of the story. Some of these occupations are identifiable but not very significant. Do you know what a snout puller is? A debeaker? A hod carrier? (By the way, the first two occupations involve working in a slaughterhouse pulling facial parts from pigs and chickens.) Some experts have estimated that about 95 percent of the workforce is employed in about 400 occupations. Four hundred is still a lot of occupations but far fewer than the 12,000 total.

For almost 50 years the *Dictionary of Occupational Titles* (U.S. Dept. of Labor, 1991) was the standard basic reference for information about occupations. However, it has been replaced by the O*NET, http://online.onetcenter.org/, a comprehensive database that provides information about 780 occupations, worker skills, and job training requirements. Each year hundreds of occupations in O*NET are updated with new research findings. O*NET is now the primary source of U.S. occupational information and its data is included in many computer-based career information delivery systems. O*NET is sponsored by the U.S. Department of Labor's Employment and Training Administration.

About Occupations

Most occupational information in the United States is compiled by the Department of Labor. More particularly, the U.S. Bureau of Labor Statistics regularly produces reports on working in America, who does it, when they do it, how much they earn, and so forth. The Occupational Employment Statistics (OES) is the primary data bank of information about occupations. Many federal government departments, such as Commerce, Education, Defense, Labor, Census, Interior, State, Agriculture, and others, contribute data to the OES.

An example of what we know about occupations can be seen in the topics used in Choices® Planner, a computer-based career information delivery system (or "CIDS" for short). Florida residents can access the program at this Web site, http://www.bridges.com/cpflorida/. Choices® Planner has 23 different *topics* for classifying occupations, such as educational level, money and outlook, skills, interests, work values, physical demands of the work, work hours, and working conditions. These topics are further divided into about 172 different *factors* that are used to describe about 700 different occupations in the program (see Table 3.1). These same topics and factors can be used in this CIDS to search for occupations. That's a lot of information about occupations. Other CIDS provide similar, detailed information about occupations.

In 1998, a federal/state initiative called America's Career Resource Network (ACRN; http://www.acrnetwork.org/network.htm) took responsibility for compiling and improving the quality of occupational information available throughout the United States. It provides quality information and resources to help youth and adults make informed career decisions. States and territories have Career Resource Networks (CRNs) designed to make available to all citizens the most current information about occupations, educational programs, financial aid for education and training, and job vacancy listings. It is wise to become familiar with and take advantage of our national and state systems of occupational information. You can explore freely information about occupations in all regions of the country.

Besides the U.S. Department of Labor and ACRN, there are many other private producers of occupational information. These include professional associations, labor unions, private authors and publishers, local governments, educational organizations, industry and commercial organizations, foreign governments, and private foundations. Besides these more formal sources of occupational information, we can find out more by talking to and observing people in occupations.

Occupations are Changing

Occupations do change constantly, and information about occupations also changes. Occupational information is very fluid and dynamic, like water that flows past the dock—the water may look the same, but it is always different. This happens because new occupations develop and long-standing occupations disappear. Before 1960, "astronaut" was not listed as an occupation, nor information

TABLE 3.1 CHOICES® PLANNER TOPICS AND FACTORS

Topic	Factor
Education level	No high school; high school; AA/AS degree; Bachelor's degree; Professional or graduate degree
Physical demands	Sedentary (up to 10 lbs.) to very heavy (above 100 lbs.)
Earnings	Ten categories (from $10,000+ to $100,000+ annually)
Aptitudes	General learning ability; verbal aptitude; numerical aptitude; special perception; form perception; clerical perception; eye-hand coordination; finger dexterity; manual dexterity
Work hours & travel	Rotating shift work; irregular hours; weekend work; overtime work; seasonal work; overnight travel; regular working hours and limited travel
Work conditions	Twenty-five categories specified, e.g., avoid indoor work
Career areas & GOE	Artistic; scientific; nature; law enforcement; mechanical; industrial; business detail; persuasive; accommodating; humanitarian; social/business; physical performing
Workplace skills	Social; complex problem-solving; technical systems; resource management
Interests	Realistic; investigative; artistic; social; enterprising; conventional
Physical abilities	Twenty-one categories specified, e.g., avoid color discrimination
Future outlook & employment	Increasing; stable; decreasing; all occupations
Apprenticeships	Yes or no
School subjects	Twenty-three categories specified, e.g., art, biology.
Fields of work	Twenty-three categories specified, e.g., avoid production occupations
Work hours & travel	Six categories specified, e.g., avoid overnight travel
Basic skills	Nine categories specified, e.g., writing, speaking, critical thinking
Career pathways	Arts & communications; business, information management, & marketing; health & related services; social & human services; engineering & industrial technologies; agriculture & natural resources
Career clusters	Sixteen categories specified, e.g., construction, financial services
Work values	Achievement; independence; recognition; relationships; support
Postsecondary programs/majors	Categories change annually based on information provided by schools
ASVAB	
Military	
Careers by gender	

Topics and factors taken from the Choices® Planner. Reproduced by permission of Bridges Transitions, Inc. Copyright © 2008 Bridges Transitions, Inc., a Xap Corporation company. All rights reserved.

system manager, instructional systems designer, robotics technician, or LAN manager. On the other hand, some occupations become outdated and disappear, such as elevator operator, radio announcer (as opposed to DJ), or steamship captain. Generally, occupations employing large numbers of people change the least.

The vast majority of occupations change very little. Indeed, there are still millions of jobs in manufacturing even though that part of the U.S. economy has declined in the past 30 years. It is a mistake to consider the occupational world as completely unstable or unpredictable.

Thomas Gutteridge, dean of management at the University of Connecticut, and Raymond Palmer, a career counselor, noted that it is *jobs that are changing, not occupations*. In other words, the lower the level of the analysis—occupation vs. job—the greater the rate of change. Gutteridge and Palmer concluded that occupations will increasingly be defined by industry and location

(Patterson & Allen 1996). For example, if your occupation is writer, teacher, or software developer, how you work and what you do will depend on the kind of industry and organization where you work—for example, state government, IBM, Chamber of Commerce. Moreover, the occupational activity may differ according to geographic region—southeast Florida, New York City, or rural Texas.

Some of the information about existing, mainstream occupations does change constantly. This is usually true of employment-related topics such as the numbers of openings, the outlook, and salaries. Other occupational information doesn't change so rapidly, such as the typical work duties, the training requirements, and the working conditions. Thus, it is best to be somewhat tentative about occupational information because it never represents all of what is really happening at any one time at any particular worksite. Don't consider occupational information as carved into stone but remain a little skeptical and questioning.

Occupational Classifications

It is useful to group and classify occupations according to some common characteristics. Table 3.2 shows some common systems of occupational classifications. We have already talked about the *Dictionary of Occupational Titles*, Occupational Employment Statistics, and Holland codes. It is important to make some additional comments about several of these classifications.

The *Dictionary of Occupational Titles* (U.S. Dept. of Labor, 1991) was for many years the most widely used occupational classification system. Many books, computer-based career guidance systems, and libraries used it to index and classify information about occupations. It was originally created in 1939 and was revised four times. About 20 percent of the 12,741 descriptions were new or revised in the last revision. As you might imagine, this classification was rather complex, including 9 occupational groupings, 83 occupationally specific divisions, and 564 groups. In addition, a nine-digit code number provided varied information about each occupation listed. Knowing the DOT numbers of occupations you are interested in learning about can be helpful for locating useful information.

TABLE 3.2   OCCUPATIONAL CLASSIFICATIONS

---

1. *Dictionary of Occupational Titles* (DOT; U.S. Department of Labor, 1977, 1982, 1986). The DOT is a true coding system in that certain digits of the occupational code reveal major and minor occupational groupings based on both the nature of the work performed and the demands of such work activities upon the workers. This is a detailed classification system with definitions of each occupation. It is organized to meet the operating need of the public employment service. The fourth edition of the DOT was updated with supplements in 1982 and 1986.

2. *Occupational Employment Statistics* (OES; U.S. Department of Labor, 2006). The OES occupational classification system is designed to provide information about staffing patterns and projected employment in U.S. industries and occupations. Survey and matrix classifications are based on the Standard Occupational Code. The OES system organizes occupational information on four levels: division, major group, minor group, and detail. It is available online at http://www.bls.gov/oes/oes_emp.htm.

3. *Standard Occupational Code* (SOC; U.S. Department of Labor, 2000). The SOC provides a mechanism for cross-referencing and aggregating occupation-related data collected by social and economic statistical reporting programs. The classification covers all occupations in which work is performed for pay or profit, including work performed in family-operated enterprises where direct remuneration may not be made to family members. Twenty-three broad occupational divisions are subdivided into 64 major groups, which are further subdivided into minor groups and units. This system is a standard overall classification system used by most federal programs.

4. *Holland Codes* (Gottfredson & Holland, 1996). The Holland codes used the RIASEC typology based on Holland's theory of vocational choice. The six types are Realistic, Investigative, Artistic, Social, Enterprising, and Conventional. All 12,000 DOT occupations are classified with three-letter Holland codes, and rated by general education (GED) level, specific vocational preparation (SVP) level, and industry codes.

Holland codes have been assigned to about 1,100 occupations in the *Occupations Finder* (Holland, 1999) and about 7,000+ DOT occupations in the *Dictionary of Holland Occupational Codes* (DHOC; Gottfredson & Holland, 1996). Table 2.3 provided some examples of occupations typically grouped into the six categories. This arrangement is important because the Holland scheme is one where popular, widely used interest inventories use the same RIASEC scheme in coding occupations (and even fields of study and leisure, for that matter—but more about that later.) Besides these two publications, Holland codes are used in Choices® Planner (Bridges Transitions Co., 2008), DISCOVER® (ACT, 2006), and other computer-based career guidance systems. Knowing your Holland code will enable you to identify and explore occupations that are compatible with your occupational personality. The *DHOC* also uses information from a sample of about 500 occupations included in census data to report occupational information for those occupations.

The Standard Occupational Code (SOC; U.S. Dept. of Labor, 2000) is used in computer-based career guidance systems such as Choices® Planner. It is a less complicated system than the DOT and is widely used in the ACRN information systems, O*NET, and Census reports. The SOC is designed to cover 822 detailed occupations where work is performed for pay or profit; both military and civilian occupations are included. It uses a four-level system with each level providing more detail. The 23 divisions are shown in Table 3.3. If you know the SOC number codes for occupations you are interested in learning more about, then you have a "key" that unlocks information for you.

TABLE 3.3   SOC MAJOR GROUPS

1. Management occupations
2. Business and financial operations occupations
3. Computer and mathematical occupations
4. Architecture and engineering occupations
5. Life, physical, and social science occupations
6. Community and social services occupations
7. Legal occupations
8. Education, training, and library occupations
9. Arts, design, entertainment, sports, and media occupations
10. Healthcare practitioners and technical occupations
11. Healthcare support occupations
12. Protective service occupations
13. Food preparation and serving related occupations
14. Building and grounds cleaning and maintenance occupations
15. Personal care and service occupations
16. Sales and related occupations
17. Office and administrative support occupations
18. Farming, fishing, and forestry occupations
19. Construction and extraction occupations
20. Installation, maintenance, and repair occupations
21. Production occupations
22. Transportation and material moving occupations
23. Military specific occupations

Industry Classifications

In learning about options for ways and places to work, most people typically think first about the kind of job they want, the "occupation." But what about the industry or the setting where the work could be performed? According to the *Career Guide to Industries, 2008–2009 Edition* (U.S. Department of Labor, 2008; also available at http://www.bls.gov/oco/cg/home.htm) there were almost 8.8 million private business establishments in the United States in 2006. The average size of these establishments varies widely. Hospitals, for example, employ an average of 543 workers, while physicians' offices employ an average of 10. Similarly, although there is an average of 15 employees per establishment for all of retail trade, department stores employ an average of 130 people.

Business establishments in the United States are predominantly small; 60 percent of all establishments employed fewer than 5 workers in 2006. However, the medium-sized to large establishments employ a greater proportion of all workers. For example, establishments that employed 50 or more workers accounted for only 4 percent of all establishments yet employed 57 percent of all workers. The large establishments—those with more than 500 workers—accounted for only 0.2 percent of all establishments, but employed 17 percent of all workers.

Understanding how industries are classified can be especially useful in thinking about career options. The Standard Industrial Classification (SIC) was developed in the 1930s to classify different kinds of businesses and employing organizations, which could then be used to obtain information about occupations and related jobs. For example, if you were interested in physical therapy jobs, you can find the names of potential employers by finding the SIC codes for hospitals, physical therapy centers, and other businesses where you can then get more information about occupations and employment.

However, the SIC system became dated with changes in the economy and it was replaced by a newer system. The North American Industry Classification System (NAICS; U.S. Bureau of Census, 2007; also available at http://www.census.gov/epcd/www/naics.html) was developed in cooperation with Canada and Mexico and significantly changed the old SIC system. NAICS groups establishments into industries based on the economic activity in which they are primarily engaged. Establishments using similar raw material inputs, similar capital equipment, and similar labor are classified in the same industry. In other words, establishments that do similar things in similar ways are classified together. In developing NAICS, every sector of the economy was restructured and redefined. For example, a new Information sector combines communications, publishing, motion picture and sound recording, and online services, recognizing our information-based economy. Manufacturing is restructured to recognize new high-tech industries. In addition, eating and drinking places are transferred to a new Accommodation and Food Services sector. NAICS classifies all economic activity into 20 industry sectors while the old SIC only used 10 (see Table 3.4).

How could you use this NAICS system in your career planning? Let's say you were interested in finding organizations involved in Professional, Scientific, and Technical Services because you wanted to work in those industries. There are six major categories of these organizations in the NAICS system:

1. accounting, tax preparation, bookkeeping and payroll services;

2. architectural, engineering, and related services;

3. computer systems design and related services;

4. management, scientific, and technical consulting services;

5. scientific research and development services; and

6. advertising and related services.

TABLE 3.4	NAICS Categories

1. Agriculture, Forestry, Fishing, and Hunting
2. Mining
3. Utilities
4. Construction
5. Manufacturing
6. Wholesale Trade
7. Retail Trade
8. Transportation and Warehousing
9. Information
10. Finance and Insurance
11. Real Estate and Rental and Leasing
12. Professional, Scientific and Technical Services
13. Management of Companies and Enterprises
14. Administrative and Support and Waste Management and Remediation Services
15. Educational Services
16. Health Care and Social Assistance
17. Arts, Entertainment and Recreation
18. Accommodation and Food Services
19. Other Services (except Public Administration)
20. Public Administration

Note: NAICS (North American Industry Classification System)

More specifically, if you were interested in working in the *sports industry* you could go to NAICS section 711 Performing Arts, Spectator Sports, and Related Industries, then to section 7112 Spectator Sports, and finally to section 71121 Spectator Sports. There you would find that this industry includes (1) sports teams or clubs primarily participating in live sporting events before a paying audience; (2) establishments primarily engaged in operating racetracks; (3) independent athletes engaged in participating in live sporting or racing events before a paying audience; (4) owners of racing participants, such as cars, dogs, and horses, primarily engaged in entering them in racing events or other spectator sports events; and (5) establishments, such as sports trainers, primarily engaged in providing specialized services to support participants in sports events or competitions. The final step would be to find the names and contact information for organizations in this industry section, 71121 Spectator Sports, so you could contact them about jobs.

Locating Occupational Information

As a college student, you are in an ideal situation to locate occupational information. The two best sources are the career library or information room in a career center or counseling center, followed by reference librarians at a school library. Both of these places are likely to have staff with expertise in using the Internet to find high quality information. Your first task is to find out where occupational information is located on your campus. Remember the distinctions we made earlier in Chapter 1 between occupational, employment, and educational information, because each of these three kinds of information may be housed in a different place. There is probably at least one staff member in the career center who has primary responsibility for managing career information resources, and that is the person who can best help you find the information you need.

If you are not at a college campus, then you will want to go to your public library. This library may have a special collection or a librarian who can assist you with career-related information searches. You may also find other occupational information at a workforce center or state CRN office, or in a public or private career counseling or vocational rehabilitation services office.

There are some particularly good and important publications with occupational information. Here are reference sources to look for when you are in the library or on the Internet.

The best U.S. Government publication is the *Occupational Outlook Handbook* (OOH; U.S. Dept. of Labor, 2007; also available at http://www.bls.gov/oco/), which is revised every two years and provides the latest information on over 250 occupations accounting for 90 percent of U.S. jobs. This information includes the nature of work, places of employment, training and other qualifications, advancement, employment outlook, earnings and working conditions, and sources of additional information. The OOH and all the other materials described here are available from the Superintendent of Documents, U.S. Government Printing Office, Washington, D.C. 20402.

Another reference book originally produced by the federal government is the *New Guide for Occupational Exploration, Fourth Edition* (GOE; Farr & Shatkin, 2006). The most recent edition of the GOE provides descriptions of over 900 occupations employing about 95 percent of the U.S. workforce. The occupations in the GOE are categorized in relation to 16 interest areas, such as "Arts, Entertainment, or Media" or "Sales and Marketing," and one can search for fields based on these 14 areas.

Finally, the *Occupational Outlook Quarterly* (OOQ; U.S. Dept. of Labor) is a government publication that describes new trends in occupations and the relationships of education and training to occupational activity. New information published in the OOQ eventually may find its way into the newest edition of the OOH, but it may take some time. It is available online at http://www.bls.gov/opub/ooq/ooqhome.htm.

Since 1995, information about the labor market, including specific job vacancies, occupations, and training opportunities, has become available through hundreds of Web sites on the Internet. For example, the U.S. Department of Labor has developed online resources about labor market and related career information at http://www.CareerOneStop.org. These include a Web site (http://www.jobbankinfo.org/) that lists job vacancies from over 1,800 state Employment Service offices, including over a million job openings. It also includes America's Career InfoNet, http://www.acinet.org/. This Internet home page is also connected by hyperlinks with other job listing sites on the net.

Private publishers also produce a great deal of reference information about occupations. Here are some of the best sourcebooks. The *Encyclopedia of Careers and Vocational Guidance* (13th edition) published by Ferguson is a five-volume set that covers over 2,500 occupations. Professional associations produce much information describing occupations in their fields, and the *Directory of National Trade and Professional Associations* (Columbia Books) published annually for 39 years includes more than 8,100 association listings. Association directories, which can include member information and accredited training programs, are often overlooked as a source of inside information about career fields.

There are many specialized publications about careers and occupations, such as *Black Collegian Magazine*, *Working Woman*, *The Collegiate Career Woman*, *Equal Opportunity Careers*, *Careers and the Disabled*, *Career World*, *Corporate Job Outlook*, and *Hispanic Business*.

Now when you go to the Internet or a career or public library and ask for assistance, you will have some ideas about the kinds of books, publications, and Web sites you can use.

KNOWLEDGE ABOUT EDUCATION AND TRAINING

Our knowledge about education and training is very extensive, but basically we can think about it in terms of the level and length of the experience. Most CIDS and other career information systems use level and length of training as a way to describe occupations. Level is defined in terms of General Educational Development, or GED. GED Levels 1 and 2 are elementary or less; Levels 3 and 4 are high school and some specialized training; and Levels 5 and 6 involve college and postgraduate training. As a college student, you'll be most interested in occupations at GED Levels 5 and 6.

The length of training is defined in terms of Specific Vocational Preparation, or SVP. SVP refers to how long you must train to master the skills of a particular job, and every occupation can be rated from 1 to 9. An occupation with an SVP rating of 4 requires 3 to 6 months of training, while one with an SVP rating of 8 could require 4 to 10 years of training. An occupation with a lower GED level can have a higher SVP rating and vice versa. Other jobs, like surgeon, could have high ratings on both measures.

We will now examine different ways that educational programs and fields of study are defined; some of the different kinds of training programs available; the differences between certification and licensure; learning as a lifelong process; providers of education and training, including financial support; and sources of educational and training information.

Classifying Educational Programs

Educational and training programs can be classified in some of the same ways as occupations. For example, Holland types and GOE clusters each group fields of study and educational training programs in terms of these two classification schemes.

Holland codes are used to classify over 900 college majors and vocational-technical training programs in the *Educational Opportunities Finder* (Rosen, Holmberg & Holland, 1994). These fields of study are also listed alphabetically and by degree level (two-year, four-year, postgraduate). GOE clusters are used in the *Guide for Occupational Exploration* to identify and group over 550 school subjects at the secondary and postsecondary level.

College Training Options

Can you name all the majors and degrees at your college or university? What should you know in thinking about educational programs in higher education? First, remember that there is often a difference between a department and a major field of study (usually just called a major). A "department" is an administrative unit of the educational institution, and it may include several degree programs and majors. Departments are located in schools or colleges. A program of study may refer to either a department or a major, depending on the organizational structure of the school.

Second, some programs of study are directly tied to occupations through certification and accreditation programs. Other academic programs, like liberal arts majors, are not directly connected to a profession or occupational activities. Table 3.5, for example, shows how the educational programs at one university are organized. Understanding a structure such as this is important in educational decision making because it is the way in which options are organized and made available to you. When compared to the occupational classification systems examined earlier in this chapter, it is clear that classifications of majors and occupations differ significantly. Only students pursuing preprofessional, certificated majors can productively think of major and occupational choice as closely related. You might notice that there are no major categories for agriculture, graphic arts, health, or forestry in this university's list. Academic program classification systems may vary widely from one college to another.

There is a widespread assumption that college training is a way to assure employment, but that is not always the case. The U.S. Department of Labor reports that from 2006–2016 only 20 percent of the jobs will require a bachelor's degree (Franklin, 2007). We will examine other training options besides college that are more directly employment-related.

TABLE 3.5   ACADEMIC PROGRAM CLASSIFICATION EXAMPLE

Degree Symbols: B-Bachelor's Degree; M-Master's Degree; A-Advanced Master's; S-Specialist; P-Professional; D-Doctoral Degree

College of Arts and Sciences

Anthropology	B	M	D
Biological Science	B	M	D
Biochemistry	B		
Chemical Physics		M	D
Chemical Science	B		
Chemistry	B	M	D
Classical Language & Literature:			
Classics	B	M	
Greek	B	M	
Latin	B	M	
Computer & Information Science	B	M	D
English	B	M	D
Geology	B	M	D
Geophysical Fluid Dynamics			D
History	B	M	D
Mathematics	B	M	D
Meteorology	B	M	D
Modern Languages:			
French	B	M	D
German	B	M	
Italian	B		
Russian	B		
Slavic Languages & Literature		M	
Spanish	B	M	D
Molecular Biophysics			D
Neuroscience			D
Oceanography		M	D
Philosophy	B	M	D
Physics	B	M	D
Religion	B	M	D
Secondary Science &/or Mathematics Teaching	B		
Statistics	B	M	D

College of Business

Accounting	B	M	
Business administration	B	M	D
Finance	B	M	
Hospitality Admin.	B		
Multinational Business	B		
Management	B	M	
Marketing	B	M	
Real Estate	B		
Risk Management & Insurance	B		

College of Communication

Audiology & Speech Pathology	B	M/A	D
Communication	B	M	D

School of Criminology and Criminal Justice

Criminology	B	M	D

College of Education

Adult Education		M/S	D
Comprehensive Vocational Educational	S	D	
Counseling & Human Systems		M/S	
Combined Program in Counseling Psychology & School Psychology			D
Early Childhood Education	B	M/S	D
Educational Administration/ Leadership		M/S	D
Educational Psychology		M/S	D
Educational Disturbances/ Learning Disabilities	B	M/S	
English Education	B	M/S	D
Evaluation & Measurement		M/S	D
Foundations of Education		M/S	D
Health Education	B	M	
Higher Education		M/S	D

TABLE 3.5 ACADEMIC PROGRAM CLASSIFICATION EXAMPLE (CONTINUED)

Program	B	M	D
Instructional Systems		M/S	D
Leisure services & Studies	B	M	
Mathematics Education	B	M/S	D
Mental Retardation	B	M/S	
Multilingual/Multicultural Education	B	M/S	D
Physical education	B	M/S	D
Reading Education		M/S	D
Rehabilitation Services	B	M/S	D
Science Education	B	M/S	D
Social Studies Education	B	M/S	D
Special Education		S	D
Comprehensive Vocational Education		S	D
FAMU/FSU College of Engineering			
Chemical Engineering	B	M	D
Civil Engineering	B	M	
Electrical Engineering	B	M	D
Industrial Engineering	B	M	
Mechanical Engineering	B	M	D
College of Human Sciences			
Textiles & Consumer Sciences	B	M	
Family & Child Sciences	B	M	
Family & Consumer Science Education	B	M	
Human Sciences	B		D
Marriage and Family			D
Movement Science		M/S	D
Food and Nutrition	B	M	
Interdisciplinary Programs			
American Studies	B	M	
Asian Studies	B	M	
Humanities	B	M	
International Affairs	B	M	
Latin American & Caribbean Studies	B		
Marriage & Family Living			D
Physics Interdisciplinary Program	B	M	
Russian & East European Studies	B	M	
Social Sciences	B	M	
College of Law			
Law			P
College of Information			
Library Science		M/A	D

Program	B	M	D
College of Medicine			
Medicine			D
School of Motion Picture, Television, and Recording Arts			
Motion Picture, Television, & Recording Arts	B	M	
College of Music			
Arts Administration		M*	
Music			D
Composition	B	M	D
Music Education	B	M	D
Music History & Literature	B		
Music Liberal Arts	B		
Music Theory	B	M	D
Musicology		M	D
Opera Production		M	
Performance	B	M	D
School of Nursing			
Nursing	B	M	
College of Social Sciences			
Asian Studies	B	M	
Demography		M	
Economics	B	M	D
Geography	B	M	D
Interdisciplinary Social Science	B	M	
International Affairs	B	M	
Political Science	B	M	D
Public Administration		M	D
Russian & East European Studies	B	M	
Sociology	B	M	D
Urban & Regional Planning		M	D
College of Social Work			
Social Work	B	M	D
School of Theater			
Theater	B	M	D
School of Visual Arts and Dance			
Arts Administration		M	
Art Studio	B	M	
Art Education	B	M/S	D
Art, History & Criticism of	B	M	
Dance	B	M	
Interior Design	B	M	

A second problem with assuming that a college degree guarantees a job is that it minimizes the importance of the person. Employers hire people—not degrees. For example, a degree in computer science will not necessarily translate into job offers. Moreover, even industries and occupations that are stable or declining continue to hire many people, sometimes thousands of workers each year.

However, college degrees do pay off in several ways. First, over the course of your working life on average, you'll earn more total income with a college degree than with only a high school diploma. Second, you're less likely to be unemployed, or you will be unemployed for shorter periods if you have a college degree. Thus, in these two ways, on average, college pays off with respect to employment. (We discuss this more fully in Chapter 7.)

What about liberal arts majors and career preparation? Much has been written about this topic over the years. A liberal arts degree can provide you with a variety of work- and job-related skills that are transferable. Majoring in a preprofessional degree will not automatically make you more job ready than someone with a liberal arts degree. Many business leaders completed liberal arts majors and they philosophically value this learning in new hires, even though front-line managers may be looking for technical skills in hiring new college graduates. Two of the most familiar professions, law and medicine, do not require a specific under-graduate major.

Your best strategy is to major in areas related to your values, interests, and skills, because this will likely produce the highest academic performance (i.e., grades), and in general, better grades keep future options open to you. In addition to completing your major degree requirements, you can do several other things to improve your employability: obtain work experience through an internship, summer job, or cooperative education; select a minor field of study that balances your major; develop a high-quality resume and/or portfolio; and network with people who already work in your areas of interest.

Noncollege Training Options

There are thousands of training programs outside of the traditional four-year college. Indeed, some have reported that noneducational organizations in the United States, for example, government agencies, business and industry, and labor unions, spend more than $60 billion annually on training. In contrast, all elementary and secondary education accounts for only about $32 billion. Here are some training options.

Vocational Education. "Voc ed" may occur at either the secondary, postsecondary, or adult education levels. Vocational education is job oriented; it is designed in response to an assessed employer need for trained workers for particular jobs in a local area. Vocational education programs may last from a few months to several years, and they usually involve completion of a certification rather than a degree. Sometimes the word *technical* is added in to this definition, making it vocational-*technical* education.

In recent years there have been some problems with vocational educational programs provided by private companies as opposed to state or local governments. These private or proprietary educational providers have not always been able to obtain a high job placement rate for students; in other words, the training programs have not been set up in response to assessed employer needs for trained workers. It is a safe bet, however, that there is some kind of training program for virtually any kind of job-related skill.

Apprenticeships. Training for many skilled and technical trades, such as electrician and steel worker, are provided through apprenticeships. Apprenticeships may involve several years of super-vised work by a highly skilled senior worker, plus a series of written examinations. This on-the-job training is intended to provide advanced learning experiences in field settings, where the trainee can develop real-life problem-solving skills related to job performance. Terms such as *helper* and *journeyman* are used to describe the different levels of apprenticeship.

Continuing Education. Virtually every occupation, whether it is a profession or skilled trade, now incorporates continuing education experiences. Because occupations and the knowledge required to perform competently in them change over time, continuing education is mandatory for people in almost any line of work. This continuing education is sometimes also called professional development, in-service training (as opposed to preservice training, which you obtain while still a "full-time" student), or staff development. Credit for continuing education is typically given in the form of CEUs, which is a standard measure for continuing education. One CEU is equal to 10 hours of time in training. In this way, a CEU is like a semester or quarter-hour of academic credit in a traditional college.

Some examples of continuing education include a half-day workshop at a community college, a two-day training program offered by a visiting consultant at the job site, completing correspondence courses, an employer-sponsored weekend MBA program, or instructional modules available through a Web-based learning tool. Distance learning is sometimes used when talking about continuing education and simply refers to the fact that the learner is in a different location from the instructor. Continuing education is increasingly being provided in innovative, nonclassroom-based instructional programs.

Military Training. The largest provider of noncollege training in the world is the U.S. Department of Defense. The armed services in this country offer many training programs in vocational and technical areas because the extensive nature and sophistication of military weapons, transportation, communication, and community-support systems requires a very highly trained workforce. It should be noted that crosswalks have been created that link civilian and military jobs and training programs to one another. Many of these crosswalks are available through state CIDS.

Credit for Prior Work. There are some schools that will provide academic credit for prior work. The system is based on a careful documentation of work-based learning and training, sometimes using a log or portfolio of prior learning. Schools that are members of the Council for Adult and Experiential Learning (CAEL; http://www.cael.org/) have agreed to incorporate a person's on-the-job training and other prior learning into the design of an educational degree program and to give credit for this prior learning. While postsecondary schools typically do not give credit for prior learning, it is something to be aware of as you acquire training experiences throughout your career.

Accreditation, Ranking, Certification, and Licensure

The relationships between occupations and training are often connected by the processes of accreditation, ranking, certification, and licensure. These terms can be very confusing for people engaged in educational and career planning, so it is helpful to compare and contrast the meanings of these four terms.

Accreditation is a designation given by a professional association or governing group to a training program. It is not a designation given directly to students or trainees. An accredited training program is one that has met standards set up by an association, board of experts, or some other recognized body. In general, you will want to complete your studies in programs that are accredited by the groups that are the most powerful and influential in a field. Completing your training at an accredited program has many advantages for you, including ease in obtaining financial aid and later employment, more prestige and credibility in the profession, and getting certified and licensed.

A word should be said here about **rankings**. Students sometimes want to know the ranking of the school or degree program they are considering and they often consult the annual report provided by *U.S. News* (http://www.usnews.com/). While it seems logical to consider this factor in planning your education, there are some problems. First, the ranking is probably based on a "reputational analysis," a fancy way of saying popularity contest. Typically, some group will ask deans, faculty, or another sample of people to rank schools or programs in their field, and the result is the ranked list. Second, the perceptions of quality may be based on history, what the program accomplished many years ago, not current conditions and information. Third, a "halo effect" can operate. Harvard always seems to get high rankings, mostly because it is Harvard. However, not all programs there are probably of equally high quality. Fourth, rankings of undergraduate programs are especially suspect. They may be mostly based on the quality of the graduate program.

Rankings may be useful in your educational planning if they are (1) based on specific outcome criteria that matter to you (e.g., salaries of graduates, percent of bar exams passed); (2) if they help you identify important characteristics of notable programs so you can use this information to evaluate other, unranked, programs; (3) if they are current; and (4) if they describe why and how the ranking was obtained.

Certification is a designation that a professional association or independent group gives to you after you have completed a specified training program, possibly including supervised field experience and perhaps an examination. Certification is a public affirmation that you have completed all the requirements as a professional in a field and that you can be designated by a name or title. Certification is typically provided by a national group, but teaching is one occupation where certification is typically provided by a state agency.

Licensure, unlike certification, is provided by a governmental agency, not a professional group (one exception is law). Licensure is often made available by a state, and it means that you can practice or offer services for a fee as a member of a particular profession or trade in that state. Hundreds of occupations require licensure for legal employment, but states may differ in the actual licensure requirements. Some states offer reciprocal arrangements with one another, so you can relocate to a state without repeating the time-consuming, expensive process of becoming licensed.

Licensed occupations have become modern-day guilds (Hoppough, 2008). About 28 percent of U.S. workers now work in a licensed field, up from 4.5 percent 50 years ago. For example, there are over 1,100 licensed occupations in California. Typical requirements include hours of classroom study, e.g., 150 hours of college coursework for accountants, and a passing score on a state licensure examination.

What can these distinctions mean for your educational and career decision making? First, it is important to note that educational and training programs don't certify or license you for anything. This is only done by national associations or boards and governmental organizations. Second, completion of an accredited training program may ease your preparation for the certification and licensure process, but it will not guarantee success for you. Third, ranking is relatively unimportant in evaluating educational and training programs. Fourth, you should inquire of educational and training providers about the past performance of graduates in completing certification and licensure requirements.

Education and Training: A Life/Career Process

When we examined Super's (1990) Rainbow in Chapter 1 (see Figure 1.1), we noted that training periods kept recurring throughout the person's career. Bolles (1981) made the same observation in regards to the "three boxes." We have seen how training is lifelong and how education can help you develop transferable skills. Education and training can be early indicators of what will happen later to a person with regards to occupational and leisure activities. For example, a person who enrolls in a welding class to learn more about the process and develop some skills for a hobby may years later start a welding business. The class experience also provided an opportunity to meet other people with similar interests, to learn something about the need for more welders and welding services in the local community, and to refocus broader career goals.

In this sense, it is important to recognize that education and training are already part of one's career; they are not something that will prepare you for some future career. If you are a college student now, you are already in your career.

Sources of Information and Support

Computer-based CIDS and other Internet-based programs have made dramatic changes in the delivery of educational information, e.g., Choices® Planner, DISCOVER®, CIS, GIS, Focus, and SIGI[3]. You can use these systems to search for educational programs that meet your criteria. Let's say you're interested in searching for bachelor's degree programs in marine biology by state, enrollment size, tuition costs, and the kinds of athletic programs available on the campus. The system will scan many thousands of combinations of options to compile a list of programs in the states you specify. You can also use the computer to get specific information about more than 5,000 programs from up to 4,000 schools that may be included in a typical database of one of these systems.

In addition to computers, most libraries and career or counseling centers will have reference books on educational and training options that are updated annually. Standard sources include *The College Handbook* (College Entrance Examination Board); *Barron's Profiles of American Colleges and Guide to Two-Year Colleges* (Barron's Educational Series); *Peterson's College or Graduate School Planners* (Peterson's, A Nelnet Company); the *College Blue Book* (Macmillan Publishing); and the 690 *Chronicle Occupational Briefs* (Chronicle).

Financial Assistance

Financial support for education and training is available in many forms. State CIDS and other computer-based career guidance systems provide lists of federal and private sources of financial support for vocational technical and higher-education training. A college financial aid office and a public library can provide reference books.

The school providing the training will likely have specialized rules and sources of financial assistance that may be especially important to you. These local sources may be fruitful for you to pursue. Employers and unions sometimes provide funds for training as a benefit of employment or membership, sometimes even for spouses and children of employees. Remember that there are some illegal and unethical operators in this field who will take your money and do nothing more than search a CIDS database, which you probably could have done better yourself. Finally, start early in the financial assistance search process. Ten months may be the best lead time in applying for financial and scholarship aid.

LEISURE TIME

In the United States, people have widely differing views about leisure time. Some view it as a positive thing and a desirable part of living. Others see it negatively and regard it as wasteful and useless. How did we arrive at such opposing views? Why is leisure an important part of career planning?

A Historical View of Leisure

Our conflicting views about leisure had their origins many years ago. The ancient Greeks, at the time of Plato and Aristotle, prized leisure as a time for learning, creativity, and sports competition by citizens. They had no word for work, because only slaves and other noncitizens were involved in labor. The fall of the Greek civilization led to a complete change in the concept of leisure. In the later Roman Empire, leisure was seen as depraved, degrading excesses in drunkenness and self-indulgence. Early Christian leaders and, later, Protestant reformers viewed leisure as idleness, and idleness was seen as moral depravity. Even today, some consider leisure the seedbed of substance abuse, antisocial acts, and financial waste. Given this brief sketch of Western cultural traditions, it is no wonder that as a society we are often very confused about the value of leisure.

Despite this low opinion of leisure by some persons, others spend a lot of time indulging in it. Jeremy Rifkin (1995), author of *The End of Work*, reported that about 51 percent of Americans, about 94.2 million adults, gave an average of 4.2 hours per week to various causes or organizations in 1992. He has noted that this third sector of the economy includes more than 1,400,000 nonprofit organizations whose primary purpose is to provide a service or advance a cause. Much of this time is volunteered (unpaid), and it represents a significant allocation of effort on the part of many citizens.

How is leisure viewed in terms of work and career by most career development experts? We defined *work* as activity that produces something of value for oneself or others. This definition included unpaid work, or leisure activities. We further defined "career" as the time extended working out of a purposeful life pattern through work undertaken by the person. With these definitions, we can include leisure as an important, significant part of our career. A definition of leisure is provided below.

> **Leisure.** *Relatively self-determined activities and experiences that are available due to discretionary income, time, and social behavior; the activity may be physical, intellectual, volunteer, creative, or some combination of all four.*

Some other important points should be considered. First, leisure is self-determined, just like other aspects of career. You choose the part that leisure plays in you life. Second, the money, time, and social relationships involved in leisure are discretionary; they are not something you "have" to do, but you "choose" to do. And, third, leisure activities may be physical, intellectual, private, social, routine, spiritual, creative, or some combination of all of these.

Viewed this way, leisure is an essential part of our career development and something that we need to better understand and know about in order to effectively solve career problems and make career decisions. As with other options for occupations and education, it is important for you to begin with knowing yourself before you start to explore leisure options.

Leisure, in relation to other occupational and educational activities, can be (1) complimentary, (2) supplementary, or (3) compensatory (Blocker & Siegal, 1981). As **complimentary**, leisure extends and magnifies your job activities. If you are a professional musician in a symphony, you could spend your weekends teaching other gifted musicians the fine points of mastering your musical instrument. As **supplementary**, leisure could enrich your life in ways that go beyond job satisfaction. It rounds you out. If you are a high school football coach, you could join a class in ceramics as a way to meet different kinds of people and enjoy solitary work. As **compensatory**, leisure could make up for deficits and dissatisfactions in your job. If you are an office manager of an accounting firm and want to be more active and work with children, your leisure might involve coaching a youth soccer team.

Leisure Classifications

How many different kinds of leisure activities are there? A book by Overs, Taylor, and Adkins (1977), the *Avocational Counseling Manual*, listed over 725 different leisure activities in a three-level classification. They classified leisure activities into nine major categories, ranging from the more concrete to the more abstract, including: games; sports; nature activities; collection activities;

craft activities; art and music activities; educational, entertainment, and cultural activities; volunteer activities; and organizational activities.

The Leisure Activities Finder, another classification of over 760 leisure activities based on two-letter Holland codes, was developed by Holmberg, Rosen, and Holland (1990). They based their groupings on Holland's six environmental models, which as we have seen have been used to classify occupations, fields of study, and now leisure activities. Each leisure option has a group label, such as collecting, nature, or entertainment, as a way of helping define the nature of the leisure activity.

Sources of Leisure Information

Information about leisure activities is everywhere. There are clubs, organizations, and online chat groups devoted to virtually every kind of leisure activity. These organizations provide demonstrations, training, organized events, memberships, and virtual communities for persons interested in the activity. There are Web sites and publications devoted to virtually every leisure activity. A virtual or physical library is one place to find out about these periodicals and publications. Your local newspaper and telephone yellow pages are a source of information about community leisure organizations, and a student activities office or Web site at a school or college will have information about school-based organizations and activities. Resorts, community recreation centers, volunteer agencies, and other community organizations can provide information and assistance to persons seeking information about leisure options. The field of leisure counseling is increasingly available to help persons assess their interests and values in order to more carefully explore leisure options available, given considerations of time, money, and social interests.

IMPROVING OUR OCCUPATIONAL, EDUCATIONAL, AND LEISURE KNOWLEDGE

There are a number of things one can do to learn more about options for solving career problems and making career decisions. We describe them in the following paragraphs.

Thinking "Better" About Options

Improving our knowledge about occupational, educational, and leisure options involves more than simply acquiring additional facts and data. It's also important to think smarter and better about these options. Here are some ways to do that.

First, develop a conceptual framework or structure (cognitive psychologists call these "schema") for thinking about options in each of the three areas. For example, Holland's six types provide a hexagonal model for thinking about options in all three areas. This chapter has reviewed other frameworks, but we like Holland types because they can be used to structure and classify self-knowledge as well as knowledge about the three areas of options. Thinking about options as types and combinations of types can free you up to think about options in new ways.

Second, think about options in ways that are neither overly rigid nor loose. For example, if you only think about occupations in terms of money or salary, you will be using a single standard that eliminates other important facts about occupational activities. On the other hand, if you think about occupations only in terms of how often they change, it will be difficult to think in useful ways about them.

Third, develop ways of thinking about options that make clear, useful distinctions among them. For example, some information about a field of study, such as, the percent of men in nursing and elementary education, may not be particularly important or useful for you in differentiating among major fields of study. You need to focus on those aspects of your options that are important to you and then examine the facts about those options. In other words, think about your values, interests, and skills as you examine the distinctions among options.

Fourth, think in complex ways about occupational, educational, and leisure options. You now know that there are many different ways to think about options. For example, options related to occupations, industries, education and training, and leisure are all simultaneously interrelated, changing, and separate. There are local, state, regional, national, and international perspectives on all these areas. This complexity is part of what makes career problem solving and decision making difficult.

Fifth, don't use information about options that is biased, superficial, or inaccurate. For example, some of the information that is available about options is produced for recruitment purposes; it is intended to put a positive spin on the option and make it more attractive. Highly stereotyped information is not reliable. It is important to censor or edit information that is not of high quality because it can confuse your thinking about career decisions.

Using Information About Options

What can you do to improve your information about occupational, educational, and leisure options? First, apply the research skills you have already developed in school to your personal career problem solving and decision making. Much of the information about your options is online in libraries or similar settings, and you have skills for finding and using computer-based indexes, databases, books, periodicals and files, multimedia resources, reference materials, and other sources. Indeed, using your research skills to develop information about your personal, life/career options may be the most important research you ever do.

Second, remember that finding information about options takes time. It is not something that you can rush along or take shortcuts to complete. A good way to look at it is if you spend, say, more than 86,000 hours working in some kind of employed position (calculated at 8 hours per day × 5 days per week × 50 weeks per year × 43 years), and you spend 100 hours in the next year studying and researching information sources related to your options, it would only be about 1/1000 of the time you spend in your occupational option. That's equivalent to about 28 seconds out of an 8-hour day. That doesn't even include the thousands of hours in learning and leisure that you will need to include in your planning. Common sense suggests that it would be important to invest the time now in this personal research in order to get the payoff of increased life/career satisfaction in the years to come.

Third, information about your options is available to you in formats that involve you in (1) reading, (2) listening, (3) observing, (4) writing, (5) visiting, and (6) talking. Think about some ways that these six actions can help you acquire information related to your options. One way you can assess your improvement in acquiring additional information about your options is to check off each time you engage in one of these six behaviors and keep track of exactly what you did. For example, you would list the resources you read, the people and associations you wrote to for information about occupations, or the information interviews you conducted. Each of these actions can be used to provide information about your options that is slightly different in nature; for this reason, it is good to use several of these behaviors to get information about each option you are exploring.

Fourth, make it a habit to constantly acquire occupational information from friends, family members of friends, relatives, acquaintances, or people sitting next to you on airplanes or buses. Church activities and volunteer organizations also provide a means to meet people working in a variety of occupations. Without such an approach, the occupations of your family members and teaching are the only occupations and jobs with which you will be directly familiar.

Fifth, make it a point to learn about and become a critical reader of sources of occupational, educational, and leisure information. They are all around us. Web-based publications, major national newspapers, popular magazines, professional and association newsletters, seminars, and television regularly carry reports about career options. These sources distill and summarize highlights from government reports, university research studies, and public surveys into informational reports that are easier to understand. If you are a college student, pay attention to the resources in your campus career center and on the center's Web site. This center is a collection point for hundreds of items each week that can inform you about your options.

Sixth, use the services of a professional career counselor, librarian, or other type of career services person to help you locate and evaluate particular sources of career information. Many public and educational libraries have a reference or adult services librarian who specializes in career information, including job vacancy listings, company and industry information, directory information, labor market trends, and so forth. In addition, career counselors can help you locate and process information about your options. They can help you clarify what the information means, whether or not you have enough of it, and where you are in the decision-making process.

SUMMARY

This chapter has introduced the topic of life/career options; the areas of occupational, educational, and leisure information. These three areas were examined in terms of organizational classifications, sources of information, and suggestions for improving the quality and quantity of information in each area. The interrelationships of these three areas were also highlighted, and suggestions were made for developing more complex ways of thinking about options in order to improve career problem solving and decision making. The goal was to help you improve the quality of information in the option knowledge domain of your Personal Career Theory.

REFERENCES

ACT. (2006). *DISCOVER*® [computer software]. Iowa City, IA: Author.

Blocker, D. H., & Siegal, R. (1981). Toward a cognitive developmental theory of leisure and work. *The Counseling Psychologist, 9*(3), 33–44.

Bolles, R. (2005). *A practical manual for job hunters and career changers: What color is your parachute?* Berkeley, CA: Ten Speed Press.

Bolles, R. (1981). *The three boxes of life, and how to get out of them.* Berkeley, CA: Ten Speed Press.

Bridges Transitions Co. (2008). Choices® Planner [computer software]. Oroville, WA: Author.

Farr, M., & Shatkin, L. (2006). *New guide for occupational exploration* (4th ed.). Indianapolis, IN: JIST Works.

Franklin, J. C. (2007, November). Employment outlook: 2006–16: An overview of BLS projections to 2016. *Monthly Labor Review,* 3–12.

Gottfredson, G. D., & Holland, J. L. (1996). *Dictionary of Holland occupational codes* (3rd ed.). Odessa, FL: Psychological Assessment Resources.

Holland, J. L. (1999). *Occupations finder.* Odessa, FL: Psychological Assessment Resources.

Holmberg, K., Rosen, D, & Holland, J. (1990). *Leisure activities finder.* Odessa, FL: Psychological Assessment Resources, Inc.

Hoppough, S. (2008, February 25). The new unions. *Forbes,* pp. 100–101.

Overs, R. P., Taylor, S., & Adkins, C. (1977). *Avocational counseling manual: A complete guide to leisure guidance*. Washington, DC: Hawkins & Associates.

Patterson, V., & Allen, C. (1996). Occupational outlook overview: Where will the jobs be in 2005? *Journal of Career Planning & Employment, 56*(3), 32–35, 61–64.

Rifkin, J. (1995). *The end of work*. New York: Putnam's.

Rosen, D., Holmberg, K., & Holland, J. (1994). *Educational opportunities finder*. Odessa, FL: Psychological Assessment Resources, Inc.

Super, D. (1990). A life-span, life-space approach to career development. In D. Brown & L. Brooks, (Eds.), *Career choice and development* (2nd ed.) San Francisco: Jossey-Bass.

U.S. Bureau of Census. (2007). *North American Industry Classification System: United States 2007*. Washington, DC: National Technical Information Service.

U.S. Department of Labor. (2000). *Standard occupational classification (SOC) system manual*. Washington, DC: U.S. Government Printing Office.

U.S. Department of Labor. (2008). *Career guide to industries, 2008–2009 edition*. Washington, DC: Author.

U.S. Department of Labor (1991). *Dictionary of occupational titles* (4th ed.). Indianapolis, IN: JIST Works.

U.S. Department of Labor. (1983). *Occupational employment statistics*. Indianapolis, IN: JIST Works.

U.S. Department of Labor. (2007). *Occupational outlook handbook, 2008–2009*. Indianapolis, IN: JIST Works.

U.S. Department of Labor. (2007). *Occupational Outlook Quarterly*. Washington, DC: Author.

CAREER DECISION MAKING

Problem solving and decision making are the essence of our lives—we are constantly involved in sorting through what we want and like in terms of what's possible. Think about it. You have probably already made a series of decisions today. What should I wear? What do I want to eat? When should I call my friend? Each of these decisions involved checking out information about yourself and your surroundings. For example, deciding what to wear might have involved assessing how you were feeling at the time—cold, sexy, grumpy—and it might have involved checking the weather forecast, how much outside walking you would be doing, and who you might be meeting during the day. In other words, the decisions you made about what to wear were based on knowing about yourself and your options.

Career problem solving and decision making also involve considering information about your values, interests, and skills and about your options in occupations, education, and leisure. In Chapter 1, we likened self-knowledge and occupational knowledge to computer data files stored in our memory that form the basis of career planning. We identified self and occupational knowledge as the base, the knowledge domain, of the Pyramid of Information-Processing Domains. Chapters 2 and 3 examined each of those areas.

Chapter 4 examines the second level of the pyramid, the decision skills domain (see Figure 4.1). The focus here is on "knowing how I make decisions." As with a computer system, the decision skills domain is like a software program that takes selected data from the files and uses it in preset ways to answer questions. The decision skills domain specifies five phases involved in decision making and helps us understand a systematic process for solving career problems.

This chapter provides information that will help you improve your problem-solving and decision-making skills in relation to your career planning. You should use this information to improve the quality of your Personal Career Theory, especially the CASVE Cycle in the Pyramid of Information-Processing Domains. After reading this chapter, you will be able to specify one or more CASVE phases with respect to your decisions about fields of study, occupations, or employment.

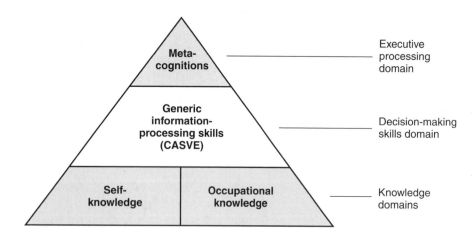

FIGURE **4.1**

Decision-Making Skills

Reprinted, by permission, from Gary W. Peterson, James P. Sampson, and Robert C. Reardon, *Career Development and Services: A Cognitive Approach.* Copyright 1991 by Brooks/Cole Publishing Company, a division of International Thomson Publishing Inc. All rights reserved.

TOPICS RELATED TO DECISION MAKING

First, we will review several topics related to the career decision-making process. These include (1) why it is important to know how to make good decisions; (2) types of career decision making; (3) basic approaches to making personal decisions; (4) barriers to effective decision making; and (5) decision making as a basic skill for general problem solving.

Importance of Good Decision Making

Sometimes we see students, who seem to have good self-knowledge and information about their options, make very poor decisions. They are constantly trying to "get it right." Other students take inventories to develop information about their interests, values, and skills and spend hours using computer-based career systems and books, and still they are unable to make a decision. In both cases, all the good effort to improve self and occupational knowledge was undermined by poor decision-making skills.

Decision making is very important because one test of our effectiveness in living is the quality of the way in which we make personal decisions. Note that the emphasis is on *how* the decision was made. This is especially true of major life decisions, such as what occupation to pursue, with whom to develop a relationship, and so on. These major life decisions, which have long-term implications covering many years, can be especially difficult, even for those with good decision-making skills. Other people know and evaluate us by the way we make important decisions. Sometimes, it is not so much the outcome of the decision that is important to others but the process that was used in making the choice. This is the position we take in this book—it is the *process*, not the outcome, that we want to focus on. Remember this point.

How do we learn to make personal decisions? Some of it is by trial and error; we learn by practice and by our past experience. Some of it is by observation; we watch others go through the decision-making process and we learn from watching them. However, most of our training for personal decision making is indirect rather than direct. You have probably never had a course on the topic, and yet much of your college coursework is designed to help you become a more effective personal decision maker. The general education courses you take in college, such as those in history, literature, humanities, biology, and psychology, are designed to both inform you about the discipline undergirding the course and to help you learn to apply that knowledge in personal decision making. For example, coursework in biology, history, geography, or economics can help you develop a personal understanding of the issues and importance of the environmental movement and ecology and to make personal decisions in this regard. The CASVE Cycle, which we will explore in more detail in this chapter, is based on the common problem-solving ideas that under gird those general education courses.

Kinds of Career Decision Makers

Sometimes it is hard to distinguish who is decided, undecided, or indecisive, with respect to career decision making. Even if we are decided on our career goals and have a career plan, we may still experience periods of uncertainty and indecision over particular aspects of our situation. Peterson, Sampson, and Reardon (1991) reviewed theory and research literature in this area and identified three states, or conditions, of career decision makers. These three kinds of individual decision makers are (1) decided, (2) undecided, and (3) indecisive.

Decided individuals are people who independently integrate knowledge about self and knowledge about options that enables them to develop a career plan that is satisfying and beneficial to themselves and society as a whole. They need to confirm a decision or to implement one. A key point is that the person has reviewed all of the relevant facts and data about self and about options in order to make a decision. In other words, a person is "decided" because of internal decision-making processes rather than of external judgments by others. However, a "false" decided person is one who has chosen an option in order to reduce immediate stress. For example, a student might indicate a psychology major on a college application form in order not to be identified as undecided by outsiders (college admissions officials), even though the student is very uncertain about which major to pursue.

Undecided individuals are people who have not made a commitment to an occupational or educational choice. Some undecided people may be considering options, but for very appropriate reasons are comfortable not declaring a first choice. Other undecided people want occupational certainty and are a little uncomfortable in not being able to declare a first choice. This lack of comfort may lead them to seek career counseling or to get more information about their occupational and educational options. Still other undecided people may have many interests and skills and are unable to make a commitment to an occupational choice due to the numerous options that fit their interests and skills.

Indecisive individuals are people who are often unable to make career decisions and continually experience considerable stress in their lives. They often find it difficult to make plans in all areas of life, and generally they focus on outside events or people in making decisions. In some cases, indecisive people find it difficult to explore options because of their anxiety; they put off or procrastinate making decisions indefinitely; they shift responsibility for the decisions to someone else; or they exaggerate the advantages and disadvantages of various options.

These three kinds of decision states are sometimes difficult to identify with respect to specific individuals, but in general they help us understand what kind of career assistance may be needed. People who are indecisive may need special assistance in their career decision making.

Problems in Effective Decision Making

The process of making personal decisions can be very difficult for some people, especially in particular situations. What kinds of things can interfere with effective decision making? The following are some of the more general problems. Being aware of these problems can help you take the necessary steps to set yourself up to succeed in the decision-making process.

Personal. We need to be in good physical, emotional, and mental condition to engage in effective decision making. If we were competing in an athletic event, we would want to be in top form and well prepared so we could succeed and have the best chance of winning the event. Being tired and run-down or stressed and anxious and unable to focus and concentrate on the decision-making activity will not ensure a good performance. This may sound fairly obvious, but career counselors find that people who have difficulty in career decision making are often not in "good decision-making condition." Their general lack of "life management skills" provides little foundation for effective decision making.

Family. Whether you're young or old, family members and relationships with significant others can interfere with effective decision making. (They can help too, of course, but here we're looking at problem areas for now.) For younger people, the problems may be with parents; for older individuals, they may be with spouses, partners, or children. Scholars who study family systems and career decision making have observed that people who are too interconnected with another family member can have difficulty separating themselves emotionally and psychologically in decision making. For example, when there is a lack of distinction between what *a significant other* thinks you should major in and what *you* think you should major in, and you can't keep it all separate, then you can have a problem. A lack of agreement among family members about things like duty, money, responsibility, guilt, values, and so forth can present problems in personal decision making. (As an aside, it is important to note that in some cultural traditions, it is considered proper and appropriate for older family members to actively participate in career decisions of younger members. We will explore these ideas more in Part Two.)

Society. Looking at the big picture, there are social, economic, historical, and cultural forces that can interfere with effective career decision making. A national economic recession, gender, or ethnic prejudice shared among residents in a community, or age discrimination can complicate one's educational or employment options and career decisions. In the case of a recession, none of the options may be very good, unless you work for a company that tries to find jobs for workers that have been "dehired."

Altogether, these three factors can make decision making even more difficult than usual, but they are all likely to be a part of many career decisions. Effective career decision makers will learn to develop strategies for overcoming personal and social factors that interfere with their decision making.

Decision Making Contrasted with Problem Solving

You have probably noticed that in the first four chapters of this book, the phrases "problem solving" and "decision making" have been used repeatedly. What are the similarities and differences between these terms? Understanding the distinction is important if this book is to be helpful.

Cognitive psychologists view a "problem" as a gap between a current state and a more desired state of affairs. The desire to remove the gap is the source of motivation to engage in the career problem-solving and decision-making process.

Problem solving, then, involves thinking or processing information that will lead to a course of action to remove the gap. This thinking process involves (1) recognizing the gap, (2) analyzing its causes, (3) coming up with different ways to remove the gap, and (4) *choosing* one of these ways to remove the gap. Thus, problem solving involves a *choice* among plausible alternative courses of action.

In contrast to problem solving, cognitive psychologists view **decision making** in a broader way. It includes the four steps of problem solving, but it adds (5) the development of a plan or strategy for implementing the chosen solution and the adoption of a risk-taking attitude and commitment to carry the plan to completion. Decision making, then, adds our feelings and behaviors to the problem-solving process. Decision making includes the *implementation* of a choice.

For example, when you were selecting a college to attend, problem-solving processes were used to select a course of action (choosing to come to your current college) and to remove a gap between a real and ideal state (able to tell anybody who asks where I'm going to college). Decision making occurred when you adopted a risk-taking attitude (your application could have been rejected; your friends could have laughed at you) and you committed energy and resources to attend your first choice (paid a housing deposit, saved money, arranged for transportation). Both problem solving and decision making are involved in career planning, and understanding the distinctions between the two can help you focus your efforts and be more effective.

Decision making is a broader life skill, the one that applies more to life/career development and planning.

THE CASVE CYCLE

The second level of the Pyramid of Information-Processing Domains pertains to decision making, and the CASVE (pronounced ka SAH' ve) Cycle will guide you through the career problem-solving and decision-making process (Sampson, Reardon, Peterson, & Lenz, 2004). Figure 4.2 shows the five phases of the CASVE Cycle: Communication, Analysis, Synthesis, Valuing, and Execution, and the order in which they proceed.

Communication

The word *Communication* is used to describe the first phase of the **C**ASVE decision-making process because this is when we receive information that communicates a gap between the ideal and current situation. This information may be communicated to us by internal or external means. Internal communications might include emotions, such as dissatisfaction, boredom, anxiety, or discouragement, and body signals, such as lethargy, headaches, and stomach problems. External communications might include a note from a dean to declare a major, questions from your family members about your plans after graduation, a layoff notice from your boss, or a newspaper article reporting that your field is becoming obsolete.

This is the "Knowing I Need to Make a Choice" phase. It involves becoming fully "in touch" with a problem cognitively and emotionally. When we become fully aware of these communications

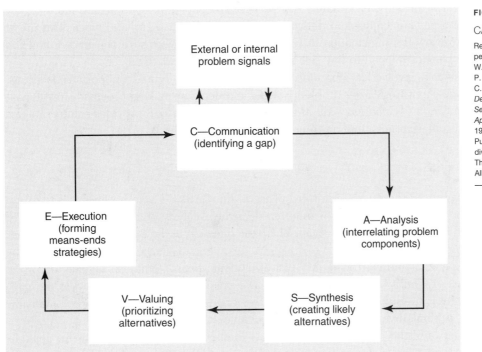

FIGURE 4.2

CASVE Cycle

Reprinted, by permission, from Gary W. Peterson, James P. Sampson, and Robert C. Reardon, *Career Development and Services: A Cognitive Approach*. Copyright 1991 by Brooks/Cole Publishing Company, a division of International Thomson Publishing Inc. All rights reserved.

indicating there is a problem or gap and can no longer ignore them, we can then begin to analyze the sources of the problem and explore its causes. The *Guide to Good Decision Making* shown in *Appendix F* provides some ways for you to think more specifically about your own "communications" in career decisions.

Analysis

The word *Analysis* is used to describe this second phase of the CASVE decision-making process because this is when good problem solvers take a moment to think, observe, research, and more fully understand the gap and their ability to respond effectively. They ask questions like "What do I need to *know* about myself and my situation to solve this problem?" "What exactly *do* I need to do to solve this problem?" "Why am I *feeling* this way?" "What do my significant *others* think about my choice process?" "Where is the *pressure* coming from to make a choice?" Good decision makers do not act impulsively to remove the tension or pain experienced in the Communication phase because they know that impulsive, thoughtless actions may be either inefficient, ineffective, or make the problem worse.

This is the "Understanding Myself and My Options" phase. During this Analysis phase, a career problem solver will often take steps to improve self-knowledge, especially in the areas of interests, values, and skills, as well as to improve knowledge about options with regards to occupations, fields of study, leisure areas, kinds of work organizations and industries, geographic areas, and so forth. In a nutshell, Analysis involves learning everything possible about all the factors that have led to creating the gap communicated in the first phase. In Chapters 2 and 3, we learned about instruments, activities, and resources that can help us improve our knowledge base for career problem solving.

The Analysis phase may include more than simply increasing one's knowledge about self and options. For example, "analysis" might involve learning about relationships or connections between self-knowledge and occupational (option) knowledge. We can draw upon the prior work of scholars and other thoughtful people for information about the connections between these two domains. Holland's hexagon and the World-of-Work Map are two examples of how this has been done. For example, if you are a Realistic type, we know that particular occupational options are more closely associated with this type, and similar knowledge exists for the other five Holland types. This might be a good time to review the information in Chapters 2 and 3 to make sure you understand the schemes that have been developed to link self and occupational knowledge.

Finally, Analysis may involve learning more about how you usually make important decisions. What is your attitude about this career problem-solving and decision-making process? How do you think about it? *The Guide to Good Decision Making* shown in *Appendix F* provides some examples related to self-talk, self-awareness, and awareness and control of self-talk.

Synthesis

The term *Synthesis* is used to describe the third phase in the CASVE Cycle because it is the time for synthesizing or processing information uncovered in the Analysis phase in order to identify courses of action to remove the problem or gap. The basic question in the Synthesis phase is "What can I do to solve the problem?"

This is the "Expanding and Narrowing My List of Options" phase. Synthesis actually occurs in two subphases: first *expanding* and then *narrowing* the possible options for removing the gap. *Synthesis Elaboration* is the subphase when problem solvers expand the list of possible options to solve the problem, to think divergently about every possible solution to the problem.

Sometimes groups use the "brainstorming" process to elaborate or expand the list of possible problem solutions. This can be difficult to accomplish, especially if you are tense, threatened, or pressured. One mental image that sometimes helps is to think of yourself fishing in a pond and using a big net to scoop up everything that you might want to keep. Obviously, not everything in the net will satisfy your needs or remove the gap (get fish for dinner), but the process is useful as one part of the problem-solving process. In career problem solving, this is the time to list all the possible occupational, major, or job options that loosely fit at least some of your values, interests, and skills.

Synthesis Crystallization is the second subphase of Synthesis. This is the subphase when problem solvers reduce the list of alternatives to a smaller number, usually three to five options. Cognitive research suggests that we can most effectively remember and work with this number of options in our minds. That is one reason why phone numbers are broken down into three- or four-digit groups. To narrow down the list of possible options, problem solvers return to the results of the Analysis phase and pick the best three to five options that remove the gap identified in the Communication phase.

At this point, you have probably noticed that the Analysis and Synthesis phases involve repeatedly checking out the quality of the information and of the decision-making processes in terms of whether or not the gap is being removed. Review *The Guide to Good Decision Making* shown in *Appendix F* to help you think more concretely about this phase of the CASVE Cycle and to prepare for the next phase.

Valuing

The term *Valuing* is used to describe the fourth phase of the CASVE Cycle. This is the "Choosing an Occupation, Job, or College Major" phase.

The first part of Valuing involves evaluating each option in terms of how it affects both the problem solver and others. For example, if Occupation A is selected, then how will that choice affect one's friends, parents, spouse, family, neighborhood, community, gender, or ethnic group? The impact of selecting each option is examined in terms of both costs and benefits to one self and others.

However, "valuing" also involves judging each option in terms of the problem solver's moral ideals, his or her sense of right and wrong. As you can see, "valuing" in career decision making at this phase involves making moral judgments of right and wrong. Each of us is ultimately faced with making choices about (1) "What is best for me personally?" or (2) "What is best for significant others in my life?" and (3) "What is best for my community at large?" Sometimes, the Valuing process might reveal options that are good for both the individual and society. Some social groups have strong beliefs about what options are most valuable. These social groups might include racial and ethnic groups, recent immigrants to the United States, religious groups, patriotic groups, and so forth.

The second phase of the Valuing process involves ranking or prioritizing the options carried forward from the Synthesis phase. The option, perhaps an occupation or college major, that best removes the gap between the existing and the ideal state of affairs identified in the Communication phase is given the first priority or ranking, the next best option is ranked second, and so forth. Review the *Guide to Good Decision Making* shown in *Appendix F* and identify some specific things to consider in the Valuing phase.

At this point, a good problem solver selects a best option and makes an emotional commitment to implement it. The career problem is then solved. One has thus successfully engaged in a career problem-solving activity. However, one must make sure that the other options ranked later in the Valuing phase would also be suitable backup options in case the first priority did not work out successfully for some reason. In other words, before we can be sure the first option selected is the best final solution, we must implement that option in the real world. This takes us to the next phase in the CASVE Cycle.

Execution

The word *Execution* is used in the final phase of the CASVE Cycle because this phase involves converting thoughts into action through the formulation of an action plan. Execution involves forming means-ends relationships and determining a logical series of steps to reach a goal. With respect to the results obtained in the Valuing phase, it is a matter of reframing the first option as a goal and then focusing on the concrete, active things that will lead to accomplishing the goal.

This is the "Implementing My Choice" phase. For many people the formulation of an action plan in the Execution phase is enjoyable and rewarding because they feel that they are finally taking positive action to solve the career problem identified in the Communication phase. They are now focused, energized, and getting feedback from outside sources regarding their actions. However, people who are indecisive may experience stress at this phase because they are having to give up their tentativeness and uncertainty in order to follow up on their commitment to their first priority. This commitment to a direction or specific goal brings with it the unavoidable risk of future failure.

Inspection of the *Guide to Good Decision Making* shown in *Appendix F* indicates three specific activities associated with Execution: (1) planning, (2), trying out, and (3) applying. **Planning** involves making a written plan for obtaining education and training, including dates and addresses. **Trying out** could include getting related experience through cooperative education, volunteering, part-time work, or taking classes to get more information about how to implement an option. **Applying** could include filling out application forms, registering, paying fees, and taking other concrete steps to implement a planned course of action.

Communication Recycled

The CASVE Cycle is a continuous cycle that repeats itself. Following the Execution phase, one returns to the Communication phase to determine whether the chosen option was a good one—if the gap between the real and the ideal state has been removed. *The Guide to Good Decision Making* shown in *Appendix F* graphically shows this process. If the problem-solving process in the CASVE Cycle has been successful, then the negative emotions originally experienced in the Communication phase will have been replaced by positive ones.

This is the "Knowing I Made a Good Choice" phase. In problem solving and decision making, people may go through the five phases of the CASVE Cycle very quickly in some cases or linger a while in one particular phase. The CASVE model can be very useful for solving both individual and organizational problems. Thinking through the five steps in a systematic way can provide a useful tool for becoming a more effective person.

IMPROVING CAREER DECISION MAKING

Each of the five CASVE phases can improve your problem-solving and decision-making skills in distinct ways. It is important to remember that the suggestions for using each phase build upon the materials in Chapters 2 and 3 on improving skills related to self-knowledge and occupational knowledge. Each layer of the Pyramid of Information-Processing Domains builds upon the lower levels.

Understanding the Process

Career problem solving and decision making are continuing *processes*, not *events*. The successful completion of the process depends on successful work in each of the five phases. The process is only as strong as the weakest phase. Our research suggests that problems in any one phase can shut down or derail the entire problem-solving process.

There are three critical places where this can happen. It can happen in the Communication phase. People become overwhelmed with the problem. They feel bad, and they're anxious, confused, frustrated, or depressed. Most of all, they're in a state of confusion and don't know how to begin or approach a seemingly overwhelming task. As a result, they never get past these feelings to move into Analysis or Synthesis.

Connected to this problem in Communication, people can become stuck in the Valuing phase. They find it impossible to make a commitment to one option after narrowing them down. When this happens, they may become frustrated, anxious, depressed, and find themselves back in the Communication phase, perhaps stewing over not yet having found the *"perfect"* occupation that meets all their needs.

A third area of difficulty is in the Execution phase. People have trouble following through on their first choice because (1) they are not able to break down Execution into smaller action steps, (2) they are uncertain about which task to do first, (3) they are overwhelmed by the ambiguity and uncertainty of the tasks, or (4) they view negative external forces as so powerful that it is pointless to even try to do anything. Therefore, it is important for us to concentrate on completing each phase of the CASVE Cycle in order to successfully solve career problems and make career decisions.

The CASVE Cycle is one of many problem-solving or decision-making models that have been described in the career literature. Using any of these models may seem a little awkward at first, but with practice, thoughtful review, and some success, using the CASVE Cycle can become almost automatic. At the early phases of learning to use this cycle, it may be important to examine decision-making problems in terms of where the CASVE process is breaking down in your situation. Sometimes, people get stuck at a particular phase, and they may have to take some extra measures to make sure they get through that sticking point. The goal is to develop a high state of problem-solving efficiency with the CASVE Cycle applied automatically to resolve important life problems.

It is also important to remember that career problems are continuous, meaning that they tend to build upon one another. Successfully using the CASVE Cycle to solve one problem will invariably lead to using the CASVE Cycle again to solve the next problem. For example, deciding which college to attend may then lead to problem solving regarding living arrangements, paying the costs, and deciding when to start school.

Improving Decision-Making Skills

Working with a counselor or career advisor, you can complete an assessment activity that can help you learn more about your skill in career decision making. Possible instruments include the Career Thoughts Inventory (CTI), the Career Decision Scale, or the Career Beliefs Inventory. A computer-based career guidance system such as SIGI³, Discover, or Choices® Planner can also help you practice and improve your career decision-making skills. In addition, career courses, workshops, individual counseling, career planning books, and other career interventions can help you become more skillful in career decision making.

You might also use the *Guide to Good Decision Making* shown in *Appendix F* to learn more about the steps you can take in solving a specific career problem and improving your Personal Career Theory (PCT). Have a trusted friend or a career counselor ask you questions about your feelings in the Communication and Valuing phases, the information sources you used in the Analysis and Synthesis Elaboration phases, and the specific actions you plan to take in the Execution phase. Have this other person share his or her views or experiences in each area of the CASVE Cycle as it relates to your situation. Talking out the CASVE phases with another person may help you get new insights into your strengths and weaknesses in decision making.

Read biographies of important people in fields you plan to enter, and analyze the ways they solved important life and career problems with respect to the CASVE Cycle. You can also conduct information interviews with people in career fields of interest to you, and try to understand how they solved work-related problems with respect to the CASVE Cycle. Such activities can accomplish two important purposes: You'll get information about career fields of interest, and you'll get practice using the CASVE Cycle.

To improve your skills in the Communication phase, such as identifying the gap between the real and ideal states or achieving a better understanding of your decision-making style, you could trace the way in which you have made several important decisions in the past, identifying common themes in past decision making; recall your feelings at the time and how they affected your decision making; develop your skills in progressive relaxation and imaging in order to obtain a clearer picture of the gap; talk with people who have recently gone through an important career change process, especially regarding their feelings at the time; and identify the role and impact of important people in your life while you were in the Communication phase of decision making.

To improve your skills in the Analysis phase, identify all the causes of the problem (either within or outside of yourself). Inventory your values, interests, and skills to make sure you know yourself well; make sure that the information you have about your options is relatively free from bias or the inappropriate influence of outsiders; write an autobiography describing important factors shaping your life; look for discrepancies between the informal and the formal information that you have about your options; and look for themes and categories that connect your personal characteristics with possible options, such as Holland codes. Concentrating on the quality of the information that you have in these areas will help you improve your skills in the Analysis phase.

To improve your skills in the Synthesis phase, such as formulating alternative choices and/or eliminating unlikely alternatives, you could find resources and obtain lists of all possible options that meet your minimum requirements; develop categories for grouping options together that have common characteristics; identify factors for each option that make an important difference in how you evaluate the option; practice brainstorming and right-brain activities; identify the factors that limit the usefulness of an option, such as cost or distance, and eliminate those options from your lists. Remember that Synthesis involves both expanding and narrowing your lists of options in order to come up with the three to five best options.

To improve your skills in the Valuing phase, such as establishing a prioritized, ranked list of three to five options, you could identify the strongest values in your family background and in the people with whom you now have the closest relationships; examine how your strongest values match up or conflict with one another; write an autobiography and trace the important decisions you have made in the past and how your values were involved in those decisions; examine the most important considerations in making prior life decisions; examine how your various life roles, such as student, child, worker, citizen, are affected by each option you have identified; talk with others to see if they have similar perceptions of the values for the options you have identified; and identify important values associated with each of your most favored options. Clarifying your values and being able to act on them consistently in public are important problem-solving skills related to the Valuing phase.

To improve your skills in the Execution phase, such as designing a plan to achieve your first option for solving a problem, you could learn about planning concepts, such as milestones, time-lines, flowcharts, budgets, and so forth; apply each of these concepts to developing a plan for implementing your first choice; put your plan into a written form, with words and narrative to explain it, and charts and graphs to show it; review your plan with important people in your life and incorporate their useful suggestions in improving your plan. Successful undertaking of these steps will assist you in improving your skills in the Execution phase.

SUMMARY

This chapter has examined the second domain of the Pyramid of Information-Processing Domains, the CASVE Cycle. This cycle for guiding a person through the career problem-solving and decision-making process was explained in detail. We explored common problems in effective decision making and examined three decision states of decision makers: decided, undecided, and indecisive. We presented observations and suggestions for improving career problem-solving and decision-making skills in the CASVE Cycle. The goal was to help you improve the quality of information in the decision skills domain of your Personal Career Theory. With respect to choosing a major, specifying an occupation, or choosing a job, after reading this chapter you should be able to answer to the question "Where am I in the CASVE Cycle?"

REFERENCES

Peterson, G., Sampson, J., & Reardon, R. (1991). *Career development and services: A cognitive approach*. Pacific Grove, CA: Brooks/Cole.

Sampson, J. P., Jr., Reardon, R. C., Peterson, G. W., & Lenz, J. L. (2004). *Career counseling and services: A cognitive information processing approach*. Pacific Grove, CA: Wadsworth-Brooks/Cole.

THINKING ABOUT MY CAREER DECISION

areer problems and decisions are among the most complex issues that most of us confront during our lives. We have been introducing a Cognitive Information Processing (CIP) approach, including the Pyramid of Information-Processing Domains and the CASVE Cycle, as devices that can help us sort our way through this process. The pyramid and the five-step cycle can be used as guides, like a map or a cookbook, to help us see where we are and where we are going in decision making. They can help us improve our Personal Career Theory.

This chapter examines the top of the pyramid, the processes involved in "thinking about my decision making." You will remember that as we have worked our way up the pyramid from the knowledge domains, including self-knowledge and occupational knowledge, through the decision skills domain—the CASVE Cycle—we have repeatedly noted how our thinking influences our career problem solving and decision making.

The top of the pyramid is the executive processing domain. This area "calls the shots." It is here that directions are given on exactly how career decision making will proceed. If you are a fan of *Star Trek*, you might like to think of this as "Command Central." We have used the example of a computer to show how the Pyramid of Information-Processing domains works in our minds. The knowledge domains are like files of information and data stored on the computer. The CASVE Cycle is like programs that prescribe when, how, and what information will be used. The executive processing domain governs this entire process. For example, it tells the system when to start and stop the CASVE process, how much information is needed from the files, and how well the process is moving along.

Another example of how executive processing works is a football team in a game situation. The knowledge domains include facts, such as the team playbook, the physical characteristics of the players, the weather, and playing field conditions. The CASVE Cycle includes the decisions that the quarterback makes in the huddle. Information has to be processed very rapidly in the huddle, so the team will rely on its game plan, which specifies what plays will be called in certain conditions. These conditions might include the game score, time left in the game, location of the ball on the field, and the player injury situation.

Executive processing in this example resides with the head coach. The head coach makes the decision to go for two points rather than one late in the game, to go for the win rather than the tie. The head coach decides when to change quarterbacks, depending on if the game is going very well or very poorly. In effect, executive processing, like a head coach, may direct that some information be ignored, that a time-out be called, or that execution in the CASVE Cycle be carried out in a risky way such as a hidden-ball trick play.

In this chapter, we will explain and analyze the executive processing domain and provide descriptions of new concepts and skills that can improve your problem solving and decision making. The chapter concludes with strategies for improving your effectiveness in the executive processing area.

THE EXECUTIVE PROCESSING DOMAIN

Having a lot of information or knowledge about yourself and your options and knowing how to use information in a decision-making situation are very important, but they are not sufficient in effective career problem solving. The missing ingredients are referred to as **metacognitive skills**, or the skills that govern *how* we think about career problem solving and decision making. Remember that "cognition" is the memory and thought process that a person uses to perform a task or attain a goal; it is the thinking process (Peterson, Sampson & Reardon, 1991). The prefix "meta" simply means "beyond" or "higher," such as "higher order thinking skills." The pyramid (Figure 5.1) illustrates the position of these higher thinking skills relative to the other two levels. These metacognitive skills help us know when to initiate the CASVE Cycle, when to get more self-knowledge information, and when we are ready to execute a choice. There are three skills that are especially important in the metacognitive area: (1) self-talk, (2) self-awareness, and (3) control and monitoring.

Self-Talk

In order to be an effective career problem solver, you must be able to think of yourself as competent and capable in this area. For example, you can make a positive statement about yourself, such as "I am a good decision maker" or "I can make good decisions for myself." Such positive self-talk does two important things for your decision making. First, it creates a positive expectation, and second, it reinforces positive behavior, such as saying "good work" following a decision-making activity.

Unfortunately, negative self-talk can create real problems in career decision making because it interferes with the effective, efficient processing of information. For example, negative self-statements such as "I'll never be able to make a career choice" or "I trust others' judgments more than my own about what is best for me" can disrupt effective problem solving. Sometimes we do a lot of

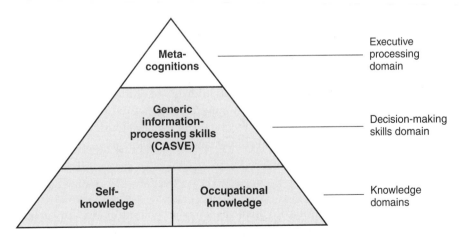

FIGURE **5.1**

Metacognitions in Executive Processing

Reprinted, by permission, from Gary W. Peterson, James P. Sampson, and Robert C. Reardon, *Career Development and Services: A Cognitive Approach.* Copyright 1991 by Brooks/Cole Publishing Company, a division of International Thomson Publishing Inc. All rights reserved.

"shoulding" on ourselves: "I *should* be a good decision maker," "This *should* be easy for me." Such negative statements tend to shut down the process or create "noise" and "static" in the system that makes it almost impossible to use whatever information is available.

Returning to our football example, coaches who are tentative or doubtful about their teams will not be able to inspire or lead their players. People with more difficult career problems may minimize their metacognitive skills as decision makers, even though they have sufficient information to make decisions. They may find they are unable to rely on themselves to solve their problems.

A particularly sad example comes to mind. Several years ago a student in a career-planning class was describing his inability to make decisions, concluding that he was a poor decision maker who would never make a successful career decision. The instructor, searching for some positive evidence of career decision-making skill to help change this negative metacognition, noted that the student was well dressed, looked nice, and could obviously make good choices about clothes. She was dismayed when the student responded that he bought the clothes directly off of store mannequins because he could not trust his judgment in selecting and buying clothes. This is an example of negative self-talk that was quite pervasive in this student's way of thinking and was influencing his ability to make career decisions. Later, we will examine ways to overcome negative self-talk and other dysfunctional metacognitions.

Self-Awareness

Being an effective career problem solver means "having an awareness of one's self as the doer of a task" (Peterson, Sampson & Reardon, 1991; Sampson, Reardon, Peterson, & Lenz, 2004). An example might be Robert saying, "I'm getting anxious about my ability to make a decision on time." Robert is aware of feelings while working through the CASVE Cycle. He is not just focusing on the specific CASVE phase, but he is aware of his feelings about the overall process of deciding as well.

A very simple example comes to mind that may further illustrate this point. Remember your first time on a bicycle? You had to concentrate very hard on the road, the peddles, the seat, your balance, and many other details about bike riding. We might look at these as "lower-order" bike-riding skills. As you developed expertise and confidence in your bike riding, you were able to devote more of your mental time and effort to focusing on other aspects of bike riding: if you were getting tired or hot, if you were riding on a safe road, if you needed more air in your tires, or how many calories you were burning on your ride. These higher-order thoughts became possible as you mastered lower-order bike-riding skills.

These same principles apply in effective career decision making. Good problem solvers are aware of their feelings as they engage in information-processing tasks. They are able to include an awareness of others' needs and to select options that are good for themselves as well as for society at large. They are able to balance self-interests and the interests of others. Several years ago, a career decision maker stuck in the CASVE process was able to break away by focusing on "what in the world made her angry." By focusing on those feelings, she eventually decided to go into environmental protection work because the loss of wetlands and coastal forests made her angry.

Control and Monitoring

Good problem solving and decision making involves knowing when to move forward and when to stop and get more information. It is the thoughtful balance between compulsivity and impulsivity in decision making. Compulsivity leads to obsessive thinking and endless processing without any action ever being taken. Impulsivity promotes "jackrabbit" decisions, with trial-and-error attempts at problem solving (Peterson, Sampson & Reardon, 1991). Both approaches generally lead to poor results.

Several years ago, a particularly compulsive student was intent on reading about all 12,700+ occupations in the *Dictionary of Occupational Titles* because she wanted to make sure she knew about all the available options before she made a decision. It took her almost a year to complete the process, with little noticeable positive effect on her ultimate choice. At the other end, an impulsive student recently requested the name of the "best-paying job for college students" because that is what he had decided to enter. Never mind that he had poor math skills and little interest in computers. Good decision makers sense when more information is needed to obtain a better understanding of the gap or the options, and they also intuitively know when they are ready to make a choice and commitment. These are examples of metacognitive skills.

DEVELOPING METACOGNITIVE SKILLS

Improving our metacognitive skills, our ability to think about our thinking, sounds at face value to be a very difficult task. However, it may be less difficult than it appears. There are specific ways that we can become more aware of ourselves as decision makers and improve our thinking skills in this area.

What Are Metacognitive Skills?

One example of a metacognitive skill is knowing when to get additional help. Good career problem solvers know when to seek assistance from outside sources. For example, they know they need help in learning how their interests and values match up with college majors, occupations, or jobs, and they seek services from a qualified helper. Sometimes, you just decide to rely on your intuition or advice from individuals you respect to make a choice after you have exhausted all the rational processes.

A second metacognitive skill is being aware of effective decision-making strategies. The important point is to be aware of how a strategy affects the decision-making process. A strategy might involve focusing on the individual steps that need to be taken to avoid becoming over-whelmed.

A third skill involves being clear about the specific problem that needs to be solved. Sometimes, relationship problems and career problems are intertwined and difficult to separate. Decision makers need to separate the issues so that the most useful skills and knowledge can be used for the problem at hand. For example, people sometimes try to solve relationship problems by making career decisions, such as "I'll make my father happy by going into business, even though I have no interest in it." It would be better first to separate the decision about which field to enter from the decision about how to improve the relationship with dad, and then see how the options selected for each decision affect the other.

As you go through the career decision-making process, a fourth important skill is monitoring how the process is going. For example, in the CASVE Cycle described in Chapter 4, it is important to pause at the end of each phase and ask, "Am I finished with this step and ready for the next one?" In looking ahead to the end of the cycle, you may also need to determine how you'll know when the problem is solved. You may not always be completely certain that you've found the ideal solution, but you know that you've expended a reasonable amount of time, energy, and resources in reaching your decision and need to take action. In CASVE terms, we would say: "Have I closed the gap between what I want and where I am?" "Can I commit and act on a choice in the midst of my uncertainty?"

Finally, good problem solvers are not their own worst enemy, but they give themselves positive self-talk, praise their good efforts, and focus positively on desirable outcomes. Such a positive attitude is an important metacognitive skill for tackling many of life's problems.

Improving Metacognitive Skills

Many of our metacognitive skills were formed at an early age, perhaps from ages four through eight. If we, as adults, happen to lack positive, high-quality metacognitive skills, then it can be difficult to learn new ones. It may take assistance from another person, perhaps a professional such as a counselor, minister, or teacher, to help us improve our metacognitive skills. However, it is sometimes possible for individuals to do this through self-directed learning activities once they learn how to identify metacognitive skills that are weak or problematic. Five techniques that can help you improve metacognitive skills hindering your career problem solving and decision making are described below.

1. **Identifying Negative Thoughts.** Some of us have negative, or self-defeating, thoughts about ourselves or the world of work that make it difficult for us to solve career problems and make career decisions. Some of those thoughts and beliefs are very popular, or they have been taught to us by important people in our lives. Nevertheless, these thoughts can present problems in career decision making.

For example, the statement, "I'm afraid I'll pick something and then change my mind" is a thought that can "freeze up" our career decision making. Being "afraid" is, itself, an emotion that is the opposite of confidence, optimism, and self-assurance, and it is an emotion that negatively impacts good decision making. Also, feeling little control over whether I'll change my mind makes it very difficult to make a choice.

We believe there are literally hundreds of these kinds of negative thoughts that can freeze or short-circuit the decision-making process, and these thoughts must be identified before they can be corrected. Of course, not all negative thoughts always shut down the process, but they can become problems at unsuspected times. In some ways, these negative thoughts are like nasty viruses that lurk in our bodies and break out periodically to make us sick. Later, we will see examples of negative thoughts that occur at various points on the Pyramid of Information-Processing Domains and the CASVE Cycle.

The Career Thoughts Inventory (CTI; Sampson, Peterson, Lenz, Reardon & Saunders, 1996a) helps people learn more about the way they think about career choices. This instrument includes 48 items or statements describing thoughts that some people have when considering educational and career choices. Completing the CTI may help you identify troublesome thoughts related to career problem solving and decision making.

By learning and exploring both positive and negative aspects of ourselves and our options, we can challenge our habitual ways of thinking about career decision making. We'll probably learn that things are not all good or all bad but combinations of good and bad. Career decision making is truly full of gray areas, and this requires us to think in more complex ways about career problems. In addition, talking out our career problems with a trusted friend or counselor can sometimes help us get our negative thoughts out there in the open, where they can be examined, challenged, and possibly changed.

Sampson, Peterson, Lenz, Reardon, and Saunders (1996b) identified a four-step sequence for changing our negative thoughts. The four steps are (1) *identify* the negative thought(s) or statements; (2) *challenge* the appropriateness, usefulness, or truthfulness of the thought-statement; (3) *alter* the negative thought, or reframe it into a more positive thought-statement; and (4) *act* in new ways that are consistent and correspond with the new, altered thought-statement. These four steps might help you remember how to improve your metacognitive skills.

2. **Train for Positive Self-Talk.** The statement, "I'm not a good decision maker" is an example of negative self-talk that a helpful friend or counselor can challenge and help a person eliminate. You can enlist your friends to help you identify and change such negative statements, and very quickly you will learn to monitor your use of these statements. You can train for more positive self-talk by first working to eliminate the negative statements, and then you can learn to start using more positive self-talk. Some people have found that reading self-help books that are intended to improve self-esteem and increase self-confidence will help them develop more positive self-talk. In addition,

professional counseling, positive religious experiences, and positive human potential groups can provide opportunities for learning more positive self-talk. Just like a good coach can help you improve your golf game, positive people can help you become more positive about yourself. Indeed, one of the things a good coach does is train you for positive self-talk about you and your sport.

3. **Reducing Either/Or Thinking.** Another metacognitive skill that helps us become better problem solvers and decision makers involves relative thinking rather than dualistic thinking. Dualistic or all-or-nothing thinking tends to freeze situations and immobilize us. For example, the statement, "All the good jobs require math" tends to shut us down, especially if we are not interested in math or have few skills in the area. Such a statement could be restated as *"Some of the better paying jobs in some organizations are held by people who have skills and interests in math as well as several other areas."* As a result of this new thinking about the relationship between jobs and math, we can now examine the matter in terms of degrees rather than all or nothing, absolute terms. In the real world of career problem solving and decision making, there are very few absolute truths that govern the process. It is almost always a matter of degrees, situations, people, timing, circumstances, and so forth, and we can function better when our thinking reflects these realities.

4. **Developing Self-Control.** We can learn self-control techniques that help us better manage the factors influencing our behavior. For example, we learn to count to 10 to avoid an outburst when our parent asks why we're not majoring in biology, or we practice deep breathing to relax before starting a job interview, or we use a calming mental image (lying on the beach) when we feel ourselves getting anxious about our career uncertainties. These self-control techniques can help us improve our metacognitive skills and ultimately improve our career decision making.

5. **Improved General Problem Solving.** The CASVE Cycle provides a general approach to problem solving that can be used in many life situations. When we can quickly and efficiently use such a strategy as the CASVE Cycle to work through career and other life problems, this will improve our career decision making. Using the CASVE Cycle without having to think about it can be compared to learning to ride a bike or drive a car—it becomes almost automatic. When that happens, we can more easily move through the decision-making process. The *Guide to Good Career Decision Making* in *Appendix F* can be useful in this regard.

In summary, remember that improving metacognitive skills involves concentrating on the *process* of career decision making, not the *event* of making a choice. Using another sports metaphor, our focus is not on winning the race (the event), but on improving our strength, using good nutrition and health, being careful about risks, and not missing practice sessions (the process). We have more control over these parts of the process of competing in the race. However, with good career problem-solving and decision-making skills, we do more than run the race well—we can win it, too.

CHANGING NEGATIVE CAREER THOUGHTS

Negative, self-defeating thoughts can occur at any place in the Pyramid of Information-Processing Domains (see Figure 1.2) and the CASVE Cycle (see Figure 1.3). Viewing these two figures together as eight areas that include all of the important aspects of effective career decision making, then we can examine typical negative thoughts in each of the following areas:

1. Self-knowledge

2. Option knowledge

3. Decision making: Communication

4. Decision making: Analysis

5. Decision making: Synthesis

6. Decision making: Valuing

7. Decision making: Execution

8. Executive processing

Good decision makers use positive metacognitions to effectively solve career problems. Negative thoughts in each of these eight areas can be reframed or restated to make them more positive or helpful metacognitions for good career decision making.

Self-Knowledge

Positive metacognitions related to *self-knowledge* pertain to how we think about our personal characteristics—for example, our interests, values, and skills. Such metacognitions have several characteristics. For example, they are clear, precise, strong, and stable thoughts or statements about the things that we are interested in, indifferent about, and not interested in. The same is true for skills and values. Taken together, these statements clearly describe what is of interest to us, what is important to us, and what we do well.

However, the clarity of these statements should not be confused with rigidity—for example, "I'll never be interested in gardening"—because the most useful metacognitions recognize the importance of time and include the idea that we may change our mind about our interests. Another characteristic of positive metacognitions is that they grow out of our personal reflection and experience rather than taking in another person's views about us. Finally, positive metacognitions about self-knowledge include information from many experiences instead of a single particularly good or bad experience. For example, getting seasick on a boat one time would not be a reason to eliminate all occupations involving working on or near bodies of water. Positive metacognitions help keep us from overreacting to any single event in life that may exaggerate how we think about our interests, values, and skills.

Here is an example of a negative metacognition about self-knowledge that needs to be changed to a more positive thought: *"No field of study or occupation interests me."*[1] As you can see, this statement is not a positive metacognition, and as a result, it tends to shut down the process of finding and using self-knowledge information to solve a career problem.

With a little work, we can change or reframe this negative metacognition to a more positive thought: *"It is possible that I haven't fully determined what my likes and dislikes are. I may need more life experience to really understand my interests. I can get more life experience from full-time or part-time jobs, volunteer work, or leisure activities."* This is a more positive thought because it keeps open the possibility of finding new interests in the future, it suggests ways to get new experiences, and it eliminates all-or-none words like "no."

You probably noticed that the more positive metacognition is longer, and this is no accident. Our experience suggests that these more positive metacognitions are, indeed, more complex thoughts and ideas, at least in their initial forms.

---

[1] Adapted and reproduced by special permission of the Publisher, Psychological Assessment Resources, Inc., 16204 N. Fl. Ave., Lutz, FL 33549, from the Career Thoughts Inventory by Sampson, Peterson, Lenz, Reardon, and Saunders, Copyright 1994, 1996 by PAR, Inc. Further reproduction is prohibited without permission from PAR, Inc.

Option Knowledge

Positive metacognitions related to *option knowledge* pertain to how we think about our options in work, education, and leisure, and also how we group these options in relation to one another. Such metacognitions have several characteristics. For example, they are positive thoughts about reading, viewing, listening, visiting, interviewing, and observing as ways to gain knowledge about options.

Another positive metacognition involves using something like Holland's RIASEC hexagon to group occupations that have things in common and to identify those that are unlike one another. The RIASEC system helps us think about similarities and differences among options at the same time. Finally, positive metacognitions help us appreciate the need to remember information about options and to realize that we can never learn *all* there is to know about all of our options.

Here is an example of a negative metacognition about occupational knowledge that needs to be changed to a more positive thought: *"Almost all occupational information is slanted toward making the occupation look good."* This statement tends to shut down the process of finding and using occupational information to solve a career problem.

With a little work, we can change or reframe this negative metacognition to a more positive thought: *"While it is certainly true that some kinds of occupational information are designed to make the occupation "look good," it is likely an overstatement to say this about most information. Occupational information may be biased in both directions, good or bad. Helping professionals, like librarians or counselors, can help me determine the quality of various sources of information. It is important to evaluate the source and purpose of each piece of information and determine its usefulness in my career decision making."* This statement is a more positive thought about the source, purpose, and quality of occupational information, and it prevents making a negative assumption about information that is needed to solve career problems and make career decisions.

Decision Making: Communication

Positive metacognitions related to the *Communication* phase in the **CASVE** Cycle pertain to expectations for successful resolution of a career problem and recognizing that career problems are simply a part of living in our society. For example, positive thoughts in the Communication phase enable us to fully appreciate all of the feelings that are associated with the career problem, such as hopefulness, anticipation, anxiety, anger, frustration, uncertainty, and resentment. Rather than being overwhelmed by these emotions, we accept them, recognize their origins, and resolve to move beyond these feelings.

Here is an example of a negative metacognition about communication that needs to be changed to a more positive thought: *"I get so depressed about choosing a field of study or occupation that I can't get started."* As with the other negative metacognitions, this one tends to shut down the problem-solving and decision-making process.

With some work, we can change or reframe this negative metacognition to a more positive thought: *"It is important for me to admit that I am feeling depressed about making a career choice, but doing nothing abut the problem is not a good idea in the long run. I may need to get help for my feelings of depression or take small concrete steps toward getting the information I need to begin the decision-making process. Such steps might include talking with people in different occupations, reading about occupations, or seeking career assistance to help me develop a plan for taking the next step."* This is a more positive thought because it acknowledges the negative feelings associated with the career problem, and then goes beyond those feelings toward concrete steps that can move the decision-making process forward. This statement helps the person avoid getting stuck or becoming overwhelmed by feelings that limit the processing of information for problem solving.

Decision Making: Analysis

Positive metacognitions related to the *Analysis* phase in the **CASVE** Cycle pertain to having the personal motivation and energy to engage the problem-solving task and the expectation of finding a good person-to-environment fit. For example, positive thoughts would be found in statements that express a desire to explore both self and occupational information in order to find good matches for oneself. In other words, the person can say with confidence, "I can figure out this relationship between who I am and what's available for me." The opposite of this latter thought is "analysis paralysis," or the belief that "I'll never get it figured out and never solve this career problem." Successfully figuring out all aspects of the career problem means that one is then ready to move on to the Synthesis phase and get lists of options that will solve the problem.

Here is an example of a negative metacognition about Analysis that needs to be changed to a more positive thought: *"I'll never understand myself well enough to make a good career choice."* Here the person has concluded that the lack of self-knowledge will make it impossible to find suitable options and choose one, and this thought can shut down the whole process of even trying to find something.

As with the earlier statements, we can change or reframe this negative metacognition to a more positive thought: *"It is important for me to be aware of my values, interests, and skills as I make career decisions. Thinking that I must have total understanding of myself before I can make a good career choice may make me feel discouraged and less likely to think carefully about my options. However, going through this career choice process will actually help me better understand myself. There are resources, including printed materials and professionals, that can assist me in gathering enough information about myself to at least take the next step in the career decision-making process."* This new, more positive metacognition enables the person to move ahead in the CASVE Cycle, and to continue to work on solutions to the career problems.

Decision Making: Synthesis

Positive metacognitions related to the *Synthesis* phase in the **CASVE** Cycle pertain to "freeing up the mind" to generate options that will draw upon the work done in the preceding four phases to solve the career problem. Information obtained from both the self and occupational knowledge domains, as well as the realization that a career problem exists (Communication) and that it can be examined (Analysis) in terms of person and environment information, leads us to Synthesis.

You will recall that there are two phases in Synthesis, Elaboration and Crystallization, so there are two kinds of positive metacognitions that can help us here. First, positive thoughts will help us make sure that no good options are missed, that all possible career solutions are on the table for review. There are no constraints or limits on our listing of possible solutions. Second, positive thoughts will also help us let go of the least likely options, to separate and critically analyze each option identified in terms of which are the best possible solutions to the problem.

Here is example of a negative metacognition about Synthesis that needs to be changed to a more positive thought: *"I can't think of any fields of study or occupations that would suit me."* This negative thought severely impedes Synthesis Elaboration because it shuts down the process of freely generating lists of possible options.

Here's how we can change and reframe this negative metacognition to a more positive thought: *"Right now I feel discouraged and that may cause me to cut myself off from developing and exploring suitable possibilities. If I think, instead, that it is possible to identify appropriate options, I may free myself up to explore and discover suitable fields of study or occupations. There are tools and resources that can help me do this."* You'll notice that this positive reframing statement incorporates the negative feelings embedded in the negative statement and then moves forward to more positive thoughts about how to proceed in solving the career problem.

Decision Making: Valuing

Positive metacognitions related to the *Valuing* phase in the CASVE Cycle pertain to the ability to prioritize or rank a list of options based on what is best for you, your family and significant others, and society. Stated another way, valuing metacognitions have to do with making a tentative first choice.

Several things may interfere with having these kinds of positive metacognitions, including inability to think about a first choice from different perspectives: self, others, society. In addition, problems in thinking about a compromise between what is best for self and also best for others can interfere with the metacognitive processes. Unwillingness to take responsibility for a choice, needing to be completely certain, and desiring to remain uncertain can also interfere with positive valuing metacognitions.

Here is an example of a negative metacognition about Valuing that needs to be changed to a more positive thought: *"The views of important people in my life interfere with choosing a field of study or occupation."* This negative thought makes it very difficult for one to make a choice because the views of other people have overwhelmed the sense of what choice is best for oneself or society.

Here is an example of reframing this negative metacognition to a more positive thought: *"The differing views of important people in my life can easily complicate my choice of a field of study or an occupation. Some of the information I may get from important people may be useful, while their other ideas make me more confused or uncertain. However, no matter what suggestions I get from others, I am ultimately the person who is responsible for and capable of making my career choice."*

In reframing the negative Valuing metacognition, we have not chosen to ignore or ridicule the ideas shared by others about what the person should do, but we have underscored the importance of the deciding person's right and responsibility to prioritize options and make the choice. Such positive metacognitions will enable the deciding person to successfully continue in the CASVE Cycle and solve the career problem and make a career decision. We move now to the last part of the CASVE Cycle.

Decision Making: Execution

Positive metacognitions related to the *Execution* phase in the CASVE Cycle pertain to the ability to think in a logical series of steps in order to implement a choice.

These execution metacognitions enable us to think in terms of means-end relationships—for example, "If I improve my grades, I can get into the accounting major." These positive thoughts also help us minimize the idea of "luck" as the explanation of good things happening in career life, strengthen the attitude of patience and persistence as paying off in the long run ("I'm willing to ride the bench for two years in order to get my shot at the starting position on the team"), and recognizing the importance of reality testing a tentative choice ("I want to get an internship to test my interest in public relations"). Such beliefs and attitudes will foster the development of positive metacognitions in the Execution phase of the CASVE Cycle.

Here is an example of a negative metacognition about Execution that needs to be reframed to a more positive thought: *"I know what I want to do, but I can't develop a plan for getting there."* This negative thought blocks the action phase of the CASVE Cycle; it keeps the person from following through on the choice that has been made. Our experience is that negative metacognitions in Execution are a major barrier to effective career decision making. It may surprise you to learn that often it is not making the choice that is the biggest problem for many people but the follow-through or execution of the choice.

Here is an example of reframing this negative metacognition to a more positive thought: *"In knowing what I want to do, I have already made good progress toward completing my career plans. That fact that I am unclear about my next step shows that I need to find information on career planning, or I need to find a competent person to help me develop a plan, so I can reach my goals."* In making this negative metacognition a more positive thought, we have demonstrated how additional information can help in the planning process and how outside, expert assistance may be needed from a counselor, mentor, teacher, or some other knowledgeable person. Positive metacognitions in Execution can help us make sure we get assistance and needed information to boost us along in the CASVE Cycle. In this way, we can assure successful career problem solving and decision making.

Executive Processing

The final aspect of the Pyramid of Information-Processing Domains and the CASVE Cycle is *executive processing*. Positive metacognitions related to the executive processing domain pertain to the ability to control, regulate, monitor, and evaluate all the preceding areas of information processing.

These metacognitions are probably the most powerful and important in effective career problem solving and decision making. They have to do with "thinking about thinking," or being aware of one's ability to solve career problems and make career decisions. Positive executive processing metacognitions, as you might expect, have characteristics in common with the metacognitions in the other seven areas. Good thinking in this area avoids *perfectionism* ("I must find the perfect job"), *"top-dogging"* ("I should or must do this better than others"), and *external forces* ("I must go into computers because that is where the best jobs will be"). Depression, anxiety, lack of self-confidence, lack of persistence, lack of a plan, and lack of self-control can all interfere with effective information processing.

Here is an example of a negative metacognition in executive processing that needs to be reframed to a more positive thought: *"I get so anxious when I have to make decisions that I can hardly think."* This negative thought almost completely shuts down cognitive information processing for the person. One literally can't think about how to solve a career problem—and perhaps other life problems as well.

Here is an example of a more positive thought to replace the negative one: *"Many people feel anxious when making important decisions. Anxiety does make it harder to think clearly. However, avoiding decision making or depending on others to make decisions for me is not a good idea. With help from a competent person, I can get the information I need and learn how to make a good career decision."* As noted before, this reframing statement pays attention to the negative emotions, but points out that unless the cycle of poor decision making is broken, things will only get worse. Also, it reminds the person that outside help might improve the situation and reinforces the idea that the person can successfully solve the problem in the long run.

Changing negative metacognitions may require persistence, motivation, and outside assistance. The *CTI Workbook*, which shows more examples of reframing statements (Sampson, Peterson, Lenz, Reardon & Saunders, 1996b), was designed to help people change negative thoughts and develop a positive plan for solving career problems and making career decisions. Metacognitions that are deep seated, pervasive, and long-standing may be more likely to require outside help. Having a "bad" attitude about career decisions may also carry over to other areas of life and personality. Counselors and other helping persons are especially trained to assist in overcoming troubling metacognitions, and the fastest, easiest course may be to consult with such a professional.

SUMMARY

This chapter examined the executive processing domain of the Pyramid of Information-Processing Domains. It described three types of metacognitive skills, self-talk, self-awareness, and control and monitoring, and suggested ways to develop and improve metacognitive skills. We discussed positive and negative metacognitions or thoughts in each of the eight areas of the Pyramid of Information-Processing Domains and the CASVE Cycle.

Effective career problem solving and decision making involve the effective use of information in four domains: self-knowledge, occupational knowledge, decision making (composed of the CASVE Cycle), and executive processing. Negative metacognitions in any of these areas short-circuit the problem-solving process. Ideas were offered on how to increase positive, helpful metacognitions in career decision making. The goal was to help you improve the quality of your metacognitions in the executive processing domain of your Personal Career Theory.

REFERENCES

Brown, A. L. (1978). Knowing when, where, and how to remember: A problem of metacognition. In R. Glaser (Ed.), *Advances in instructional psychology* (Vol. 1, pp. 77–165). Hillsdale, NJ: Lawrence Erlbaum Assoc.

Peterson, G., Sampson, J., & Reardon, R. (1991). *Career development and services: A cognitive approach*. Pacific Grove, CA: Brooks/Cole.

Sampson, J., Peterson, G., Lenz, J., Reardon, R., & Saunders, D. (1996a). The Career Thoughts Inventory (CTI). Odessa, FL: Psychological Assessment Resources, Inc.

Sampson, J., Peterson, G., Lenz, J., Reardon, R., & Saunders, D. (1996b). *Improving your career thoughts: A workbook for the Career Thoughts Inventory*. Odessa, FL: Psychological Assessment Resources, Inc.

Sampson, J. P., Jr., Reardon, R. C., Peterson, G. W., & Lenz, J. L. (2004). *Career counseling and services: A cognitive information processing approach*. Pacific Grove, CA: Wadsworth-Brooks/Cole.

Social Conditions Affecting Career Development

CAREERING IN A CHANGING WORLD

In Chapters 1 to 5, we focused on the idea of "career" and how the Pyramid of Information-Processing Domains and the CASVE Cycle could help us understand and improve our thinking about career problem solving and decision making, our Personal Career Theory (PCT). The goal was to learn how to become better career problem solvers and decision makers and to improve the ways we think about and use career information. In a word, we have been examining the person and how the person *thinks* about career.

In Part Two, we examine some of the forces, outside the person, that affect careers: the increased use of technology, global economic markets, changing work organizations, alternative ways of working, and the relationships between men and women at home and at work.

Chapters 6 to 10 will help us refine our thinking about the part of the pyramid that deals with understanding our options: the occupational knowledge domain. We will examine very large, powerful forces in terms of the way they may *limit or increase our options. Stated another way, these macrolevel forces—meaning large, high-level forces—impact all areas of our PCT, the Pyramid of Information-Processing Domains, and the CASVE Cycle.*

However, our individual perception and interpretation of these macrolevel forces is related to our metacognitions, which, we have already learned, influence how we solve career problems and make career decisions.

THE ROLE OF GENERAL EDUCATION COURSES

The liberal studies courses taken in college should affect your thinking about careers. White (2005), writing in the *Wall Street Journal*, noted that future chief executives may require a broader liberal-arts education and wider international experience. Paraphrasing comments by a former corporate recruiter, White suggested that for future CEOs it's about maturity and leadership rather than how many accounting courses they took. Furthermore, international experience is a "big deal."

As a college student, you have taken (or will take) courses in general education or liberal studies. What role do these courses play in career planning? Are they simply courses to "get out of the way" until you get into your major? General education courses, apart from those in your major, are intended to broaden your appreciation of what is happening in the world that affects the way we work and live.

Such knowledge directly affects the way we learn to think about our careers. For example, courses in the social sciences provide opportunities to learn about ethnic groups, communities, organizations, and human behavior. Courses in the humanities help us learn about cultures, languages, and the communication of ideas and values, and courses in the sciences help us learn about technology and problem solving. "Clearly students need to have emphasized the intrinsic value of studying history and culture, mathematics and science—*learning broadly about those things that make us what we are and the world about us what it is*" [italics added] (Johnston, Reardon, Kramer, Lenz, Maduros, & Sampson, 1991, p. 192).

Some experts have suggested that general knowledge, apart from technical skills and direct knowledge learned in the major, has a powerful impact on employment success. Gardner (1998) argued that of the total jobs available, 75 percent require general skills and knowledge (a good liberal arts education), and 25 percent require specific skills and knowledge (technical competencies, programming skills). While technical skills might be very helpful in obtaining a job offer, general knowledge skills may contribute more to your long-term employment success (Gardner, 1998).

In terms of the Pyramid of Information-Processing Domains, general education courses provide knowledge about work options, such as labor market trends, social changes, and work styles. These courses help you sharpen and clarify your knowledge about work options. In terms of the CASVE Cycle, these courses help you learn about and clarify the societal "gaps" to which you might want to dedicate your career or prioritize the values on which you will base your career decisions. Such courses might help you understand an "issue" that motivates you to commit to a particular career objective, e.g., global warming, homeless children, family entertainment.

General education/liberal studies courses can enable students to develop more complex and accurate ways of thinking about careers in many ways, including the following:

- A course in world **history** can increase understanding of the decline of nationalism, the rise of tribalism, and the increase in global economic power in relation to geography, culture, technology, and population; such historical interpretations can be helpful in developing schema regarding strategic career planning.

- A course in **sociology** or **economics** can increase understanding of the ways that organizations develop and function, particularly work-related organizations; such knowledge can be helpful in developing career schema regarding work attitudes and organizational culture, because most work is done in organizational settings.

- A course in **science** or **humanities** can increase understanding of the ways that technology has affected work organizations and jobs, which has resulted in new ways of working; such knowledge can be helpful in developing schema regarding work and leisure, unemployment, occupational change, part-time work, and job hunting.

- A course in **communication, sociology,** or **psychology** could increase understanding of gender and interpersonal relationships in relation to work and family life; such knowledge can be helpful in developing and negotiating successful work and family relationships now more complex in the modern world.

NEEDED: NEW CAREER METACOGNITIONS

Jerry Hage (1995), an industrial and organizational psychologist, has studied issues associated with modern work for many years and he argues that we must develop more complex ways of thinking about life in this modern world:

People must learn to live in complex role-sets, each with a large number of role-relationships in which negotiations about role expectations or behavior become one of the major capacities for successful role performance. Furthermore, to adjust to the constant changes in society that provides the context for both the family and the workplace, people in post-industrial society need to have complex and creative minds, be adaptive and flexible, and know how to understand symbolic communications. (p. 487)

If Hage is correct, we have no choice but to think in more complex ways about our careers. In our view, the Cognitive Information Processing approach provides ways to help us do this.

As you read Part Two, you should be constantly thinking about your metacognitions (your thoughts, beliefs, and attitudes) regarding your PCT, how you think about yourself and your career, and whether the information in these five chapters requires you to reframe or modify your thinking. Remember, metacognitions refer to the process of thinking about thinking. Here are some thought-provoking questions to ask yourself:

- How can I fully use this information about the sociology of work, economic changes, diversity in the workplace, and alternative work styles to sharpen my PCT career metacognitions and become a more effective career decision maker?

- How does this information relate to my gender? My ethnic group membership? My religious preferences? My spirituality? My identification with my community?

- How will this information affect my "careering" as I finish school, look for a good job, make plans for a significant personal relationship or family, and undertake job changes (voluntary or forced)?

- How can I develop a strategic plan for my career in light of the powerful, rapidly changing socioeconomic forces affecting persons today?

Two metaphors are useful as we begin Chapter 6. First, think of your career as a ship sailing on the sea. These macrolevel forces are like the tides, the wind, the ocean currents, and the temperature—they are the forces that may require you to make adjustments to your ship as you go "careering" over the horizon. They will directly cause you to make changes in the way you sail your "career ship."

Second, in Chapter 1 we examined Roe's formula (see Table 1.1) explaining "occupational choice." Roe observed that the general state of the economy (**E**); family background (**B**); chance factors (**C**), such as technological inventions, new laws; and one's friends, peers (**F**) and marital situation (**M**) all combine to shape a person's career options. These are the conditions affecting career behavior that we will explore in Part Two.

THE VISION: "TO HAVE A SUCCESSFUL CAREER"

Almost every college student working through a career problem or decision is really pursuing the vision of "having a successful career." *Webster's* (Mish, 1997) defines *vision* as "something seen in a dream or trance; something imagined or revealed, as to a prophet." In a real sense, we are each prophets for our career; we have the potential to develop a vision, a dream, of what we want and where we will end up.

As we learned in Chapter 1, a career is *not* something that a person has or possesses. As the cover of our text suggests, it is better to think of career as a course, a journey, a process, a path, rather than a destination or prize. If we substitute the word *life* for the word *career*, we come closer to the meaning of career. Therefore, a career is something we pursue or seek, not something we have or possess. This is an important reframing of the career metacognition and changes the common understanding of a "successful career." Make sure you fully grasp this thought.

The word *successful* is vague and fuzzy because to be a *success* in something is truly an individual matter. Mary Decker Slaney set 36 national records and 17 official and unofficial world records at various distances, but after four tries she never won an Olympic medal. However, we can still say she had a *successful* running career. Our vision of having a successful career is doomed to frustration if we are not clear and specific about what *success* means to us.

In this information age, we may have to think differently about what a successful career entails. For example, it may be appropriate to substitute the word *satisfying* for the word *successful*. Satisfaction is based more on internal factors and one's state of mind, whereas success is often based on many external factors over which we may have little control.

Elizabeth McKenna (1997), in *When Work Doesn't Work Anymore*, suggests that men and women (especially women) "have to figure out who they are and what their own definitions of success are (apart from business achievements) in order to negotiate the emotional contract they have made with their careers. And no matter what the decision, there are trade-offs" (p. 38). She noted that success on the job often comes at the price of success in family and personal life. McKenna believes that future generations will "have a different definition of success than we have" (p. 251) and a very different way of working.

REFRAMING THE CAREER METACOGNITION

Figure 6.1 provides a graphic image to illustrate the point we want to make, and we are indebted to the psychologist Kurt Lewin (1951) for presenting this idea. He noted that it is important to distinguish between the "world out there" and what we actually see (or perceive). The larger circle shows the broader environment (the "real world") in which our careers unfold. This real world or force field includes technology and the global economy (Chapter 7), changes in work organizations (Chapter 8), alternative ways of working (Chapter 9), and family-career adjustments (Chapter 10). You might think of this as a stage with all kinds of varied sets and props where actors do their thing.

The smaller shaded circle indicates that we each view the broader environment in our own unique ways using our metacognitions. We can learn to view this "real world," this force field, in new and different ways, depending on our goals, aspirations, interests, values, and skills. You are the principal actor in your career. The chapters in Part Two are intended to help us to learn more about "the real world" and to improve the quality of our "psychological world" in relation to career problem solving and decision making.

Technology and the New Global Economy

Changes are taking place that will continue to impact the way we "career" in the future. Here are some examples of events that have affected even the work of career counselors.

Technology has changed the way many organizations conduct business. For example, in the banking industry, computers are set to automatically move money to and from accounts when certain preset conditions exist. This occurs throughout the world, 24 hours a day. While you sleep, your money is moving around various world exchanges, searching for the highest interest-bearing accounts. The Internet makes it possible for individuals and organizations to have instant contact

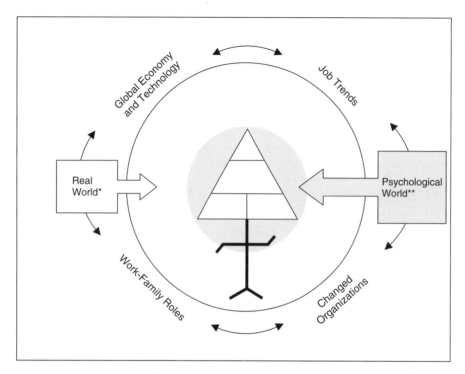

FIGURE **6.1**

Career Metacognitions in a Force Field

*<u>Real World</u>: Constantly changing social and physical events experienced by the person; the nonpsychological experiences impacting a person's career, e.g., technology and the global economy, changes in work organizations, alternative ways of working, changing career and family roles.

**<u>Psychological World</u>: The person's psychological world, or "life space"; the person's *perception* of the social and physical events in the Real World as either positive (supporting) or negative (restraining) forces having an impact on the person's achievement of goals.

with one another, at little cost. Financial experts were shocked when one bank employee, working alone at a computer, was responsible for financial transactions that caused the collapse of one of the largest banks in the United Kingdom.

Richard Judy and Carol D'Amico (1997) tell us that the pace of technological change in the economy has never been greater. Moreover, it will increase in an exponential manner. According to them, the "creative destruction" brought by technology to national economies, organizations, and individual workers will be even more powerful in the 21st century than in the past. It is virtually impossible to underestimate the impact of technology on careers.

Trade agreements between nations can dramatically change the way products and services are sold. For example, the North American Free Trade Agreement (NAFTA) between Canada, Mexico, and the United States eliminated many barriers to economic exchanges. In effect, this means that there are no economic borders between these countries, although there are still political ones. As a result of NAFTA, some U.S. companies sell their products or services, such as computer parts or software training, to businesses and organizations in new places that were off-limits before. Products are manufactured in one country and packaged in another.

The United States has entered into many new trade agreements in recent years, especially in the Pacific Rim (the countries that surround the Pacific Ocean), the former Soviet Union (including Russia and former communist countries), South and Central America, and the Middle East (such as Egypt, Israel, and Saudi Arabia). Other trade agreements are pending with Africa. These new trade agreements between nations increasingly affect the kinds of jobs available to us.

Even the authors, who are college faculty and staff in a southeastern university, have been impacted by international economic developments. One consulted with people in Turkey about how to improve job training and employment of Turkish citizens. That required considerable time taking a "crash course" in Turkish history, culture, customs, and current issues. This text has been translated into Chinese and is being used in the People's Republic. In the past ten years, visitors from more than 40 foreign nations have come to observe our career center's career planning and placement services, especially the use of computers. Although some of these visitors have many different ideas about "successful career" and what it means, they are anxious to learn from the American experience how to help citizens plan careers and find jobs in the new market economies developing around the world. It turns out that the field of career counseling knows no borders in a global economy.

Changes in Work Organizations

Work organizations, including businesses, government agencies, schools, and community centers, are changing the way they function. Increasingly, they are organized differently, they communicate internally and externally in new ways, they treat employees differently, and they think about their customers and products in new ways. These organizational changes are having a dramatic impact on the ways in which we "career," and we will examine them in more detail in Chapter 8.

One example is when organizations significantly cut personnel and then purchase the same services from an outside organization. This is typically called *outsourcing*. For example, Company A, a medical supply service, decides to eliminate its human resources department and contract with Company B, a firm that specializes in HR services, to provide these services to Company A (for example, to maintain employee leave records, advertise positions, screen resumes, keep payroll records). Company A has reduced the number of employees, which saves Company A money, but the work still gets done by Company B.

Alternative Ways of Working

Many people have grownup with the idea of working a 40-hour week in a professional job—that just seemed to be the natural order of things. Of course, physicians, nurses, plumbers, and police officers work odd schedules, but most of us assumed we would have regular weekday jobs. Perhaps nothing else in the career world has changed as much as the "way" we work. Work patterns include options such as flextime, part-time, job sharing, temporary, and home-based work/telecommuting patterns. We will examine these issues and others in detail in Chapter 9 and focus on how they affect our career planning.

Job sharing occurs when one job is shared between two people. Each person typically works 20 hours per week at separate times, although they probably share two or three hours of time on the job each week for joint meetings with supervisors and other staff members. This arrangement is ideal for someone with child care or elder care responsibilities where a 40-hour job might be difficult or impossible. A person completing an educational degree might find it impossible to work full time and attend classes full time. A person might have leisure or entrepreneurial interests that make it difficult to work full time and still pursue these outside interests. A job share typically carries one-half the insurance and other benefits available with the position. This arrangement provides some extra support that might not be otherwise available to the part-time worker.

As you contemplate your career journey, be mindful that alternative work arrangements might give you some options regarding *when* and *how* you work as well as *how* you engage in other important life activities.

Career and Family Roles

Sociologists have noted that the patterns of work for men and women common today in the United States are only about 100 years old. Before the industrial revolution, both men and women worked on the farm or in the shop and shared childcare and housekeeping duties. With the rise of manufacturing and industry in the late 1800s, men increasingly left the farm to pursue higher-paying jobs in city factories. Women were left at home to care for children and manage the domestic responsibilities. In the past 50 years, beginning during World War II in the 1940s, women have increasingly taken jobs outside the home. The dual-career family, or in some cases the dual-earner family, where both the man and woman are working outside the home, has had a huge impact on the way most of us work today and will work in the future. We will explore these topics in more detail in Chapter 10.

Relocation is a critical issue that may add complexity in career planning for a dual-career couple. When both partners are engaged in career, and relocation opportunities impact one career, the trailing spouse or partner can face considerable difficulties. The same kinds of opportunities may not be present in the new location. Successful relocation in dual-career situations require considerable skill in negotiation and compromise. In cognitive terms, it means that both people are able to perceive a "win" no matter which option is selected.

THE FOUR MACROLEVEL FACTORS

In Part Two, we will look at the "market economy" and how things are changing in this regard. A market is created when one person's wants or needs create a demand for a product or service that another person can satisfy. The market involves the exchange of goods and services between people, typically involving money. *In a market economy, jobs are created because one person is willing to spend money for goods or services. Jobs follow from what someone wants, needs, or is willing to pay for.*

In the present day, market economies—also known as capitalism—are springing up throughout the world. Moreover, there are markets for everything: baseball cards, money, hamburgers, steel, and knowledge. Someone once joked that we could become a nation of hamburger sellers, because that's how we all like to spend our money. Right now, markets are the largest seedbed of career development for people.

In our analysis, we have emphasized the distinct nature of the four macrolevel changes affecting work today: (1) global economic markets, (2) changing work organizations, (3) alternative ways of working, and (4) the relationships between men and women at home and at work. In reality, however, these four influences are impossible to separate, and they have all been affected by technology. Altogether, they function as a complex system where each factor affects the others and vice versa. The phrase "everything affects everything" applies here. Focusing on the independent nature of these four factors in Part Two will make it easier to analyze and understand them.

You might notice that the progression of these four factors moves from the most broad and distant to the most specific and immediate. We will begin by looking at global economic events and trends and then examining how these factors are affecting work organizations and the way individuals work now and in the future. We will conclude with the impact of these changes on the lives of men and women in contemporary America.

Finally, the perspective we will take in Part Two is one of change, how things about career and work are changing in the modern world. This reflects some age bias (the authors are all old enough to have experienced many of these changes in their work lives), but many college students born after 1988 may not see these macrolevel factors as changes because they haven't experienced anything else. The present-day world with its technological advances, global economy, instant communication, and changing social roles is all they know.

STRATEGIC CAREER THINKING

The term *strategic thinking* may not be a familiar one, so first we should define it. Years ago, business organizations began to use the concepts of strategic thinking and strategic planning to ensure that their organization was headed in the right direction (Cope, 1987; Omahe, 1982). When "thinking strategically," an organization asks itself the following questions:

- Where does our organization want to go?

- Are we in the right business relative to other businesses we could be in?

Cope defined strategic thinking for an organization as "the process of developing a vision of where the institution wants to go, and then developing managing strategies (plans) on how to get there" (quoted in Hoadly & Zimmer, 1982, p. 16). Note that strategic thinking begins with the process of developing a vision. *Put another way, strategic thinking is doing the right things (effectiveness), whereas operational planning is doing things right (efficiency).* Sometimes organizations get so caught up in being efficient and doing things right that they lose sight of doing the right things, of being effective. In other words, effectiveness is doing the right things and thinking strategically, while efficiency is doing things right and operational planning. *Organizations can fail for being either ineffective or inefficient.*

The process of strategic thinking applied to organizations can also be applied to individuals. By thinking strategically about your career, you can (1) formulate a vision of what being "successful" means for you, (2) get yourself organized and prepared to do the "right things," and (3) implement a plan to do "things right." Strategic career thinking means setting your course and charting your way through important social issues, such as the global economy, changing organizational cultures, alternative ways of working, and changing roles of men and women.

Thinking and planning your career in a strategic way means that you can set your career direction in light of the internal forces, such as your interests, values, and skills, in relation to the external forces existing in society.

Your task is to develop a vision of your career, based partly on your intuitive, subjective judgment about where the four social forces we examined are taking us as individuals and a society.

As you read the next four chapters, interpret the facts presented in light of your own experience and the other things that you know or have

learned about the future. Critically analyze the information in light of your strategic career plan. How does it change how you think about your life/ career in the future? Be proactive and forward-thinking in light of the facts that are presented in these chapters about work organizations and work roles, especially with reference to your Personal Career Theory.

A Case Application: Becoming a Manager

In conclusion, let's examine how the social conditions we have briefly sketched would possibly affect a beginning manager's vision of a successful career and how to pursue certain elements of strategic thinking. This is not a far-fetched idea because college students often find themselves in positions managing projects, programs, or people.

With respect to the global economy, a new manager might do the following:

- Consider getting educational and work experiences in multicultural settings

- Take courses in world history, sociology, economics, and languages to learn more about world-wide changes and issues

- Travel to different countries; learn about his or her own cultural traditions

- Develop friendships with persons from other countries

- Learn about how management is done in other countries

- Look for work opportunities in multinational organizations

- Use the Internet to communicate directly with people around the world

These activities will help in developing a better vision of the existence of macrolevel problems and opportunities for a beginning manager.

With respect to changing organizational cultures and strategic thinking, a new manager might do the following:

- Interview other managers to learn about their actual work histories and experiences in different kinds of organizations

- Seek to complete graduate training from an accredited program and pursue professional certification (if appropriate) as a manager

- Learn about different kinds of managers and management philosophies, both from direct experience and reading

- Research the advantages and disadvantages of being a manager in different kinds of organizations and agencies

- Study the occupations and organizations that employ managers, and learn about the laws, inventions, and policies that are affecting those areas

- Learn about the characteristics of family-friendly organizations and other employee-centered practices

This would help in developing a better vision of what a practicing manager might do and the settings where it might be done.

With respect to changing personal work styles and strategic thinking, a new manager might do the following:

- Develop a vision of how the roles of parent, spouse/partner, worker, student, child, leisurite, citizen, and so forth will be incorporated into one's life over the next 10 or more years

- Examine how significant people in one's life will be involved in shaping a career

- Understand the importance of leisure activities in one's life and how these activities may be selected in relation to work activities and organizational policies

- Learn about alternative workstyle patterns and employer benefit options, and set priorities on when and how these would be incorporated into one's career plan

This will be helpful in developing the vision of a time-extended plan for balancing work and other life roles in one's career.

With respect to changing roles of men and women and strategic thinking, a new manager might do the following:

- Develop a shared career vision with one's spouse or partner

- Learn about successful patterns of balancing work and family life given different kinds of career options and organizational characteristics

- Learn about effective child care options

- Learn about alternative work styles within different kinds of industries

- Study the kinds of stressors—for example, eldercare, relocation, childcare—that affect relationships in dual career situations

- Study the trends and issues in work and family life for single parents

The purpose of this research and learning would be to develop a vision of how work and family life might be balanced in the work of a manager.

SUMMARY

We have introduced four external, social forces that are affecting the ways individual careers are developing now and in the future. We began with a review of general education/liberal studies courses in relation to strategic career planning and suggested the need for new career metacognitions in the information age.

"Having a successful career" is the vision that many people bring to the career-planning process. The vision of a successful career can be framed within four social conditions: (1) technology and the changing global economy, (2) changing organizational cultures, (3) alternative ways of working, and (4) changing roles of men and women.

The idea of strategic career thinking is one way to project one's career vision into the future, accounting for the changing social conditions that will affect future career behavior. The process of career visioning and strategic thinking was illustrated by examining the thinking processes of a management trainee. The next four chapters of this text will help you improve the part of your Personal Career Theory having to do with occupational knowledge. This, in turn, will enable you to develop new metacognitions for solving career problems and making career decisions.

REFERENCES

Cope, R. G. (1987). *Opportunity for strength: Strategic planning clarified with case examples* (ASHE-ERIC Higher Education Report No. 8). Washington, DC: George Washington University, Clearinghouse on Higher Education.

Gardner, P. D. (1998). Are college seniors prepared to work. In J. N. Gardner, G. Van der Veer, & Associates (Eds.), *The senior year experience* (pp. 60–78). San Francisco: Jossey-Bass.

Hage, J. (1995). Post-industrial lives: New demands, new prescriptions. In A. Howard (Ed.), *The changing nature of work* (pp. 485–512). San Francisco: Jossey-Bass.

Hoadly, J. A., & Zimmer, B. E. (1982). A corporate planning approach to institutional management: A preliminary report on the RMIT experience. *Journal of Tertiary Education Administration, 4,* 15–26.

Johnston, J., Reardon, R., Kramer, G., Lenz, J., Maduros, A., & Sampson, J. (1991). The demand side of general education: Attending to student attitudes and understandings. *Journal of General Education, 40,* 180–200.

Judy, R. W., & D'Amico, C. (1997). *Workforce 2020: Work and workers in the 21st century.* Indianapolis, IN: Hudson Institute.

Lewin, K. (1951) *Field theory in social science.* New York: Harper & Row.

Omahe, K. (1982). *The mind of the strategist: The art of Japanese business.* New York: McGraw-Hill.

McKenna, E. P. (1997). *When work doesn't work anymore: Women, work, and identity.* New York: Delacorte Press.

Mish, F. C. (Ed.) (1997). *Merriam-Webster's collegiate dictionary* (10th ed.). Springfield, MA: Merriam-Webster.

White, E. (2005, April 12). Future CEOs may need to have broad liberal-arts foundation. *The Wall Street Journal,* p. B4.

WORKING IN THE NEW GLOBAL ECONOMY

The world is getting smaller. Communication across continents and nations is easier, long-distance travel is an experience shared by ever-increasing numbers, and business organizations have become multinational companies. Increasingly, we live and work in a "global village." Some have gone so far as to describe the world as "flat" (Friedman, 2005). This is the stage on which our careers will unfold.

This chapter will examine how factors and trends in the global economy shape the ways we work, play, and learn during the next 10 years. Changes in work activity and production are occurring throughout the world, and we will look at projected economic changes. We will explore the scope and shape of the U.S. labor force as it has been affected by international changes in the world of work, especially the services industry. Finally, we will analyze these macrolevel changes in light of Cognitive Information Processing theory, the Pyramid of Information-Processing Domains, and the CASVE Cycle to see how we might improve our metacognitions for career problem solving and decision making.

As you read about these changes in global and U.S. economies, keep in mind your Personal *Career Theory and how your strategic career thinking can be improved.*

INTERNATIONAL CHANGES IN WORK ACTIVITY AND PRODUCTION

Peter Drucker, Robert Reich, Jeremy Rifkin, and Thomas Friedman have all written books on the world economy. Their works can help us understand the place of individual lives and careers in the global economy.

Drucker's Post-Capitalist Society

Peter Drucker was a management consultant who wrote 35 books about trends in the working world. His views are widely read and often controversial, and his book *Post-Capitalist Society*, is no exception. Drucker (1993) argued that the world is once again in a period of enormous transformation. The earlier transformations included the Reformation, the Renaissance, and the American Revolution.

This time it is not, however, confined to Western society and Western history. Indeed, it is one of the fundamental changes that there is no longer a "Western" history or, in fact a "Western" civilization. There is only world history and world civilization—but both are "Westernized." It is moot whether this present transformation began with the emergence of the first non-Western country, Japan, as a great economic power ... or with the computer—that is, with information becoming central. (p. 3)

Drucker predicted that by 2010 or 2020 the world will be nonsocialist and postcapitalist. Its primary resource would be knowledge (i.e., useful information); nation-states would be replaced by megastates; and it would be a society of organizations, each devoted to a specific task. One of the leading groups in this new world society would be the "knowledge workers," who know how to allocate knowledge and information to productive use.

The knowledge society [where knowledge workers will be employed] must have at its core the concept of the educated person. It will have to be a universal concept, precisely because the knowledge society is a society of knowledges and because it is global—in its money, its economics, its careers, its technology, its central issues, and above all, in its information. (p. 212)

Tomorrow's educated person will have to be prepared for life in a global world. It will be a "Westernized" world, but also increasingly a tribalized world. He or she must become a "citizen of the world"—in vision, horizon, and information. But he or she will also have to draw nourishment from their local roots, and, in turn, enrich and nourish their own local culture.

Post-capitalist society is both a knowledge society and a society of organizations, each dependent on the other and yet each very different in its concepts, views, and values. Most, if not all, educated persons will practice their knowledge as members of an organization. The educated person will therefore have to be prepared to live and work simultaneously in two cultures—that of the "intellectual," who focuses on work and ideas, and that of the "manager," who focuses on people and work. (pp. 214–215)

In reflecting on Drucker's last point, we are reminded of Holland's Investigative and Enterprising types from Chapter 3 and the fact that they are located in opposite points on the RIASEC hexagon. Success will come easier to those who develop I (investigative) and E (enterprising) skills.

In summary, Drucker believed that future careers would occur in a global context where people having management and information-processing skills will work in an information society. Moreover, these knowledge workers will find themselves at work as members of organizations and teams, each seeking to accomplish its own limited objectives. This vision is complex and requires some thoughtful reflection for more complete comprehension. We will see Drucker's ideas reinforced by other writers in this chapter.

Reich's Global Enterprise Webs

Robert Reich, a former U.S. Secretary of Labor, is a political economist and a faculty member at the University of California at Berkeley. He has written several books about economic life in contemporary America and what government and business should do to make it better. His ideas also have implications for college students and their career planning.

In 1992, Reich wrote an important book, *The Work of Nations: Preparing Ourselves for 21st-Century Capitalism*. His basic idea was this:

As almost every factor of production—money, technology, factories, and equipment—moves effortlessly across borders, the very idea of an American economy is becoming meaningless, as are the notions of an American corporation, American capital, American products, and American technology. A similar transformation is affecting every other nation, some faster and more profoundly than others. (p. 8)

However, Reich also noted that there is one aspect of our American economy that remains American, and that is its workforce (this includes all of us). We are *relatively* immobile; it is not easy for masses of us to cross national borders. While money, technology, factories, and equipment can be quickly moved to other countries, people are another matter. So, if the American economy is to succeed in the future, it is the American people who must develop their work knowledge, skills, and attitudes relative to those of citizens in other countries. This is an important point. No matter how much attention is devoted to the global economy, we, as American workers, are the important ultimate stakeholders in this matter.

Reich described the new business organizations as *"global enterprise webs."* To understand this, we have to go back in history. Early in the 20th century, business organizations looked much like a big pyramid—with lots of salaried workers at the bottom, managers in the middle, and top executives in a small area at the top. The power and control of the organization was vested in a few people at the top, while vast amounts of material, buildings, people, and other resources were lodged at the bottom. Business organizations were organized like the army—lots of infantry, guns, and tanks at the bottom and a few generals at the top running the show.

The heyday of these organizations occurred in the 1950s. Reich reported that about 500 of the largest American corporations produced half of the nation's industrial output, created about 40 percent of the nation's corporate profits, and employed more than one out of every eight nonfarm workers. The biggest companies were *very* large. General Motors, for example, produced goods and services equivalent in value to those produced by the country of Italy. These big companies were the basic American economy in that day. These kinds of business organizations were effective in their time, producing high volumes of materials, goods, and services, but they are now becoming outmoded.

In the modern world, these big, cumbersome, rigid organizations have been increasingly replaced by small groups of information workers who create high value for business organizations by quickly *identifying and solving problems*. These workers are joined by a strategic broker in a headquarters who helps them identify work projects and communicate effectively among themselves. In order for these workers to be effective, they have to be able to communicate directly and quickly with each other, often horizontally rather than vertically. A big bureaucracy with a large number of middle managers just slows things down. These information workers are involved in projects like developing software, designing a new marketing strategy, designing a new employee training program, finding a biological discovery, or developing a new financing scheme.

Reich described these enterprise webs as high-value business enterprises, and they are very complex, flexible work organizations, which also may be very temporary. These new enterprise webs are best understood in terms of a spider's web, where each connecting point is a place where information is exchanged by the workers. This is a very different kind of business model compared to the earlier pyramid organization.

In the new enterprise web, speed, or time, is very important—in other words, who will correctly identify and solve the problem *first*? The knowledge needed to do this work can be obtained from anywhere in the world though computer networks and international travel. These enterprise webs are often global in nature. The idea of speed or time is also important, and we examine this theme further in Chapters 8, 9, and 10.

Reich described enterprise webs as having many different kinds of shapes that constantly change and evolve. Here are some of the most common ones he identified:

- *Independent profit centers.* This web eliminates middle management and pushes authority for product development and sales down to engineers and marketers (problem identifiers and solvers). For example, Reich noted that in the 1990s, Johnson & Johnson comprised 166 separate, autonomous companies. As another example, you may have noticed that your textbooks are often published by small, semiautonomous publishing companies operating under a larger publisher. Each little company has the responsibility to find and publish books on its own. (This text, for example, is custom published by Cengage Learning, a global publisher of information which has five separate publishing divisions.)

- *Spin-off partnerships.* In this web, strategic brokers at headquarters look for good ideas that bubble up from groups of problem solvers, which are then spun off as new business organizations. Reich noted that Hitachi is actually more than 60 companies, only 27 of which are publicly traded on the stock market. This means that almost half of the companies are small and perhaps temporary.

- *Spin-in partnerships.* In this web, good ideas bubble up outside the organization from independent problem solvers. Reich noted that this kind of web is common in the software industry, where hundreds of small companies are regularly bought up by big ones such as Microsoft and IBM. The owners of the smaller companies get rich and the big companies get a steady flow of new products and ideas.

- *Licensing.* In this web, the strategic brokers at headquarters contract with independent businesses to use a brand name to sell special services or products. A good example of this is the franchise arrangement, where ownership and control is left in the hands of the licensee. Much economic activity in America today is based on this kind of web, for example, Starbucks.

- *Pure brokering.* This is the most decentralized kind of web, and it occurs when strategic brokers contract with independent businesses for problem solving as well as production. Let's say a computer company contracts with one company to make its computer and with another to deliver it, and another to advertise it on the Internet. This new company sells millions of dollars worth of computers within weeks of its startup and has fewer than 40 engineers, technicians, and accountants on its staff. This kind of outsourcing is becoming more common. Reich noted, for example, that in the 1990s General Motors bought half of its engineering and design services from 800 different companies.

Reich reminded us that these Web-like business organizations and relationships are shaping the new global economy. They can be very complex structures, with various profit centers, licensees, suppliers, dealers, and spin-offs. Reich noted that even IBM, which in an earlier time had been a very exclusive kind of American company, has joined with dozens of other companies and more than 80 foreign-owned firms to share problem solving, problem identifying, and strategic brokering. It provides services in over 170 countries and has 319,000 employees. Think about it: Is IBM still an American company? Many other companies have also created hundreds of alliances with other organizations to create enterprise webs that will produce marketplace value.

These enterprise webs are linked by computers, telephones, facsimile machines, and satellites, throughout the world. Power and wealth flows through this technology to the places on the globe where the problem solving, problem identifying, and strategic brokering are most effective. This may be to places outside the United States, including India, Ireland, Japan, China, Europe, or South Korea.

Products created by global webs are typically the combined work of many different nations. Friedman (2005) provided a good example with the Rolls-Royce organization. Most people know this as a British company and the manufacturer of a shiny, hand-made car with a uniformed driver. However, Rolls-Royce hasn't made cars since 1972 and the brand was licensed to BMW in 1998. Today it is a technology company that builds power systems for airplanes, ships, and other industries. Rolls-Royce has customers in 120 countries and employs about 35,000 people. Forty percent of its employees are outside the United Kingdom and they represent about 50 nationalities in 50 countries speaking 50 languages. It outsources and offshores about 75 percent of its work to a global supply chain. Friedman noted that a new manager in this company could be working with a team that is one-third in India, one-third in China, and a sixth in Palo Alto and Boston. Such a job would require some special skills.

In summary, global webs, whether headquartered in the United States, Western Europe, or Japan, have many characteristics in common. For example, the global enterprise webs have no clear connection to any particular nation. Indeed, many have much larger economies than most nations in the world. In addition, such webs involve "an international partnership of skilled people whose insights are combined with one another and who contract with unskilled workers from around the world for whatever must be standardized and produced in high volume" (Reich, 1992, p. 132). Multinational corporations, then, are global and their profits are shared with problem solvers, identifiers, and brokers around the world.

Rifkin's End of Work

Another important writer in this area is Jeremy Rifkin, an American economist who has produced more than a dozen books on the macrolevel forces impacting the world economy. His most important book, written in 1995, is *The End of Work: The Decline of the Global Labor Force and the Dawn of the Post-Market Era*. Rifkin's basic idea was that the global economy is undergoing fundamental changes that will lead to a steady decline in traditional, 40-hour-per-week "jobs." This will happen as computers, robots, telecommunications, and other technologies replace human beings in every area of work. Virtual companies and factories will replace workers in Rifkin's view, and this means that every nation will have to rethink the idea of *work*. These are powerful ideas, and they obviously have strong implications for individual career planning.

According to Rifkin, the coming of the "Third Industrial Revolution" has been brought about by the rapid advancement of technology throughout the world. The increased use of the *microchip* is the source of this change. (By the way, the first Industrial Revolution involved the introduction of the steam engine, and the second involved the use of oil.) Rifkin cited many reports to show that in every area of the economy—agriculture, manufacturing, services—and in every nation, machines are increasingly doing the work of people. News reports carry information about this phenomena every day as companies reduce their workforce, restructure their operations, and re-engineer the workplace.

Rifkin cited a survey of 2,000 corporate executives from the world's leading industrial nations. In this study, 94 percent of the respondents reported that their companies had been through a reorganization in the past two years resulting in permanent workforce reduction. More than 66 percent of these business leaders predicted that downsizing and re-engineering will increase in the future. The companies surveyed employed 18 million people, or more than 6 percent of the workforce in the six leading industrialized countries in the world. "In the United States alone, that means that in the years ahead more than 90 million jobs in a labor force of 124 million are potentially vulnerable to replacement by machines" (p. 5). The scope of this change is difficult to ignore.

What does this mean for individual workers? The loss of jobs may mean that increasing numbers of people will experience unemployment or underemployment during their lives. Rifkin reported that in the mid 1990s, more than 8.7 million people were unemployed, 6.1 million were working part-time and wanted full-time employment, and more than 1 million were so discouraged that they stopped looking for a job altogether. These are sobering reports for college students and other people seeking traditional jobs.

Sounding a theme described earlier by Reich, Rifkin explained how the Japanese company Toyota led the way in introducing "lean production." The guiding principle, according to Rifkin, was the combination of new management techniques and sophisticated machinery to produce more cars with few resources and less labor. This was accomplished by management bringing together teams of workers with different specializations who shared ideas about how to improve production directly with one another. The factory floor became a laboratory where changes were made immediately in order to make continuous improvements. Technology helped the team make these improvements by reducing the numbers of people involved in the process, speeding up the process, producing more specialized products, using less space, requiring less inventory onsite, and making a less expensive product. Using this approach, each worker naturally developed a variety of skills, and important information was shared among all workers. Lean production is very different from the older-style craft and mass-production models.

The production model developed in Japan also places a high priority on "just-in-time" production, or stockless production. Ironically, Rifkin noted that an American supermarket provided the beginnings for this idea. Here, the amount of product stocked on the shelves provides customers just what they want, when they need it, and in the right amount. The American fast-food restaurant provides another example. Just-in-time models have now also been incorporated into health care, education, retail clothing, and many other areas of the economy. Wal-Mart would never have been created without the scanners used by clerks at the point-of-sale, which inform suppliers about what and how much product to include in the next shipment. Rifkin noted that corporate re-engineering is only in its early stages and will increase as companies faced with global competition use even more sophisticated technologies to reduce production costs, including labor, and increase productivity and profits.

Does Rifkin have any solutions to the problems he identifies? The full exploration of this topic goes beyond the scope of this chapter, but we'll give a brief look at his ideas. First, Rifkin suggested that in this postmarket era, we must move to shorten the work week, perhaps to 30 hours. This was almost accomplished in the United States in the late 1930s, and it is already being implemented in some European countries. The immediate benefit is the creation of jobs for more workers. Second, Rifkin predicted the development of a more powerful Third Sector, which will contribute to what he calls the "social economy." This Third Sector, also known as the independent, nonprofit, or volunteer sector, will balance the Public Sector (government) and the Market Sector (business).

The Third Sector, or social economy, includes all those volunteer and community organizations that feed the poor, protect the environment, teach reading, run midnight basketball programs, care for the elderly, operate museums, promote women's civil rights, and build churches. (Readers will recall that Drucker also discussed the increasing importance of such organizational memberships in his book.) Rifkin indicated that about 80 percent of economic activity was made up of the Market Sector, 14 percent from the Public Sector, and 6 percent from the Third Sector. Surprisingly, the last includes about 9 percent of national employment. "More people are employed in third-sector organizations than work in either the construction, electronics, transportation, or textile and apparel industries (p. 241)," and it is growing twice as fast as the government and private sectors.

Few college students are aware of the paid employment opportunities in this Third Sector. Crosby (2001) noted that nonprofits, organizations that are neither businesses nor part of governments, employ more than 10 million people. Charities, foundations, private schools, churches, professional and trade associations, many scientific institutions, and more than half of U.S. hospitals are in the Third Sector. Perhaps it seems like a contradiction to think of having a good job in a nonprofit organization, but the reality is that these organizations can be desirable places to work. The U.S. Department of Labor does not report salary differences between occupations in the nonprofit and profit or government sectors of the economy, so it is not possible to provide facts about salaries in these three areas. (It should be noted that nonpaid work in this sector can also be important, because it provides opportunities to satisfy needs that might not be met in paid employment and it also provides opportunities to develop skills for future paid work activities.)

Rifkin cited a 1992 Gallup survey indicating that 51 percent of Americans gave their time to various causes and organizations. There are more than 1.4 million nonprofit organizations in the United States, and their primary goal is to provide a service or advance a cause. It is good that Rifkin reminds us of this rich, growing area of economic life, because many interesting and important individual careers can flourish in the Third Sector. This is much more than an American phenomenon. As Rifkin sees it, "The third sector is emerging in every region of the world. Its meteoric rise is attributable in part to the increasing need to fill a political vacuum left by the retreat of both the private and public sectors from the affairs of local communities" (p. 283). This Third Sector is another aspect of the global economy.

What are the implications of the development of a social economy for individual strategic career planning? What are the implications of the dramatic increases in the use of technology and biogenetics for career development? These are the macrolevel forces that people will wrestle with in the coming years as they think about their individual career development.

Friedman's Flat World

Thomas Friedman (2005) has written several books about how work has changed because of technology innovations and the global economy. He identifies three historical periods of globalization. The first began in 1492 with Columbus' trip to the new world and lasted until 1800 with ships traveling the world's continents seeking trade. The second era lasted from 1800 to 2000 and was marked by multinational companies using new forms of transportation, e.g., steam and rail, and new forms of telecommunications, e.g., satellites, PCs, telephones. But Friedman views this third period as very different because it is marked by the capacity of individuals to use new software to collaborate and compete globally. Unlike the two earlier eras, this one is not driven by European and American individuals or companies but includes persons in China, India, South Korea, Turkey, Japan, South America, and other parts of the world. Friedman believes that this most recent phase of globalization has truly shrunk and flattened the world – individuals who have the skill and knowledge can now directly participate in the global economy.

The global, Web-enabled playing field permits all kinds of new collaborative efforts in education and work and does it in real time with no regard for distance. This, in turn, has led to new forms of business leadership and organizational behavior – new ways of working. Friedman suggests that 3 billion people outside of Western Europe and North America are now able to compete and collaborate in the new global economy. He argues that the discovery and innovation brought about by these changes are simply unprecedented in world history. For example, he notes that there are more cell phones in use in China than there are people in the United States and that the South Koreans far exceed American's use of the Internet.

What does all this mean for U.S. college students and their career planning? There are numerous implications, e.g., international experience, ethnic cultural understanding, information technology skills, constant training, but the bottom line is to develop job skills that cannot be outsourced. We explore this topic further in this chapter.

Offshoring and Outsourcing

A discussion of global changes in work and production impacting U.S. jobs would not be complete without mention of the offshoring and outsourcing phenomenon. Friedman offered a distinction between these two terms. He described offshoring as the movement of an entire factory to another location where exactly the same goods were produced as before but the costs were less. Outsourcing means taking some specific organizational function, e.g., research, call center, accounting, human resources, and having some other organization do the work and then return the output. Advances in medical technology and the rise in medical tourism mean that surgeries can be performed in India for a fraction of the cost in the U.S., e.g., $3,000 vs. $39,000 for a hip replacement (Colvin, 2004). High technology start-ups are especially prone to this activity. Google won't say how many of its 3,000 workers are outside the U.S. but it has offices in Toronto, London, Tokyo, Hamburg, Paris, Milan, Sydney, Amsterdam, Dublin, and Madrid (Krantz, February, 2005). Such changes mean that the white-collar, middle class worker as well as the factory production worker is faced with the flow of jobs to global markets where the basic issue is the cost or salary of the worker (Thottam, 2004).

THE CHANGING AMERICAN LABOR FORCE

Given these changes in the global economy, how are American jobs being affected? In this section, we will learn about which occupations are growing and which are declining. We will examine these general labor market trends with reference to the implications for individual career planning. We'll also focus on the earnings gap. The goal is to help you develop "mental maps" of how the labor market works (Wegmann, Chapman & Johnston, 1989). This, in turn, should help you improve your strategic career thinking.

U.S. Labor Market Trends Through 2016

Given this brief review of economic global trends and changes in the nature of work, what is happening in the United States regarding job changes? What are the trends in the growth and decline of occupations? Where are the jobs? What industries are growing? What is the labor market for college graduates?

To begin to answer these questions, we examined the work of Jerome Pikulinski (2004), an economist with the Division of Occupational Employment Statistics, Bureau of Labor Statistics. He reported that most new and emerging occupations were in firms with fewer than 100 employees. For many college students, this means that you might find yourself working at a job in a relatively small organization that is not well known. Pikulinski further noted that no single state in the U.S. or occupational group dominated in the creation of new and emerging occupations. However, health-care, management, and production occupations were the three most frequent occupational classifications noted in his report.

Who works? We consulted a special issue of the *Occupational Outlook Quarterly (OOQ)*, "Charting the Projections: 2006–2016," for information about the U.S. labor force. The *OOQ* is one of the publications produced by the Bureau of Labor Statistics (BLS) in the U.S. Department of Labor, which has been studying the American workforce for many years. The economists and statisticians working there provide useful information to answer such questions. Toossi (2007) indicated that 164.2 million persons will be working or looking for work in 2016.

The labor force (those 16 and older who are working or looking for work and who are neither in the military or in prison) in 2002 included about 67 percent of the U.S. population, and this is projected to be 65.5 percent in 2016. The labor force will continue to age, with the 55-years-and-older group growing at five times the rate of everyone else.

Who works? Toossi (2007) reports that an average of 59 percent of women and 72 percent of men will be employed in 2016. Who doesn't work according to BLS? This group includes those who are incapacitated, ill, in prison or the military, under 16, or discouraged job hunters.

Two views. Figure 7.1 illustrates the two ways in which job growth can be viewed, numeric change and percent change. Numeric change is the actual number of jobs gained or lost over a decade. Percent change is the rate of job growth or decline during the decade.

The upper chart shows the projected increase in employment for accountants and auditors compared with that for environmental engineers. In numeric terms, more than 11 times as many new jobs are projected for accountants and auditors as for environmental engineers between 2002 and 2012. Percent change tells a different story. As the lower chart shows, employment of environmental engineers is expected to grow about twice as fast as that of accountants and auditors.

In general, occupations expected to grow at a fast rate will not produce large numbers of jobs. This has implications for those who want to use labor market forecast information in their career planning. Should they pay more attention to occupations that grow rapidly or those with the most jobs? What do you think about this?

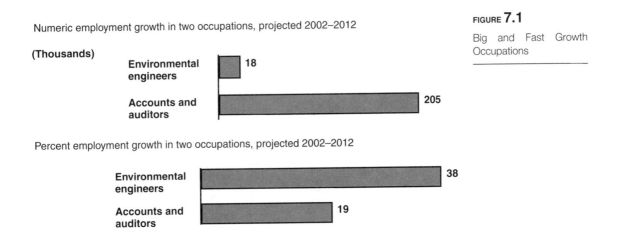

Numeric employment growth in two occupations, projected 2002–2012

FIGURE 7.1

Big and Fast Growth Occupations

(Thousands)

Percent employment growth in two occupations, projected 2002–2012

Employment trends. Before continuing, we should pause a moment and reflect upon the accuracy of these labor market forecasts by BLS. In general, the economists who study labor markets and issue projections are very accurate in their forecasts, possibly underestimating the trends slightly. On the whole, BLS employment projections are quite accurate. Alpert and Auyer (2003) observed that occupations projected in 1988 to have the most rapid growth were underestimated, and those projected to have little growth or slight declines experienced greater declines than anticipated. The direction of employment change was predicted accurately 70 percent of the time.

Moreover, the projections themselves can affect the forecast outcomes. For example, if a shortage of engineers is forecast, which leads to increased enrollment in engineering programs, then the projected shortage will decrease somewhat. In addition, economic recessions impact occupations in different ways—for example, career counselors have more work to do, whereas some workers have less to do. The following factors can also affect economic forecasts:

- Natural disasters—earthquakes, hurricanes

- World political events—war, trade agreements, terrorism

- Changes in government spending—homeland security

- New welfare or student aid programs

- Technological inventions and breakthroughs

- New laws, e.g., balancing the federal budget

In general, it is wise to keep these things in mind as you read about labor market forecasts.
Tables 7.1, 7.2, 7.3, and 7.4 outline the following helpful information:

1. The 20 occupations that will employ the most people through the year 2016;

2. The 20 occupations that will grow the most rapidly through 2016; and

3. The 20 occupations with fastest growth, highest earnings, and lowest unemployment through 2012.

These data are based on an analysis of Occupational Employment Statistics (see Chapter 3 for a review of the OES topic). We'll also examine Holland codes (see Chapter 2) for these occupations.

Occupations that employ the most people. Table 7.1 shows the 20 occupations expected to have the most job openings each year through 2016 (Dohm & Shniper, 2007). We might call these "big growth" occupations. As a college student, the first fact that will probably get your attention is that only four occupations listed require a college degree: postsecondary teachers, computer software engineers, accountants and auditors, and elementary school teachers. The registered nurse

TABLE 7.1   BIG GROWTH OCCUPATIONS, 2006–2016

Standard Occupational Code (SOC) Number and Occupational Title	2016 Employment (thousands)	Percent+ Change	Holland Codes
29-1111 Registered nurses	3,092	24	SIE
41-2031 Retail salespersons	5,034	12	ESR
43-4051 Customer service representatives	2,747	25	ESC
35-3021 Combined food preparation and serving workers, including fast food	2,955	18	REC
43-9061 Office clerks, general	3,604	13	CRS
39-9021 Personal and home care aides	1,156	51	SRE
31-1011 Home health aides	1,171	49	SRC
25-1000 Postsecondary teachers	2,054	23	IRS
37-2011 Janitors and cleaners, except maids and housekeeping cleaners	2,732	15	RES
31-1012 Nursing aides, orderlies, and attendants	1,711	18	SER
43-3031 Bookkeeping, accounting, and auditing clerks	2,377	13	CSR
35-3031 Waiters and waitresses	2,615	11	ECS
39-9011 Child care workers	1,636	18	ESA
43-6011 Executive secretaries and administrative assistants	1,857	15	CES
15-1031 Computer software engineers, applications	733	45	IRE
13-2011 Accountants and auditors	1,500	18	CEI
37-3011 Landscaping and grounds-keeping workers	1,441	18	RIS
25-2021 Elementary school teachers, except special education	1,749	14	SAE
43-4171 Receptionists and information clerks	1,375	17	CSE
53-3032 Truck drivers, heavy and tractor-trailer	2,053	10	RCS

Source: Occupational employment projections to 2016, published in the *Monthly Labor Review*, November 2007
Note: These 20 occupations account for almost 45 percent of projected new jobs 2006–2016.
Note: RIASEC Code order: S = 32, E = 27, R = 25, C = 22, I = 9, A = 3; same code order as in 2002

occupation typically requires an associate degree, and the other 16 occupations require associate degrees or short-term to moderate on-the-job training. However, you should keep in mind that the management and supervision of all these workers probably does require advanced training.

Dohm and Shniper (2007) noted that only four of the occupations gaining the most new jobs through 2016 pay at $46,360 or higher (registered nurses, postsecondary faculty, software engineers, and accountants/auditors), three pay at $30,630–46,300 (executive secretaries/administrative assistants, elementary school teachers, and heavy truck drivers), and 13 pay at $30,000 or lower. This is consistent with the idea that many of these occupations do not require education beyond the high school level.

College students should be especially interested in growth in employment in professional and related occupations. These include (1) education, training, and library work; (2) healthcare and technical work; (3) computers and mathematical science; (4) community and social services; (5) legal; (6) life, physical, and social sciences; (7) architecture and engineering; and (8) arts, design, media, entertainment, and sports. The first three areas are expected to grow rapidly and gain many new jobs.

Finally, occupations with the most openings ("big growth") are not new, different, or unique but familiar and common. There can be something very reassuring about this fact for persons involved in career planning. The more things change, the more they stay the same.

Table 7.1 also shows the Holland summary code order of SERCIA for these 20 occupations. (An earlier 10-year projection from 2002 showed the same code order.) In order to determine Holland codes for these projections, we consulted the *Dictionary of Holland Occupation Codes* (Gottfredson & Holland, 1996) to find the three-letter Holland code for each occupation listed (you may want to review information about Holland's theory in Chapter 2). We then calculated this summary code by giving each RIASEC letter 3 points for first position, 2 points for second position, and 1 for third.

As a result, we see that the predominance of the Holland S and E codes shows that the occupations that will employ large numbers of people in the future will draw upon the social and enterprising skills of workers, their "people" skills.

Occupations that grow most rapidly. Table 7.2 shows the 20 fastest-growing occupations in the United States (Dohm & Shniper, 2007). This list is based on the percentage growth of the occupations. We just saw data pertaining to "big growth" occupations, but the focus here is on "fast growth." Eleven of the 20 fastest-growing occupations are associated with health services or the provision of personal or social and mental health services, and 14 require education beyond the high-school level. Twelve of them have earnings above $30,630 annually.

In examining these BLS reports, we noticed that only computer software engineers, home health aides, and personal and home care aides appeared on the lists for both big growth and fast growth occupations. Computer software engineers ranks 4th on fast growth and 15th in big growth,

TABLE 7.2   FAST GROWTH OCCUPATIONS, 2006–2016

Standard Occupational Code (SOC) Number and Occupational Title	2016 Employment (thousands)	Percent Change	Holland Code
15-1081 Network systems and data communications analysts	402	53	RSI
39-9021 Personal and home care aides	1,56	51	SRE
31-1011 Home health aides	1,71	49	SRC
15-1031 Computer software engineers, applications	733	45	RIC
29-2056 Veterinary technologists/technicians	100	41	ISR
13-2056 Personal financial advisors	248	41	ESC
39-5091 Makeup artists, theatrical and performance	3	40	AER
1-9092 Medical assistants	565	35	SCR
20-1131 Veterinarians	84	35	IRE
21-1011 Substance abuse and behavioral disorder counselors	112	34	SEA
39-5094 Skin care specialists	51	34	SEA
13-2051 Financial analysts	295	34	CIE
21-1093 Social and human service assistants	453	34	SCE
33-9031 Gaming surveillance officers and gaming investigators	12	34	RES
31-2021 Physical therapist assistants	80	32	ESC
29-2052 Pharmacy technicians	376	32	RIE
19-4092 Forensic science technicians	17	31	RIE
29-2021 Dental hygienists	217	30	SAI
21-1023 Mental health counselors	130	30	SAE
21-1023 Mental health and substance abuse social workers	159	30	SEC

Source: Occupational employment projections to 2016, published in the *Monthly Labor Review*, November 2007
Note: Many fast growth occupations relate to health care and the elderly.
Note: RIASEC Code order: S = 36, R = 24, E = 23, I = 16, C = 12, A = 9; E has moved from 5th to 3rd in code order since 2002

home health aides ranks 3rd in fast growth and 7th in big growth, and personal and home care aides ranks 2nd on fast growth and 6th in big growth lists. The social conditions associated with an aging population in the United States contribute to the growth in these latter two occupations.

Table 7.2 also lists Holland codes for the 20 fastest-growing occupations. The summary code is SREICA, which is slightly different than the code order for 1996–2006 of SIERCA. It is somewhat surprising to see that the Realistic area has become more prominent in the latest projections.

Anne Fisher (2005) took BLS projections a step further and eliminated blue-collar jobs and those employing fewer than 1,000 people nationwide (Table 7.3). She found that occupations in the IT area along with those in health care and accounting or financial management will grow rapidly. For example, Fisher found that PricewaterhouseCoopers hired 3,100 new accounting graduates in 2005 and Ernst & Young added 4,000. But perhaps the greatest growth will be in the environmental area where the U.S. will begin exporting expertise to India, Asia, and Europe.

Occupations that have it all. Finally, we will take a brief look at the occupations projected to have faster than average employment growth, above average earnings, and below average unemployment through 2012. Table 7.4 shows the results of this analysis. The occupations represented in this table include a diverse group, e.g., teachers, managers, and construction trades workers. Note that the jobs shown in the table are projected annual openings, and the median salaries mean that half the workers will make more and half will make less than the number shown. While these

TABLE 7.3   FAST GROWTH PROFESSIONAL OCCUPATIONS

Occupational Area	Category	Growth Rate (percent)
Environmental engineer	Not specified	54.3
Network systems & datacom analysts	Technology	41.9
Personal financial advisors	Financial/management	36.3
Database administrators	Technology	33.1
Software engineers	Health	27.8
Emergency management specialists	Financial/management	27.8
Biomedical engineers	Technology	27.8
PR specialists	Not specified	27.8
Computer & infosystems managers	Financial/management	25.6
Comp, benefits, and job analysts	Technology	25.6
Systems analysts	Technology	24.9
Network & systems administrators	Technology	24.9
Training & development specialists	Not specified	22.3
Medical scientists	Health	22.1
Marketing & sales managers	Financial/management	21.3
Computer specialists	Technology	20.8
Media & communication specialists	Not specified	20.6
Counselors, social workers	Not specified	20.6
Lawyers	Not specified	20.6
Pharmacists	Health	20.2

Source: Bureau of Labor Statistics and Fisher (2005)

TABLE 7.4 FAST GROWTH, HIGH WAGE, LOW UNEMPLOYMENT OCCUPATIONS

Occupation	Job Openings	Median Annual Earnings 2002
Registered nurses	110,119	$48,090
Postsecondary teachers	95,980	$49,090
General and operations managers	76,245	$68,210
Sales representatives, wholesale and manufacturing, except technical and scientific products	66,239	$42,730
Truck drivers, heavy and tractor-trailer	62,517	$33,210
Elementary school teachers, except special education	54,701	$41,780
First-line supervisors or managers of retail sales workers	48,645	$29,700
Secondary school teachers, except special & voc. ed.	45,761	$48,950
General maintenance and repair workers	44,978	$29,370
Executive secretaries and administrative assistants	42,444	$33,410
First-line supervisors or managers of office and administrative support workers	40,909	$38,820
Accountants and auditors	40,465	$47,000
Carpenters	31,917	$34,190
Automotive service technicians and mechanics	31,887	$30,590
Police and sheriff's patrol officers	31,290	$42,270
Licensed practical and licensed vocational nurses	29,480	$31,440
Electricians	28,485	$41,390
Management analysts	25,470	$60,340
Computer systems analysts	23,735	$62,890
Special education teachers	23,297	$43,450

Source: *Occupational Outlook Quarterly*, Spring 2004

occupations generally have low unemployment, those with higher levels, e.g., truck driver, carpenters, electricians, are dependent on a strong economy or seasonal growth.

Growth in industries. Thus far, we have examined growth in occupations through 2012 or 2016, but what about industries? In individual career planning, it may be more useful to focus on the industry rather than the occupation in planning for your future employment. Industries vary widely in size and scope. For example, the public and private education industry employed 11 million workers in 1996, whereas manufacturers of clocks and watches employed fewer than 8,000. Later in this chapter we'll examine the services industry in more depth, and in Chapter 9 we'll discuss employment opportunities in the staffing services industry.

Figueroa and Woods (2007) reported that industry employment growth is concentrated in the services sector, which includes professional and business services (see Table 7.5). In terms of employment, the health care and social assistance industry sectors will have the most rapid growth rate in the economy through 2016. Organizations in these industries include hospitals, elementary and secondary schools, physician offices, postsecondary schools, community social agencies, home health services, and child daycare services. However professional and business services are projected to provide the greatest number of jobs during the period. Firms in this industry help organizations respond to globalization, technology changes, and other challenges.

TABLE 7.5	INDUSTRY GROWTH AREAS, 2006–2016				
Industry description	**NAICS Code**	**Thousands of jobs**		**Change, 2006–16**	**Average annual rate of change, 2006–16**
		2006	**2016**		
Food services and drinking places	722	9383	10,407	1,024	1.0
Offices of health practitioners	6211, 6212, 6213	3,508	4,365	857	2.2
Construction	23	7,689	8,470	781	1.0
Management, scientific, and technical consulting services	5416	921	1,639	718	5.9
Individual and family services	6241	974	1,687	713	5.7
Hospitals, private	622	4,427	5,119	692	1.5
Employment services	5613	3,657	4,348	692	1.7
Retail trade	44, 45	1,539	16,006	687	0.4
Residential care facilities	6232, 6233, 6239	1,317	1,829	513	3.3
Local government educational services	NA	7,339	8,450	512	0.6

Source: Bureau of Labor Statistics, *Monthly Labor Review*, November 2007

Holland Codes and jobs. In Chapter 3, we pointed out that Holland's RIASEC theory provided a way to classify occupations. Figure 7.2 shows what has been happening in the economy over five decades from 1960 to 2000 (Reardon, Bullock, & Meyer, 2007). Inspection of this figure shows that Realistic jobs have held constant in employing the most people, but the percentage has been declining over the years. Think about the reasons for this in terms of the decrease in manufacturing jobs in the United States. Note that very few people work in the Artistic area and this has remained constant, which is also true of the Investigative area. Note also that the Enterprising area has been increasing slightly.

Following up on this theme, Figure 7.3 shows how annual income varied in 1990 across the six RIASEC kinds of work. (We believe this may still be representative of how income is distributed across the RIASEC areas today.) Remember that the Investigative area of work requires more

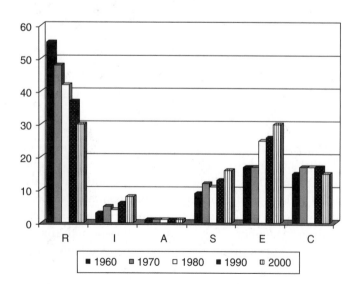

FIGURE 7.2

Employment and Six Kinds of Work

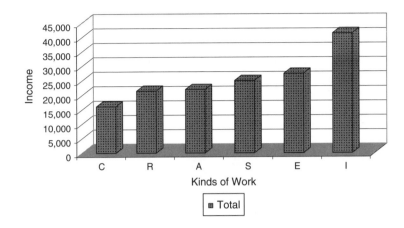

FIGURE 7.3

Income and Six Kinds of Work

education and training than the other five areas, so this figure provides some data supporting the idea that education pays.

The forecast for college graduates. In Chapter 3, we noted that those with college degrees earn more than high school graduates over the course of their working lives, and they will be unemployed for shorter periods of time. What are some other important facts associated with the employment of college graduates in the global economy?

Dohm and Wyatt (2002) reported that more than one million students earned college or graduate degrees in 2000. Of those aged 25–34, the 2000 census revealed that almost 30 percent have completed four or more years of college.

What are the benefits of a college degree? In a nutshell, Dohm and Wyatt (2002) reported that college graduates have more career options, better promotion opportunities, higher earnings, and lower unemployment. Because employers are increasingly classifying positions simply as "college preferred," college graduates can enter a field unrelated to their major. Dohm and Wyatt reported a 1997 survey indicating that about 55 percent of graduates were in jobs related to their degree four years after graduation.

The median weekly earnings in 2000 for those with a college degree was $834 compared to $507 for those with high school or equivalent education. But not all college graduates earn high salaries because 17 percent with a bachelor's degree earned less than the median for high school graduates. This is because there is a widening disparity in earnings among all educational groups, and the geographic location of the job, the nature of the industry, the specific occupation, and the nature of the organization (public vs. private) all contribute to income differences.

The Bureau of Labor Statistics predicts that the professional and related occupations group, which employs large numbers of college graduates, will grow faster and add more workers than any other occupational group through 2010 (Dohm & Wyatt, 2002). The most significant source of these jobs will be the replacement of workers leaving their positions. Millions of baby boomers will retire by 2010 and college graduates will fill their positions.

Finally, we should note that the phenomenon of *educational upgrading* is occurring in many occupations because of the large numbers of college graduates available for jobs. Stated another way, there is an increasing level of educational attainment in many occupations. This change has been especially noticeable in the health and protective service occupations and in occupations that usually are considered desirable and well paid, such as airline pilot and flight attendant (Dohm & Wyatt, 2002). Employers increasingly prefer college graduates because jobs are becoming more complex in the global economy, college graduates are more motivated and have better problem-solving skills, learn tasks more quickly, and have better communication skills.

THE SERVICES INDUSTRY

What exactly do we mean by services? Is it just health care and social work? It is important to fully understand the services industry because this is where the U.S. economy is growing and where many of us will find employment. It is expected that employment in the services industry will increase from 76 percent of total jobs to 79 percent in 2016 (Figueroa & Woods, 2007).

Henkoff (1994) pointed out that the services industry has an image problem. Sometimes, it is viewed as less important and worthwhile than manufacturing. You can touch the results of manufacturing, but you only experience the results of services (e.g., an airplane ride or telephone call). Services brings to mind what George Ritzer (1995) called "McJobs," including-low paid burger flippers and floor sweepers who work in highly controlled and tightly scripted jobs. However, the services industry also includes highly paid brain surgeons, defense lawyers, movie stars, and accountants.

Anthony Carnevale and Stephen Rose (1998) suggested another way of thinking about the services industry, which they call the "Office Economy." College students who fear "being stuck in an office all day" may be alarmed by their views. Carnevale and Rose believe that the new economy demands skills in office work more than in technology. They reported that office work employs 41 percent of all workers, pays the highest salaries, is growing the fastest, employs over half of college graduates, and captures 50 percent of all earnings. Office work includes accountants, managers, sales representatives, and brokers, which account for 44 percent of office jobs.

Carnevale and Rose concluded that the office has become the new model for the American economy. The office accounts for almost 60 percent of jobs for people with college degrees, 50 percent of all earnings, and most of the job growth in the last two decades. They noted that the office economy has been especially beneficial for women and African Americans.

Henkoff (1994) provided three examples of successful companies in the services industry, and we'll profile them briefly.

Progressive Insurance

Progressive is an automobile insurance company—it may insure a car in your family. Rather than simply selling policies, however, the company now sees itself as a helper in dealing with human trauma. Henkoff described the following scene.

> The crash occurred at an intersection in Tampa. The two cars are smashed, but no occupants are seriously hurt. However, they are scared. Moments after the accident, a young man, Lance, dressed in casual clothes arrives and begins to assume command of the situation. He calms the victims, advises them on medical care, repair shops, police reports, and legal procedures. He is a senior claims representative at Progressive and is part of the company's 24-hour Immediate Response program. He invites the policyholder into an air-conditioned van equipped with chairs, a desk, and phones. Even before the tow trucks have cleared the area, Lance offers his client a settlement package.
>
> Lance has been heavily trained in negotiating and grief counseling, as well as the details of the insurance business. He leads a six-member team of adjusters, and his salary is partly determined by a profit-sharing program used by the company. This company understands the link between employee loyalty, customer satisfaction, and profits, and makes extra efforts to keep Lance happy in his job.

This brief description of Lance and his work provides a good example of what is happening in the services industry. We'll discuss some of these topics about organizational culture more fully in Chapter 8.

Johnson Controls

Johnson Controls might have built the thermostat or energy system used in your house or apartment. However, this company has moved into managing other companies' buildings. Here's what happened. The engineers who designed the heating/cooling systems for buildings have now moved away from their desks and out into the buildings to ensure that occupants of the buildings—their customers—are always comfortable. Johnson Controls, however, expanded beyond heating and cooling and moved into lighting, security, and cleaning operations of office buildings. Henkoff described the work of an engineer, Tina, who heads a four-member team that spends half its time out in the field helping schools become more energy efficient. The company realized that this market is worth billions of dollars in the United States alone (review Table 7.1 to examine the growth in jobs for janitors/cleaners). Service means doing something that customers cannot or do not want to do for themselves. This explains why Johnson Controls, ServiceMaster, and Merry Maids have become so successful.

Taco Bell

We're all familiar with what Taco Bell does, and many of us have eaten there. What we probably don't know is that Taco Bell serves 35 million customers per week at over 6,500 restaurants. It employs 166,000 persons at company-owned and franchised businesses. So how is it in the service industry? A senior vice president stated, "We've changed the way we think about ourselves, moving from a company that prepares food to one that feeds hungry people" (Henkoff, 1994, p. 56). The shift toward "services" reflected in this statement is unmistakably clear.

In order to carry out this shift, Taco Bell moved food preparation out of its kitchens to suppliers. It also began to operate with no manager on the premises but moved to self-directed teams ("crews"), who manage everything associated with the point of access (POA). Regional managers oversee as many as 30 POAs and 250 employees. Their pay, linked to sales results and customer satisfaction scores, can top $100,000.

While there are many examples of work in the services industry, we hope these three illustrate the scope of the work included in this area. New ways of thinking about the services industry, including the idea of sales, can introduce new schema for individual career planning.

STATE LABOR MARKET INFORMATION

In strategic career planning, geographic location can sometimes make an important difference in analyzing labor market information. Economic conditions can vary greatly across states in terms of the factors we have discussed in this chapter, e.g., big growth occupations, fast growth occupations, big growth industries.

It is beyond our purposes here to speculate about the similarities and differences between state and U.S. economic data with respect to labor market forecasts or Holland's typology and the amount of education and training associated with high-employment jobs. However, these data do point out the value of thinking critically about the kinds of jobs available in various geographic regions of the United States, and how you might use something like the RIASEC typology to guide your strategic career thinking.

We should note that labor market reports are often produced for geographic regions, counties, and cities within states. These may be obtained from a local employment service office or a state department of labor. In Florida, for example, the Agency for Workforce Innovation provides this kind of information (http://www.labormarketinfo.com/index.htm). Many other states have similar services, and you can search for directory information at America's Career InfoNet http://www.careeronestop.org/.

A CIP PERSPECTIVE

We have examined information related to the emerging global economy, as well as some of the trends in the U.S. labor market. Along the way, we have raised questions that might be considered by those engaged in strategic career planning for themselves. Now we want to review what we have learned by examining it in light of the Pyramid of Information-Processing Domains and the CASVE Cycle. Our goal is to improve the quality of your PCT for solving career problems and making career decisions.

Self-Knowledge

What interests, skills, and values are most relevant in this emerging global economy? A review of information in this chapter suggests several things to us, but individual readers can think of others in light of their unique career history and goals (their PCT, we would say). In general, Holland's Social, Enterprising, Investigative, and Artistic types appear to be in a "good place" with respect to the changing labor market. It is especially apparent that Social and Enterprising interpersonal skills, essential in good teamwork and leadership, will be highly valued.

The nature of the global economy would appear to reward people with skills in languages, history, and experience in ethnic diversity and multicultural traditions. Technology-related skills, including computers, telecommunications, systems analysis, biology, business, and economics, would also appear to be essential in the global economy.

Rifkin's discussion of the developing social economy suggests that personal values, which include community welfare and social service, will be important. Indeed, there will be jobs for college graduates in this Third Sector.

In general, it is important to constantly explore new interests and develop new skills or to find meaning in a variety of work options. Adaptability, flexibility, compromise, and personal growth are traits that will most likely be rewarded in the new global economy.

Option Knowledge

Understanding the nature of the new kinds of work organizations in the global economy will be essential. We'll examine this topic more closely in the next two chapters.

Among other things, Drucker told us about knowledge workers, Reich told us about global enterprise webs, Rifkin told us about lean production, and Friedman told us how individuals with technology skills can participate directly in a global economy. These ideas and others make us mindful of the constant need to learn more about the contemporary world, which is changing so rapidly. Indeed, the need for constant learning is one of the most important lessons in this chapter.

While global economic statistics may show job stability, local economies might show change. For example, larger, dynamic cities, such as Atlanta, Orlando, Boston, Dallas/Ft. Worth, and San Francisco Bay may provide rich possibilities for individual career development.

Decision Making

Our individual career planning skills will be increasingly important in the global economy. One reason is because of the increasing rate of speed in which work projects will be completed and jobs will develop and change. Indeed, people will be actively involved in one stage or another of the CASVE Cycle throughout their lives. Career decision making will be virtually continuous, as new training, work, and lifestyle options rapidly emerge. In this chapter, we have learned that periods of unemployment may be increasingly common for most people. For example, we can look at the Execution stage of the CASVE Cycle and be aware that we constantly need to keep our resumes up to date and be ever ready to move into a job-hunting process.

Executive Processing

Many of the ideas presented in this chapter have suggested that careers will be more complex con-structions in the future. This means that our individual PCTs will need to become more complex as well.

Careers will no longer be tied to a single company or organization, and individuals will take much more personal responsibility for independently managing their careers. This will require us to think strategically about our career life, to be flexible, to have a sense of timing, and to constantly scan the environment for new information. As we will learn in Chapter 10, careers will also require complex thinking to balance family relationships, organizational roles, leisure pursuits, and personal goals.

In a word, *career development in the future will require us to think globally and work locally*. What do we mean by this? We will need to be ever mindful of the global economy and the changes occurring there that will affect the way we work in the future and the strategic direction of our careers. However, we must work locally in the immediate job situation at hand, mindful of the services we provide our clients and customers, the need to constantly improve our job skills, and to actively work in some phase of the CASVE Cycle to solve career problems and make career decisions.

Here is how to put these new career metacognitions to work:

- Constantly monitor market trends in your chosen industry or occupation.

- Read the "Business" section of your newspaper, watch business news on television, and read the *Wall Street Journal* to keep informed about labor markets.

- Access the best Internet sites that provide business forecasts and market outlooks.

- Make it a habit to pay attention and inquire about the local economy—recent business successes, new growth areas, new industries.

- Select a place to live on the basis of the quality of life and the work opportunities in your area of interest.

- Identify with a community through service and organizational memberships in order to strengthen your personal sense of identity.

As we have suggested throughout this book, such positive thinking helps individuals solve career problems and make career decisions.

SUMMARY

In this chapter, we have introduced some of the important career themes to emerge from the developing global economy. We also examined some of the facts associated with understanding the labor market and trends in the U.S. economy, including states and local communities. Finally, we reviewed this new information in light of the Cognitive Information Processing paradigm that undergirds this book. This information should help you improve the part of your Personal Career Theory (PCT) having to do with occupational knowledge. This, in turn, will enable you to develop new metacognitions for solving career problems and making career decisions.

REFERENCES

Alpert, A., & Auyer, J. (2003). The 1988–2000 employment projections: How accurate were they? *Occupational Outlook Quarterly*, *47*(1), 2–21.

Carnevale, A. P., & Rose, S. J. (1998). *Education for what? The new office economy*. Princeton, NJ: ETS.

Colvin, G. (2004, December 13). Think your job can't be sent to India? Just watch. *Fortune*, p. 80.

Crosby, O. (2001). Helping charity work: Paid jobs in charitable nonprofits. *Occupational Outlook Quarterly*, *45*(2), 11–23.

Dohm, A., & Shniper, L. (2007, November). Occupational employment projections to 2016. *Monthly Labor Review*, pp. 86–106.

Dohm, A., & Wyatt, I. (2002). College at work: Outlook and earnings for college graduates, 2000–10. *Occupational Outlook Quarterly*, *46*(3), 3–15.

Drucker, P. F. (1993). *Post-capitalist society*. New York: HarperCollins Publishers.

Figueroa, E. B., & Woods, R. A. (2007, November). Industry output and employment projections to 2016. *Monthly Labor Review*, pp. 53–85.

Friedman, T. L. (2005). *The world is flat*. New York: Farrar, Straus, & Giroux.

Fisher, A. (2005, March 21). Hot careers for the next 10 years. *Fortune*, p. 131.

Gottfredson, G., & Holland, J. (1996). *Dictionary of Holland occupation codes* (3rd ed.). Odessa, FL: Psychological Assessment Resources.

Henkoff, R. (1994, June 27). Service is everybody's business. *Fortune*, pp. 48–60.

Krantz, M. (2005, February 11). To start up here, companies hire over there. *USA Today*, pp. 1B–2B.

Moncarz, R. (2002). Training for techies: Career preparation in information technology. *Occupational Outlook Quarterly*, *46*(3), 38–45.

Pikulinski, J. (2004). New and emerging occupations. *Monthly Labor Review*, *127*(12), 39–42.

Reardon, R. C., Bullock, E. E., & Meyer, K. E. (2007). A Holland perspective on the U.S. workforce from 1960–2000. *Career Development Quarterly*, *55*, 262–274.

Reich, R. (1992). *The work of nations*. New York: Vintage Books.

Rifkin, J. (1995). *The end of work*. New York: Putnam's Sons.

Ritzer, G. (1995). McJobs. In R. Feller & G. Walz (Eds.), *Career transitions in turbulent times* (pp. 211–217). Greensboro, NC: ERIC/CASS Publications.

Thottam, J. (2004, March 1). Is your job going abroad? *Time*, pp. 26–34.

Toossi, M. (2007, November). Labor force projections to 2016: More workers in their golden years. *Monthly Labor Review*, pp. 33–52.

Wegmann, R., Chapman, R., & Johnson, M. (1989). *Work in the new economy*. Alexandria, VA: American Counseling Association.

ORGANIZATIONAL CULTURE AND EFFECTIVE WORK

In Chapter 7, we learned how socioeconomic trends, including the emerging global economy and the growth of technology, are affecting organizations. In this chapter, we will focus more specifically on organizations, because they are the settings where most of us will spend our time working. The organizational context is sometimes overlooked in career planning, but we believe that a better understanding of organizations is essential for career growth. As in Chapter 7, we will focus on what several authors have to say about this topic. Along the way, we will examine several related subjects:

- The changed social contract

- Characteristics of organizations

- Organizational culture

- Kinds of organizations

- Past and present organizational structures

- Leadership in organizational development

- The relationship between career development and organizational development

We will then conclude with a CIP perspective on the nature of changing organizations and the implications for your career planning.

As you read about organizational culture and effective work, try to think about how your Personal Career Theory (PCT) and strategic career thinking can be improved by this information. How will this information affect occupations you are interested in, and how will it affect the ways you think about working? How will it impact the type of questions you might ask in a job interview? What new more complex career metacognitions will this information enable you to develop? What will be the organizational context of your work?

THE CHANGED SOCIAL CONTRACT

The big story related to the changing culture of organizations pertains to the changed "social contract" between individuals and work organizations. Under terms of the old social contract, it was understood that if workers were loyal to the organization and dedicated their working lives to producing its products and services, then the organization would maintain them as employees and pay them benefits in retirement. *Loyalty would be repaid with economic security.* It was a contract for life.

However, the nature of this social contract has changed, and many organizations now view workers like other parts of the production process, just like the machines, buildings, and money. As William Morin, president of one of the nation's largest human resources consulting firms said years ago, "We've broken the whole mommy and daddy syndrome. Nobody else is responsible for your happiness. You have to see yourself as a business. *That* is your job" (Henkoff, 1993, p. 46). For many this is a dramatic new way of thinking about careers and working, something emphasized throughout this book.

Productive work is a commodity that the organization purchases in the marketplace, just like it buys electricity, water, and raw materials for production. Loyalty and long-term commitments are no longer part of the social contract between workers and the organization. Indeed, some have suggested that the only thing workers might reasonably expect from an organization is ongoing training to enable the worker to become more productive and competitive in the marketplace (Gutteridge, Leibowitz & Shore, 1993).

The new social contract is based on the employee's opportunities for training and development, and loyalty may be more to the profession than to the organization. For example, Malcolm Ballantine (1994) observed that a group of British police officers found it easier to relate to their work team than to the organization. However, not all organizations have discarded the old social contract, and over generalizing about employers can be misleading. Examining employee turnover rate is one way of examining the organization's commitment to workers. Such matters have to do with understanding the culture of an organization, the focus of this chapter.

What about job security? The idea has changed from job security to *employability security*, meaning that the worker develops skills and competencies that someone is willing to pay for in the marketplace. As Feller and Whichard (2005) noted: "Skills and competencies tied to adding value to an organization's core mission, increasingly determine the quality of jobs workers can expect to attain" (p. 41). Although it is still developing today, workers under the new social contract have strong commitments to their work skills and to their coworkers (or teammates). This appears to be the nature of the new social contract. We will return to these ideas throughout Chapters 9, 10, 11, and 15 when we examine the job campaign.

CHARACTERISTICS OF ORGANIZATIONS

Peter Drucker, Edgar Schein, Susan Mohrman, and Susan Cohen, wrote on the issue of organizations in relation to career planning.

Drucker's View

Peter Drucker (1993), who consulted with many organizations over the years in order to help them improve their effectiveness, noted that "organizations" have not been studied by social scientists until relatively recently. He pointed out that an organization is not a "community," "society," "class," "family," "clan," or "tribe." Organizations are not outgrowths of geographic location, wealth or status, marriage, or royalty. However, armies, churches, hospitals, universities, and labor unions *are* organizations, because "organizations are special-purpose institutions. Organizations are effective because they concentrate on *one task*" (p. 53).

Drucker further noted that organizations function best when they have a clear purpose and the specialists working in the organization know exactly how to align themselves with this larger purpose. "Only a clear, focused, and common mission can hold the organization together and enable it to produce results." He suggested that an excellent example of a modern organization is the symphony orchestra, where 250 specialists forego their specialization and play together from one piece of music. Because most of us work in organizations, it is important that we understand the essential task(s) of the organization, its mission.

Sandroff (1993), writing in *Working Woman* magazine, shared this example from American Express. Like other modern organizations with too many good business ideas and goals, American Express decided to set fewer goals in order to encourage a clear sense of purpose. Employees were asked to clear their desks of all work that did not directly pertain to the company goal of "improving cardholder satisfaction. Workers evaluated every assignment in terms of improving cardholder satisfaction, and some common work tasks done in the past were deemed irrelevant. This is an example of an organization and its workers having a clear understanding of purpose. One of your tasks in seeking employment is to develop an accurate, clear understanding of the purpose of the organization where you seek to work. Erin White (2005) in a *Wall Street Journal* article noted that culture clash was one of the primary reasons that new hires failed on the job.

What is the relationship of individuals to organizations? In one way, the contribution of any one person can be swallowed up, because organizations exist to produce goods and services for the outside world. In another way, however, each person's contribution is important and valued. This is because organizations are social systems, and each part (person) is both independent and inter-dependent at the same time. People become involved with organizations because of *decisions* by both the individual and the organization. Organizations look for competent, dedicated members, and in this sense they compete among themselves for new members.

Organizations are also always *managed*, which is how decisions are made. As with the symphony, there is a conductor who controls things, an arranger who writes the music, and a manager who makes sure members are paid and can travel. However, Drucker (1993) noted that modern organizations have a new factor to consider. They must be able to function in rapidly changing conditions, to constantly invent new ways to accomplish their tasks, to *constantly improve*. As we shall learn, these facts of modern organizational life are also played out in the careers of those who work in them.

ORGANIZATIONAL CULTURE

Edgar Schein (1985), a professor of management at the Massachusetts Institute of Technology, is one of the foremost experts on organizations in the United States. He has researched organizational culture for over 40 years.

Schein's definition of "organizational culture" is somewhat complex. Let's break it down into some manageable parts.

1. Schein views culture as a characteristic of a stable social group that has a history, and where members have shared important experiences in solving group problems.

2. These common experiences have led the group members to have a shared view of the world and their place in it.

3. This shared view has worked successfully long enough as to be taken for granted by the group, and has it now dropped out of members' awareness. They take this shared view for granted as members of the group.

4. "Culture" may be viewed as a learned product of group experience, and it is found in a group or organization with a significant history.

As a new member, or employee, in an organization, it is important for you to learn the culture of the organization. Indeed, the members of the organization will watch you closely to see if you are able to understand and adopt their organizational culture. Why? Because most members have a history of experience in solving the organization's problems, and it is important to them that you learn from those prior experiences, to adopt their shared view. It is important to add this factor to your developing PCT.

In many organizations, there is more than one culture, and each department or work team may have its own subculture. It is essential that you learn about the various cultural traditions in a new organization, especially those held by top managers and your supervisor, if you want to be accepted and succeed as a member.

Organizational culture is practically observable in many ways. Schein offers six examples:

1. *Regular behaviors*, such as common ways that members greet one another, courtesies extended to senior members of the organization, where people sit at meetings or have lunch, or how members dress; the artifacts the organization uses to represent or symbolize itself, including the furniture, colors, art, nature of publications and Homepage.

2. *Norms*, such as how hard one works in the organization, if one is willing to work evenings or weekends, if working more than 40 hours per week is the norm; beliefs about use of time and working hard are key elements of organizational culture.

3. *Dominant values*, such as customer service is No. 1, our products are of highest quality, employee family life is important, or members should have leisure interests; organizational culture usually reflects the values of the founder, the way things "ought" to be; in this way, leadership is directly tied to organizational culture.

4. *Philosophy*, such as the overall guiding views toward employees, the local community, serving others, making money, or working hard; a key basic philosophical assumption relates to the nature of the relationship between the individual and the group, e.g., the boss and co-workers are basically out to get me.

5. *Rules*, such as learning the ropes as a new employee, understanding and accepting supervisor's feedback, managing time, and getting along with coworkers; how new employees are oriented.

6. *Feeling or climate*, such as the physical layout of the facilities, the manners in which employees treat customers and coworkers, or the level of trust. Is the climate marked by tension, happiness, competitiveness, or some combination of these things?

As you review these six indicators of organizational culture, think about organizations where you have worked or volunteered. How would you evaluate an organization's culture using these six topics? We will look at specific ways to assess an organization's culture in Chapter 15 when we analyze the first day on the new job.

Increasing Diversity in Organizations

Organizational culture in the workplace is also being impacted by several demographic changes now taking place in the United States. Some of these changes are related to history, some to public policy, and others to sociology. The workplace is increasingly being composed of more diverse groups, and these changes have an impact on organizational culture (Howard, 1995).

1. **More older workers.** The labor force is growing most rapidly in the 55-and-older age group. This will happen as baby boomers (born between 1946 and 1964) continue to age, live longer, and seek income to offset health costs and other expenses. The workforce growth rate of this group will be five times the overall labor force growth rate. Conversely, the 16- 24-year olds, including college graduates, will be decreasing in workforce participation through 2016.

2. **More immigrants.** Foreign born workers have come to play an increasingly role in America's workforce. Since 1960, when the share of foreign-born worker was 1 in 17, the numbers have increased to 1 in 8 workers (Mosisa, 2002). The greatest influx in immigrants has come from Latin American and Asia. This is a very different group of workers than those who entered this country from Europe in the early 1900s. Many of these immigrants will take positions in the natural and applied sciences, while others will take low-level jobs in the services industry. The skills and training of immigrants vary widely by country of origin and whether their immigration is legal or illegal. The Census Bureau reports that 43 percent of population growth in the U.S. from 2000 to 2006 was from international migration. Asian immigrants accounted for 23 percent and immigrants of Hispanic origin about 52 percent (Franklin, 2007).

3. **More varied ethnic and racial groups.** A recent report in the *Monthly Labor Review* (Toossi, 2007) indicated that participation in the labor force will vary by group through 2016. White participation will drop to the level in 1986; Asians will be at about the same in 2016 as 2006; blacks will increase slightly; white non-Hispanic participation will drop below 1986 levels; and Hispanic participation will be the strongest through 2016. Large numbers of immigrants coming to the U.S. now and in the foreseeable future are Hispanics searching for better and higher paying jobs. Indeed, 92 percent of human resource managers tie diversity recruiting to their organizational strategic staffing plan (Koc, 2007).

4. **More people with disabilities.** The passage of the Americans with Disabilities Act (ADA) in 1990 was a dramatic effort to increase the entry of people with disabilities into the workforce. The ADA prohibits discrimination in all employment practices, including job application procedures, hiring, firing, advancement, compensation, training, and other terms, conditions, and privileges of employment. It applies to recruitment, advertising, tenure, layoff, leave, fringe benefits, and all other employment-related activities. Conditions that might impair a person functioning in a work environment include mental retardation, cancer, multiple sclerosis, cerebral palsy, blindness, orthopedic impairments, arthritis, and emphysema. The ADA requires organizations to provide "reasonable accommodations" to remove a barrier to functioning in an environment or to adapt the environment so that the person can function on a "level playing field." More information about this topic is available at the ADA Hot Links and Document Center at http://www.jan.wvu.edu/links/adalinks.htm.

5. **More women.** The participation of women in the labor force has nearly doubled over the last 54 years. In 2002, 67.4 million women age 16 and older were in the labor force. The positive change over the last half century in the female labor force participation rate has greatly affected the social and economic condition of women, their families, and our nation's economy (Employment Policy Foundation, 2005). There are many interesting factors involving career planning associated with this labor market trend, and we will review them more fully in Chapter 10.

Howard (1995) indicated that organizations are reporting new, increasing needs associated with workforce diversity and team-based approaches to work. It would seem clear that workers who are knowledgeable about diversity issues, and who are able to work effectively with diverse groups of coworkers and customers or clients, will be valuable assets to organizations. Moreover, the culture of some organizations may be especially receptive to diverse groups of workers, such as older persons, immigrants, ethnically and racially diverse persons, and women.

Ethnic Culture and Organizational Culture

In Chapter 7, we focused on the increasing global economy and the development of multinational corporations. As an aside, it is worth noting that half of the world's largest economies are either nation-states or multinational corporations (Centron & Davies, 2008). As business organizations have become involved in global enterprise webs (Reich, 1992), they have sought to accommodate themselves to the diversity of ethnic and national cultures represented by the new employees. Managers and workers increasingly find themselves coping with this diversity.

For example, how do workers in different countries approach work? U.S. workers are more than twice as likely as Europeans to work 50+ hours a week (Deangelis, 2007). Indeed, U.S. workers lead the industrialized world in the hours worked each week (International Labour Market, 2003). U.S. workers now lead workers in Canada, France, Germany, Japan, and the United Kingdom, in that order, and they are working about a week longer each year than they did ten years ago. The cultural value placed on work has changed in a short period of time.

Geert Hofstede (1984), a professor at the University of Maastricht in the Netherlands, conducted a study of people working in sales in a major multinational American corporation operating in 39 countries. He studied the work-related values of these employees, and he found that work attitudes and values could be attributed to cultural differences among the 39 countries. He found four major categories for classifying cultures: (1) power distance, (2) uncertainty avoidance, (3) individualism, and (4) masculinity.

1. **Power distance.** This category refers to the relationship between the boss and subordinates, the social power difference between the two. Hofstede found that in some countries, such as Philippines, Mexico, Venezuela, and India, there were strong, clear status differences between bosses and employees, while in others, New Zealand, Denmark, Israel, and Austria, there were not. In the United States, social power distance was minimized.

2. **Uncertainty avoidance.** This category refers to the ways different cultures handle stress and anxiety. Hofstede found that the workers in various countries differed significantly in this area. Those avoiding uncertainty had lower job stress, less resistance to change, greater readiness to live day by day, and stronger ambition for advancement. Those who were prone to uncertainty had greater fear of failure, less risk-taking, higher job stress and anxiety, and more worry about the future. A person working with someone from a different country might find differences in approaches to work activities in the area of uncertainty avoidance.

3. **Individualism.** This category refers to the ways different national cultures emphasize the individual or group (collectivism). Countries having highest scores for individualism were the United States, Great Britain, Australia, and Canada, and countries having highest scores on collectivism were Peru, Colombia, and Venezuela. Countries high on individualism placed importance on employees' personal lifestyle, emotional independence from the company, freedom and challenge of jobs, and working for a small company. Countries high on collectivism were emotionally dependent on companies, frowned on individual initiative, considered group decisions better than individual ones, and had managers who sought conformity and orderliness.

4. **Masculinity.** This category pertains to cultures that maintain differences between men and women in the workplace. Those in countries scoring high in the masculinity category tended to believe in independent decision making, aspired for recognition, and had stronger achievement motivation. Those scoring lower in masculinity were more likely to believe in group decision making, valued security, had lower job stress, and preferred shorter work hours.

How can these ideas impact your individual career planning? These differences between national cultures may affect employee attitudes, interpersonal relationships, and reactions to supervision. An organization founded in the United States may experience "culture shock" as it expands into South America, the Middle East, or Southeast Asia. However, we caution you to use these ideas about national culture as general guidelines because unique organizational and individual differences exist in all cultures.

Typical Organizational Problems Involving Culture

Our understanding of some common organizational problems (Schein, 1985) can be improved if we pay attention to organizational culture. It is important to briefly focus on some of these topics because they can help us improve our individual career development.

1. **New Technologies.** In Chapter 7, we focused on the increasing importance of technology in the global economy. However, the culture of an organization may significantly slow the introduction and effective use of technology. For example, computers could bring new information about products, production, and staff to *all* members of an organization, information that was once only seen by top managers or bosses. The people in power in the organization may resist these technological changes because of their loss of control and status. Almost all organizations that are introducing new technologies into the workplace are also having to deal with issues of organizational culture. This includes schools, hospitals, sports teams, government, and business organizations. For us, it stands to reason that new employees in the organization who understand the language of technology, know how to use it effectively, and are willing to continue to improve their skills in this area, will be able to adapt to the new culture in most organizations.

2. **Intergroup Conflicts.** In joining an organization, one quickly becomes aware that subgroups in an organization can have a culture of their own. These groups might be based on physical location, common occupation or job, similar ethnic background, or rank. "Once a group acquires a history it also acquires a culture" (Schein, 1995, p. 39). When sales and engineering or research and marketing have disagreements, these problems may be viewed as intercultural conflicts. In multinational organizations, these problems can become even more complex. A good example involves payoffs between customers and suppliers; in some ethnic cultures these are viewed as normal, and in others they are viewed as kickbacks and bribery. As a new employee in an organization, it is important for you to identify different cultural groups and to balance the cultural values of various groups. It is likely that longer-term success in an organization involves first aligning yourself with the dominant cultural group and then the smaller subgroups.

3. **Communication Breakdowns.** Ineffective communication in an organization can occur in group discussions in meetings, in e-mail exchanges, and direct one-to-one interviews. Some might view communication problems as semantics or defensiveness, but social psychologists view these problems as cultural differences, real differences in how people view their history and their group. It almost goes without saying that people from different cultural traditions will have some difficulties in communication, in fully understanding what another person really means in his or her communication. As we find ourselves in organizations working with people from other cultures, including people in different occupations, we may encounter communication problems related to culture.

4. **Training Problems.** Every organization spends considerable energy in making sure members "fit" properly. This may be done through training programs, informal socializing, or special orientations. If these efforts are not successful in helping new members learn the culture of the

host organization, employees may feel lost and uncomfortable, and the organization may suffer in productivity. Learning an organization's culture is an ongoing process for new members. Organizational culture helps determine who is "in" and who is "out." It helps the group determine who is a member.

In summary, Schein and others have provided us a rich understanding of organizational culture and how it provides the background from which our career portrait will emerge. Many issues associated with work, including staff relationships, training, and negotiating job offers, have their roots in organizational culture.

KINDS OF ORGANIZATIONS

People might find themselves working in many different kinds of organizations. We will examine some of the most common ones.

Profit-Making Organizations

In Chapter 7, Rifkin (1995) noted that about 80 percent of economic activity is in the market sector of the economy. These organizations include Fortune 500 companies, as well as small family-owned businesses and self-employment (being an entrepreneur).This is the largest sector of the economy and has the most jobs. The most common term for such organizations is "private enterprise" or "business," but it is important to note that this might include schools and even some charities, religious organizations, and social service organizations. For example, Embry-Riddle Aeronautical University is a private college that makes a profit for its owners. The chamber of commerce in a town or state is a good place to get lists of profit-making organizations.

Nonprofit Organizations

Most churches, charities, and social service organizations are included in what Rifkin (1995) called the "service sector" of the economy. He noted that about 9 percent of U.S. employment is in this area. Such organizations include the Red Cross, the Humane Society, the Sierra Club, the Environmental Defense Fund, and even the Educational Testing Service, which administers the SAT and GRE tests. However, this is only part of the story about this group of organizations. The nonprofit group also includes the National Football League, the Motion Picture Academy of Arts and Sciences (it puts on the Academy Awards), and the National Basketball Association.

Nonprofits employ more than 10 million people. They include nearly every kind of occupation, e.g., managers of volunteers, fundraisers, event planners, grant writers, foundation officers, communications directors, credit counselors, social workers, community organizers, and executive directors. Large nonprofits rival large corporations in facilities and resources, but small ones may have limited budgets and limitations requiring improvisation. One example of such an organization is The Brother's Brother Foundation, which shipped over $262 million in medical books, supplies, and shoes around the world at a cost of less than $1 million in 2006. It employs a staff of 10 (Barrett, 2007). The intangible benefits, such as starting a new program, seeing people helped or a problem solved, seeing a volunteer have a good experience, can be very rewarding. Volunteering is probably the best way to see what this kind of work is like.

Entrepreneurial Nonprofits

Not surprisingly, there is an emerging form of organization that is a combination of the first two. Shuman and Fuller (2005) described it as a form of nonprofit that is actually using its profits to advance its ideas. For example, the YMCA operates health clubs to support its youth outreach programs. The American Red Cross draws blood and sells it to hospitals and health centers. Good Will Industries raises more than a billion dollars through the collection, refurbishment and sale of secondhand clothing and household items, and another half billion from fees for contracts and services. Planned Parenthood has 850 clinics that provide family planning information and services that generated over $306 million in 2004. And many of us have done business with the Girl Scouts, which generates millions from the sale of cookies. Other nonprofits operate all kinds of business enterprises in order to generate income to further their organizational goals.

Governmental Organizations

Rifkin referred to government as the "public sector" of the economy and indicated that about 14 percent of economic activity is in this area. Sometimes when we think of government jobs, we think first about federal employment, but the truth is that state and local governments have experienced rapid growth in recent years. Indeed, counties, cities, and municipalities have grown significantly. In 2004, federal employment represented 2.2 percent of all employment, state government 3.5 percent, and local government 10.6 percent (Department of Labor, 2005). There are hundreds of agencies, offices, bureaus, departments, and sections in the executive, legislative, and judicial branches of federal and state government, and each of these has its own organizational culture.

Quasi-Governmental Organizations

Quasi means "semi" or "sort of," and this is a good kind of description of such government organizations. Before it was "privatized," the U.S. Post Office was a quasi-governmental organization. These kinds of organizations are not governmental in the strict sense, because they have boards that are elected by the organization members and the boards are accountable to the members. However, much of their funding typically comes from governmental organizations (tax revenues). Water management districts in Florida or rural electric cooperatives in Texas are examples of quasi-governmental organizations.

Public schools are in a special category of organization in this regard. Public schools receive most of their funding from local and state tax funds, but local school boards and/or local superintendents make many decisions about employment and programs. Public colleges and universities operate in a similar fashion.

Associations

In state capitals and other geographic locations with a high concentration of government agencies, one will typically find the headquarters for hundreds of trade and professional associations. Such groups are a combination of nonprofits and quasi-governmental organizations. These groups represent their members before the legislature and other governmental boards, and they try to influence laws and public policy in directions that will benefit their members. Within the service industry, only legal professionals, health care workers, and a group that includes accountants, engineers, and others pay more than associations (Harris, 1993).

For example, Florida's 1,000 largest associations have an economic impact of $3.5 billion annually and generate about 10,800 full time jobs. About 400 have headquarters in Tallahassee, the state capitol, where up to 5,400 jobs exist (Hodges, 2007). Meetings and conferences are a big part of the economic impact.

The yellow pages of the phone book includes a listing of associations, and you might be surprised to see the names of organizations appearing there. You can also locate information about associations in directories such as the annual *NTPA Directory, 2008* (National Trade and Professional Associations of the United States; Colombia Books, 2008). This book provides detailed contact and background information on over 7,500 trade associations, professional societies, technical organizations, and labor unions in the United States, as well as the 20,000+ executives who run them. Virtually every product or service available in the economy is supported by an association.

In summary, it is important to note that these categories of organizations are not rigid, and it would not be unusual for any single organization to fit into more than one category. However, the categories can be useful in helping you learn about some of the basic kinds of organizations where employment might be found and to quickly understand some of the defining characteristics of the organization's culture.

PAST AND PRESENT ORGANIZATIONAL STRUCTURES

Organizations have been changing in terms of their shape and structure. We will examine these changes such as the shift from the triangle to the diamond and the move away from "boxes."

The New Diamond

We have often referred to the triangle shape of organizations and how it is changing. The old structure of organizations is shown in Figure 8.1. It shows the top 15 percent of the workers in the organization, the executives, officers, and department heads, in the smallest part of the figure at the top of the triangle. Most workers found their careers unfolding in the lower parts of the triangle because there was not enough room for everyone to move to the upper levels of management in the organization.

Feller and Whichard (2005) suggested that this new diamond-shaped organization is a dramatic departure from the old triangle shape. While the top of the diamond is still reserved for the top executives and managers, this is only 5 to 10 percent of the workers in the organization, a smaller number than before. The bottom portion of the diamond shows the 15 to 40 percent of the workers that might be employed as contract workers or temporary employees. We will discuss this topic more fully in Chapter 9. The most significant segment of the diamond is called the core workers, who make up 50 to 80 percent of the organization's

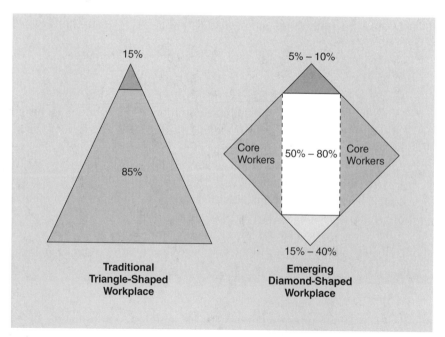

FIGURE 8.1

Traditional Triangle to Emerging Diamond Shaped Organization

Adapted by R. Feller and reprinted, by permission, from William A. Charland, Jr. *Career Shifting* Copyright © 1993, William A. Charland, Jr., Published by Adams Media Corp.

workforce. These core workers will be involved in leading teams, supervising coworkers, and monitoring quality control, and those who excel will move to positions in the far right and left points of the diamond. These workers will enjoy higher earnings and more job security because of their contributions to the success of the organization.

As we have emphasized throughout this chapter, individual career planning will be impacted by shifts to diamond-shaped organizations. Besides Holland's (1997) Social and Enterprising areas, the development of skills related to oral and written communication, teamwork, lifelong learning, leadership, and self-directed career decision making will be rewarded in this new organizational model.

No More Boxes

The combined impact of technology, the global economy, and the growth in knowledge is changing the structure of modern work organizations. Wenger and Snyder (2000) discussed what they called "communities of practice" which are groups of people bound together by shared expertise and passion for a joint enterprise. They may connect via e-mail networks or meet regularly for lunch, and as a result of these contacts, end up sharing experience and knowledge in free-flowing, creative ways that generate new approaches to solving problems. Susan Mohrman and Susan Cohen (1995) tell us that new organizations will be flatter, giving rise to the use of teams and other horizontal means of connecting workers. They described these new organizations as "high-involvement" organizations, in which workers are empowered to affect performance of the organization. Using our schema, these are the kinds of organizations that will welcome Holland's Social and Enterprising types.

In the past, organizations have often been described in terms of an organizational chart, with boxes showing people and the nature of the relationships among them (Mohrman & Cohen, 1995). An organizational chart for Florida State University, minus the vice president for academic affairs and all the deans of the schools and colleges, is shown in Figure 8.2. (This is the employing organization of the authors.) This figure shows the organization broken down into boxes (with names omitted), and the interrelationships among members of the organization are shown by the connecting lines. Career advancement means moving up in the triangle-shaped organization, which we described earlier. The advantages of this organizational structure have to do with stability, knowing the rules of the organization, and simplicity. The boss (in this case, the president) is clearly identified.

The structure of organizations represented in this model is changing, however, and the new structures emphasize interconnections and teamwork among members. Modern organizations rely on more sophisticated approaches, such as Total Quality Management (TQM) (Deming, 1986) which focuses on serving the end user (customer) and the performance of work teams (rather than individuals). At Target stores, for example, customers are called "guests" and teams have names like "guest services," "merchandise," and "merchandise flow."

Figure 8.3 shows a team-based model of an organization. Unlike the old box-line structure, members of this new organization belong to one or more teams, and this is how they identify with the organization. One's value in this kind of organization is based on the competencies and skills that have been developed and the varied ways these are used to contribute to the organization. This is sometimes called "multiskilling," meaning that the worker has accumulated varied skills that can be used in many jobs in the organization. One's value is reflected in salary and career growth. Employees relate directly to one another in the organization with whom they work rather than having to go through a third person (a supervisor). In this model, employees have to deal with more diverse groups of coworkers. This includes working with more subcultures in the organization to get things done. Much of this employee contact is through electronic means rather than face-to-face meetings. Obviously, the more workers know about various cultures, the more effective they can be in contributing to the team and the organization.

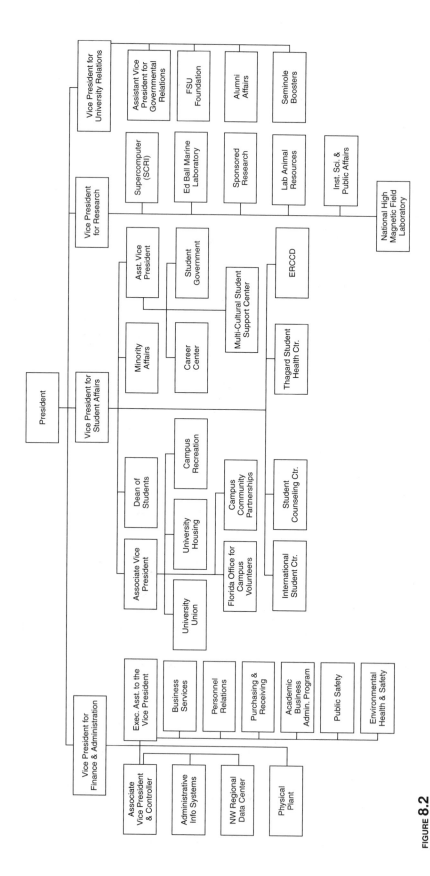

FIGURE 8.2

Partial Organizational Chart of Florida State University

Adapted from Florida State University 1993–1994 Fact Book, Budget and Analysis Department, Florida State University, Tallahasee, FL

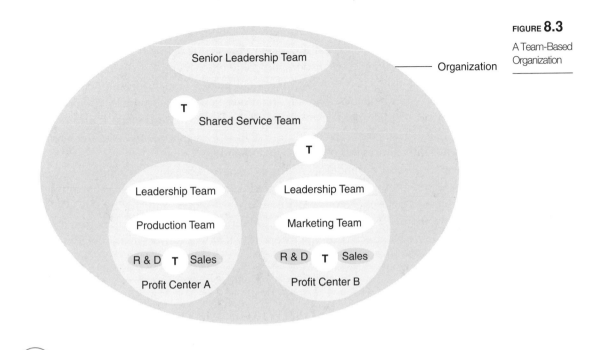

FIGURE **8.3**

A Team-Based
Organization

Organization

Senior Leadership Team

T Shared Service Team

T

Leadership Team

Production Team

R & D T Sales

Profit Center A

Leadership Team

Marketing Team

R & D T Sales

Profit Center B

(T) indicates a team linking other teams

This is one of the areas where liberal studies coursework and service learning pay off, by providing you with a broader perspective in solving problems and by giving you more diverse experience in how organizations function. These are powerful new metacognitions, or ways of thinking about yourself, as you make decisions about organizations in which to work. This is what William Morin meant when he said, "You have to see yourself as a business. *That* is your job."

Workers in these new flat organizations will need interpersonal skills (Enterprising and Social types in Holland's terms) that can help them manage conflicts and participate effectively in a team of coworkers. The irony is that these workers will need to make strong commitments, albeit temporary ones, to the work of the organization (including spending extra time completing tasks) and to coworkers, even though the old social contract no longer exists. This will be difficult to accomplish and will require new ways of thinking about the relationship of employees to an organization. It represents an unfinished model for what careers will be like in the future.

Leadership in Organizational Development

The founder or founders of a successful organization are the first source of its culture. Organizations are created when founders recognize that a group working together can accomplish more than individuals working alone. Realizing that 8 of the 10 richest people in the world is an entrepreneur and not a U.S. citizen brings home the idea of how important it is to understand the global nature of organizational culture (Zakaria, 2007). An organization's beliefs about its core mission, its history, its reasons for existence, its favorite methods for getting things done, and its ideals about how members should treat one another are typically established by the founder(s). The history of the organization, as told through personal stories, gossip, documents, and old news reports, are ways in which leaders continue to shape and mold the culture of the organization. Listening to such stories and reading such reports are ways to learn about an organization's culture. We will say more about this in Chapter 15.

Schein (1985) has analyzed the close link between organizational culture and leadership. Indeed, he describes organizational leadership as "culture management." The leader's vision of what the organization should be and do is designed to inspire and guide other members. Sports teams provide a good example of the relationship between organizational culture and leadership. Sports teams have a clear, single purpose—to win games. Winning traditions, hard work, expertise, risk-taking, and self-sacrifice are elements of the culture of a successful team. However, leadership is also essential. This includes the work of the head coach, the assistant coaches, the senior members of the team, and the captains who transmit the culture of the team to new members.

As we saw in Chapters 7 and 8, modern organizations are increasingly relying on individual members to provide leadership in work teams, task forces, committees, and other groups. Because organizational leadership is so closely connected to culture, it is important for us to understand these relationships as we assume roles as employees in work organizations. Our personal career development will increasingly be affected by the extent to which we can become effective leaders and managers of the culture in our work settings.

CAREER DEVELOPMENT AND WORKFORCE DEVELOPMENT

The relationship between the career development of individual employees and the overall development of an organization is a vital one. Indeed, these two factors are often very closely linked. An organization can renew itself, change, and grow in new directions through the management and direction of the careers of its workers. This is sometimes called "workforce planning," and it is different from individual career planning, the primary focus of this book. Workforce planning is something that the organization does for itself to make sure it grows properly, while career management is something that individuals in an organization do with respect to their interests, values, skills, and goals (Herr, Cramer, & Niles, 2003).

In the past, career development was part of the old social contract between the organization and its employees, but we have learned that this contract has been broken in many ways. Today, individuals may use career development in the form of organizational programs such as human resources, training and development, supervision, and the organization's career resource center. They can also voluntarily seek lateral moves in the organization in order to further develop their skills. Of course, the strength of the relationship between career development and organizational development depends on the culture of the organization. Organizations with a culture of *"people development"* are more likely to have organizational career development programs.

In an early study of what is happening in this area, Thomas Gutteridge, Zandy Leibowitz, and Jane Shore (1993) surveyed 1,000 large U.S.-based organizations and 96 U.S. government agencies to learn what was happening in organizational career development. Nearly 70 percent of the organizations had or were launching career development programs.

How do organizations get involved in career development? The implementation of a career development program in an organization may take many forms, and there is no one best way for it to occur. Here are some of the most common program activities found in organizations (Inkson & Arthur, 2002):

- *Individual career counseling.* This may be provided by professional staff, personnel workers, outside consultants, supervisors, or peers.

- *Group career counseling.* This may take the form of career workshops or special topics seminars on self-assessment, resume writing and interviewing, preretirement, or new employee orientation.

- *Assessment.* This can include job performance appraisals and reviews, self-assessment activities, psychological testing, and assessment center work.

- *Career information*. This could include a career resource center; researching career paths and career ladders in the organization; job posting or bulletin boards, phone message systems, or Web pages; messages about scholarship programs and training/development activities.

- *Training and development*. This can include job enrichment, job rotation, career sabbaticals, tuition reimbursement, in-house training, or external degree programs.

- *Organizational career planning*. This can include the development of labor force projections for the organization and the development of employee skill banks, such as how many employees have PowerPoint presentation skills.

- *Special programs*. This can include targeted presentations for special groups of employees, minorities, women, people with disabilities, preretirees, plateaued workers, outplaced (fired) workers, young managers, high-performing workers, management trainees, dual-career couples, science/technology workers, and support staff.

In reviewing these career development program activities, you might be surprised to see how many of them are also available in a college career services program. These are things you can learn how to do and participate in while still in college. The existence of a comprehensive, effective career development program might be one of the factors to consider in accepting a job offer from an organization. In researching potential employers, find out what organizations are doing in this area for their workers. If nothing else, it can help you see how your individual career development is linked to the future growth of an organization that might employ you.

A CIP Perspective

Let's review what we have learned about work organizations in light of the CIP Pyramid of Information-Processing Domains and the CASVE Cycle. Use this knowledge to improve the quality of your Personal Career Theory (PCT) for solving career problems and making career decisions.

Self-Knowledge

How does information about organizations relate to information about the interests, values, and skills that comprise self-knowledge? One thing seems clear—those working in the new kinds of organizations will constantly have to cultivate their interests, talents, and skills in order to enhance Person-Environment (P-E) matches. These P-E matches, such as those in Holland's RIASEC typology, are no longer stable because individuals and organizations are changing. This means that people will have to make adjustments and compromises in adapting their interests and skills. Moreover, those who value "security" have been negatively impacted by the loss of the old social contract between employers and workers. Individual job security is no longer part of the contract.

We also learned that Holland's Social and Enterprising types, especially the interpersonal, team-building, leadership, and conflict resolution skills associated with those types, will be increasingly valued by organizations. Individuals would do well to enhance their interests and skills in these areas to assure career growth opportunities. In analyzing an organization's culture, individuals will first have to assess themselves in terms of preferred supervision and leadership style, the agreement between organizational and personal philosophy and values, and so on. It is out of this improved self-knowledge that one can then more accurately analyze the culture of an organization in making career decisions.

Option Knowledge

Schein introduced us to the idea of organizational culture, a rich body of information that can be added to what we have already learned about schema for occupations, industries, educational training programs, and leisure in Chapter 3. Organizational culture is the context in which many of our careers will unfold, and our career growth will be related to our ability to understand and effectively act on this knowledge. We know that organizations are increasingly becoming more diverse in terms of worker characteristics, and we will likely find ourselves working in teams with people very much unlike ourselves. Individuals with varied experiences and skills in ethnic and cultural diversity will be sought by organizations.

Increased knowledge about organizations helps us understand the differences between business, government, nonprofit, and other kinds of organizations. Emerging new organizational structures also have implications for career planning. All of this information helps us move to more complex schema, beyond just occupations, when thinking about our career options. This kind of thinking helps us improve our PCT. This chapter also helped us understand more about the place of leaders in organizations and how career management is related to organizational change and individual career growth.

Finally, we believe it is important to remind ourselves that Holland's environmental typology using the six RIASEC categories can help us understand organizational culture. Indeed, Holland first used RIASEC types to study colleges and universities in terms of their dominant characteristics. RIASEC theory provides a way to describe organizational cultures or environments as well as personal interests.

Decision Making

Knowledge of organizational culture can have a very important impact on the kinds of educational and career decisions we will make. Besides exploring occupations and job descriptions, employment decisions will certainly be affected by our perceptions of organizational culture. Persons will have to pay attention to their feelings and instincts as they visit organizations on second and third interviews, and they will have to sharpen their skills in reading the signs of organizational culture.

How does one go about choosing organizations, environments, and cultures? In some ways, person–environment matches may be like choosing a fraternity, sorority, or club. Viewed holistically, an organization is more than a sum of its parts. "I know a Phi Gam when I see one," someone might say. "He'll never be a TKE," another says. Ultimately, choosing an appropriate culture is highly subjective in nature.

Decisions about career growth will be increasingly tied to decisions about the work we want to do in the organization—how we want to retrain ourselves, new skills we want to develop, new roles we want to play in the organization, the option of home-based work. Moreover, these decisions may be related to the matter of remaining with the organization itself or choosing to become an independent contractor who is self-employed. This will bring added complexity to individual career decisions, and the time for making these decisions will be shortened as organizations change more quickly.

Executive Processing

Given all these changes in the global economy and organizations, is the idea of career now dead? Douglas Hall (1996) a professor of organizational behavior at Boston University, who has spent a lifetime studying careers and organizations, believes "career" is still alive.

> The career as we once knew it—as a series of upward moves, with steadily increasing income, power, status, and security—has died. Nevertheless, people will always have work lives that unfold over time, offering challenge, growth, and learning. *So if we think of the career as a series of lifelong work-related experiences and personal learnings* . . . , it will never die [italics added]. (p. 1)

Hall et al. believe that in the new career, the "notions of caregiving, mentoring, caring and respect, connection, and co-learning (that is, learning through relationship with others), especially co-learning with others with whom one regards as different, provide the clues to growth and success" (p. 4). In this idea of career, personal development becomes a person's most powerful career development tool (p. 265). In CIP terms, this new career schema is based on personal learning and growth. These ideas should be incorporated into your Personal Career Theory (PCT).

As we learned in Chapter 7, careers will be more complex psychological constructions in the future, especially given the changes in the nature of organizations discussed in this chapter. Understanding an organization's purpose and how the organization is structured may require new cognitive schema for individuals seeking to develop successful careers. The difficulty will be balancing individual needs and expertise with an organizational culture emphasizing teamwork and group goals. Organizations will be changing constantly, and individuals will have to learn new things about organizations and be flexible in adapting to these changes in a continuing basis.

In this chapter, we reported Henkoff's (1993) admonition that you have to see yourself as a "business" in this new organizational culture. In effect, you have to think of yourself as an entrepreneur, even if you work in an organization for someone else. This is a new career metacognition for many, and it will probably add some complexity to your PCT.

We introduced the idea of "employability security," the idea that your career effectiveness is tied to your ability to use a wide variety of skills and to produce value in numerous ways. As long as you keep increasing your skills and knowledge, as well as your ability to use both effectively, you can make yourself employable and can engage in career growth.

Ultimately, however, the career schema you develop for yourself in this new age will be most adaptive if it helps you define yourself in several roles, including family, leisure, community, and spirituality, as well as work.

SUMMARY

In this chapter, we introduced some of the important ideas associated with organizational behavior, including organizational culture and structure. We believe that organizations provide the context in which much of individual career growth occurs. However, the rapidly changing nature of organizations makes it difficult to adjust career planning accordingly. The implications of emerging trends in organizational life for building your Personal Career Theory were highlighted throughout this chapter. Finally, we reviewed this new information in light of the Cognitive Information Processing paradigm that undergirds this book.

REFERENCES

Ballantine, M. (1994). *Career development in mid-career: Practice and problems from a British perspective*. Paper presented at the National Association of Career Development Conference, Albuquerque, NM.

Barrett, W. P. (2007, December 10). Your charity dollars at work. *Forbes*, pp. 180–181.

Cetron, M. J., & Davies, O. (2008, March-April). Trends shaping tomorrow's world. *The Futurist*, pp. 35–52.

Colombia Books. (2008). *National trade and professional association directory*. New York: Author.

Deangelis, T. (2007, April). America: A toxic lifestyle? *Monitor on Psychology*, pp. 50–52.

Deming, W. E. (1986). *Out of crisis*. Cambridge, MA: MIT Press.

Department of Labor. (2005). *Industry at a glance*. Washington, DC: Author.

Drucker, P. (1993). *Post-capitalist society*. New York: HarperCollins Publishers.

Employment Policy Foundation. (2005). *Handbook on 21st century working women.* Washington, DC: Author.

Feller, R. & Whichard, J. (2005). *Knowledge nomads and the nervously employed: Workplace change and courageous choices.* Austin, TX: PRO-ED.

Franklin, J. C. (2007, November). An overview of BLS projections to 2016. *Monthly Labor Review,* pp. 3–12.

Gottfredson, G., & Holland, J. (1996). *Dictionary of Holland occupation codes* (3rd ed.). Odessa, FL: Psychological Assessment Resources.

Gutteridge, T., Leibowitz, Z., & Shore, J. (1993). *Organizational career development.* San Francisco: Jossey-Bass.

Hall, D. T., & Associates. (1996). *The career is dead … long live the career.* San Francisco: Jossey-Bass.

Harris, W. (1993, July 28). Strength in numbers. *Tallahassee Democrat,* p. 3D.

Henkoff, R. (1993, July). Winning the new career game. *Fortune,* p. 46.

Herr, E. L., Cramer, S. H., & Niles, S. G. (2003). *Career guidance and counseling through the lifespan: Systematic approaches* (6th ed.). Boston: Allyn & Bacon.

Hodges, D. (2007, December 4). Associations have huge impact. *Tallahassee Democrat,* p. 6A.

Hofstede, G. (1984). *Culture's consequences: International differences in work-related values.* Beverly Hills, CA: SAGE.

Holland, J. L. (1997). *Making vocational choices: A theory of vocational personalities and work environments.* Odessa, FL: Psychological Assessment Resources, Inc.

Howard, A. (Ed.) (1995). *The changing nature of work.* San Francisco, CA: Jossey-Bass.

Inkson, K., & Arthur, M. B. (2002). Career development: Extending the "organizational careers" framework. In S. G. Niles (Ed.), *Adult career development: Concepts, issues, and practices* (3rd ed., pp. 285–304). Tulsa, OK: National Career Development Association.

International Labor Market (2003). *Key indicators of the labor market* (3rd ed.). Geneva, Switzerland: Bureau of Publications, International Labour Office.

Judy, R. W., & D'Amico, C. (1997). *Workforce 2020: Work and workers in the 21st century.* Indianapolis, IN: Hudson Institute.

Mohrman, S. A., & Cohen, S. G. (1995). When people get out of the box: New relationships, new systems (pp. 365–410). In A. Howard, *The changing nature of work.* San Francisco: Jossey-Bass.

Mosisa, A. T. (2002, May). The role of foreign-born workers in the U.S. economy. *Monthly Labor Review,* pp. 3–12.

Reich, R. (1992). *The work of nations.* New York: Vintage Books.

Rifkin, J. (1995). *The end of work.* New York: Putnam's Sons.

Sandroff, R. (July, 1993). The psychology of change. *Working Woman,* pp. 52–56.

Schein, E. (1985). *Organizational culture and leadership.* San Francisco: Jossey-Bass.

Shuman, M. H., & Fuller, M. (2005, Jan. 24). Profits for justice. *Nation,* pp. 13–22.

Toossi, M. (2007, November). Labor force projections to 2016: More workers in their golden years. *Monthly Labor Review,* pp. 33–52.

Wenger, E. C., & Snyder, W. M. (2000, January). Communities of practice: The organizational frontier. *Harvard Business Review, 78,* 139–146.

White, E. (2005, March 29). Savviest job hunters research the cultures of potential employers. *Wall Street Journal,* pg. B1.

Zakaria, F. (2007, October 22). The end of exceptionalism. *Newsweek,* p. 35.

ALTERNATIVE WAYS TO WORK

The emerging global economy, the increased use of technology, and changes in organizational culture and structure are having profound impacts on the way we work in the United States. If you consider regular, permanent jobs the crystal vase that has been knocked off the table by the cat, the new ways to work are the little pieces of the broken vase.

Our individual places of employment are increasingly linked by communication networks to other work sites around the world. Those in business may be pursuing markets for products and services in a score of different nations. Moreover, the teams in which we work today have changed job descriptions in many ways. The focus in this chapter is on *how* the forces reviewed in Chapters 7 and 8 have altered the ways we work. A good understanding of this issue will help you develop new, more complex schema related to career planning and employment and help you to improve the quality of your Personal Career Theory.

Here are the topics we will cover in this chapter:

- The nature of *job creation*. Why are the forms of employment changing?

- *Alternative ways to work* and the growing *contingent workforce*, including the various kinds of employment options associated with it

- The *social forces* that are influencing regular and contingent jobs and how all of this is affecting *retirement*

- *Problems* associated with these new ways of working

We will conclude with a *CIP perspective* and a summary.

As you read about these alternative ways to work, try to think about how your PCT and strategic career thinking can be improved by this information. How will this information affect occupations you are interested in, and how will it affect the ways you might think about working. In what kind of job will you work? How will this new way of working differ from what you have thought about in the past?

JOB CREATION

Where do jobs come from? Before looking at the alternative ways in which we work, it is probably useful to take a few minutes to think about why and how jobs are created. What events or factors lead employers to create jobs? (You might want to review the definitions of *job* and *position* in Chapter 1.)

Sar Levitan and Clifford Johnson (1982), the economists who wrote *Second Thoughts on Work*, explained that jobs are created by the public's desire for goods or services. In effect, jobs are the outcomes of our consumer wants, rather than our needs. When we want more clothes, cars, college degrees, elder care, or child care, people who provide these things will take the necessary steps to produce more of them. Producing more can be accomplished in two basic ways. The providers can *either* have the present workers do more, by working more hours or days each week, *or* the providers can hire more workers, by creating new jobs. Of course, when these wants decrease, jobs will be lost as providers cut back on production.

The demand for many things in the United States is very strong—the economy is growing at a modest rate. In the past, employers would respond by hiring more workers, but today, organizations often have their employees work more overtime. This is becoming the standard because a full-time worker costs up to 40 percent more in pensions and benefits; he or she can sue when they're passed over for promotions; and they cannot be laid off easily when times are bad (Phillips, 1994).

In an effort to control labor costs, organizations have resorted to many new schemes to meet the public's increased wants and to increase the production of goods and services. Among other things, organizations are using contingent workers, who may be likened to rented furniture or a leased automobile. In effect, they are disposable, and the employer has no obligation beyond paying the salary. This is a new way of working in America because in the past we believed that when profits and demand were up, the "good jobs" would return. Now we are moving to "just-in-time" employment as well as "just-in-time" manufacturing.

There are many alternatives to permanent, full-time positions. As you read about these different ways of working, think about your occupational and employment goals and how they might be affected by this information.

ALTERNATIVE WAYS TO WORK

Permanent Full-Time Positions

The most common way of working is 40 hours per week in a regular, permanent job. However, given all that is happening in the economy, it seems a little awkward to talk about "permanent" jobs. Historically, the general view was that these positions were filled for life, unless the employee really messed up or chose to leave the organization. While jobs are no longer as permanent as before, these kinds of positions for core workers still make up the backbone of most organizations. In Chapter 8, we saw the new diamond-shaped work organizations and saw that core employees comprise between 50 and 80 percent of the workers in these emerging organizations.

Employees in permanent positions are working directly for the organization. Permanent employees typically have full benefits: health insurance, child care services, retirement programs. These employees may also have certain protections with respect to layoffs: they are last to be fired, and their salaries are drawn from more secure funds within the organization. In organizational charts, these positions are in boxes, and there are lines showing relationships to other positions in the organization.

Permanent employees are not typically thought of as part of the contingent workforce, which we will examine later in this chapter. In recent years, organizations have begun to experiment with programs to provide more flexible arrangements for work by people in regular positions.

Part-Time

Part-time work is defined as 1 to 34 hours per week and involved 25 million workers in 2006 (Torpey, 2007). This is the most widely used alternative way to work, and it is increasing relative to other kinds of part-time workers. Part-time work is an easy tool for employers to use in making workforce adjustments to accommodate shifting customer demands, and it is desirable to workers who have personal responsibilities away from the jobsite. A part-time job has the advantage of a regular paycheck, but it may not include benefits such as health insurance.

When you study an organization as your possible employer, it might be helpful to know how many workers are part-time, particularly in an area where you would be working. Also, because it is so widespread, it might be a way to begin working for an organization you're interested in; some organizations use part-time work to screen for full-time workers.

Flextime, Compressed Workweeks, or Comp Time

Flexible scheduling, or flextime, is also widely practiced in organizations. One of the most common practices involves permitting employees to set their work schedules.

There are many ways to "flex," including the following:

1. Working 4 days a week at 10 hours per day (sometimes called a "compressed week")

2. Working from 6:30 A.M. to 3:30 P.M.

3. Taking a half-hour for lunch

4. Working longer hours on some days and a half day on others

5. Working Saturdays and Sundays

Organizations offer such flextime arrangements to help employees meet family obligations, schedule medical care, and so forth. However, an organization might have a policy that requires all employees to be available from 9 a.m. to 3 p.m. weekdays, for example, or on all Mondays. Local communities like flextime because it reduces traffic at peak hours and places fewer strains on the community infrastructure. An organization's approach to flextime might also reveal something about its culture regarding alternative ways to work.

Another approach to flextime involves the compressed workweek, or working more hours on some days in order to have some days off. For example, a person might work 1 extra hour for 9 days in a 10-day work period, and then take every other Friday off. Related to this is compensatory time off, or "comp time," which means that the hours worked beyond what is required can be accumulated and used later for a vacation.

Overtime

Before discussing overtime work, it might be useful to distinguish between hourly and salaried employees in an organization. Hourly workers typically include blue-collar workers and clerical staff whose work arrangements may be covered by labor union work rules. Their basic way of working is controlled by a time card or clock. (In some organizations, certain managers and professional staff may also be hourly workers.) Hourly workers are sometimes called nonexempt or included, meaning that they must conform to federal wage and hour laws, or they are included in a collective bargaining agreement with a union. These workers are protected from abuse by employers, and any work beyond the maximum of 40 hours per week must meet certain requirements, including higher pay.

On the other hand, exempt employees, including most senior managers and professional staff, are not limited to 40 hours of work per week. Indeed, in some organizations such workers may spend up to 60 hours working at their job, at home, and/or at the worksite.

As we noted earlier, organizations have an option to meet the increased demands for goods and services by having employees work more hours or days—to work overtime. Hetrick (2000) noted that, not surprisingly, when the U.S. economy experiences growth, particularly coming out of a recession, there is a parallel rise in overtime. Many people who work in hourly jobs are regularly faced with a dilemma when employers want them to work more hours each week, because these extra hours cut into time available for spouse/partner relationships, family activities, or leisure pursuits. Declining overtime work, however, can be interpreted by employers as poor commitment to the organization or lack of interest in the job.

Dr. Arlie Hochschild (1997), who studied a large U.S. company, found that although most workers *said* they wanted more time away from their jobs, they most often *chose* to spend more time on the job, working overtime. (This might have been an instance of workers *saying* what they *wanted* and *choosing* what they *needed*.) A similar thing happens with exempt employees, the senior executives, and managers. We will return to some of the reasons for this apparent contradiction in Chapter 10.

When you research an organization, learning about the numbers of workers on overtime and how many hours managers and professional staff work each week can provide insights about the organization's culture.

Shift Work

The shift to lean production and just-in-time production has caused some organizations to move to 24-hour work schedules. The "graveyard shift" was once limited to blue-collar workers and hospital staff, but this has changed. Nowadays, college graduates should anticipate doing some shift work in their careers. For example, banks and other business organizations may need to operate on a 24-hour basis because what happens in Tokyo financial markets at 2 a.m. Eastern time may require immediate action in New York. Shift work includes night, evening, and weekend work. Torpey (2007) noted that night and evening shift workers reported working this way because they liked the nature of the job, but 27 percent did shift work for personal preference, family, child care, or salary reasons. There are many issues associated with shift work, including the health and safety of shift workers.

Moonlighting or Multiple Job Holding

The Bureau of Labor Statistics (2002) reported that 5.7 percent of all U.S. workers had multiple jobs, about 7.8 million persons. About 35 percent reported moonlighting in order to make extra money, 28 percent to meet or payoff expenses, 17 percent enjoyed the second job, and 5 percent to build a business or get experience in a different job. Moonlighting can take several forms, including (1) holding two part-time jobs, (2) working a part-time job in addition to a full-time job, or (3) working more than one full-time job. Moonlighters are typically from low- and - middle income families. Moonlighting is most often associated with jobs in services, entertainment, public administration, protective services, and teaching.

Moonlighting can be a person's best option for making more money, learning a new job, or taking care of family members. However, moonlighting can also be an indication of financial stress, poor quality job market, and high costs of work.

Job Sharing

Job sharing is a relatively common alternative to full-time, regular work, although the BLS does not keep track of this kind of part-time work. It occurs when a single job is shared by two people. Given a regular full-time position of 40 hours per week, each person in the job share typically works 20 hours per week at separate times, although they probably share two or three hours of time on the job each week for joint meetings with supervisors and other staff members. Like other part-time work, there can be several advantages to job sharing:

- Handle child-care or elder-care responsibilities that would be impossible when working 40 hours per week

- Complete an educational degree more quickly by taking additional classes during regular work hours

- Pursue leisure or entrepreneurial interests that are difficult to handle while working full-time

- Maintain insurance and other benefits available in the regular full-time position

- Reduce stress and time pressures related to job and family conflicts

From an organizational perspective, job sharing may provide a way to retain highly valued employees by accommodating their changed life situations. It also provides opportunities for more flexible staffing arrangements. However, people participating in job sharing have to work closely with their partner, communicate effectively about work projects so these are completed properly, and be flexible about making necessary adjustments to work schedules.

Telecommuting

Telecommuting, flexiplacing, or telework is an alternative way of working that appears to be growing rapidly, and it can be either for someone else or for one's self. It involves working from a remote site away from the office or the employer's workplace. Home-based work is the most common arrangement (Mariani, 2000), although not all home-based workers telecommute. Telecommuting could be done wherever one has access to the Internet in a plane, train, cab, telecenter, or hotel room. This way of working has been most clearly impacted by technology, including notebook computers, fax machines, cellular phones, PDAs, the Internet, e-mail, and voice mail. BLS data show that about 13.7 million people worked at home for an employer at least once a week in 2004 (Torpey, 2007). However, only about 25 percent had a formal arrangement to do this and many people spend less than 15 hours per week doing it. Less that 1 percent of wage and salary workers, about 575,000, work entirely at home.

Godinez (2003) reported that employers want independent workers who are paid by the assignment, and advances in technology make it possible for workers to have fully functioning home offices. In addition, some young professionals got their start during the technology boom in the 1990s which makes them confident enough to telecommute from home. New technological innovations—desktop videoconferencing, expanded Integrated Services Digital Network (ISDN) lines, improved automobile fax machines, and expanded videoconferencing sites in places like FedEx Kinko's Copy stores—make it more cost-effective for organizations to include more workers in telecommuting programs.

However, one person's perk in telecommuting may be another person's problem. There can be problems in communication and team building when the workers seldom see each other face to face. Other problems involve liability insurance for injuries sustained from working at home. The cost of equipping a home office can be $3,500, and studies show that employees are footing most of the bill (Stafford, 1998). Does the employer pay for the computer needed at home, more phone lines, a printer, PDA, fax machines, office furniture, cell phone, insurance, training, and so forth?

A perk can involve ease in managing home and job responsibilities, more flexible time. Sometimes, it is also an attractive option in recruiting new hires for an organization. Telecommuters reporting satisfying arrangements worked roughly half-office and half-home, which provides workers with opportunities for "face-time" in the office, as well as flexible control over daily schedules, particularly in meeting family needs. This new way of working places a premium on self-motivation and independence; an ability to avoid distractions in the home; the ability to effectively use, even rely on, technology; and willingness to be left out of informal office communication loops. Most telecommuters have a set of rules for the family, meaning that when they're in the office with the door shut, no one is allowed to interrupt them; otherwise, they can find it very difficult to separate work from personal life (McChristy, 2002).

Some reports indicate that organizations may not have formal policies about telecommuting and this is certainly an area to explore with potential employers. A recent analysis of 46 studies involving 12,883 employees by Gajendran and Harrison (2007) provided some encouraging information about this way of working. They found that telecommuting had small but beneficial effects on work outcomes such as a higher sense of autonomy, lower work-family conflict, more job satisfaction, and less stress. In addition, it had no negative effect on workplace relationships unless it was more than 2.5 days per week. High quality human resource management policies would be important in minimizing any negative effects. This is apparently a rapidly growing way to work that many college graduates will encounter.

Independent Contractors, Self-Employeds, Freelancers, or Consultants

These workers function like entrepreneurs. Independent contractors are defined as someone who obtains customers on their own to provide a product or service. These workers consider themselves to be consultants or freelance workers, and business owners such as shop owners or restaurant owners are not included (Cohany, 1996).

In 2005, independent contractors accounted for more than 7 percent of all workers (10.3 million) (Torpey, 2007). A more recent report indicated that 82 percent of independent contractors prefer this alternative work arrangement (U.S. Department of Labor, 2005). Cohany (1996) noted that independent contractors were more likely to be men, white, have a bachelor's degree, and be 25+ in age. They were also more likely to work part-time and hold managerial, professional, sales, or precision production jobs. Dan Pink further examined this trend in his book, *Free Agent Nation* (2001) and suggested that tens of millions of Americans have taken on this role.

In some cases, there is confusion about whether a worker is an employee or an independent contractor. The Internal Revenue Service's Web site (www.irs.gov) has information on distinguishing between an employee and independent contractor. Some of the points of distinction are shown in Table 9.1.

Because about 7 percent of the workforce is self-described as independent contractors, including freelancing and consulting, and because many of these workers are in the services industry, college graduates are likely to find increasing opportunities in this way of working. Several years ago, one state social services administrator reported to a college class that independent contractors were replacing state employees—social workers, and rehabilitation counselors—in providing these services. Thinking of oneself as a self-employed contractor is an increasingly common way to view work or one's relationship to an employer. Also, it is important when talking with employers about jobs that the nature of the work relationship is clear—will you be an employee or an independent contractor?

Contract Workers

Contract workers are defined as working for a company that contracts them out to a client's work site for services (Polivka, 1996). Of 60,000 households surveyed by Cohany (1996), about 625,000

TABLE 9.1	DISTINGUISHING BETWEEN EMPLOYEES AND INDEPENDENT CONTRACTORS

Employee	Independent Contractor
• May be trained to work in a certain way	• Receives no training
• Hired, supervised, paid by employer	• May hire, supervise, pay others
• Relationships continue beyond specific tasks	• Relationships limited to completion of tasks
• Hours are set by employer	• Hours are set by the worker
• Work times specified by employer	• Work when and for whom they choose
• Paid by the hour/week/month	• Paid by the job or commission
• Materials & equipment furnished by the employer	• Supply their own materials and equipment
• Do not make profits or losses	• Can make profits or incur losses
• May be fired by the employer	• Cannot be fired as long as contract specifications are met
• Can quit job at any time	• Cannot quit until job is satisfactorily completed or restitution provided

Source: Internal Revenue Service

individuals or 0.5 percent of the population, worked for contract firms. Cohany indicated that these workers were often male and most often employed in the services industry in a professional specialty or service occupation.

These new ways of working represent a complex set of arrangements for thinking about jobs, and it is important for job hunters to develop useful schema for thinking about these aspects of employment knowledge. This information helps you improve the quality of your Personal Career Theory (PCT). Knowledge about these employment options can be of critical importance in your strategic career planning.

THE CONTINGENT WORKFORCE

The Bureau of Labor Statistics categorizes the area of contingent work as the *personnel supply services industry*, which is one of the fastest growing areas of the economy as we learned in Chapter 7. The American Staffing Association reports that 3 million people are employed by staffing companies daily, and 79 percent work full time (the same as the rest of the workforce). Moreover, 12 million temporary and contract employees are hired by staffing firms each year (http://www.americanstaffing. net/statistics/pdf/Staffing_Facts_2007.pdf). These workers once did low-level clerical work, but the demand for temporary workers in managerial, professional, and technical occupations is strongest in industries such as financial services, health care, telecommunications, and information technology.

This area of labor force information is somewhat turbulent today, because new work arrangements and programs are being created on a continuing basis. We will now discuss recent developments and the employment options that are open to you. We will also define the terms used in this area, such as *outsourcing, employee leasing, temporary services, interim* or *on-call workers, interns* and *co-ops*, and compare and contrast them where appropriate. See Table 9.2 for a sample list of terms associated with contingent workers.

There is increasing likelihood that entry level jobs will be contingent work. The word *contingent* refers to uncertainty, possibility, chance, unforeseen conditions, dependent, conditional, and unpredictable

TABLE 9.2	EMPLOYMENT TERMS ASSOCIATED WITH CONTINGENT WORKERS	

Process Terms	Job Titles
employee leasing	consulting workers
temporary services	temporary staff, temporaries, temps
contract employment	interns and co-ops
self-employment	co-employees
freelancing	hourly partners
flexible staffing	consultants
outsourcing	subcontractors
other personnel services (OPS)	independent contractors
	on-call workers
	short-timers
	per-diem workers
	flexible staff
	interim
	extra workers
	supplementals
	peripherals

(http://www.merriam-webster.com/dictionary, 2008). When these words are added to *work*, a picture emerges of what is meant by *contingent workforce*. The Bureau of Labor Statistics defines contingent workers as those "who do not have an implicit or explicit contract for ongoing employment."

Until recently, organizations used contingency workers primarily to fill in for employees who were absent, fired, or on maternity leave, but contingent workers are now part of the culture in many organizations. The work of contingent workers is uncertain, unplanned, and dependent on changing conditions and employer's immediate needs. It is work that is not expected to last longer than a year. This is the increasing nature of work being done in the United States and throughout the world today.

Many organizations want a specified number of workers for a specified time, and when the need passes, they don't want them around anymore. In Chapter 7, we introduced the idea of "just-in-time-production," and this idea has now been transferred to "just-in-time-employment." This is the nature of the contingent workforce in the U.S. economy.

How did this situation develop? You will recall that in Chapters 7 and 8 we outlined how the emerging global economy and the increased use of technology, among other things, has impacted organizations. As organizations have reengineered and restructured themselves, the result has been "downsizing," or a reduction in employees working in the organization. There are many different terms used to describe this downsizing process (see Table 9.3). This is how organizations have become "leaner" (Rifkin, 1995). Unfortunately, it is apparent that many workers in the future will find themselves labeled with one of these terms more than once during their career.

The Bureau of Labor Statistics Studies

The most important federal study of contingent and alternative ways to work was conducted by the Bureau of Labor Statistics (BLS) and reported in the *Monthly Labor Review* (Polivka, 1996). In this study, 50,000 households were surveyed by the Census Bureau for BLS. This report on "Contingent and Alternative Employment Arrangements" included 5.4 million workers (representing 4.0 percent of total employment) who don't expect their job to last. The important news is that 96 percent of jobs

TABLE 9.3 COMMON TERMS ASSOCIATED WITH LOSS OF EMPLOYMENT	
curtailed	outplaced
dehired (one of our favorites)	pink-slipped
displaced	reduction in force
downsized	riffed
excessed	right-sized
fired (the original term)	terminated (sounds permanent)
laid-off	surplused

were not filled by contingent workers. This means that even though more workers are employed in time-limited jobs than before, and the rate of such employment is increasing, the actual number of such jobs is relatively small.

For us, the findings of this study emphasize how important flexible staffing is to organizations, and it is instructive to job hunters to know that part-time and temporary work may be a doorway to permanent employment.

Outsourcing

As organizations have laid off regular, permanent employees, they have, at the same time, contracted with other companies to do the work previously done by those laid off. The "new" workers are hired on a contingency basis and are called contingent workers. A good example is cleaning and janitorial services, which we examined in Chapter 8. Let's say Dollar Down Securities fired its janitorial staff, then turned around and contracted with ServiceMaster to clean its buildings. It is possible that the same people would continue doing the work in the same buildings, but they would now be working for a different employer. Every kind of job is affected by growth in the contingent workforce—hourly pay jobs, technical jobs, and top professional positions—located throughout the world. Organizations call this outsourcing.

Using our janitorial example, outsourcing cleaning and janitorial services would enable Dollar Down Securities to save money on health insurance, payroll taxes, and retirement benefits. These costs might be taken over by ServiceMaster. The trend toward outsourcing has exploded, and many other functions previously thought to be core internal elements of an organization are now contracted outside. This can include all personnel and staffing services, accounting and financial services, research and development, legal services, and marketing. In the case of personnel, for example, a firm specializing in this area would conduct employee performance reviews, health care and retirement benefits administration, training and development, new employee recruiting and orientation, and the like, for a fee to the client.

What does this trend toward outsourcing mean for workers? The good news is that the work or job is still there to be done, but the employer may change. The bad news is that the work or job may change more quickly, and workers will have to be flexible and change their expectations about the nature of employment arrangements—their positions are less permanent now because an organization may choose to go "outside." It also makes it difficult to know exactly how to seek employment in such an organization because it is unclear exactly who is employing the workers.

Employee Leasing

In this outsourcing arrangement, an organization fires its employees and then hires a leasing firm to take over the personnel administration using the same employees. Sometimes this is called a master vendoring partnership, co-employment, or managed staffing. This administrative work includes employee records, insurance and benefits programs, payroll, government reporting, hiring/firing, taxes, and workers' compensation. The leasing company then "leases" the employees back to the original organization. This program can make it easier for an organization to remove ineffective workers and to avoid costly litigation and training activities. The leasing company now handles these functions.

Staff leasing is increasingly used by small companies with 5 to 50 workers that do not want to take on all the difficulties and expenses of personnel administration (Miracle, 1995). This arrangement is relatively common in Florida, which has more small businesses than most other states.

It is unclear what benefits might come to the workers in this kind of arrangement, other than the fact that specialists are handling personnel matters. Indeed, staff leasing is invisible to most workers (Miracle, 1995). Job application procedures might also be complicated because the company that you want to work for is leasing its employees from another employer, and it is unclear whom you would actually be working for.

Temporary Services

One of the most common types of outsourcing or contingency work is through temporary employees, or "temps." The growing staffing services industry (discussed in Chapter 7) makes extensive use of part-time workers and temps. Temps are defined as contingent workers when they do not expect to stay with their current employer for more than one year or the job has a specified ending date.

An important distinction should be made here regarding temporary employment and working for a temp agency. If one has continuing employment with a temporary services company, then the work is permanent, not temporary or contingent (Polivka, 1996). This means that one can have permanent employment with a temp agency. This gets confusing, but it is an important point to remember when developing new schema for new ways to work.

In temping, the person actually doing the work is known as an *employee* or a *contractor*, and the temporary help organization is known as the *employer*. The organization for whom temporary employment services are being provided is known as the *client*. In our example, Dollar Down Securities is the client and ServiceMaster is the employer of janitorial staff. These services are provided at no charge to the employee, but the client pays the employer for these staffing services.

In contrast, it might be noted that private employment agencies, who act as your agent in helping you find employment, do not hire you as a contingent employee. In this regard they are different from temporary services. Also, private employment agencies may charge a fee to job hunters, but temp agencies do not. Public (government) employment services also do not charge job hunters a fee.

It is very important to understand these schema related to temp work, to know which is the employer, the client, and the employee. Effective use of these terms is important in researching organizations, applying for jobs, and understanding the work culture of an organization.

Temp work once targeted assembly-line and clerical workers, but today lawyers, accountants, engineers, scientists and other professionals make up the fastest growing segment of the temporary work force and a third of employees in staffing services companies. The Bureau of Labor Statistics (Thottam, 2004) predicts that between 2002 and 2012, 1.8 million new jobs will be added to the staffing services industry, a 54 percent increase. The vast majority of temp employees work about 40 hours per week. Hourly wages are higher for temps but this may be offset by reduced benefits.

In spite of the numbers of workers involved, temporary services companies, increasingly called staffing companies, are big business. Here are some facts:

- Manpower Inc., a world leader in the employment services company, based in Milwaukee, Wisconsin, has over 4,500 offices in 78 countries and serves over 400,000 clients. It is currently ranked 131st on the Fortune 500 list of largest companies and placed 4.4 million persons in positions in 2006 (http://www.manpower.com).

- Manpower, like other staffing companies, is constantly training its employees to learn something new and different, to obtain more work-related experience. Such organizations are a major source of corporate training today.

- Besides Spherion and Manpower, there are more than 140 national staffing companies with over 15,000 offices, including, Adecco, Interim, Kelly Services, Office Team, and Olsten Corporation. The American Staffing Association, http://americanstaffing.net, provides information about this industry.

In reflecting on the information in the preceding paragraphs, we think it is especially important to note that only 1 percent of the workforce was employed by a staffing agency in 1995, but other observers place this number as high as 30 percent. It is difficult to know for sure what is happening in this area, and more research is needed. Some organizations have taken "temporary" out of their name because the jobs are often not temporary.

Many college students already have experience working with a temporary services organization, perhaps in retail or office staffing. They will want to watch the staffing services industry closely, because a temporary staffing company may become a highly viable method for finding professional employment in the future.

Eve Broudy (1989) offered some advantages in temping for professionals, including mobility, flexibility, and visibility. *Mobility* is a way to sustain career growth while being moved from one organization (or place) to another. It is a way to stay active, occupied, and working while looking for a more permanent position. *Flexibility*, Broudy indicated, applies to temp work in numerous ways. For example, it provides a tryout work experience without a long-term commitment. It can also provide opportunities for part-time work while making a career change. Moreover, it safeguards an employee from getting stuck with a nasty boss or work situation—it puts the employee in control. *Visibility* pertains to keeping oneself exposed to potential employers and maintaining opportunities to network in one's area of interest. Being "invisible" provides a sure guarantee for career stagnation, and temping can be an antidote for this.

Temporary workers are increasingly being used by organizations as a pool for finding permanent employees. This is called a "buyout" or "temp-to-hire," meaning temporary to permanent employment status. The American Staffing Association reported that 72 percent of temporary employees obtained permanent jobs while working for a staffing company. When organizations create new full-time jobs, they often first look inside to part-time workers or temporary staff to fill the position. This is why 75 percent of jobs are never advertised. An organization looking for permanent employees may first look at temps to fill the positions, even though it may have to pay a fee to the temporary services company if it hires the temp. However, Broudy cautions temps against moving too quickly to pursue full-time employment because both the temp agency and the client may react negatively.

Broudy suggested that temporary companies can be like a career lifeline. They promote your interests, seek to find work for you, and handle all the paperwork associated with your employment. Howard Figler (1988) described these as "interim jobs," which provide you with a regular income at a level that permits financial survival. You accept interim jobs not intending to stay in them on a permanent basis. A temp company will determine your interests, skills, and career goals, as well as the hours available to work, in order to make a good match with a client. As the employer, it is essential to the effectiveness of the staffing services business that the employee and client find the job placement a mutually beneficial one. In this way, the temp employer can expect to obtain repeat orders from the client. In Chapter 11, we will examine some of Broudy's suggestions for deciding on a temporary service company.

So what does all this information about the temporary staffing services industry mean to you? First, college students should realize that temporary and staffing services companies might be very good organizations to use in launching a career. These organizations will represent you, coach you, and train you for various kinds of jobs. They will help you network in your field of interest and get needed initial job experience. Second, because some organizations use temps as a way to screen for regular, permanent positions, signing on with a temp agency may be an avenue to full-time employment. Third, job hunters should sign up with more than one temporary service company, because these employers have staffing contracts with different clients. Finally, college students should realize that they will probably find themselves unemployed during their careers, and temporary services employers can help provide a means for returning to the workforce.

On-Call Workers

This area of the contingent workforce includes substitute teachers and construction workers (Polivka, 1996). On-call workers are defined as being in a pool of workers who are only called to work as needed, which might be for one day or up to several weeks. In the survey of 60,000 households regarding alternative work forms, 1.7 percent (2 million) reported working on-call. Cohany (1996) reported that on-call workers had similar characteristics with regular workers and often worked in the construction or services industry in professional, service, or laborer occupations. A substantial number of on-call workers are contingent.

Interns and Co-ops

Internships and cooperative education programs provide a specialized kind of contingent work for college students. In an internship or co-op position, a student provides services to an organization related to the student's academic training. In this situation, the internship or cooperative education office functions somewhat like a temporary services agency, and the organization is the client. Because the person is participating in the program as a student, this is a specialized kind of temporary work experience. Clients have "positions" available for interns that provide their organization with an opportunity to observe the intern/employee as a potential permanent employee. Like other kinds of temporary positions, these internship positions may also provide students with career mobility, flexibility, experience, and visibility.

The National Association of Colleges and Employers (1998) tried to clarify the meaning of "internships." Given that the Fair Labor Standards Act (wage and hour law) requires employers to pay at least minimum wage to employees, NACE cited U.S. Department of Labor (DOL) criteria for determining when a learner/trainee may be *unpaid*:

1. The training is similar to that provided in a vocational school.

2. The training is for the benefit of the student.

3. The student does not replace a regular employee, but works under the close supervision of one.

4. The employer provides the training and derives no immediate benefit from the student's activities.

5. The student is not necessarily entitled to a job after the training period.

6. The employer and student understand that the student is not entitled to wages for time spent training.

Therefore, an internship should be mostly for the benefit of the student as a learner.

Is an unpaid intern the same as a volunteer? DOL regulations define a "volunteer" as one who provides services to a public agency for civic, charitable, or humanitarian reasons without promise or expectation of compensation for services rendered (National Association of Colleges and Employers, 1998). Thus, private sector business internships would not be considered volunteer positions.

Organizations are increasingly looking at interns when recruiting students for full-time, permanent positions. Indeed, a report by the National Association of Colleges and Employers (2007) revealed that 88 percent of employers responding to a survey were using internships and/or cooperative education programs to create a pool of quality job candidates. They like to "test-drive" their job candidates before offering permanent employment. Employers reported to NACE that about 30 percent of new hires in 2005 came from their own internship programs (Collins, 2007). The current benchmark is 53 percent of eligible interns and 64 percent of eligible co-ops, respectively, are converted to full-time hires (Collins, 2006). More information can be obtained about cooperative education from a college career center and the Cooperative Education and Internship Association (CEIA; http://www.ceiainc.org/).

WHAT ABOUT RETIREMENT?

These alternative ways of working have important implications regarding retirement planning. Some college students today may want to retire at age 55. Is this good planning? In Chapter 1, we noted that the three boxes of life—education, work, and leisure (retirement)—are no longer viable. With the changed social contract and the increasing new ways of working, this will be even more true in the future.

In many ways, our current view of "retirement" is a completely new phenomenon. For example, two-thirds of all people who have ever lived past 65 are living today (Varchaver, 2005). Generations ago, and in many parts of the world today, people just died—retirement wasn't an option. Today, nearly 80 percent of baby-boomers want to continue working when they reach retirement age, and 42 percent want to rotate between work and leisure. As many as 56 percent dream of a radical shift in working, while 17 percent never want to work for pay again (Varchaver, 2005).

The options for flexible work, a national health care system, and other social policy matters will shape the options that today's college students have in retirement. This underscores the importance of viewing career planning as a lifelong endeavor, as we have emphasized in this text.

PROBLEM AREAS

Persons with alternative work arrangements have varied reactions to their situations. Some would prefer more traditional arrangements and others are quite satisfied. Among independent contractors, on-call workers, and temp agency workers, the latter are least satisfied with the alternative work arrangements (Bureau of Labor Statistics, 2005).

Independent contractors may be abused by employers in several ways. For example, they may work next to permanent employees, doing the same job but not getting benefits or unemployment compensation. In effect, they are doing the same job for much less pay. A review of some of the topics in Table 9.1 can help determine whether one is truly an independent contractor or an employee. Employers may be breaking federal and state laws by categorizing workers as independent contractors when they are not.

S. N. Houseman (1997) concluded that some organizations may use contingent staffing as a way to avoid paying benefits to workers, including health insurance and pensions. In addition, part-time workers and temporary workers may not be able to receive unemployment insurance when their job ends. This raises questions about the social safety net for workers who are unemployed.

A CIP PERSPECTIVE

In this chapter, we have examined information related to the emerging new ways of working in the U.S. labor market. Along the way we have focused on alternative ways of working and the rise of the contingent labor force. Now we want to review briefly what we have learned by examining it in light of the Pyramid of Information-Processing Domains and the CASVE Cycle. Our goal is to help you improve the relevance and quality of your PCT for solving career problems and making career decisions.

Self-Knowledge

This chapter has focused on the enormous changes taking place in the way Americans are working today. The nature of jobs is changing. We have emphasized the introduction of alternative work-styles and the emerging contingent workforce.

Ironically, the more some things change in the workforce, the more other things stay the same. Even though these new jobs may be temporary and part-time, they can still be classified according to Holland's RIASEC codes. The bottom line is that Holland's typology applies well to these new ways of working.

These new ways of working place a premium on multiskilling, on workers being able to do a variety of things that will add value to the organization's products and services. With respect to work values, it is becoming clear that the idea of job security is changing to employment security. In working with a temporary staffing company, you may actually work several jobs in one year, each in a different organization. However, the employment might be continuous and could even include benefits. Flexibility, mobility, and adaptability become new aspects of employability skills.

Option Knowledge

The new ways of working require the development of new schema related to employment. There is a new language associated with jobs and positions, and we learned about many of these developments in our review of the permanent and contingent workforce. We counted more than 15 different new terms used in this area, including outsourcing, temporary staffing, contingent workforce, job sharing, flextime, employee leasing, and outplaced.

The development of the contingent workforce and the temporary staffing industry has made it difficult for job hunters to identify who administers the job application and employment services for many organizations. For example, few of the workers in contemporary organizations may actually work for the "client" and instead are working for a temporary staffing company or an employee leasing firm.

Ann Howard (1995) even suggested that the whole idea of a "job" is now outdated because it was a concept created in the industrial age to package work in factories and bureaucratic organizations, which is irrelevant in team-based work. The new schema of "job" is still emerging, but we have some glimpses of what it will be like.

- A job will be a loose collection of constantly changing work tasks that are both general and specific.

- A job will involve using knowledge (useful information) to solve unusual problems.

- A job will require maintaining a few core skills but primarily expanding into roles that involve interacting with others in the organization.

Howard concluded:

> Post-industrial work in adaptive organizations will be cognitively demanding and complex. It will be fluid and constantly changing; in this environment, tying down stable jobs will be difficult. Uncertainty and invisibility will enhance the abstract nature of work, but interconnections to others will engender new roles and relationships. (p. 524)

In Chapter 3, we learned about occupations and ways to classify occupations. In this chapter, we have learned about the many different ways in which occupations can be packaged, the many different ways in which a person may actually work in an occupation. By learning more about work organizations and ways of working, we have added a necessary level of complexity to our understanding of occupations. One of the key ideas in individual career development in the future will involve piecing together part-time and temporary jobs into a coherent career tapestry. The idea of "just getting a job" includes learning about the different ways that jobs are structured and managed. This knowledge improves the quality of your PCT and makes you a more informed career problem solver and decision maker.

Decision Making

The process of deciding how to work, full-time or part-time, permanent or contingent, follows the same CASVE stages of decision making that we learned about earlier. Whether the gap is finding a job or choosing a way to work, a person must carefully analyze the links between self-knowledge and the available options. Synthesis elaboration, as we have learned in this chapter, means that there is an increasing array of different ways to work in jobs. The valuing phase means choosing the way of working that is best for you, your family and important friends, and your important reference groups. Work values, which we examined in Chapter 2, can be examined with respect to alternative ways of working. This chapter should make you more aware of the rapidly changing nature of work options and the likelihood that you will have more frequent opportunities to make career decisions in the future because of the lack of stability in jobs.

Executive Processing

In moving away from the idea of permanent full-time employment, you will probably have to develop new career metacognitions that involve flexibility, self-reliance, adaptability, teamwork, and continuous learning. The new ways of working increase employment ambiguity and complexity; therefore, you have to develop confidence in yourself as a good decision maker. You have to be psychologically comfortable in these new conditions, to develop the career identity of a self-employed person. These new metacognitions are essential for effective career planning and should become part of your PCT.

In many organizations, workers are like rented packages of skills that can be used and then discarded. The new employer might be the temporary staffing company, which acts as an agent to help the employee market job skills. More importantly, this arrangement is not related to organizational profits and success—it has become a new form of permanent employment for many people.

SUMMARY

This chapter focused on alternative ways to work, including part-time, flextime, telecommuting, and independent contractor, and the contingent workforce, involving work that has specified time limits. This includes temporary and on-call work. We began the chapter with a brief excursion into the nature of job creation in order to understand why forms of employment are changing.

Along the way, we examined some of the social forces that are influencing regular and contingent jobs and how this is affecting retirement. There are various kinds of problems associated with these new ways of working, and we examined some of these, too. Finally, we concluded this chapter with a CIP perspective of the new ways of working in America. The constant theme in the chapter was to help you improve the quality of your PCT for solving career problems and making career decisions.

REFERENCES

Broudy, E. (1989). *Professional temping*. New York: Macmillan.

Bureau of Labor Statistics. (2005, Fall). Preferences of workers in alternative arrangements. *Occupational Outlook Quarterly*, p. 36.

Bureau of Labor Statistics (2002, September). Twenty-first century moonlighters. *Issues in Labor Statistics*, Summary 02–07.

Cohany, S. R. (1996, October). Workers in alternative employment arrangements. *Monthly Labor Review*, pp. 31–45.

Collins, M. (2006, December). College recruiting and hiring: What to watch in 2007. *NACE Journal, 67*, 14–16.

Figler, H. (1988). *The complete job-search handbook*. New York: Henry Holt.

Gajendran, R. S., & Harrison, D. A. (2007). The good, the bad, and the unknown about telecommuting: Meta-analysis of psychological mediators and individual consequences. *Journal of Applied Psychology, 92*, 1524–1541.

Godinez, V. (2003, November 5). Market drives workers to self-employment. *Tallahassee Democrat*, pp. 2E–3E.

Hetrick, R. L. (2000). Analyzing the recent upward surge in overtime hours. *Monthly Labor Review*, pp. 30–33.

Hochschild, A. R. (1997). *The time bind: When work becomes home and home becomes work*. New York: Henry Holt & Co.

Houseman, S. N. (1997, Spring). New institute survey on flexible staffing arrangements. *Employment Research, 4*(1), 1, 3–4.

Howard, A. (1995). Rethinking the psychology of work. In A. Howard (Ed.), *The changing nature of work* (pp. 513–555). San Francisco, CA: Jossey-Bass.

Levitan, S., & Johnson, C. (1982). *Second thoughts on work*. Kalamazoo, MI: W. E. Upjohn Institute for Employment Research.

Melchionno, R. (1999, Spring). The changing temporary work force. *Occupational Outlook Quarterly*, pp. 24–32.

Mariani, M. (2000). Telecommuters. *Occupational Outlook Quarterly, 44*(3), 10–17.

McChristy, N. (2002, July-August). Stories from the road: Working effectively on the move. *OfficeSolutions, 19*(7), 16–18.

Miracle, B. (1995, June). Lease-a-worker. *Florida Trend*, pp. 6–9.

National Association of Colleges and Employers. (1998). Legal Issues. *Spotlight, 20*(15), 3.

National Association of Colleges and Employers. (2007, June). *NACE 2007 recruiting benchmarks survey: A report on key measures for college recruiting and experiential education*. Bethlehem, PA: NACE.

Phillips, B. J. (1994, October 18). Even these good economic times aren't bringing more good jobs. *Tallahassee Democrat*, p. 13A.

Pink, D. H. (2001). *Free agent nation: The future of working for yourself*. New York: Warner Books.

Polivka, A. E. (1996, October). Contingent and alternative work arrangements, defined. *Monthly Labor Review*, pp. 3–9.

Rifkin, J. (1995). *The end of work*. New York: Putnam.

Stafford, D. (1998, June 10). Rise of telecommuting raises questions. *Tallahassee Democrat*, p. 3D.

Thottam, J. (2004, April 26). When execs go temp. *Time*, pp. 40–41.

Torpey, E. M. (2007, Summer). Flexible work: Adjusting the when and where of your job. *Occupational Outlook Quarterly*, pp. 14–27.

Varchaver, N. (2005, July 11). Pitchman for the gray revolution. *Fortune*, pp. 63–72.

Williams, L. (1997, November 17). Americans not rushing headlong into retirement. *Tallahassee Democrat*, p. 3A.

U.S. Department of Labor (2005, Fall). Preferences of workers in alternative arrangements. *Occupational Outlook Quarterly*, p. 36.

CAREER AND FAMILY ROLES

In Part Two, we learned how the increasingly competitive global economy and the use of technology have impacted organizational culture and the way we work. If we were geologists, we could think about these macrolevel forces as if they were giant plates shifting on the earth's crust, creating earthquakes and tidal waves. In many ways, these social forces have produced "careerquakes" (Bolles, 2008) in the way we engage in careers.

That, however, is not the end of the story. There is another huge shift that has been affecting organizations and the way we work, and this is related to the movement of women into work roles outside the home. Altogether, these macrolevel forces have added complexity and change to the way we engage in career. Perhaps more than anything else, these forces have impacted the Personal Career Theory (PCT) that we use to solve career problems and make career decisions. That is the focus of this chapter which explores the following topics.

- A historical review of the changes in labor force participation among women and men with the resulting impact on organizational and family life

- Living in a dual-career relationship

- Strategies for managing work and family life, including individual and organizational responsibilities

- A case study analysis of what happened at Amerco, a family-friendly corporation

- A CIP perspective on career/family factors related to career

As you read about these issues involving gender and ways to work, try to think about how your PCT and strategic career thinking can be improved by this information. How will this information affect the kind of work-family balance you value, and how will it affect the ways you think about family roles and relationships while working outside the home? What kind of life-career will your spouse/partner have? How will this affect the way you work?

SETTING THE STAGE: GENDER ISSUES AT HOME AND AT WORK

Some years ago, instructors asked 200 students enrolled in an undergraduate career course to indicate what information about career planning they expected to receive in the course (Gerken, Reardon, & Bash, 1988). No one checked either of the two survey items about obtaining marriage or family information related to career planning. Apparently these students' metacognitions regarding career did not encompass spouse/partner and family relationships. Many students still do not connect these personal relationships with career planning, and that can be a problem. In this chapter we will provide information and ideas to help you broaden your thinking about career (your PCT) to include family and other relationships.

At the outset, we should remember that in 2016 women will represent 59 percent of the U.S. labor force, with men 13 points ahead at 72 percent (Toossi, 2007). Both have a stake in finding solutions to work-family balance problems. Using a different national sample, Bond, Thompson, Galinsky, and Prottas (2002) found the proportion of women and men in the workforce was 51 percent men and 49 percent women, even more equal than the Department of Labor report cited above.

Another factor in the lives of American workers is the expanded role of fathers in the home. While the total time mothers and fathers spend each week with children has not changed from 1992–2002, fathers are doing 42 minutes more of household work on the days they are at the job. Mothers have decreased their time in housework by the same minutes, but they still do more than fathers, especially in cooking and childcare. Horrigan and Herz (2004) found that on the days they worked, employed men worked about an hour more than employed women, 8.0 versus 7.1 hours. Employed women spent about an hour more per day than men doing household activities and caring for household members. About 1 in 5 workers did some or all of their work at home. (Note that adults in households without children spent about 1.4 hours more per day in leisure and sports activities than those with children.)

In Chapter 7, we examined how employment and income varies across Holland's (1997) six RIASEC areas. Figure 10.1 shows how the distribution of men and women varies across these six areas in the 2000 census report. Note that women are dispersed more evenly over the six areas than men, who are primarily concentrated in the Realistic (R) and Enterprising (E) areas. Women are at 15 percent or higher in Realistic, Social, Enterprising, and Conventional areas.

Finally, in setting the stage for this chapter, we note that income also varies by gender, and this has many, varied implications in career planning for both men and women (Weinberg, 2008). Examination of 2000 Census data indicates that there is a substantial gap in median (half above and half below) earnings for women in comparison to men that is unexplained by the fact that women have fewer years of work experience, work fewer hours and less full-time, and take more leave from

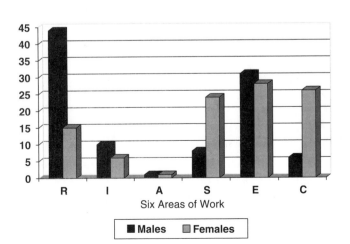

FIGURE 10.1

Percent of Employment Across Six Areas for Men and Women, 2000 Census

U.S. Bureau of Census

the job. When these factors, along with the occupation, industry, race, marital status, and job tenure are considered, women still earn about 73–80 percent of what men earn.

In the remainder of this section, we will look at the movement of women into work roles outside the home, and examine the impact of this on family and work life. Then we will look at changes in men's roles at home and work.

Women and Mothers in the Labor Force

From the time of the first colonists, women helped build America by working long, hard hours on farms and in their homes. In 1900, only about 20 percent of women were working outside the home, usually because they were unmarried or widowed (Matthews & Rodin, 1989). The Industrial Revolution drew men from jobs on the farm and in small stores to factories, and women were left to work at home. During World War II in the early 1940s, many women were recruited into the workforce as teachers, factory workers, and businesspeople, and some remained there after the war was over.

The Bureau of Labor Statistics reported that *60 percent of women with children under 6 were employed outside the home in 2006* (U.S. Department of Labor, 2007). Karen Matthews and Judith Rodin (1989) described this phenomenon as "a natural experiment of enormous proportions." In this regard, we continue to learn from this experiment with respect to new ways of participating in work and family life.

In recent years, the steady increase of working mothers in the labor force, especially those with young children, has stopped (Cohany & Sok, 2007). In 2005, the participation rate for mothers with preschoolers was 60 percent, down from 64 percent in 1997. For married mothers with infants, it was 53 percent in 2005, and for married mothers with school-age children 75 percent. Interestingly, the workforce participation rate for married women with a college degree declined from 71 percent in 1997 to 62 percent in 2000 for two reasons. First, married women with college degrees typically have husbands with a similar education who are likely to be relatively high earners, and this provides these women with more options regarding employment. Second, women with college degrees are likely to have a longer workweek (42 hours on average; 45 hours for those with professional degrees), and these heavier work hours provide an incentive to take the "off ramp" from a job.

The movement of mothers into the workforce has impacted work organizations, family life, and virtually every social institution. For women, there is evidence that increased tensions associated with labor force participation will lead to more stress-related illnesses, such as heart disease and mental illness (Matthews & Rodin, 1989). At the same time, the workplace can reward women with increased personal accomplishments, higher self-esteem, more interesting social contacts, and increased income.

Without a doubt, the biggest unresolved problem associated with women's employment is connected to childcare. Women appear to be feeling the primary impact of this issue. There are many questions here. What should be governments' role in establishing policies and laws pertaining to work and family life? What responsibilities do employers have to support family members in care giving? And what roles should spouses assume as mothers are employed in more stressful, demanding jobs? We will explore these topics further as we move through this chapter.

A Family/Career Issue—Not a Women's Issue

As we have learned in using the CASVE Cycle in Chapter 4, the schema used to frame an issue or problem can be of critical importance in finding solutions. One thing seems clear to us: *Problems associated with women working outside the home are not only women's issues, but they are shared by men, families, and the broader society.* Scarr et al. (1989) were very clear about this with respect to one aspect of women's employment: They concluded, "Child care is not a women's issue; it is a family issue" (p. 1404).

The movement of women into the labor force along with men has had many effects on family life. Donna St. George (1996) observed that as parents lose their jobs, children are affected by increased family stress and uncertainty. There is longstanding research showing the link between unemployment and child abuse, domestic violence, and divorce.

There is more spillover from job to family than vice versa. Jackson (1998) reported a study by the Families and Work Institute, *National Study of the Changing Workforce*, which indicated that economic "productivity is far more likely to be hurt these days by job-related stress than by family problems stemming from child care or elder care" (p. 3A). This study involved more than 3,000 employees. What are some of these job-related problems? Employees reported working almost 10 percent more hours than 20 years earlier; 33 percent brought work home once a week or more; and job insecurities were higher. One respondent noted, "While I don't necessarily spend more time at the office, I check my e-mail and voice mail at home at night, and I spend more time thinking about the office."

Bond et al. (2002) found 45 percent of men and women reporting "some" or "a lot" of interference between jobs and family life. This was significantly higher than 25 years earlier. When supportive work-life policies and programs were in place, employees exhibited more positive work outcomes as well as life outcomes.

It seems clear that the movement of women into the labor force has had a significant impact on work organizations, families, men's roles, children, and on women themselves. However, this natural experiment, as Matthews and Rodin described it, is still ongoing, and much of the data about its impact and outcomes are conflicting and unclear. At the very least, the social changes associated with women working outside the home impact every aspect of career development in all sectors of society.

Men and Women Feeling Overworked

In a national study of 1,003 employed adults, Galinsky, Kim, and Bond (2001) sought to determine the extent, causes, and consequences of feeling overworked. They theorized that feeling overworked is often an *acute* condition which subsides when work demands decrease. Galinsky et al. found nearly half (46 percent) of the respondents reported feeling overworked often or very often during the preceding three months. It is not surprising that employees working more hours each week feel more overworked. In addition, those who had the greatest pressure to work fast and hard felt more overworked ("never have enough time to get everything done" was a common response). Employees most frequently using technology, e.g., mobile phones, felt most overworked, partly because employers found them accessible during nonwork times. Finally, employees with poorer quality jobs, e.g., less autonomy, more wasted time, few learning opportunities, felt more overworked.

What happens when employees feel overworked? Galinsky et al. (2002) concluded that they are more likely to make mistakes, to feel angry toward employers for expecting them to do so much, to resent coworkers who work less hard, and to look for a new job. Overworked employees felt more work-life conflict with a resulting negative impact on both family and work activities. They felt less successful in relationships with others, and they were more likely to have sleep problems. Altogether, feeling overworked negatively impacted an employee's physical and mental health.

"Sandwich Generation"

Contemporary workers are sometimes described as being in the "sandwich generation." What does this mean? While not a new phenomenon, this term is used to describe middle-aged people who have simultaneous demands of caring for aging parents and supporting dependent children (Pierret, 2006). Several factors have led to increased attention to this issue: (1) more middle-aged people have living parents, (2) the parents live farther away which complicates care-giving, (3) women are having children at a later age so parents are older and children are still young, (4) children are supported longer than in previous generations, and (5) women are working outside the home. It is apparent that women have been especially impacted as dual caregivers. Pierret (2006) found that one-third of 45–56 year-old-women were helping both parents and children to the tune of about $18 billion dollars and 2.4 billion hours each year. It is no wonder that many American workers say they don't have the time to properly care for both young children and elderly parents (Park, 2005). The lesson to take from this is that care giving will be an increasing role in the lives of many workers in the future.

Changing Family Systems

In Chapter 8, we talked about organizations as social systems and noted that such systems have interdependent elements that have interrelated functions and share common goals. If we take a systems view of a dual-career family situation, we see each individual as separate but also inter-connected with other members in pursuit of common goals. Therefore, if one member charges off on his or her own, then the entire family is impacted. The nuclear family in the United States is commonly thought to consist of a husband/father, wife/mother, and at least one child. The extended family includes other relatives, such as grandparents.

Family systems are changing in the United States. For example, Dr. Vernon Zunker (2006) reported that there are increased numbers of single-parent families, increased numbers of divorces, more remarriages leading to reconstituted and blended families, more people marrying later in life, more women working outside the home, and fewer children in families. It is worth noting that only about 3 percent of families fit the definition of a "traditional family," where the male was the sole provider or breadwinner and the mother stayed at home (Barnett & Rivers, 1996).

Advancing one's career while taking care of children requires strategic thinking and balancing several life roles. The two basic options for parents (usually mothers) are the *career primary option* and the *career-family primary option*. The latter group of workers is willing to change their work schedules, and perhaps their career goals, to accommodate the needs of their children. They may do this by working flexible hours, switching to part-time, changing a career path, dropping out of the workforce completely for a period of time, or starting their own business. This decision is usually made after the birth of a second child because child-care demands become too overwhelming, and the old arrangements are no longer sufficient (Kantrowitz & Wingert, 1993). There is considerable controversy about this *career-family primary* option, but it appears to be one way to create a new family system that balances work and family alternatives. Although women may pursue this most often, small numbers of men are increasingly choosing this *career-family primary* option as well. We will explore this topic later in this chapter.

FOUR GENERATIONS VIEW WORK/FAMILY BALANCE

In an effort to learn more about gender and generational differences in work/family attitudes and values, the Families and Work Institute (FWI; 2004) surveyed four groups of adults in 2002: Generation Y, 18–22; Generation X, 23–37; Baby Boomers, 38–57, and Matures, 58+. Table 10.1 summarizes some of the findings regarding childcare, career advancement, gender roles, and job retention. The FWI researchers also found that dual- and family-centered workers, compared to those who were work-centered, reported better mental health, greater life satisfaction, and higher job satisfaction.

Boomers were more likely to be work-centered than people in other generations. Gen-X and Gen-Y were more likely to be dual-centered or family-centered. This finding has important

TABLE 10.1 GENERATIONAL VIEWS OF WORK/FAMILY BALANCE				
Work/Family Balance Issue	Gen-Y (under 23)	Gen-X (23–37)	Boomer (38–57)	Mature (58 or older)
Work centered	13%	13%	22%	12%
Family centered	50%	52%	41%	34%
Dual centered	37%	35%	37%	54%
Time with children under 18 per workday	—	3.4 hrs.	2.2 hrs	—
Endorse traditional gender roles (woman as homemaker; man as breadwinner)	37%	40%	40%	51%
Leave current employer within year	70%	43%	—	—

implications for the development of policies and programs in work organizations regarding balance in home and family life. These data provided evidence that most American workers are rejecting the work-centered style of their father's workplace. Gen-X men led the way in spending time with children under 18, and the few Gen-Y fathers in the sample seemed to have a similar priority on family life. FWI researchers speculated about these generational differences, noting that younger men have first-hand experience with a working mother outside the home, they have seen "permanent" jobs replaced by "employment at will," and they were impacted by 9/11.

FWI (2004) researchers found that among college-educated men and women, Gen-Y, Gen-X, and Boomer groups desiring to move into jobs with more responsibility declined by 16 and 21 percent from 1992–2002, respectively. This change in career ambition is relatively dramatic and has been noted by organizations seeking to fill top management positions. Adjustments to workplaces and jobs may be required in order to attract younger men and women into higher-level positions. Only 39 percent of workers would like to have jobs with greater responsibility.

Consistent with the findings reported earlier by Horrigan and Herz (2004), Families and Work Institute (2004) researchers found that married men employees were spending more time on workdays doing household work than 25 years ago, 1.9 versus 1.2 hours. Married women employees had reduced their time in homemaking from 3.3 hours per workday in 1977 to 2.7 hours in 2002, and this time was being made up by their spouses.

This report by the Families and Work Institute regarding generational views of work and family life provides important information for career planning. It helps us understand how attitudes about balancing work and family life differ across generations. Gen-Y workers need to understand that their supervisors and managers from other generations may have different values regarding working extra hours, taking care of family members, and career advancement. These differences can form the basis for supervisory discussions and mentoring.

FACTORS AFFECTING WOMEN'S CAREERS

The careers of women have been affected by a number of factors over the years. These include low pay, stress, traditional sex-role expectations, occupational stereotypes, glass ceilings, harassment, and entrepreneurship in the workplace. If you are a woman, think about your personal occupational and employment goals as you read about these factors. If you're a man, imagine what it would be like if some of these factors impacted your career goals.

Stay-at-Home Mom. Jason (2004) reported a Census Bureau study that revealed 5.4 million U.S. mothers stayed at home in 2003. The analysis showed that 20 percent of them lived in households with incomes of $100,000 or more while 2.3 percent were in households earning less than $10,000. Mothers who stay at home are either in the top 5 percent or the lower 25 percent of income. About 88 percent of the women reported they stayed at home to care for children. About 98,000 dads also stayed at home, but only 16 percent indicated it was to care for children. The high cost of child care is a consideration in whether or not a parent stays at home with children.

More recently, the PEW Research Center (2007) reported that full-time work has lost some of its appeal to mothers with children 17 and under. Only 21 percent say full-time work is an ideal situation for them, down from 32 percent who said this in 1997. Sixty percent say that part-time work would be ideal, and 19 percent prefer not to work at all outside the home. Interestingly, these views are not shared by fathers, with 72 percent of whom think the ideal situation for them would be a full-time job. (This is related to the male breadwinner role discussed in the next section.)

Glass Ceiling and Stereotypes. As women entered work organizations in increasing numbers in the 1980s, many of them experienced the phenomenon of the "glass ceiling." The term refers to artificial barriers based on attitudes and organizational bias that prevent qualified women from advancing into mid- and senior-level management positions (Vega, 1993). When women are unable to enter such leadership positions in organizations, they cannot directly influence the missions, policies, plans, strategies, and activities of an organization. Only 1 percent of chief executives of Fortune 500 companies are women (Joyce, 2005), and only 17 women lead Fortune 1000 companies. To become CEOs, women must first reach positions in organizations that generate revenues or have profit-loss responsibilities. However, women with an aggressive, risk-taking style, and wanting to get to the top may be viewed more negatively than men with the same traits (Joyce, 2005).

Harassment. Zunker (2006) cited reports concluding that sexual harassment was the single most widespread occupational hazard women faced in the workforce. This included sexual remarks, suggestive looks, deliberate touching, pressure for dates, unwanted letters and calls, pressure for sexual favors, and actual or attempted sexual assault. A study of 2,000 recent college graduates reported similar rates of harassment and discrimination, up to 30 percent for women (Gardner & Lambert, 1993). These women graduates indicated great surprise in the prevalence of harassment they encountered on the job and indicated they were unprepared for it.

FACTORS AFFECTING MEN'S CAREERS

The movement of women into the workplace and other areas of society has caused men to reexamine many of their roles, beliefs, and values. Zunker (2006) cited research indicating that many men have not had an easy time adjusting to the egalitarian movement toward equal rights for women. Boys are expected to be masculine, and this includes behavioral traits such as being active, aggressive, independent, and brave. These traits are not always compatible with the new social situations at work and at home that involve teamwork, negotiating, shared power, and compromise. Let's examine some of the other changing social factors currently affecting men's careers.

Breadwinner. Perhaps the most powerful gender stereotype or schema associated with men working is the concept of "breadwinner." From earliest times in food-gathering societies, men have been viewed as the hunters who came back from the forest with food that had been trapped or killed in order to feed the family. In the industrial society, men went off to work in the factory in order to buy bread to feed the family. Males were expected to go out and obtain what was necessary for family survival. Men have perceived career success in terms of achievement, status, power, and control in their work. These schema have dominated the male idea of career. However, the role of breadwinner has been modified today somewhat, because women are also assuming more responsibility for this role in family life.

There appears to be some complex forces operating with respect to the breadwinner role for men. For example, Cohany and Sok (2007) reported that women who had husbands paid at the top and bottom 20 percent of income levels had the lowest participation rates in the workforce, 48 percent in 2005. This suggests that the male breadwinner role is still alive and well as these women choose not to work outside the home. At the same time, a new code for men may be emerging. Orecklin (2004) found that 64 percent of Gen-X men preferred a female boss or had no preference, and 80 percent agreed or strongly agreed that they would feel comfortable dating a woman who earned significantly more.

Androgyny. While masculinity is often associated with social power, group leadership, physical toughness, lack of intimacy, logical thought, and ambition, femininity is often associated with submissiveness, frailty, emotions, nurturing, and limited physical strength (Zunker, 2006). However, these distinctions are breaking down in modern life, and androgyny, or the presence of both masculine and feminine qualities in each person, provides both men and women with opportunities to move beyond the traditional gender stereotypes. Along with androgyny, the fear of femininity creates problems for men who no longer find themselves the primary breadwinners in their families. The thought of being an androgynous male is quite unappealing to these men and makes it difficult for them to incorporate child care and housework into their life/career roles.

Traditional Male Careers. Men tend to work in traditional occupations, meaning that at least 30 percent or more of the workers are of the same sex. Figure 10.1 showed that men tend to work mostly in Realistic and Enterprising occupations, e.g., engineers (89 percent), dentists (81 percent). In reality, some of the most segregated occupations by gender are those dominated by women, including preschool and kindergarten teachers (98 percent) and registered nurses (93 percent). Unlike women, most men have been unwilling to move into nontraditional occupations, and this tends to limit their occupational alternatives (Zaldivar, 1996). In particular, it may exclude jobs in health care and education.

Stay-at-Home Dad. Steven Church (2004) reported on how growing numbers of men are slowing down their professional growth in order to spend more time with their families, something an earlier generation of women did. Younger men (Gen-X as we identified them earlier) are following a different parenting model. Church noted a study by the Society for Human Resource Management where men ranked the need to balance work and family life higher than their female colleagues did. Church also noted a U.S. Census study that found a 54 percent increase from 1986 to 2003 in the number of married men staying home while their wives worked. However, this percentage change must be viewed in light of the numbers involved—3.6 million men out of 58.6 million married couples. Orecklin (2004) reported slightly different numbers based on a different poll. In this survey, 22 percent of Gen-Xers in their 20s through early 40s were stay-at-home dads.

Technology. With advances in technology, men are increasingly doing business from home as free-lancers, entrepreneurs, or telecommuters (Martin, 2003). High-speed Internet access and personal digital assistants have created a 24–7 work mentality in a virtual office, which provides for more flexible work hours and more time with family. However, this also creates some areas of stress.

Orecklin (2004) found that 75 percent of men polled indicated they were concerned with keeping up with changing job skills involving technology. Bond et al. (2002) reported that nearly two thirds of workers use computers for their jobs daily, and more than a third sometimes use a computer at home for job-related work. Not surprisingly, workers who use cell phones, beepers, pagers, or e-mail report the most spillover from jobs into home life, especially if they use technology to stay in touch with family and friends.

In summary, it is apparent that men, like women, are finding themselves in some uncharted areas regarding work-family balance. At the same time, there is evidence that younger men are creating new models for balancing these conflicting values.

DUAL-CAREER FAMILIES: PROBLEM AREAS

We have briefly explored some of the trends in the employment of women and men in contemporary America and some of the factors that are affecting their careers. Now we will focus on the nature of the spouse/partner relationship in relation to their separate and mutual careers. As you review this material, think about how it applies to your life/career goals. How will these ideas improve your strategic career thinking?

Families in which both parents work are called dual-career or dual-earner families. The term *dual-career* is usually reserved for families in which both spouses hold professional, managerial, or technical jobs. Following the definition of "career" presented in Chapter 1, in a dual-career both people are engaged in the time extended working out of a purposeful life pattern through work undertaken by the people. Obviously, this is a much more complicated career situation, because each person is effectively seeking to manage the two careers embodied in the relationship. The issues surrounding such careers and strategies for implementing them are the focus of this section.

Child and Elder Care

Bond et al. (2002) reported that dual earner families have increased from 66 percent in 1977 to 78 percent in 2002. Couples with children spend 91 combined hours per week at work, and 6.2 hours with their children. Surprisingly, both of these numbers reflect increases from 1977, and this probably means that working parents have less time for themselves. Throughout this chapter, we have stressed the time demands on employed couples, and the care of other family members, including children and aging parents, is a major source of difficulty.

Travel and Relocation

Another problem area for dual career couples involves travel and relocation. When one spouse or partner is traveling, then the load of care giving shifts to the one remaining at home.

One of the most difficult issues for dual-career couples involves relocation and the possible dislocation that it brings. This could result in a decreased standard of living, because the jobs that trailing spouses have to take in the new location provide less salary and benefits. There are also changes in housing, climate, children's schools, and closeness to other extended family members that can be positive or negative. International moves significantly complicate relocation issues because laws in most countries prevent spouses from working.

When one partner gets a promotion or transfer, the "trailing spouse" can be left in the lurch. In the past, women appeared to be more willing than men to be the "trailing spouse." In order to make it easier for dual-career couples to relocate and to implement transfers of workers, organizations are increasingly contracting with management-consulting firms to provide spouse relocation assistance. This is designed to help the trailing spouse more quickly find employment.

Handling Stress in Dual Careers

How are men and women in dual careers handling the stress? Barnett and Rivers (1996) spent four years studying dual career full-time working couples in the Boston area. They found them to be tired and stressed but also healthy and happy. More specifically, the research indicated that women weren't having levels of depression and anxiety that homemakers of the 1950s experienced, and fathers were more involved in their children's lives than many of their own fathers had been. The biggest problem for dual-career couples involved inflexible employers who did not want to acknowledge that employees' personal lives were affected by their work and who failed to offer family-friendly benefits.

STRATEGIES FOR MANAGING WORK AND FAMILY LIFE

In this section, we offer some additional thoughts about managing dual-career relationships at home and at work. Men and women can use some of these strategies directly in their lives, and others will require organizations to change their cultures to help reduce home/work conflicts that affect working men and women and their children.

Individual Strategies

What are some of the personal and individual activities that people can use to achieve more balance in work and family life?

Clarifying and Limiting Roles and Relationships. It seems clear that problems arise when dual-career partners do not have a shared schema or vision regarding home and family life. Typically, one partner believes the other should take a secondary role in career aspirations and effort.

In the process of clarifying dual-career roles and relationships, partners might review their roles and relationships, e.g., child, student, worker, spouse/partner, homemaker, citizen (Super, 1990), and share views about which ones are essential in their dual-career relationship. It is probably not possible to fully engage in more than several of these roles at any one time, especially without the support and role sharing of another person, members of an extended family, or contracted home-making services (e.g., nanny, maid).

Developing Social Support Systems. Support systems for dual-careers include a variety of arrangements, ranging from car pools to help with transportation to caregivers going into the child's own home. Social networks of extended family members, friends, neighbors, and associates exchange time and care-giving services with one another.

Given all that is happening at work and at home, who will survive these changes? What kinds of individuals will be successful? Jerald Hage (1995), whose ideas were first introduced in Chapter 6, suggested that individuals who can continuously redefine their life roles by renegotiating who will do what, when, and how are most likely to succeed. The fact that so many of these negotiations end up in divorce court is evidence of how far we need to go in this area. More specifically, Hage concluded that individuals who can use the following higher-order cognitive processes have the best chance to prevail.

1. Those who are able to engage in highly creative problem solving using new symbols, relationships, and techniques. For example, how does one become both a father and a mother and a worker outside the home?

2. Those who can use complex images of themselves—more than a simply a person of one gender, race, religion, or nation—to view social problems at home or work from multiple vantage points that take into account another person's view. The capacity to do this makes it easier to negotiate new role relationships.

Judith Warner (2005), writing in her new book *Mommy Madness*, observed that finding a "balance" in life is hard, stressful, and expensive. The harsh realities of family life in our culture, with few structures in place that allow women and men to balance work and childcare or eldercare, means that "career choices" are nonexistent or very limited. "It almost never occurs to them that they can use the muscle of their superb education or their collective voice to change or rearrange their social support system. They simply don't have the political reflex—or the vocabulary—to think of things in this way" (Warner, 2005, p. 2). In the following section, we'll examine some organizational and governmental responses to this problem.

Our book stresses the importance of using Cognitive Information Processing Theory in solving career problems and making career decisions.

College students must develop more complex PCTs in this regard, which should include strategies for social change.

Organizational and Governmental Strategies

Is the matter of work-life balance an individual problem or is it a national problem? Some suggest that it is a problem that needs to be addressed at the societal level by organizations and governments. With respect to business organizations, how is the cost of such programs balanced with the benefits? The Employment Policy Foundation (2005) reported that compliance with the Family Medical Leave Act cost employers $21 billion dollars in 2004. However, a study by Arthur and Cook (2004) found that 231 work-family human resource policies adopted by Fortune 500 companies suggested these initiatives positively affected shareholder return. Furthermore, innovative programs attract and retain better and more talented workers, and they actually do help employees balance work and family life. In sum, the benefits may exceed the potential costs. In this section, we examine some of the things affecting career and family roles that you can look for in researching potential employers.

Family-Friendly Organizations. These organizations provide various kinds of child-care arrangements for workers. They have been motivated to do this in order to retain valued employees. These programs include the following elements provided by the employing organization (Zunker, 2006):

- *Emergency care*. Provides temporary care for children when the employee's regular arrangement fails or when the child or elder is sick.

- *Discounts*. Arranges for a discount on regular child-care fees.

- *Vouchers*. Pays some portion of the charges or offers special assistance to help employees pay for child care.

- *Referral service*. Offers a list of approved daycare and elder-care centers to employees.

- *On-site day care*. Provides child daycare centers that are located at the work site, often in the same building.

- *Flexible benefits*. Fees for day care are deducted from employees' salary and are not considered part of taxable income; benefits for domestic partners.

- *Alternate work arrangements*. Flextime, job sharing, telecommuting, work from home, compressed workweeks, sabbaticals.

- *Leisure support*. Vacation childcare, vacation banks, fitness club memberships.

In researching organizations for possible employment, and in considering job offers, you can use this kind of information about family-friendly organizations in assessing how supportive the employer might be in helping you manage a dual-career relationship.

Increasing women and family-friendly people on corporate boards. Catalyst (www.catalystwomen.org), an organization based in New York City, has long sought to increase the numbers of women on corporate boards of directors. They consider this the only long-lasting solution to making private companies adopt policies that are more supportive of family needs. In a recent study, Catalyst (2007) reported that in 2007 women held 14.7 percent of the seats on boards of Fortune 500 companies. Given these numbers, it is no wonder that organizations have difficulty adopting policies and programs supportive of people in dual careers and/or seeking to solve work-family problems.

Obtaining lists of family-friendly companies. Organizations that have developed model family-friendly programs are available on the Internet. For example, WFC Resources (formerly the Work-Family Connection), www.workfamily.com/, which helps organizations develop policies and programs that promote work/life balance for workers, identifies the 100 Best Companies for Working Mothers, and rates companies in terms of several family-friendly categories. Magazines, such as *Working Mother* (www.workingmother.com) and *Career Woman* (www.careerwomen. com) also provide lists of companies with family-friendly benefits and descriptions of their programs. Job hunters can examine the programs of organizations on these lists to learn what kinds of services and accommodations might be available from employers. This might be a factor in deciding to accept or reject a job offer.

Developing national policies regarding leave and child care. The United States was slow to develop national policies on childcare and maternal leave. Scarr, Phillips, and McCartney (1989) reported that among 100 industrialized countries, the United States was the sole exception to the rule of providing paid, job-protected maternal leave as national policy. In 1994, the federal government did pass the Family and Medical Leave Act, which allows workers to take up to 12 weeks of *unpaid* leave during any 12 month period for the birth or adoption of a child, the employee's serious health condition that limits the ability to work, or serious illness of a family member. This law was updated in January 2008. It remains to be seen whether or not this national program can be enhanced in the future to become more like those of other nations.

Developing on-ramps for women's careers. Organizations seeking management and leadership talent in the future will need to retain and reconnect with highly qualified women. Hewlett, Luce, Shiller, and Southwell (2005) reported that more than 58 percent of college graduates are now women and 45 percent of graduate and professional degrees are awarded to women, and these trends are projected to increase. Organizations have made it easy for women to leave (off-ramp) but difficult to return to work (on-ramp). It is apparent that women who minimize their needs as mothers to the needs of demanding workplaces will have more success in their occupations (Conant, 2007).

How can organizations change this situation for women? Hewlett and Luce (2005) suggested that employers need to make it attractive for them to return by creating reduced-hour jobs, providing flexibility in the workday, changing the timelines for tenure or partnership status, removing the stigma of taking time off, offering outlets for altruism such as eldercare or childcare, and nurturing women's ambition.

Public policy changes. Warner (2005) identified a variety of possible governmental strategies: (1) tax subsidies encouraging corporations to adopt family-friendly policies; (2) government mandated child-care standards; (3) affordable, flexible, high-quality, part-time day care; (4) developing vouchers or tax credits for part-time workers to make child care affordable; (5) progressive tax policies that transfer wealth back to the middle class so workers do not have to work excessive hours to achieve financial security. Rubin (2004) further noted that moving away from the "breadwinner-homemaker" model to a "dual-earner/dual-career" model means recognizing children as public goods and work-family balance as a public problem rather than a private problem. In comparison to 12 European countries and Canada, it is apparent that the U.S. has a long way to go in this regard (Rubin, 2004).

Overcoming the complex, difficult problems associated with gender, relationships, and work will require solutions drawn from many elements in society, including individuals, couples, organizations, and governments. In the next section, we will examine what actually happened to workers regarding home-career issues in one company.

AMERCO: CASE STUDY OF A FAMILY-FRIENDLY COMPANY

In order to find out what really goes on regarding work-family issues in a big, family-friendly company, Dr. Arlie Hochschild (1997), a sociologist, spent three years living and working with employees at all levels in an organization. In order to protect the workers and the company, she gave it a fictitious name of "Amerco." Let's examine some of the findings that emerged from her research.

Amerco was a Fortune 500 company with over 21,000 employees that competed globally for markets. Like modern organizations we have learned about in Part Two, Amerco had instituted a team-based approach to management and become a "leaner" organization. It was also very profitable. Even though Amerco had won awards for its family-friendly programs, such as flextime and telecommuting, it was losing many of its most highly trained women faster than it was losing men. Top management felt that the work-family balance was not right and wanted to find out why women were leaving. Hochschild discovered many things about the Work-Family Balance program at Amerco:

- Despite available options, 99 percent of Amerco employees worked full-time, which was 47 hours per week.

- Flextime was the most popular family-friendly program—25 percent of all workers used it, including 33 percent of working parents.

- Less than 1 percent shared a job, and only 3 percent of parents with young children took advantage of part-time work options.

- Workers with young children actually put in more hours at work than those without children.

Hochschild wondered why Amerco's workers were not taking advantage of these family-friendly programs. Did they need the money? Were they afraid of being laid off? Did they not know how to use the programs? Were the programs just for show? The answers to all these questions seemed to be "no." Hochschild came to *the conclusion that the family-friendly programs were not being used at Amerco because working families were not asking to use them.* Why weren't they asking?

The answers that Hochschild began to uncover at Amerco are somewhat unsettling, because they do not fit with many of our established ways of thinking about this matter.

- The declining quality of home life led many people to find "pink slips" at home, whereas harmony and orderliness were found at work. Poor marriages, lack of friendliness, child-care needs, and other problems at home made work a better place to spend time, according to 50 percent of Amerco workers. Work was a refuge from family problems.

- Workers felt more "at home" at work because they were more appreciated and competent there.

- The crush on time led to increased efficiencies in home life, including the outsourcing of many home services. Ironically, the workplace had become less hurried and more relaxed than the home.

- Amerco's corporate culture believed that time at work (face-time) was a sign of commitment, just as much as the production accomplished with that time. In effect, this belief undercut the family-friendly programs.

- The idea of a "family man" at Amerco had come to mean a worker who was not a serious player, and men avoided using family-friendly programs because it was understood that participation in such programs would self-sabotage their career.

- Amerco had far more power over families' time than families had over Amerco; consequently, parents stole time from their children, not the company, in order to get things done. Ironically, the higher the parents' income, the more time the children spent in childcare.

- Although parents were spending more time at work (first shift), and the time at home was more rushed (second shift), parents were then forced to spend additional time (third shift) coping with their children's negative emotional reactions to the compressed time at home. This third shift contributed to making work at home more difficult.

Unfortunately, Hochschild did not uncover any easy solutions to the career time binds at Amerco. She found parents using three strategies. First, some just minimized the problem and made do with less time, less fun, less support, and less understanding. Second, some readjusted their ideas about being a good parent or spouse and paid others to take care of the children, clean the house, or mow the lawn. Third, some divided themselves into the real self with little time to get things done and the potential self who was always available to do things. To illustrate this last point, Hochschild told of a man who had purchased thousands of dollars of fishing equipment years ago that had never been used.

Readers should know that Amerco stopped the Work-Life Balance program after Hochschild completed her study. The company decided to put greater focus on flextime and flexplace so workers were offered a chance to work long hours at different times of days and locations, but nothing was done to help them work shorter hours (Hochschild, 2005).

We can learn a great deal from the workers' experiences at Amerco. First, we realize that finding a balance in work-family life is very complex and difficult. Second, it is apparent that some segments of society still adhere to traditional gender models of work and family. Moreover, there may be gaps between policies (what is said) and practices (what is done) in this regard. Third, work at Amerco provided compelling social attractors for both men and women. People felt better at work, and it is apparent that making family life attractive can be difficult. Fourth, providing sufficient time for child care and nurturing was a source of considerable stress in finding an optimum life-work balance.

Now we will analyze the matter of career and family issues from a CIP perspective.

A CIP PERSPECTIVE

In this chapter, we have examined information related to gender and work-family roles. We believe this topic is very important relative to successful career planning and employment. Let's examine what we've learned in light of the Pyramid of Information-Processing Domains and the CASVE Cycle. Our goal is to help you develop a more useful PCT for solving complex career problems and making career decisions.

Self-Knowledge

This chapter focused on the impact of work on family life and vice versa. Both women and men are increasingly recognizing the importance of fully clarifying personal and career values in solving career problems and making career decisions.

Throughout this book we have used Holland's (1997) RIASEC theory to help us think about ourselves and our options. These ideas also have application in considering work-family options. The Holland code for homemaker is SEC, and men or men who have a personal code including these three letters might find caring for children or family members and managing a household to be a good match for them, at least for a period of time. The point is that self-knowledge about our personality and interests from a Holland perspective might be useful in deciding whether or not to engage the homemaker role at some point.

Option Knowledge

The schema regarding women and men at work, separately and in dual-career situations, present new ways of thinking about careers. The option of a dual career is relatively new in contemporary careers, and it affects men and women in various ways. However, the nine roles that Super (1990) identified (see Chapter 1)—child (son or daughter), student, worker, spouse or partner, homemaker, leisurite, parent or grandparent, annuitant/pensioner, and citizen—remain the basic roles for any life/career, including persons in dual-career situations. Career remains an important vehicle for defining our self-concept, as well as our lives at work and in other social relationships.

Thinking about career options in relation to gender would not be complete without mentioning the role of organizations and public policy. The United States has been very slow to develop national policies regarding work and family life; indeed, it is unique in this regard among industrialized nations. The lack of public policy has not served citizens well, or organizations for that matter. There is evidence that more organizations want to become family-friendly, because it gives them some advantages in retaining good employees. At the same time, there is some evidence that the culture of many organizations does not reward women (or men) who make substantial commitments to family life. In exploring career and work options, you need to examine closely the culture and history of organizations in this regard.

Decision Making

The values and priorities that men and women attach to family and career are played out in decisions about having children, how the children will be cared for, how employment relocation options are handled, and how time for independence and leisure is created within work-family roles and relationships. These would typically occur in the Valuing phase of the CASVE Cycle.

In dual-career situations, decision making is ideally carried out on the basis of negotiated agreements, assuming both individuals have equity in the decision. This is a more complex kind of decision making because two people and a relationship are involved. However, the CASVE Cycle could still be used as a guide to help a dual-career couple go through the process of making decisions about issues such as childcare, elder care, or relocation. For example, the process of agreeing on the nature of the gap in the Communication phase could help clarify the issues associated with a possible relocation move:

- How are we feeling about our present circumstances?

- Are we happy?

- Do we need more income?

- Do we need a bigger house?

- Do we need to live farther away from (or closer to) our parents?

- Do we need to live in a different climate?

- Does one of us need a better job?

A couple could have the same discussions about topics in the Analysis, Synthesis, Valuing, and Execution phases of the CASVE Cycle.

Throughout this chapter, we have emphasized the idea of making career decisions in order to achieve balance in life roles. However, we noted that the Work-Life Balance program at Amerco was not continued. Perhaps a new understanding of balance is needed. Elizabeth McKenna (1997), a former top publishing executive, suggested that there is something very wrong with our work culture, which requires men and women to make choices that are not congruent with their personal values or needs. Workers sometimes come to feel that they are at fault for not "fitting in," but in reality it is the organization that obsessively wants more work from them. Perhaps a more humanized work environment is needed, one that respects the values of workers.

Executive Processing

Negative thinking makes it more difficult to cope effectively with the dual-career issues discussed in this chapter. There is also evidence that college students and teenagers have not developed metacognitions that will enable them to effectively grapple with complex dual-career issues. As we indicated earlier, we need more complex metacognitions to build effective PCTs that will enable us to solve these kinds of career problems and make effective career decisions.

For example, at the beginning of this chapter, we noted a study of college students who failed to see connections between "career" and family or spouse/partner relationships (Gerken, Reardon & Bash, 1988). The reality, of course, is that 70 percent of men and 56 percent of women were employed outside the home in 2002 (U.S. Department of Labor, 2004). These data reinforce the need for college students to develop new metacognitions for addressing work-family issues.

Hage (1995) helped us understand that people who will have successful careers in the Information Age will be able to think in complex ways about their life roles, to negotiate new creative solutions to role-related problems at home and work, and will be able to move beyond simple categories in their thinking about career problems. At earlier times in our history, less complex ways of thinking about career were sufficient, but new solutions are needed now. In CIP terms, these are new metacognitions, new schema, that we have the freedom and challenge to create and use in solving career problems.

Perhaps most important, however, is the need to deal with the uncertainty about work-family roles and relationships. Matthews and Rodin (1989) described the movement of women into the workforce as "a natural experiment of enormous proportions." There are many signs available in society that individuals and organizations are not dealing with matters related to gender and work very effectively. At the same time, there is abundant evidence that both women and men are benefiting from the new ideas emerging about blending home and family life.

SUMMARY

This chapter has examined issues associated with the movement of women into the workplace outside the home and the impact of this change on men and social organizations. We looked at factors affecting the ways men and women work in contemporary America, and we examined issues associated with dual-career couples. Issues associated with the time binds brought on by work and family needs were explored in the case study of Amerco, a family-friendly company. The chapter concluded with a CIP perspective on gender and work and offered suggestions for building a more effective Personal Career Theory for solving career problems and making career decisions.

REFERENCES

Arthur, M. M., & Cook, A. (2004). Taking stock of work-family initiatives: How announcements of "family-friendly" human resource decisions affect shareholder value. *Industrial & Labor Relations Review, 57*, 599–613.

Barnett, R., & Rivers, C. (1996). *She works he works*. New York: Harper Collins.

Bolles, R. (2008). *A practical manual for job hunters and career changers: What color is your parachute?* Berkeley, CA: Ten Speed Press.

Bond, J. T., Thompson, C., Galinsky, E., and Prottas, D. (2002). *Highlights of the national study of the changing workforce: Executive summary.* New York: Families and Work Institute.

Catalyst (2007). Women gain Board committee chairs in the Fortune 500. Retrieved February 25, 2008 from http://www.catalyst.org/knowledge/files/census_board.pdf.

Church, S. (2004, November 26). More Gen-X dads choose their family over career. *USA Today*, p. 10B.

Cohany, S. R., & Sok, E. (2007, February). Trends in labor force participation of married mothers of infants. *Monthly Labor Review*, pp. 9–16.

Conant, E. (2007, May 28). Trying to opt back in. *Newsweek*, p. 42.

Employment Policy Foundation (2005, April 19). FMLA cost employers $21 billion in 2004 (News Release). Retrieved April 26, 2005 from http://www.epf.olrg/news/pring_nrelease.asp.

Families and Work Institute (2004). *Generation and gender in the workplace* (Issue Brief). Watertown, MA: American Business Collaboration.

Galinsky, E., Kim, S. S., & Bond, J. T. (2001). *Feeling overworked: When work becomes too much (Executive summary).* New York: Families and Work Institute.

Gardner, P., & Lambert, S. (1993, Winter). It's a hard, hard, hard, hard, hard, hard world. *Journal of Career Planning & Employment*, pp. 41–49.

Gerken, D., Reardon, R., & Bash, R. (1988). Revitalizing a career course: The gender roles infusion. *Journal of Career Development, 14,* 269–278.

Hage, J. (1995). Post-industrial lives: New demands, new prescriptions. In A. Howard (Ed.), *The changing nature of work* (pp. 485–512). San Francisco: Jossey-Bass.

Hewlett, S. A., & Luce, C. B. (2005, March). Off-ramps and on-ramps: Keeping talented women on the road to success. *Harvard Business Online,* retrieved May 3, 2005, at www.womenscareersreport.hg\br.org.

Hewlett, S. A., Luce, C. B., Shiller, P., & Southwell, S. (2005, March). *The hidden brain drain: Off-ramps and on-ramps in women's careers.* Cambridge, MA: Harvard Business Review Research Report.

Hochschild, A. R. (1997). *The time bind: When work becomes home and home becomes work.* New York: Metropolitan Books.

Hochschild, A. R. (2005). Personal communication to R. Reardon, May 6, 2005.

Holland, J. L. (1997). *Making vocational choices.* Odessa, FL: Psychological Assessment Resources, Inc.

Horrigan, M., & Herz, D. (2004, October). Planning, designing, and executing the BLS American time-use survey. *Monthly Labor Review*, pp. 3–19.

Jackson, M. (1998, April 15). Stressed employees bring problems home. *Tallahassee Democrat*, p. 3A.

Jason, S. (2004, December 1). Census: 5.4 million mothers are choosing to stay at home. *USA Today*, p. 3A.

Joyce, A. (2005, February 27). Women at the top work in the spotlight. *Tallahassee Democrat*, p. 2E.

Kantrowitz, B., & Wingert, P. (1993, February). Being smart about the mommy track. *Working Woman*, pp. 49–51, 80–81.

Martin, J. (2003, May 12). Work-at-home fathers becoming less unusual. *Crain's Chicago Business, 26*(19), 10–11.

Matthews, K. A., & Rodin, J. (1989). Women's changing work roles. *American Psychologist, 44,* 1389–1393.

McKenna, E. P. (1997). *When work doesn't work anymore: Women, work, and identity.* New York: Delacorte Press.

Orecklin, M. (2004, August 23). Stress and the superdad. *Time*, pp. 38–39.

Park, A. (2005, February 21). Between a rocker and a high chair. *Business Week*, p. 86.

PEW Research Center (2007, July 12). Fewer mothers prefer full-time work. Author. Retrieved July 12, 2007, from http://pewresearch.org/assets/social/pdf/womenworking.pdf.

Pierret, C. R. (2006, September). The "sandwich generation": Women caring for parents and children. *Monthly Labor Review*, pp. 3–9.

Rubin, B. A. (2004, October). Review of *Families That Work*, by J. C. Gornick and M. K. Meyers. *Industrial & Labor Relations Review*, 58, 147–149.

Scarr, S., Phillips, D., & McCartney, K. (1989). Working mothers and their families. *American Psychologist*, 44, 1402–1409.

St. George, D. (1996, January 28). America's downsizing affects more than workers. *Tallahassee Democrat*, p. 6A.

Super, D. (1990). A life-span, life-space approach to career development. In D. Brown & L. Brooks (Eds.), *Career choice and development* (2nd ed., pp. 197–261). San Francisco: Jossey-Bass.

Toossi, M. (2007, November). Labor force projections to 2016: More workers in their golden years. *Monthly Labor Review*, pp. 33–52.

U.S. Department of Labor. (2007, Summer). Parents and work, 2006. *Occupational Outlook Quarterly*, p. 48.

U.S. Department of Labor (2004, October). Time-use survey results. *Monthly Labor Review Online*. Retrieved March 2, 2005 from http://stats.bls.gov/opub/mlr/2004/10/lmir/htm.

Vega, J. (1993, Spring). Crack in the glass ceiling? *Career Woman*, pp. 43–45.

Warner, J. (2005). *Mommy madness*. Retrieved February 16, 2005 from http://www.manbc.msn.com/id/6959880/site/newsweek/.

Weinberg, D. (2007, July/August). Earnings by gender: Evidence from Census 2000. *Monthly Labor Review*, pp. 26–34.

Zaldivar, R. A. (1996, July 15). Come on guys and ride the glass escalator into "women's work." *Tallahassee Democrat*, p. 1A.

Zunker, V. (2006). *Career counseling* (7th ed.). Pacific Grove, CA: Brooks/Cole.

Implementing a Strategic Career Plan

LAUNCHING AN EMPLOYMENT CAMPAIGN

This chapter deals with how to approach a job campaign. CIP is the basic theoretical model used in this text, so in this chapter we will apply it to the job-hunting process.

Are college seniors concerned about employment? There is considerable evidence that they are. Denise Smith and Linda Gast (1998) reported that 76 percent of college seniors responding to a senior transition survey were concerned about finding a job and adjusting to work. Other publications attest to the fact that seniors and recent college graduates have anxiety about transitions from college to employment because "their expectations of the workplace (and their lives) do not match reality" (p. 191).

The negative economic climate in the United States over the past several months has clearly affected college recruiting expectations (NACE, 2008, March 19). Overall hiring expectations are still positive for the Class of 2008, with employers expecting to hire 8 percent more graduates from this year's class compared with their actual number of hires from the class of 2007. However, this is significantly lower than the 16 percent they expected to hire six months earlier. The job market for college graduates is expected to remain strong because of increased demand for products and services as well as replacements of current workers. The National Association of Colleges and Employers (NACE) is a good source of job forecast information because it connects staff at nearly 2,000 college and universities and more than 3,000 HR/staffing professionals in college relations and recruiting.

We begin Part Three by discussing the basic idea of a job campaign and the nature of employment problems. After reviewing how job-hunting methods have changed over time, we will examine how CIP theory can be used to guide the development of a job campaign. We will conclude with some specific suggestions for job-hunting strategies in the temporary staffing services industry.

WHAT IS A JOB CAMPAIGN?

Why do we use the word *campaign*? The word is often connected to military or political terms, as in a "political campaign." When we combine campaign with job, we're thinking about a similar operation in magnitude and scope. A job campaign involves thinking about many things:

- Identifying goals and objectives

- Finding resources for identifying potential employers

- Specifying employers and/or job targets

- Considering alternative work settings and ways of working

- Preparing letters and resume(s)

- Contacting employers

- Interviewing with employers

- Making on-site visits

- Maintaining a record-keeping system

- Choosing the best job offer

Perhaps the most important metacognition associated with a job campaign is the need for an active approach—being passive will not produce results. Passive approaches include (1) relying heavily on the Internet for job leads or listings, (2) assuming that the good jobs will be advertised, (3) using the same resume and cover letter for applications, (4) waiting until a month before graduation to get the campaign started, (5) paying a head hunter or employment search firm to run your job campaign, (6) waiting to research information about the employer until after receiving an offer, (7) not applying for jobs if you don't meet all the listed qualifications, and (8) not fully using the resources in your college career center (Connelly, 2007).

A job campaign has been equated with actually having a job; it takes time, preparation, commitment, teamwork, and skill. People engaged in a job campaign often report how much time it takes—up to eight hours every day for weeks and months at a time. People begin their job campaigns at different places, meaning that some have very clear job targets, whereas others are more vague. Moreover, some job campaigns are anticipated (graduation from college), whereas others are not (just laid off from a job).

In Part Three, we view a job campaign as involving a series of activities. In Chapter 12, we examine how written communications, including resume writing, letter writing, record keeping, and use of the Internet, contribute to a successful campaign. Chapter 13 explores topics related to verbal communication, including job interviews, social networking, and information interviews. Chapter 14 examines a critical phase of the employment campaign that is sometimes overlooked— the process of negotiating with prospective employers and deciding between or among job offers. Finally, Chapter 15 explores the transition from college to full-time professional employment, which requires careful planning with respect to budgets, time management, networking, and relationships with supervisors.

THE NATURE OF EMPLOYMENT PROBLEMS

In Chapter 1, a "problem" was defined as a gap between an existing and a desired state of affairs. Stated more simply, it is the difference between *where you are* and *where you want to be*. Here are some examples of gap statements about employment that could lead to a job campaign:

- "I'm about to finish school and I need to get a job."

- "This job is going nowhere. I need to find an employer who will give me the opportunity to get into management."

- "With a new baby, I don't want to work full-time. It is necessary that I earn *some* money. I need to find a part-time job and good child care."

For each of these employment problems, a person needs to figure out how to remove the gap between the existing and desired state of affairs—to move from a present condition to a more desired situation. We will begin by discussing employment problems in general and why we sometimes feel uncertain or overwhelmed when we think about beginning a job search. Our ultimate goal will be to help you use the skills and knowledge gained in previous sections of this text to help you successfully conduct your employment campaign.

Daily living requires solving numerous problems, some simple and some complex. The employment problems we just listed tend to be complicated. For example, we receive numerous complex and ambiguous cues about employment. We are often overwhelmed by information about training opportunities, possibilities for advancement, or the changing job market. Having so much information, some of it conflicting, makes it more difficult to make employment choices.

Also, no matter what our choice may be, there is uncertainty of the outcome. Having selected several potentially appropriate employers, researched the organizations, and prepared a resume and appropriate cover letters, there is no guarantee that we'll get a position with any of the organizations. Several authors in this field have described job hunting as the process of "seeking rejection," not a task that most of us would choose to engage in on a regular basis. Finally, solutions present new problems in that one problem often leads to one or more related subsequent problems. Landing a new job can lead to questions and problems dealing with moving to a new location, selling one's house, employment for a spouse, and so forth (Peterson et al., 1991, 1996).

A BRIEF HISTORY OF JOB HUNTING METHODS

There have been many changes over the years in the way job campaigns are conducted. It is important to remember that job hunting is a relatively recent social invention, and there is a great deal remaining to be studied about this social process. Richard Bolles, the author of *What Color Is Your Parachute?* (Bolles, 2008), described some of these ideas in his newsletter.

Early 1900s. Frank Parsons, the originator of vocational guidance whom we introduced in Chapter 1, described how he would stop at each shopkeeper's store on his way to the Vocations Bureau (career center) in Boston to pick up the day's job notices. He then took them to the Bureau, where they were made available to job seekers. This idea of collecting job notices in a central place was new. Parsons also introduced the idea of matching people to jobs.

1929. Groups of job hunters first began to meet during the Depression to share stories about job hunting with professional counselors. These job-hunting groups had names like Thursday Night Club, Man Marketing Group, and later, Job Club. This was a new idea at the time but a common practice today.

1960. Bernard Haldane, an executive recruiter, studied the success rates for various job-hunting methods and reported that fewer than 5 percent of openings are filled by employment agencies, 15 percent are filled by applications or responses to "help wanted" ads, and 80 percent are filled through recommendations of friends already employed by the organization, by "tips," or other contacts. This laid the foundation for the concept of the "hidden job market."

1965. The practice of sending a cover letter with one's resume when applying for jobs was first introduced (Bolles, 1994). (We'll talk about this more in Chapter 12.)

1966. Networking—using friends, relatives, or other workers to learn about jobs—as an effective job-hunting technique was introduced. Networking proved to be 11 times as effective as using newspaper ads (Bolles, 1994). (This is covered in Chapter 13.)

1970. What Color Is Your Parachute? was first published by Richard Bolles. This book is one of the 100 top-selling books of all time in this country, with over 8 million copies in print (Bolles, 2005).

1973. Job Clubs were born through the work of Nathan Azrin (Azrin & Besalel, 1980), a behavioral psychologist. These groups were highly successful in helping people find jobs; they became a national network to help the unemployed. The groups emphasized that job hunting was a *learnable* skill.

1979. Robert Wegmann, a sociologist at the University of Houston, conducted research and found scientific evidence to support many of our beliefs about job hunting: (1) self-esteem is crucial to a successful job campaign; (2) job hunting is inherently discouraging and almost everyone needs some kind of social support; (3) there are facts to be learned about job hunting; (4) telephone and interviewing skills can be practiced before they are used; (5) the more time spent attempting to get interviews, the more interviews are obtained; and (6) the more interviews obtained, the greater the likelihood of getting a job offer (Wegmann, Chapman & Johnson, 1985).

1996. The Internet becomes an increasingly popular resource for job hunters, and it is now one of the most frequent search options among Internet users. Typing in the word *employment* in any of the popular search engines available on the Internet produces a listing of hundreds of sites with employment-related resources.

1997. One-stop career centers were described by Matthew Mariani (1997). These centers were developed in response to initiatives of the Education and Training Administration of the U.S. Department of Labor, and they are quite different from the old employment service centers. One-stops were designed to simplify the process of a job campaign by putting many services for customers in one place.

1998. In Chapter 9, we noted that a report by the National Association of Colleges and Employers (1996) revealed that 70 percent of employers emphasizing hiring college graduates are using internships and/or cooperative education programs to create a pool of quality job candidates.

This brief historical review helps us understand that some of what we know and believe about job campaigns is based on relatively recent ideas and scientific knowledge. With this background, we can now examine a CIP approach to a job campaign.

EMPLOYERS AND APPLICANTS

Employers and college graduates view the employment process in different ways, and it is useful at the outset of Part Three to compare and contrast these views (Nunamaker & Riley, 2007). Employers regularly report that applicants fail to conduct sufficient research to answer such simple questions as "why do you want to work here?" In addition, employers complain that students don't attend on-campus information sessions, fully utilize services of the campus career center, exhibit professionalism (e.g., write thank-you notes), use strong presentation skills in interviews, or establish a positive impression (e.g., e-mail and voice-mail addresses, Facebook images). Finally, employers note that some students project a sense of entitlement with respect to raises and promotions.

In contrast, college graduates had difficulty comprehending the time line of the interview process and the use of online application procedures. They wanted more information about the organizational culture and the extent to which community service was expected, support was provided for personal and family living, and whether or not vacation days are actually taken by employees. One issue left unresolved was the role of parents in the job campaign process. While a few employers are sending employment information to parents, most wanted the communication to remain exclusively between the applicant and the employer (Nunamaker & Riley, 2007).

But employers and college graduates also have something in common—they are both looking for a high quality interpersonal match that will enable the organization to solve its problems and perform better, and will provide the applicant with a positive working situation for the future. According to a NACE survey, the average cost-per-hire for the employer was $6,177 in 2005, which means that mistakes in finding a good employment match can be costly to the organization (National Association of Colleges and Employers, 2006).

THE CIP APPROACH TO JOB HUNTING

Employment problem solving and decision making can easily be placed in the context of the Pyramid of Information-Processing Domains and the phases of the CASVE Cycle. As with other career choices, job hunters need certain knowledge about themselves and their employment options. This is the base of the pyramid. Next, they need to follow certain steps in using that knowledge to obtain employment. This relates to the middle of the pyramid—the CASVE Cycle—or the process you typically use in solving important problems. Finally, the top of the pyramid is concerned with how thoughts influence the way people solve employment problems. These thoughts (positive or negative) influence the way you go about problem solving and decision making, as well as what you think about yourself and what you know about your options. In the following sections, we will describe the job campaign from a CIP perspective.

Knowledge of Self

The self-knowledge necessary to make an appropriate *employment* choice is somewhat similar to the knowledge necessary to make an appropriate *career* choice. The values, interests, and skills that you considered in making a general occupational choice can now be applied to an employment campaign.

Values motivate us to work. Clarifying your values helps you identify potential employers and work settings that will give you the opportunity to satisfy your values. Determining that an employer and a position appear to offer what you value can help confirm your decision to seek employment with that organization and provide the basis for the quality of the "match" that an employer might ask you about in an interview.

Interests indicate what work activities we enjoy or prefer doing. *People generally end up doing what they are interested in doing.* Clarifying your interests can help you identify specific positions that will allow you to engage in activities you enjoy. By defining and clarifying your interests, you can better identify those employers that are a good match with your personal characteristics.

Skills indicate work tasks (behaviors) that we can successfully perform. This knowledge of the match between your skills and the needs of the organization confirms that pursuing employment with this organization makes sense.

Knowledge of your values, interests, and skills can help you clarify what type of organization, industry, or position offers you the most of what you want in a job. As a result of completing the activities in the first part of this book, you have begun to compile this type of knowledge. However, it is important to remember that this knowledge will continue to evolve and be revised as you gain experience and learn more about jobs. In addition, your search for employment may also be influenced by external factors, such as family, geographic location, and related issues. These are discussed in the next section.

In addition to values, interests, and skills, employment preferences, family situation, and job target may also influence your employment choice. By reviewing occupational information and reflecting on your past paid and unpaid work experience, you can further clarify future employment preferences. For example, a person imagines what it would be like to work irregular hours after reading an occupational description and conducting an information interview with a manager in a retail business. The person may remember how working irregular hours in a summer job influenced his or her lifestyle.

A person's family situation may also influence an employment choice. Family situations include the desire to live close to family members, the employment opportunities for a spouse, fiancée, or partner, the preferences (or bias) of family members, family employment contacts, or the existence of a family business. For example, before accepting a promotion that would involve relocation, you might want to consider the potential impact of such a decision on significant others in your life, whether that be parents, your partner or spouse, your children, or others who are close to you. For some cultural groups, it may be very important to include family members in the employment problem-solving and decision-making process.

Specifying a job target or targets is a very important aspect of the job campaign. Your self-knowledge and your knowledge of options enable you to answer the question "What do I want to do?" We will discuss this in more detail later in this chapter and in the next chapter, but here is a brief summary of what is involved:

1. Consider and specify job families, work settings, and occupational titles of interest to you. These topics were reviewed in Chapters 3 and 7. Examples for each of these areas might be fund-raising, nonprofit agency, and development officer.

2. Consider and specify the geographic location where you want to do the work.

3. Consider and specify who employs people who do what you want to do. This involves researching potential employers in library materials, the Internet, networking contacts, and the like.

Although no position is likely to be an exact match for your values, interests, skills, employment preferences, and family situation, the job offer you accept should provide the best opportunity available to match the factors that are most important to you. Now that we've examined factors related to self-knowledge, we'll look at knowledge about employment options.

Knowledge of Employment Options

In Chapter 3, we focused on the occupational knowledge needed to make a career choice. Another part of career choice is knowledge about specific employment options. The information in Chapters 6 through 10 provided information about the "real" world of work, and this is vital in launching an employment campaign. Information about employment in terms of geographic location, certification and licensure factors, education/training, and leisure issues all apply to employment choices.

Knowledge about employment options is different from more general occupational knowledge in several ways. First, employment information includes specific data about an organizational structure and culture. Second, jobs across different industries can vary widely. Being a biologist and working for either a timber company, a state forestry service, or a forest preservation association can represent very different kinds of work. Third, employment information typically includes information about geographic location. Finally, as noted in Chapter 10, various family issues, including child care and leave policy, may be an important aspect of your employment decisions.

Knowledge of Specific Jobs

Similarities and differences exist between occupational knowledge and employment knowledge. In general, employment knowledge is more specific than occupational knowledge. For example, work tasks for accountants are described broadly to reflect a range of typical employers, whereas the work tasks for a specific accounting position may be much narrower to reflect the needs of a specific organization.

Using again our accounting example, a job hunter is better prepared to research a *specific* employer and position by becoming familiar with the *general* work tasks of accountants. This strategy can help the applicant to clarify missing or conflicting data in the recruitment literature, to ask more focused questions in an employment interview, and to demonstrate to the interviewer that the applicant has the ability to prepare carefully for important tasks. Most of the categories of occupational information identified in Table 3.1 also relate to specific positions.

Knowledge of Employers

In researching employers, the classification systems described in Chapter 3 can be especially helpful. For example, you can use the *Dictionary of Occupational Titles* (U.S. Department of Labor, 1991) to obtain a "definition" of an advertised position. Employers sometimes review these DOT definitions when they create a new position. Similarly, employers can be grouped into manageable concepts via the 20 major industrial categories of the *North American Industry Classification System* (NAICS, see Table 3.4). Using the *Dictionary of Holland Occupational Codes* (Gottfredson & Holland, 1996), it is possible for an individual to identify potential employers by linking their Holland codes with NAICS codes. Instead of being overwhelmed with numerous options, individuals can begin identifying employers that already hire individuals with their interests. Since many print, personal computer, and Internet resources reference these codes, familiarity with these classifications can help individuals to more quickly find and organize the information they need.

In designing a job campaign, it may be useful to know that employers are evaluating potential new hires in terms of teamwork, critical thinking and analytical reasoning, and oral and written communication. Moreover, 63 percent of business executives believe that recent college graduates do not have the skills to be successful in today's global economy (Peter Hart Research Associates, 2006). An effective job campaign should address these matters that are important to employers.

Location

What is the relevance of geographic location in designing a job campaign? Kaihia (2005) reported that five hot job sectors are in South Florida (healthcare), Washington, DC (technology), Raleigh-Durham, NC (life sciences), California (entertainment), and Southern California (accounting). While jobs exist almost anywhere, it is clear that economic activity is sometimes concentrated in particular regions of the nation, which means more employment opportunities than ordinary are available there.

Education and Training

We have repeated several times that ongoing education and training are pertinent for remaining employable. In most technically oriented occupations, further education and training are essential. Employers differ in the amount and type of education and training opportunities they offer their employees. In researching employers, you may want to find out the type and amount of education and training opportunities typically provided to employees. When education and training benefits are considered, a lower salary offered by one employer may actually be "worth more" than a higher salary offered by an employer with limited education and training benefits. Typical education and training benefits include tuition reimbursement, on-site training, off-site training, and distance-learning programs.

Leisure

Chapter 3 described the interaction between work and leisure in career planning, and Chapter 8 discussed organizational culture and the quality of the match between a person and a job. Students may want to know what kind of work/life balance can be obtained in a job. We should add that the boundary line between work and leisure can become very blurred. For example, learning to play golf or tennis may be a good strategy for enhancing opportunities for networking within an organization or with customers.

Family

As we noted in Chapter 10, work has a major influence on family life. The interaction between work and family life varies depending on the organizational culture. Two important factors are child care and parental leave policy. In an effort to enhance productivity, some employers offer child care at the work site, making it easier for workers with children to locate child care and to manage transportation. Employers also vary in terms of leave policies for pregnancy, infant-care leave, caring for sick children, and attending to parental responsibilities, such as coaching Little League.

Knowledge About Employment Decision Making—The CASVE Cycle

This is a good place to stop and review the CASVE Cycle as a tool for helping you obtain and use the right information at the right time in the job campaign.

In the *Communication* phase of your job campaign, you become aware that an employment decision needs to be made. Internal cues, such as anxiety, or external cues, such as statements from trusted friends or the completion of a training program or degree, signal that employment problem solving and decision making needs to begin.

For example, college seniors often come into a career center the week before graduation to ask about opportunities for interviewing with prospective employers. In this case, they responded to the cues too late. The beginning of their senior year would have been a better time to ask these questions.

In the *Analysis* phase of your job campaign, you use self-knowledge and knowledge of employment options to better understand the gap between where you are and where you want to be. You begin the Analysis phase by reflecting on what you know, obtain information, and reflect on what you have learned. Generally, a more accurate understanding of yourself and your employment options leads to a more effective job campaign.

In the *Synthesis* phase, you first expand and then narrow the employment options you are considering in your job campaign. The goal is to avoid missing potentially appropriate options (expansion or elaboration) while reducing the number of options to a small enough list to avoid being overwhelmed when you finally choose (narrow or synthesize).

There are two methods of expanding your employment options:

1. Generate a list of potential employers and positions that you have considered in the past—your aspirations.

2. Use information resources to generate options, such as print or electronic directories or job banks. When considering potential employers and positions, it is important to remember that self-employment is an increasingly viable option for some individuals.

After generating a comprehensive list of potential positions, you then narrow your options by considering what you learned in the Analysis phase. What was most important to you? Keep only those employers and positions that offer a reasonable chance of helping you to narrow your gap in employment.

In the *Valuing* phase, a small number of employment choices are prioritized, and a first choice is identified for real-world exploration. There may also be good second and third employment options. Your task then is to consider the costs and benefits of each position for yourself and your significant others. Some individuals also consider the costs and benefits relative to their cultural group, community, and society at large. After considering the costs and benefits, the job offers are prioritized, and ultimately one position is accepted and the remaining positions are declined.

Simultaneous consideration of employment offers are most likely to occur in high-demand occupations, such as software engineer, in selected geographic areas. The Employment Decision-Making Exercise in *Appendix L* can be used when considering simultaneous job offers.

In the *Execution* phase of your job campaign, actions are taken to make the transition to employment. The first step in Execution involves developing your job search tools, including the resume(s), cover letter(s), and interviewing skills. It is also very important to set up a record-keeping system to help you keep track of your job campaign. When offers are received, it is important to inform an employer in writing (by letter, fax, or e-mail) that you will accept the position that has been offered. If multiple employment offers exist, then the other offers should be declined in writing. These activities will be discussed in more detail in Chapters 12–14.

The final phase of the CASVE Cycle involves a return to *Communication* to determine if internal and external cues indicate whether or not the original employment gap has been successfully closed.

Understanding How Thoughts Influence a Job Campaign

At the top of the Pyramid of Information-Processing Domains is the *executive processing domain*. As we saw in Chapter 5, the metacognitive skills in this domain influence how we think and subsequently act in designing a job campaign, and they include the following components: (1) self-talk, (2) self-awareness, and (3) control and monitoring.

Self-talk. Self-talk is the conversation that we have with ourselves about our past, present, and future capability to complete a specific task, in this case employment problem solving and decision making. Table 11.1 shows some of the practical outcomes of positive and negative self-talk.

Negative self-talk generally makes it more difficult to do the following:

- Clearly write a career objective for a resume.

- Accurately identify skills on a resume.

- Be motivated to identify potential employers and position openings.

- Follow through with networking opportunities.

- Be motivated to research an employer.

- Positively articulate your potential contributions in an employment interview.

- Respond with clarity and enthusiasm to questions posed by an employment interviewer.

- Follow through with interview thank you letters.

TABLE 11.1   PRACTICAL OUTCOMES OF POSITIVE AND NEGATIVE SELF-TALK

Positive self-talk can help you do this:	Negative self-talk often leads to this:
• Stay motivated even when no job offers are coming	• Discouragement when quick responses to job applications don't come through
• Overcome shyness and lack of confidence in job hunting	• Fear of rejection by employers
• Actively seek job offers even when rejections are received	• Failure to get the information needed to sustain your job campaign
• Think clearly and realistically about the good and bad points of job targets and offers	• Hanging out with other frustrated job hunters and singing the "Can't Get a Job" blues
• Make better use of the opinions of important people in your life	• Procrastination or not getting started in your job campaign
• Get outside help in your job campaign when needed	• Confusion about the good and bad points of job targets and offers
	• Despair from the negative opinions of people in your life

One of the assumptions or myths associated with ineffective job hunting is the *"Wallflower Syndrome."* This job-hunting myth is drawn from a party situation where some persons sit and wait for other persons to ask them to dance. The negative self-talk includes "I'm not a good dancer," "I'm not popular," or "Nobody likes me," and the result is the Wallflower Syndrome. Sure enough, they don't dance. The alternative positive self-talk, "I want to dance, and I'll ask someone to dance with me," is likely to produce different outcomes. The Wallflower Syndrome is equally ineffective in a job campaign. Assuming that others will do the work— for example, you must wait to be chosen by an employer, an employment agency will find you a position, employers will find your resume on the Internet, the career center will send your resume to employers who will hire you—in most cases is not likely to produce the desired outcome.

For some individuals, a job campaign may provoke more anxiety than an occupational choice or the choice of a college major. The reason for this potential difference is the specificity of each type of decision. Choosing an occupation and related program of study is a general, future-oriented choice. Failure to obtain an employment position related to an individual's program of study is a possibility, but is typically far enough in the future to cause limited anxiety for most people. A job campaign, however, often results in the possibility of specific and immediate rejection from potential employers. As a result, failure is concrete and easily perceived.

Job applicants are often aware that they are likely to receive many rejections before actually receiving a job offer. As noted in the section on the Communication phase of the CASVE Cycle, a little anxiety may be motivational, but too much anxiety may lead to self-defeating coping behaviors, such as procrastination. In dealing with rejections, we sometimes advise job hunters that the ratio of employment rejections to offers can be 20 to 1. A positive reframing statement would be "I need to get my 20 rejections in order to get an offer," or "I'm thankful for 'no's' because they probably signal a poor person-environment fit."

Tom Jackson (1992, p. 50), a popular job search and resume book author, described the job hunting process as a series of "no's." The best job search looks something like this:

No, No, No, No, No, No, No, No, No, No, Yes!!

You have to be willing to encounter a series of "no's" before you get to the employer who will say "yes." The faster you get through the "no's," the sooner you'll get to the "yes!"

In summary, if individuals expect to do poorly (or to fail) in a job campaign, they have little motivation to prepare for and follow through with the steps in the process, such as resume writing and interviewing. Also, negative self-talk is likely to influence individuals' perceptions of their capabilities to perform successfully in a particular position. Subsequent awareness that a person is not making good progress in obtaining employment only reinforces negative self-talk.

Employment interviewers often remark that some applicants are poorly prepared for interviews, even though they were aware of the importance of preparation and had the time and resources available to prepare effectively. Employment interviewers also remark that some applicants have a difficult time explaining how their capabilities and characteristics relate to employer needs reflected in a specific position. Self-awareness of negative thoughts is a key strategy for limiting the potentially harmful impact of negative thinking in a job campaign.

Self-awareness. Effective problem solvers are aware of themselves as they are doing a task (in this case processing employment information). Self-awareness includes an awareness of the interaction among thoughts, feelings, and behaviors, especially the debilitating impact of negative self-talk on a job campaign. Examples of self-awareness might include the following:

- Negative emotions, such as depression, anxiety, panic

- Lack of emotion or caring about an employment problem—no motivation

- Persistent negative thoughts about employment choice—predicting future failure and using absolute terminology ("never" and "always")

- Failure to initiate or persist with job campaign behaviors

- Repeating job campaign behaviors that are ineffective

Self-awareness also includes the reactions of significant others (such as family and friends) to your job campaign. Possible feedback from significant others might include the following:

- "You're proceeding too slowly or too haphazardly in your job campaign"

- "You're proceeding too fast—caution and planning is needed"

- "You're failing to seek or consider ideas from significant others, such as mentors"

- "You're targeting an inappropriate employer or position in your job campaign"

Another assumption or myth associated with ineffective job hunting is the *"Lone Ranger Syndrome."* This job-hunting myth comes from the cartoon character who rides off and solves all kinds of problems by herself or himself. As we have noted, a successful job campaign involves other people. (We'll talk about this more in Chapter 13.) A successful job campaign is not a one-person operation but requires the assistance of friends, family, mentors, supervisors, and colleagues. While it is important to consider input from significant others, not all input may be helpful. Be aware of the extent to which this input may be negatively influencing your thoughts related to job-search activities. Review the information in Chapter 5 about ways to improve your self-awareness of the impact of career thoughts on feelings and behavior.

Control and monitoring. Effective problem solvers and decision makers know when to stop and get more information and when to continue on with the next step in the process. *Control* refers to an individual's ability to purposefully engage in the next appropriate problem-solving and decision-making task in a job campaign. *Monitoring* refers to an individual's ability to judge when a task has been successfully completed and when to move on to the next task or when additional assistance with a task is needed. Effective problem solvers and decision makers are aware of what they know and what they *need* to know, and they are aware of the sequence of steps that must be completed in a successful job campaign.

Two additional assumptions or myths associated with ineffective job campaigns are the *"I'll do anything"* and *"Looking under the light"* syndromes.

"I'll do anything" sounds like a good schema to use in a job campaign, but in reality it is highly ineffective for several reasons. Neither employers or supporters involved in your job campaign know what you want or how to assist you, which reduces their positive impact on your campaign. The lack of a job target or goal results in confusion and wasted time and energy, and you may end up applying for all kinds of unrelated jobs. Also, you are unable to specify precisely how your interests, skills, and values match up with job requirements in your resume or cover letters.

The "Looking under the light" myth involves looking for jobs in the wrong places. There is the story of the person frantically looking for lost keys on the street corner under the light. A passerby asks if she can be of assistance and is told about the lost keys. When the helpful passerby asks how and where the keys were lost, she learns that they had been lost in the park, but, the searcher explains, it is easier to look for them under the streetlight. Jobs are posted in the career center, on the Internet, and in newspapers, and they are easier to find there, but many jobs are "hidden" and not posted in places where they are easy to find.

Good control and monitoring in executive processing enable you to use schema that lead to a successful job campaign. Reframing the four syndromes, "Wallflower," "Lone Ranger," "I'll do anything," and "Looking under the light," are examples of where that can be done.

In concluding this section on using a CIP approach in conducting a job campaign, we offer some suggestions to help you have a more positive job search experience:

1. Get positive support from friends and career services professionals, especially those who can help you reframe negative metacognitions into more positive thoughts.

2. Reward yourself when you make progress in your job campaign, for example, do something you enjoy when you successfully complete research on eight possible employing organizations.

3. Take care of yourself physically, because job hunting takes energy; get plenty of sleep, eat well, and exercise.

4. Avoid negative people, especially those who have been unsuccessful in protracted job campaigns.

5. Keep good records of everything happening in your job campaign—costs, people, dates.

6. Join a job hunters' club provided by an employment services agency, church, school, or community organization.

7. Consider part-time or temporary work as a way to stay involved and continue networking while you continue your job campaign.

We will now examine the temporary staffing services industry in relation to an employment campaign.

JOB HUNTING IN THE TEMPORARY STAFFING SERVICES INDUSTRY

In Chapter 9, we discussed the personnel supply services industry, sometimes also called the temporary workforce. This is an important area to explore because many employing organizations and increasing numbers of jobs are available in this area of the economy.

Claudia Allen (1998) reported that about half the employers responding to a survey use staffing services to fill positions. Melchionno (1999) noted that about 90 percent of companies use temporary help. Employment campaigns in the 21st century will need to account for this phenomenon. We will (1) review some of the common terms used in this field, (2) describe some of the special employment trends and issues in this area, (3) present a brief review of job hunting tips, and (4) conclude with lists of some of the largest companies in this industry.

Temp Terminology

Here are definitions of terms you will hear in using temporary staffing services as part of your employment campaign.

Contingent workforce. The word *contingent* means uncertain, accidental, chance, dependent, and unforeseen; in a nutshell, contingent work depends on the employer's needs. Some employers are now using contingent workers to fill 30 to 80 percent of their needs. Contingent workers do not have a contract or commitment for ongoing employment—the work is time-limited, which means they are not "permanent" jobs.

Other words associated with *contingent* workers include temporary services or staff, temps, employee leasing, flexible staffing, outsourcing, freelancing, consultants, co-employees, on-call workers, independent contractors, flexible staff, supplementals, peripherals, or interns.

Temps. Temps are contingent workers who do not expect to stay with the current employer for a period of more than one year or beyond a specified ending date. An important distinction must be made regarding *temporary employment* and *working for a temporary services company or temp agency*. If one has continuing employment with a temporary services company, then the work is permanent, not temporary or contingent. This means that one can have permanent employment with a temp agency.

Temping. The person actually doing the work is known as an *employee* or a *contractor,* and the temporary help organization is known as the *employer.* The organization for whom temporary employment services are being provided is known as the *client.* The client pays any fees for the employment service. The services are provided at no charge to you (the employee), but the client pays the employer for these staffing services.

Private employment agency. This company acts as your agent in helping you find employment. The agency does not hire you as a contingent employee, unlike a temp agency, and may charge you (the employee) a fee for its services.

Client organization. This is the organization that uses the temporary workers provided by the staffing services company. Temp agencies provide temporary workers on a contract basis to client companies.

Trends

- Employers create more "temp" than permanent jobs.

- About 20 percent of employers (clients) use temp jobs to screen for permanent employment. This can lead to a "buyout" or "temp-to-hire" wherein an employee moves from temporary to permanent employment status.

- Almost every worker can expect to be unemployed at some time in his or her life, and temporary staffing companies can help a job hunter fill in these employment gaps.

Job-Hunting Tips

In seeking employment with a temporary staffing services agency, here are some guidelines to follow for a successful job campaign.

1. Be clear and honest about the kind of work you want, because the temp agency will use your preferences to develop a successful match with a potential client. It is in the agency's interest for you to succeed in the job.

2. It is generally advisable to apply to and be on the roster with several different temp agencies instead of just one. In this way, you have several employers pursuing your job interests. Different agencies have contracts with different clients.

3. Be aware that you might start in low-level jobs with an employer, but keep negotiating and working collaboratively with the temp agency to get you into higher-level positions.

4. Try to get all the leadership, teamwork, computer, and training experiences that you can with a temporary employment agency.

5. In reporting work experience on your resume, remember that the temp agency is your employer and that your job description would describe your duties and name the client and location.

6. In researching client organizations, try to find out which temporary staffing agency has the hiring contract for that organization—for example, Spherion could have the staffing contract for MCI, Manpower might have General Motors.

Hiring Companies

The Yellow Pages of a phone book will have listings of temporary staffing organizations under the heading of Employment Contractors or Temporary Help. There are hundreds of such companies, and more are created every year. Below are the names of some of the organizations that might be most interested in hiring people with technical and college training.

- Adecco
- Fidelity Staffing Service
- Interim Personnel
- Kelly Services
- Aquent
- Manpower
- Olsten Staffing Services
- Professional Staffing Group
- Spherion
- Temporary Solutions

The American Staffing Association, http://www.americanstaffing.net/index.cfm, can provide additional information about this industry.

Temp Work Checklist

This list of factors might be important for you to consider in seeking employment in the temporary staffing services industry. If many of these items apply to you that might indicate that you would be a good candidate for this kind of employment.

- You do not need a lot of job security right now.
- You are willing to start at lower-level positions in an organization in order to develop inside information about permanent positions.
- You are willing to work for different organizations (clients) in different locations in a short period of time.
- You want to make yourself visible to employers who might be looking for someone with your skills.
- You are relocating to another city and don't want to accept "permanent" employment right away.
- You want a decent income and secure health benefits.
- You desire a more flexible lifestyle that temping can provide.
- You would benefit from having an "agent" who can help you market your skills in the community.
- You want to maintain a stable work history without getting stuck in jobs you don't like.
- You are interested in a more relaxed hiring process with an organization as a "temp."
- You would like to get training in new job skills areas, such as word processing or database creation.
- You would like to try out new occupations or industries at less risk.

- You have skills—consulting, information processing, technical, professional—that would enable you to function as an independent contractor.

- You do not want to make long-term commitments to a permanent employer.

This section has provided some basic information about the contingent workforce and the temporary staffing services industry. There is evidence that increasing numbers of college graduates will find their first jobs in this industry, ultimately working in many different public, private, and nonprofit organizations.

Mende (1998) provided an overview of life as a temp and reported that a temp may have many different jobs over the course of a few months—teacher, puppeteer, photo processor, technical editor, product demonstrator—and the work is not in a particular office or place. Temps have to think of themselves as more than their jobs, which might mean the development of a new metacognition. Temps need to think of each assignment as an "adventure," something unpredictable as well as important; a positive attitude is essential.

We close Chapter 11 with this thought: *"The best jobs don't always go to the best qualified but to the best job hunters."* In other words, jobs go to those who can sell an employer on a match between the applicant and the job. Employers want the best person for the job, and this might not be the most talented, highly trained person. They are looking for the best "match," a competent, dependable employee who can do what the position requires now.

SUMMARY

This chapter introduced the idea of the employment campaign, explored perceptions of employers and applicants of the employment process, and applied the basic elements of Cognitive Information Processing theory to employment problem solving and decision making. We have expanded on ideas introduced in Chapters 1 through 5 on specific processes of the job campaign. Definitions were presented with employment examples, followed by an exploration of the nature of job-hunting problems. The Pyramid of Information-Processing Domains was reviewed in relation to conducting a job campaign, and the CASVE Cycle was applied to the steps involved in making employment choices. The goal was to help you to improve the quality of your PCT related to employment issues. The chapter concluded with employment campaign strategies that can be used in the temporary staffing services industry.

REFERENCES

Allen, C. (1998, Spring). NACE employer benchmark survey. *Journal of Career Planning and Employment*, 58(3), 25–30.

Amundson, N. E. (1996). Supporting clients through a change in perspective. *Journal of Employment Counseling, 33*, 155–162.

Azrin, N., & Besalel, V. (1980). *Job club counselor's manual: A behavioral approach to vocational counseling*. Baltimore, MD: University Park Press.

Bolles, R. (1994, December). A history of ideas and events in the job-hunting field during the twentieth century. *Newsletter about life/work planning*, pp. 1–12.

Bolles, R. (2008). *A practical manual for job hunters and career changers: What color is your parachute?* Berkeley, CA: Ten Speed Press.

Broudy, E. (1989). *Professional temping*. New York: Macmillan.

Connelly, A. R. (2007, December). How not to find a job. *Counseling Today*, p. 29.

Gottfredson, G., & Holland, J. (1996). *Dictionary of Holland occupation codes*. Odessa, FL: Psychological Assessment Resources, Inc.

Jackson, T. (1992). *The perfect job search*. New York: Doubleday.

Kaihia, P. (2005, March). Features/what you're worth. *Business 2.0, 6*(2), p. 99. http://proquest.umi.com/pqdweb?

Kleiman, C. (1997, February 5). Job hunters should track the "gazelles." *Tallahassee Democrat*, p. 14D.

Mariani, M. (1997). One-stop career centers: All in one place and everyplace. *Occupational Outlook Quarterly, 41*(3), 2–15.

Melchionno, R. (1999, Spring). The changing temporary work force. *Occupational Outlook Quarterly*, pp. 24–32.

Mende, B. (1998, Winter/Spring). Another way to work. *Managing your career*, pp. 10–13.

National Association of Colleges and Employers. (1996). Two out of three employers use work/study programs to "test-drive" prospective employees. *1996 employer benchmark survey*. [on-line], 1–3. Available: <http://www.jobweb.org/>

National Association of Colleges and Employers. (2006, fall). Employer benchmark survey: Executive summary. *NACE Journal*, pp. 36–39.

National Association of Colleges & Employers. (2008, March 19). Job outlook 2008 spring update: Hiring outlook remains positive, but down from fall projections. Retrieved from http://www.naceweb.org/pubs/spotlightonline/2008/c031908.htm.

National Association of Colleges and Employers (2008). Class of 2008 steps into good job market. Retrieved February 25, 2005, http://www.jobweb.com/studentarticles.aspx?id=1219.

Nunmaker, T. D., & Riley, F. M. (2007, May). Employers and student candidates: How they see each other. *NACE Journal*, pp. 26–31.

Peter Hart Research Associates. (2006, December 28). How should colleges prepare students to succeed in today's global economy? Washington, DC: Author.

Peterson, G. W., Sampson, J. P., Jr., & Reardon, R. C. (1991). *Career development and services: A cognitive approach*. Pacific Grove, CA: Brooks/Cole.

Peterson, G. W., Sampson, J. P., Jr., Reardon, R. C., & Lenz, J. L. (1996). Becoming career problem solvers and decision makers: A cognitive information processing approach. In D. Brown & L. Brooks (Eds.), *Career choice and development* (3rd ed., pp. 423–475). San Francisco, CA: Jossey-Bass.

Sampson, J. P., Jr., Peterson, G. W., Lenz, J. G., Reardon, R. C., & Saunders, D. E. (1996). *Career Thoughts Inventory workbook*. Odessa, FL: Psychological Assessment Resources, Inc.

Smith, D. D., & Gast, L. K. (1998). Comprehensive career services for seniors. In J. N. Gardner, G. Van der Veer, & Associates, *The senior year experience* (pp. 187–209). San Francisco: Jossey-Bass.

Smith, L. (1994). Landing that first real job. *Fortune, 129*(10), 58–59.

U. S. Department of Labor (1991). *Dictionary of occupational titles* (4th ed.). Indianapolis, IN: JIST Works.

Wegmann, R., Chapman, R., & Johnson, M. (1985). *Looking for work in the new economy*. Salt Lake City: Olympus.

WRITTEN COMMUNICATIONS IN JOB HUNTING

As we have emphasized many times, the process of career decision making and job seeking is grounded in information processing. While technology has made an impact on the way we communicate with prospective employers, it has not eliminated the need for various forms of written communication. How you present your qualifications in cover letters and in your resume should take into account your self-knowledge—your skills, interests, and values—and your knowledge of the job options you are pursuing. For example, if your job target is a position as a pharmaceutical sales representative, it is important to know how your personal qualities match up with this type of position and be able to describe that effectively in your written communications with prospective employers.

We begin with a discussion of the following:

- The various types of letters used in the employment-search process

- Resumes

- Strategies for writing career objectives

- The distinction between resumes and vitae

- The role of references in the job-search process

- Methods for effective record keeping

- Job searching on the Internet.

As you read about how written communications are used in a job campaign, concentrate on how your Personal Career Theory (PCT) and strategic career thinking can be improved by this information. How will this information affect the kind of job campaign activities you will pursue, and how much time will you devote to these activities? How and when will you begin preparing these materials? Our goal is to provide information and knowledge that will help you to improve your PCT and the skills needed in solving employment problems.

LETTERS IN THE JOB SEARCH PROCESS

The most common letter used in the job-search process is often referred to as a cover or application letter. This is often the first piece of information the employer sees and is generally accompanied by a resume. A letter that precedes the cover letter is called a letter of inquiry or a *"prospecting"* letter.

Letter of Inquiry

One type of letter that is less well known than the standard cover letter is the letter of inquiry. Many times in the job-search process, you may not know if opportunities actually exist with a prospective employer you have identified in your search. Some writers suggest that you begin by sending a "letter of inquiry" or information-seeking letter before you formally apply to the organization. After preparing a list of organizations that might have the position you are seeking, a letter of inquiry is sent in which you approach the employer requesting employment information. It is important to research the organization as much as possible so as to lend credibility to your inquiry letter.

A sample letter of inquiry is included in Table 12.1. In these days of "instant" communication, this type of letter is probably used less frequently. Much of what you might hope to learn through such a written inquiry can be learned through an e-mail or phone call. The main advantages of this type of job-search correspondence are that it has the potential to help you learn useful information and gives employers a chance to see your written communication skills. What you learn from these types of inquiries can improve what you include in your job application or let you know that it may not be worth

TABLE 12.1   SAMPLE INQUIRY LETTER

Ronald B. Carter
P.O. Box 1056
Tallahassee, FL 32303

April 10, 2008

Rita Monroe
Jackson Communications Company
1010 Western Drive
Denver, Co 79036

Dear Ms. Monroe:

I read with interest your profile in the Executive Suite section of *Business Week*. I am very impressed with the rapid growth of Jackson Communications in the telecommunications field.

During my senior year, I received advice from several people here in Tallahassee about the direction my career might take, and I have decided that an organization such as Jackson Communications is where I would like to begin. I feel my education and experience fit well with the kinds of entry-level opportunities that are potentially available with your company.

During the semester break, I expect to be in Denver, and I would appreciate the opportunity to meet with you to explore opportunities with your organization. I know your schedule is busy, but I would appreciate 30 minutes of your time, any day between May 5th and May 10th. I will accommodate my schedule to yours. I appreciate your willingness to consider this request.

Sincerely,

[signature here]

Ronald B. Carter

Enclosure

your time to apply after all (for example, you learn by mail or phone contact with the employer that they've just merged with a multinational corporation and they're laying off 3,000 employees).

Cover Letter Format

As we noted, the most common type of job-search correspondence is the traditional cover letter. This basic form of communication has remained essentially the same over the years, despite all the changes in the workplace and the new methods available for communicating with employers. Although there are a variety of styles, formats, and content elements, there are two basic formats that may help you in writing your letter of application. These are often referred to as the "broadcast" and the "targeted" approach.

Broadcast Approach. In this type of cover letter, job hunters announce their availability to many employers in their field without composing a separate letter for each one. Job hunters who are seeking employment across a fairly wide geographic range and who have numerous job targets often find themselves using this approach. In using this format, you're essentially playing the numbers game—that is, if I send out many letters, I can hopefully count on at least a few positive responses.

Although the broadcast letter is not typically used to pursue a specific job lead, it is wise to personalize the letter. Some examples include: "I am writing to present you with my qualifications for a position as a sales representative at ..." or "I am very aware of the changing role of the nurse in today's (hospital, clinic, etc.)." By inserting the appropriate word or phrase, you can tailor each correspondence with much less effort than with individually composed letters. Determine and state your exact interest in the organization and explain why it, in turn, should be interested in you. The more you know about the organization, the easier it will be for you to tailor your letter to the organization's needs and interests.

Emphasize your positive assets and skills in your letter. Be as specific as possible about the type of position you are seeking, and tie this to your knowledge of the organization and its business, product, or service.

Targeted Approach. This type of cover letter is typically used to investigate a specific job lead. You may be answering a newspaper ad, responding to an Internet listing, or following up on a suggestion offered by your career center or an employment services office, a relative, friend, or faculty member. Because you are aware of the opening, you construct the letter to show how your abilities and qualifications can be applied to meet the employer's needs. In this letter you are constructing a match between your career goals and background and the needs of the employer. You are literally selling yourself to the employer.

You can also refer to specific information you discovered through conversations or by doing research about the organization. You can include this type of information with statements such as "My academic background, together with my work experience, have prepared me to function especially well as an Account Executive for American Express" or "I am impressed by your continual growth through grant-funded activities."

When writing your letter, it is always important to first identify the correct contact person in the organization, although in some cases this is not possible. For example, you may find yourself replying to a box number from a listing in the newspaper. Directing your letter to the key executive or manager in the department to which you are applying is advisable, but in some larger organizations, you may be required to apply through the Human Resources or Personnel Department, for example, Manager of Employment, Recruitment, or Human Resources.

Here are some more tips on preparing your letters:

1. Thoroughly read and reread job ads to determine what potential employers are seeking in applicants. Try to speak to the "needs" of the organization evidenced through the ad—some reading between the lines may be necessary so that you can tailor your response most effectively.

2. Answer the ad as soon as possible after it appears. However, make sure that you allow yourself enough time to prepare the best-written response.

3. Be as innovative and creative as possible in describing how your skills and interests match up with the needs of the organization in order to make your letter stand out amidst the mass of letters the organization is sure to receive.

4. Follow instructions in the job listing carefully; note where the response should be directed and what to include (e.g., resume, statement of geographic preference, etc.). Answer all questions, with the exception of responding to a request for salary requirements. In this case, it is advisable to avoid the question and simply indicate that it is open or negotiable.

5. State when you would be available to meet for an interview and include a phone number and e-mail address where you can most often be reached.

6. Be brief! Letters should be individualized, concise, truthful, and factual.

7. Always consider the reaction of the employer by putting yourself in his or her place. Try to determine what accomplishments and skills would be most attractive to a particular employer.

8. Be straightforward, professional, and businesslike—remember you are selling yourself. As with the resume, stick to the facts.

9. Remember that the primary purpose of the letter is to get you in the door for the interview—make sure the letter has impact!

10. In today's electronic age, you may find that you are doing all of your employer correspondence via e-mail, especially if you learn that this is their preferred mode of communication. However it is important to note that all the guidelines related to professionalism in business communications should be followed, even when sending your letters via e-mail. Avoid e-mail "slang," abbreviations, and similar formats that are typically used for more social exchanges via the Internet.

Table 12.2 provides a sample cover letter outline that you can use in drafting your letter. Although the majority of the letters written for your job campaign will be cover letters for specific jobs, there are additional forms of written communication that are important and are described below.

Interview Appreciation Letter

Interviews should always be followed up with a thank-you letter expressing appreciation for the interviewer's time. Thank you notes are one of the most powerful and overlooked job-search tools (Farr, 2004). Not only is this an accepted courtesy, your letter can also serve to refresh the memory of your meeting in the mind of the interviewer. When an on-site visit to the employer is involved, the appreciation letter may accompany your expense account for the visit.

Format Suggestions. When writing your appreciation letter, the following list may help structure your written communication.

- Express appreciation for the interviewer's consideration and arrangement of the meeting.

- State the date of the interview and the name of the interviewer.

- Reiterate your interest in the employer and the position by mentioning new points or assets you may have forgotten to address in the original interview or become aware of afterwards.

- Ask any questions you may have that were not answered in the original interview.

- Express your anticipation of receiving word regarding the employer's decision.

- Be sure to include your contact information.

TABLE 12.2 SAMPLE COVER LETTER OUTLINE

Today's Date

Ms. Jane Blank, Title
Organization
Street Address
City, State, Zip Code

Dear Ms. Blank:

1st Paragraph • Tell why you are writing; name the position, field, or general career area about which you are asking. Tell how you heard of the opening or organization.

2nd Paragraph • Mention one or two of your qualifications that you think would be of greatest interest to the organization, slanting your remarks to their point of view. Tell why you are particularly interested in the employer, location, or type of work. If you have had related experience or specialized training, be sure to point it out and emphasize how your are a good fit for the position. Refer the reader to the enclosed application form or resume. If appropriate, mention that the Career Center has or will send full credentials to provide additional information concerning your background and interests.

3rd Paragraph • Close by making a request for an opportunity to visit the employer, suggesting a possible date and time. Indicate that you will follow up with a phone call (when you reach the city, for instance) for a confirmation of the appointment unless you hear beforeh and that the reader does not wish to meet with you. If, instead of wanting an interview, your request is for further information concerning the opening, you can ask them to reply via e-mail or enclose a self-addressed, stamped envelope. Make sure your closing is not vague but makes a specific action from the reader likely.

Sincerely,

(Your Handwritten Signature)

Type Your Name

Enclosure

Letter of Acknowledgment

Once you have received an offer from an employer or institution, it is important to respond as soon as possible. While an immediate "yes" or "no" is not essential, prompt acknowledgment of the offer is expected. This process may occur over the telephone or via e-mail, but in the event that you need to respond in writing, the following information is generally included in this type of letter:

- An acknowledgment that you received the offer.

- Expression of appreciation for the offer.

- Indication to the employer of the date by which you expect to make your decision.

Letter of Acceptance

Once you have decided to accept an offer, the employer should be notified immediately. It is not necessary to wait until the offer expiration date before contacting the recruiter or hiring officer in the organization selected. Employers will appreciate your promptness as it allows them to assess more efficiently the status of their personnel selection processes. You may acknowledge acceptance of an offer by phone, but it is always important to follow up with a written confirmation that includes the following information:

- Acknowledge the letter, verbal offer, or telephone call of the dated offer.

- Be as specific as possible, mentioning starting salary and supervisor's name. Be sure to list and detail all items (benefits, performance reviews, moving expenses, etc.) agreed to in the offer.

- State when you will be able to report to work. Acknowledge if the offer is contingent on any events, such as award of a degree, passing of physical examination, certification, and so forth.

- Express appreciation to the contact person and anyone else who has been particularly helpful in the recruiting process.

- Ask if any other information is required or if additional details should be attended to prior to reporting for work.

Job Offer Rejection Letter

As a matter of courtesy, a letter declining a job offer is due to those organizations whose offers you are rejecting. Despite the possibly negative nature of the correspondence, it is vital that other employers know your decisions. A letter declining an offer often includes a telephone call, but the letter makes your decision a matter of record and helps to avoid any later confusion arising from verbal communication.

The types of information in a letter of declination include the following:

- Express appreciation for the offer.

- Mention name of potential supervisor.

- State the exact position for which you were being considered.

- Decline graciously.

- Briefly explain reason for choice, sticking to the facts.

- No profuse apology is necessary—re-express appreciation.

Here are some more "do's" related to job-search letters.

Do

- Follow rules of layout and format of a standard business letter.

- Address your letter, whenever possible, to an individual, along with their correct title.

- Spell, punctuate, and paragraph your letter correctly.

- Write in your own words and in conversational language.

- Hand-sign rather than type your signature (unless you're sending electronically).

- Print on good-quality paper.

- Be brief, concise, and to the point.

- Take advantage of any link to the employer that can put your foot in the door or give you an edge over the competition.

The appearance and tone of your letter and resume can say more about you than you can gracefully say about yourself. For further assistance in the development of your letter(s), review resources in the career center or library on your campus, check local bookstores for publications on letter writing, and explore Internet sites devoted to this topic. Finally, we suggest you have drafts of your letter(s) critiqued by a career services professional or friend with relevant skills.

RESUME WRITING

The most widely recognized form of written communication used in a job campaign is the resume. We will examine the purpose of a resume; the style of a resume, including length and format; alternative forms of resumes; the organizational approaches and categories of a resume; sample resumes; and issues regarding resume critiques and reproduction. As you learn about resume preparation, remember that writing a resume will require some time and effort on your part.

Purpose of a Resume

Many years ago, resumes were actually called "qualifications briefs." As a self-marketing tool, it should be unique in both content and format to highlight facts about an individual as they relate to a job or position. A resume is a summary of one's personal, educational, and work experience qualifications. Remember the purpose of a resume is to help secure an interview. It should not be a complete life history.

Resumes can be used by candidates applying for work, internships, graduate schools, or scholarships/fellowships. Sometimes they are even used to apply for mortgage loans.

Style of a Resume

While it is true that there is no absolutely one correct way to design a resume, there are certain traditions in resume writing that have become standard. The descriptions presented here are intended to help you create a resume that will serve your individual needs and represent your qualifications.

The style in which you choose to write your resume will give it tone and a personal flavor. The style can either enhance your resume or detract from it. Don't forget—a resume is a sales device and must present a positive image. Keep in mind that while a resume is an essential tool in the job campaign, it is not meant as a substitute for the interview (even though it usually precedes the interview). Because of this, and because the resume is a summary, you may (and most people do) use incomplete sentences (e.g., "analyzed survey data," "led small group recreation activities," "supervised staff"). Some people feel that the resume should be action oriented and reflect a somewhat assertive and confident job seeker. Others are more comfortable with a neutral tone, showing qualifications and interests without much attention to assertiveness or self-promotion.

Length. Most resumes are usually one to three pages in length. The resume should be as long as necessary to present your qualifications concisely. One-page resumes are most preferred for traditional age (18 to 23) college students applying for staff-level positions, according to 73 percent of employers surveyed by the National Association of Colleges and Employers (NACE, 1996). Two-to three-page resumes are appropriate for individuals with more education and work experience applying for executive-level positions (NACE, 1996). A variation on the resume—a "vita"—is generally much longer. Vitae are discussed later in this chapter.

Format. The format of your resume should attract attention and create interest in those reading it. In constructing a resume, choose appropriate categories for your information and order them from most to least relevant to your objective. Use capital letters, underlining, boldface, indentations, and white space to emphasize important information. However, once you've selected a format, be consistent within categories. The resume should be easy to follow and pleasing to the eye. Some other factors that may affect your resume format are employers who use resume-scanning systems and the posting of resumes on the Internet.

Alternative Resumes

Resumes for posting on the Internet. A common form of job hunting involves posting resumes on the Internet. Distributing your resume via the Internet may or may not increase your chances of securing an interview, but it may be a base you want to cover in your job campaign, especially if you are seeking technology-oriented positions. The Riley Guide is a very useful resource on this topic because it maintains quality and currency. It is online at http://www.rileyguide.com/eresume.html. There are a few recommendations to consider before posting your resume on the Internet:

1. No line of text should be longer than 65 characters, including spaces.

2. Pay close attention to your choice of words throughout your resume. Employers who search for online resumes typically use keyword search programs to find resumes of interest. If your resume does not include these keywords, it will not be retrieved during the search process. To select keywords, consider the specific skills and qualifications necessary for success in the position you're seeking.

3. Keep in mind that the information you place in your resume will be available to anyone in the world with access to the Internet who wants to see it, so avoid including information that you wish to keep confidential, such as your postal address and phone numbers. Use your e-mail address as a point of contact.

Scannable resumes. Some employers use scanning technology to handle the large number of resumes they receive. This is done by a system that scans the resume into computer memory. Employers can then search the resume for specific keywords or skills that match those necessary for a particular job. When constructing a scannable resume remember the following tips:

1. Specify skills you have obtained, using nouns as opposed to verbs—for example, "responsible for training" should be worded "trainer for new employees."

2. Use lots of white space to aid the computer in recognizing the information.

3. Avoid using underlining, boldfacing, varied fonts, or other fancy formatting options. These can result in the computer misreading information and potentially could cost you an interview.

4. Use words that everyone will be able to recognize. Scanning programs may not be designed with a thesaurus, so technical words may be overlooked.

5. Do not fold or staple a resume that will be scanned. If you are concerned about whether an employer included in your job campaign scans resumes, you may wish to call in advance to check.

HotJobs (http://hotjobs.yahoo.com) is an example of a company that provides resume-scanning systems for employers. Such systems can scan and analyze a resume in seconds and categorize it in terms of 80,000 skill/school combinations. This is a valuable time-saving service for a large organization with 150,000 jobs.

Organization

In organizing the information in your resume, there are two basic approaches: chronological or general, and functional.

Chronological or general. A chronological resume lists, describes, and dates the details of each job and educational experience separately. Table 12.3 shows an example. Listings under each category are placed in reverse chronological order, starting with the most recent schooling or job. This approach is most appropriate if you have extensive uninterrupted work experience in the area

TABLE 12.3   SAMPLE RESUME–ALICE HARRIS

ALICE HARRIS
aharris34@hotmail.com

Present Address	**Permanent Address**
FSU Box 3035 Tallahassee, FL 32313 (850) 644-8190	1305 Iroquois Dr. Ft. Pierce, FL 34946 (305) 465-5525

CAREER OBJECTIVE

To utilize my strong interpersonal and organizational skills in a competitive sales program and eventually advance to a management position.

EDUCATION

Bachelor of Science, April 2008, Florida State University, Tallahassee, FL
Major: Advertising   **Minor**: Business
Overall GPA: 3.5   Major GPA: 3.7

EXPERIENCE

Securities Agent Trainee, A.L. Williams Co., Boca Raton, FL, 05/07-08/07

Learned securities industry by co-managing accounts and compiling research on client investment options.

Undergraduate Student Assistant, FSU College of Communication, Tallahassee, FL, 09/06-12/06

Advised undergraduates on course selection and assisted the dean in carrying out administrative duties.

Sales Associate, Circuit City Department Store, Atlanta, GA, 05/06-08/06

Assisted customers with product selection and provided product information; received award for monthly sales totals; managed departmental inventory.

Account Executive, Advice Advertising Agency, Tallahassee, FL, 01/06-04/06

Developed marketing strategies for local businesses, supervised media and market research; managed accounts.

Data Entry Operator, FSU Center for Professional Development, Tallahassee, FL, 09/05-12/05

Helped organize professional workshops; entered data on conference activities; maintained record system.

HONORS/ACTIVITIES

- President/Founder, Association of Black Communicators
- Sigma Chi Iota, Minority Honor Society
- Dean's List, four semesters
- Advertising Club

REFERENCES AVAILABLE UPON REQUEST

in which you seek employment. It is also the most common approach. Employers are generally more familiar with this format.

One variation on the chronological format, which has become more popular, leads off with a summary statement of relevant skills and qualifications. This section is then followed by the more traditional chronological arrangement of information. An example of this format is shown in Table 12.4. By including this type of section, you quickly call an employer's attention to those qualifications that relate most directly to the type of position you are seeking.

Functional. A functional resume consists of selections from your total experience of only those parts that relate to the job you seek. Under each category you list qualifications, skills, experiences,

TABLE 12.4	SAMPLE RESUME—NED ALLEN

NED ALLEN
215 Canopy Road, Apt. 155
Tallahassee, FL 32306
(850) 366-1111
nallen45@hotmail.com

QUALIFICATION

- Strong written and oral communication skills
- Dependable and enthusiastic worker
- Familiar with database and spreadsheet applications

EDUCATION

Bachelor of Science, **Multinational Business Operations & Finance,** December 2008

Florida State University, Tallahassee, FL   **Overall GPA:** 3.8

EXPERIENCE

Coordinator, USTA Under 16 National Tennis Tournament, Tallahassee, FL, November 2007

- Helped in the organization and coordination of the tournament.
- Responsible for tournament financial accounts and concessions.

Assistant Coach, Florida State University Summer Tennis Camp, Tallahassee, FL, June 2007

- Trained and supervised participants.
- Prepared and coordinated activities.

Receptionist, Marquee Sports Facility, Saint-Raphael, France, July-August 2006

- Answered the phone and helped manage financial records.
- Coordinated recreation activities for members.

HONORS

2007, 2006, 2005, ACC Academic Honor Roll

2007, 2006, 2005, FSU Dean's List

2007, 2006, 2005, Winner of the Golden Torch Award for best team GPA

Phi Eta Sigma National Honor Society, 2005-Present

Beta Gamma Sigma Honor Society for Accredited Business Programs, 2006-Present

ACTIVITIES

FSU Tennis Team, 8/05-Present

Camp I AM SPECIAL-Camp counselor for children with disabilities; served as head counselor & tennis coach for 3 years

Play golf in free time

REFERENCES AND PORTFOLIO AVAILABLE UPON REQUEST

and so forth that logically support your job objectives in functional areas such as management, research, writing, teaching, sales, or human relations. This approach is more difficult to construct, but it may be more effective in documenting the skills or functions you want to perform, especially if your background is varied. This approach may also be more appropriate if you have significant time gaps in employment and education.

Categories of a Resume

As stated earlier, certain traditions in resume writing have become standard. The following categories have come to be regarded as typical in resume writing.

Identification. Your name (generally in all capital letters or in bold), full address, and phone number(s) with the area code should be the first items on your resume. If you are at a temporary address, you can include this in addition to or in place of your permanent address, depending on the circumstances. You may also choose to include your e-mail address or fax number if you wish to be contacted in this manner. The main purpose of the information in this section is to make it easy for employers to get in touch with you at any time of the day.

Career Objective. The career objective section of resumes is probably the most controversial and most difficult one to prepare. Employers, career counselors, and job-hunting books have often given very different opinions about how to handle this part of the resume, including some that suggest you omit it completely. Furthermore, while the other sections of the resume are easy to put into words—they are part of your personal history databank—writing a career objective involves projecting out into the future, putting down on paper in a concise form what you want to do with your life! Some individuals get to the end of their education and training without giving much thought to this topic. The following paragraphs clarify some of what you may have heard about career objectives.

A career objective is designed to state as concisely as possible the type of position or opportunity you are seeking. In scope, it should be broad enough to cover any suitable employment and to interest a wide array of employers, yet specific enough to give an element of sound career direction to your resume. Your career objective should be guided by the self-knowledge you developed through the earlier activities and exercises in this class. What skills, interests, and values are reflected in the type of position you might be seeking? If you are a skilled writer, with an interest in travel, who values variety, your objective might be something like this:

> Seeking a position where I can use my writing skills as a features editor for a travel magazine.

Another strategy for developing your career objective involves focusing externally on things like the following:

- Position title
- Occupational or functional area
- Kind of organization
- Specific population to serve or manage

An example of this type of objective might be:

> Seeking a counselor position in a rehabilitation hospital, specializing in elder care.

In writing your objective, you may also combine your self-knowledge with your knowledge of specific options or types of organizations:

> To work for an environmental organization using my planning and technical skills.

If you are planning to seek employment in several different areas where the same objective would not be appropriate, consider writing a resume for each area. Do not try to mix diverse objectives in one statement. It will make employers think you don't know what you really want to do. Likewise, don't write a statement that is so vague that you aren't telling the employer anything of value—for example:

> Seeking a challenging position where I can apply my skills and knowledge and advance to my full potential.

An objective like this is basically a waste of space. The best objectives are personal, action oriented, and specific. They communicate what you have to offer the employer, and they show that you've done your homework on the field you want to enter. They are generally no more than one to two lines in length.

If you are having trouble writing your career objective, several activities might be helpful. Review your self-assessment exercises. What skills, interests, and values do you want reflected in your objective? Review your knowledge of options by examining occupational literature for fields you're interested in and employer literature for organizations you're interested in. Read specific job announcements for positions in your field. Review sample objectives in one of the many job hunting and resume books found in the career center or library on your campus.

As an alternative to putting the objective on the resume, you could omit it and use your cover letters to specify an objective targeted at a particular employer or position. This approach allows you to use language that matches the type of position you are seeking. The main disadvantage of this approach is that cover letters and resumes can get separated, creating a void for employers when it comes to information about your job interests and objectives.

Remember, whether you put the objective on the resume or leave it off, it is still important to give it some thought. When those in your circle of job-hunting contacts or prospective employers ask you "What are you interested in doing?" or "What type of position are you seeking?" you should have some fairly concrete ideas in mind. It never works to your advantage to say, "I'll do anything." The problem with that statement is that most job hunters really don't mean it (there are some jobs they wouldn't do!), and it makes narrowing down their job targets almost impossible. The Valuing stage of your job campaign should leave you with three to five well-focused job targets. You may add to these at any time, but you need a manageable number to start your job search.

Education. This section should begin with the highest level of training (even if your graduation date is some months in the future) and continue with all other schools attended, degrees earned, or training received. It is not necessary to include high school. However, if some items in the high school background show high honors or generally reinforce the career objective, then that data should be included. You should list the names of schools, dates attended or graduation date, degrees earned, and major/minor subjects. If your G.P.A. is good (3.0 or higher), you may wish to list it. You could include your G.P.A. in your major if that is higher. If your G.P.A. is not your "strong suit," leave it off, but be prepared to talk about it. Employers may still ask!

The possibilities for expansion in this category are unlimited, and you may decide to list selected courses you have taken as well as special projects, academic honors you have received, academic specializations, and activities in which you have participated. Beware! If you have a long list of these items, it might be wise to select only the most important and omit the others or include them in separate resume categories, such as "Honors/Awards," "Activities." Including all of these items under the "Education" category might distract from your degree and give your resume a cluttered appearance.

Experience. This category reflects your contact with specific employers in paid and unpaid work experience. It is permissible to include internships, volunteer work, summer jobs, special projects, or military experience under this category. If you have several experiences directly related to your objective, you may want to list those under "Related Experience" and your other experiences under "Other" or "Additional Experience."

List position titles, names of organizations, locations (city and state), dates, and duties for each entry under "Experience." Again, in presenting this information, choose a format where the most relevant material to your objective comes first in the resume. Here are two different examples:

Holiday Inn: Atlanta, GA

Desk Clerk (01/08–present) or

Desk Clerk—Holiday Inn; Atlanta, GA

January 2008 to present

Employers are mainly interested in the degree of responsibility you held and the skills you demonstrated. Try to outline your duties in such a way that the information about that experience is presented in the most positive way, and at the same time relate the experience to your professional objective. Here is an example:

McDonald's; Orlando, FL

Crew Chief, 09/07–08/08

- Managed daily food preparation and other operations
- Supervised five staff members
- Compiled inventory data and maintained stock
- Assisted in selecting, hiring, and training new employees

Positive-Quality/Action Word Lists. Use the positive-quality word list and positive-action word list in Table 12.5 to help you identify skills and accomplishments connected to your work experiences. Remember, any experiences, including those gained through student activities and volunteer work, may demonstrate your dependability, resourcefulness, and responsibility. Choose whatever shows your qualifications and experience to your best advantage. In describing your work experiences and in identifying your skills, action verbs are an indispensable tool. When selecting action verbs for your resume, make sure that you can provide detailed examples in an interview of when, how, and where you applied these skills in your previous experience. This list is by no means complete. You should add all the positive-quality and positive-action words that best describe your unique qualifications.

Personal. Experts once varied in their recommendations on whether or not to include personal information on your resume, or on what to include if you do have this category. However, because such personal information, e.g., your birthdate, marital status, physical characteristics, health, religion, and the like, has been ruled a basis for discrimination in hiring, employers do not like to see it in job application materials. Moreover, such personal information can be used by cyberthieves "phishing" for information that will compromise your identity. For these reasons, we advise against including personal information, especially related to your social security or driver's license numbers, in any of your job campaign materials unless it is clearly relevant to the job requirements.

Other Categories. The categories we have just outlined are standard for a resume. However, there are many more possible categories that might be included. If you have information that you feel is important but does not fit any of the above categories, create other categories for this information. Here are some possibilities:

- Activities
- Awards/Honors
- Background
- Certifications
- Computer skills
- Languages
- Memberships
- Special Skills
- Workshops/Seminars

Sample Resumes

Besides the two sample resume formats in Tables 12.3 and 12.4, additional samples can be found in career center libraries, online, and in the resume-writing books in most college and commercial bookstores. Don't get hung up on the search for the "perfect" format. You may find that none of the

TABLE 12.5   POSITIVE-QUALITY AND POSITIVE-ACTION WORD LISTS

Positive-Quality Words

ability	consistent	judicious	preference	sound
academic	developing	knowledgeable	productive	special
accuracy	effective	major	professional	stable
administrative	effectiveness	management	proficient	substantially
building	efficient	mature	proven	successful
capability	enlarging	maturity	qualified	technical
capable	executive	original	record	thorough
capacity	expanding	particularly	resourceful	thoroughly
competence	experienced	pertinent	responsible	versatile
competent	extensive	positive	significant	vigorous
completely	increasing	potential	significantly	well-rounded

Positive-Action Words

accomplish	contribute	explain	mobilize	repair
account	control	facilitate	model	report
achieve	coordinate	formulate	motivate	research
act	correct	furnish	negotiate	review
administer	counsel	guide	operate	schedule
advertise	create	handle	order	select
advise	dance	hire	originate	sell
analyze	delegate	implement	organize	serve
appraise	demonstrate	improve	paint	solve
appeal	decrease	increase	perform	speak
arrange	decide	initiate	persuade	staff
assemble	design	influence	photograph	start
assign	determine	inspect	plan	structure
assist	develop	install	play	submit
attend	devise	instruct	predict	supervise
audit	diagnose	interpret	prepare	supply
authorize	direct	interview	present	synthesize
budget	discover	invent	preside	talk
build	document	investigate	produce	teach
calculate	draft	judge	program	test
catalogue	draw	landscape	promote	train
chart	edit	lead	propose	translate
clarify	engineer	learn	provide	travel
collect	entertain	listen	publish	tutor
communicate	establish	make	purchase	type
compete	estimate	manage	qualify	understand
complete	evaluate	manufacture	raise	verify
compile	exercise	market	read	write
compose	exhibit	measure	recommend	
conduct	experiment	meet	recruit	

samples seem appropriate for the presentation of your unique qualifications. You may also, however, discover that all the samples seem like the best way for you to proceed. Confused? Pick and choose whatever is useful and consistent with your individual needs and objectives and presents your qualifications well to prospective employers—then create your own original resume. The final document should be one you're proud of and about which you're comfortable talking to prospective employers.

Critiquing Your Resume

We recommend that you have several people whose opinion you respect critique your best draft copy. You may also bring your resume to the career center on your campus, and a staff member can review it with you. Use the Resume Critiquing sheet in *Appendix K* as a guide in the analysis of the document.

Reproducing Your Resume

Your resume is only good if many people see it, and this means that you will need to make many copies, perhaps hundreds (this goes back to the cost issue we brought up earlier). There are several considerations in reproducing your resume in quantity.

Preparing the original. To reproduce your resume, your will need a good, clean, high-contrast original copy. Most people use word-processing software to create this original.

A word-processed original is typically done on a personal computer. A typeset original (called a camera-ready copy) is done by a professional with a typesetter. Names of typesetters and word processors and their fees can be obtained from your career center or by consulting the yellow pages in the telephone book. There are differences between typeset and word-processed resumes in both appearance and cost, and only you can decide which best suits your situation. If you are purchasing resume services, examine the quality of work produced by the vendor—shop around.

Another development in the preparation of resumes is the fairly widespread availability of resume-writing software packages or templates. These usually provide several preset formats to guide you through the resume preparation process, as well as other helpful tips on preparing your resume. Some people like having the resume sections already laid out in the template so all they have to do is "fill-in-the-blanks." Others prefer using standard word-processing software to create their resume document. The downside of using templates is that your resume tends to look like everyone else's and the pre-set format may restrict your options for arranging and highlighting information in a way that best presents your qualifications. We discourage the use of preset formats in resume development but you can decide what approach to resume development works best for you.

Making copies. If you do your resume using word-processing software, use the best printer available (high quality laser printers are recommended). If your resume is typeset, the print shop usually reproduces it for you.

Resume Do's and Don'ts

Before you begin the task of actually writing your rough draft, thoroughly familiarize yourself with the "Do's and Don'ts" outlined here. By following these tips, you should increase the probability of producing a clear and readable account of your unique qualifications. Use the self-knowledge gained in Part One as you think about how you want to market yourself to prospective employers.

Do's

1. *Be brief, clear, and concise.* A resume stands a much better chance if it is easy to read and well organized.

2. *Be consistent.* Experiment with the arrangement of headlines, captions, indentations, blocks of text, and the use of capitals and underscoring. Then choose a layout that is readable and appealing to the eye, and stick with it. Make use of the white space surrounding the words for emphasis.

3. *Be positive.* Start statements or phrases with verbs denoting positive activity, such as "successfully introduced," "initiated," and so on. (See the Table 12.5 Positive-Quality/Action Word Lists for ideas. Avoid the use of the personal pronoun "I.")

4. *Be honest.* Many organizations consider your resume to be part of a job application, and false information on an application or resume is grounds for immediate dismissal. Besides reflecting a lack of personal integrity, false resume information is just bad practice in a job campaign.

5. *Be careful.* Double-check for typographical errors and mistakes in grammar, spelling, or punctuation. Do not hesitate to consult a dictionary or use the spell check feature on the computer. Errors in copy editing may suggest careless and shoddy workmanship, and most employers immediately eliminate any resumes with errors.

6. *Be neat.* Prepare your resume on 8.5 × 11 inch paper, then have it printed or photocopied. Use lots of white space when typing your resume to avoid the cluttered look. Make sure you get a clear, unmarred copy. Use a laser or other high-quality printer to produce your original copy.

Don'ts

1. Don't state salary requirements.

2. Don't give reasons for changing past employers.

3. Don't limit geographical considerations unless necessary.

4. Don't expound on philosophy or values.

5. Don't offer any negative information.

You will find that there are many different ideas in the literature on what is best in writing a resume. Almost everyone seems to have an opinion about what should be included in a resume. The http://www.amazon.com site listed over 600 different books related to resume writing. This is a huge collection and an indication of the numerous and varied points of view that exist on this topic. The titles listed included books on almost every kind of resume issue or topic imaginable. The information in this chapter is a distillation of what the authors think is most important to know about this topic, especially for a college student seeking employment after graduation.

Resume vs. Vita

For typical college graduates completing bachelor's degrees, the accepted format for resumes is a one- to two-page document that focuses primarily on education and experience and, second, on any additional activities and honors that enhance qualifications and skills in the eyes of prospective employers.

A resume should be brief and concise. Its purpose is to get you an interview. A vita, on the other hand, is a complete, cumulative record or history of your academic and professional accomplishments. The word *vita* is Latin and literally means "life."

Occasionally, on some position announcements, you may see at the bottom a request to send a copy of your vita. Vitae have their origin in the academic job search process. They are primarily used by people with advanced degrees who are seeking positions in colleges, universities, or similar organizations. They may also be used by persons applying to graduate school.

The focus of a vita is on areas of accomplishment that are traditionally valued by academic institutions, such as:

- Publications

- Presentations

- Research

- Consultations

- Grant writing

- Fundraising
- Certifications or licenses
- Professional development activities
- Professional leadership activities
- Teaching
- Service

The length of a vita may be anywhere from 2 to as many as 100 pages—as is the case with some college faculty! It is unlikely that a recent undergraduate would have a need for a vita. Books devoted to the academic job search include sample vitae. If you're in doubt about whether to send a resume or a vita when applying for a particular position or seeking admission to graduate school, check with a career services professional or someone in the field to ensure that you follow the most appropriate format in your application.

REFERENCES AND LETTERS OF RECOMMENDATION

In many of the written forms of communication used in a job campaign, the issue of job references comes up. You may use both your letters to employers and your resume to communicate information about the availability of references. References in the job-search process usually consist of three to four individuals who can speak to prospective employers about your qualifications and personal characteristics, particularly as they relate to a specific position.

For recent graduates, these are usually some combination of current and former employers, as well as individuals on campus such as faculty, student organization advisors, or other staff that know you fairly well. For more experienced job hunters with a lengthy work history, references will usually be drawn from their most recent employers. "Personal references" are rarely requested. These may be neighbors, people who knew you growing up, people in your religious group, and similar types of individuals.

Employers are generally more interested in references who will speak honestly and accurately about your qualifications as a prospective employee. They are interested in your work habits, and they may want to verify information on your resume. The most important thing for you to do is to *ask* your references if they're willing to serve in this capacity *before* you put them on a list and give it to employers.

Some references might be willing to write specific letters for each position you apply for (this is the ideal option), and others may prefer to simply write "To whom it may concern" letters that are more generic in nature. In the latter instance, you would keep these letters yourself and send copies of them when requested by employers. Another alternative is to put reference letters on file with your career center's credentials service (this is described in more detail later).

When presenting reference information on your resume, several formats can be used:

1. One option is to simply include "References available upon request" at the bottom of the resume. This is the most common practice.

2. Another alternative is to state "Credentials available from Career Services, State University, Anytown, FL 32306-2490. If you choose this option, contact the appropriate office to get more information on how to set up a credentials file. This file allows you to keep letters of recommendation on file with the career center. These letters can be mailed by the career center to potential employers or graduate schools for a small fee upon your request.

TABLE 12.6	SAMPLE REFERENCE PAGE

REFERENCES

for Ms. Jane Jones

Ms. Alice Smith, Program Coordinator
All-American Foundation
Koger Building, Room 122
Tampa, FL 32309
(813) 487-1111

Mr. Tony Mason, Vice President for Operations
Leon County Civic Center
515 W. Pensacola Street
Tallahassee, FL 32304
(850) 942-1111

Dr. Lynn Smith, Professor
College of Education
Room 120 Stone Building
State University
Jacksonville, FL 32306-1059
(850) 644-1111
lsmith@coe.fsu.edu

3. A third alternative is to list on a separate page the names, titles, addresses, and telephone numbers of people (three to five) who can attest to your experience or knowledge of subject matter. You may also include their e-mail addresses, if available. A sample reference page is shown in Table 12.6. As a courtesy, remember to send copies of your resume to your references so they are informed about the materials you are using in your job campaign and can address any questions raised by potential employers.

RECORD KEEPING IN THE JOB CAMPAIGN

It should be apparent by now that the job campaign is an information-intensive and paper-intensive process. For example, if you are working with 5 prospective employers and you have 10 bits of information about each of them, that's 50 pieces of information to catalog and file. You will be keeping up with many documents in the process of the job campaign, including the following:

- Your own letters of inquiry, application, thank you, acceptance

- Resume(s) and career objective statements

- Lists of job contacts and referrals (information interviews and social network contacts)

- Business cards

- Notes from telephone and personal conversations

- Past and future dates of contacts with employers

- Copies of job announcements and position descriptions

- Employer literature

- Printouts from Internet sites

- Receipts, invoices, and costs associated with your job campaign

- Return correspondence, e-mails, and phone messages from employers

The most successful job hunters develop some kind of cataloging system that helps them maintain this information is usable and easily retrievable form.

As you make contacts through your networking and information interviewing, you need a record of whom you spoke with (name, title, phone, address, etc.), what was discussed, and what follow-up is needed, by whom and by when. Similarly, if your contacts give you additional referrals, you need to repeat this process with those individuals. For those employers you contacted regarding specific vacancies, you need to note when letters were sent, when additional phone calls need to be made, and what action is needed next on your or the employers' part.

Before you begin sending any written correspondence as part of your job search, it is important that you devise some way of keeping track of when and what you have sent. For instance, if you send a letter to Mr. Jones asking for an interview and offer to call him during the week of June 6, you need to have that date on record so you can be sure to meet that commitment. Also, if you are sending out 40 letters to various employers, it can be critical to know what you have said in a particular letter to be able to follow it up with accuracy.

Store copies of all the letters that you send out either in an electronic file or a more traditional paper file. Keep another folder for the letters you receive that call for further action to be taken on your part, and keep a separate folder for your rejection letters. This method can be especially helpful because you have immediate reference to all your letters for use when composing other letters. Also, you can look back over the letters you have sent and see which ones were the most effective in generating interviews.

The format used and the type of information included in any record-keeping system may vary slightly from one job hunter to another, but it's critical that you develop a system for tracking what employers you've contacted, by what means, on what date, nature of the contact (phone, mail, or in person), what responses were received, and what follow-up, if any, is needed. One example of a record-keeping form is shown in Table 12.7. Copy this for your own use, or adapt it in a manner that fits your system.

We have now outlined the standard ways that written communications are used in a job campaign. We have seen several different kinds of letters used in job campaigns, an analysis of resume types and content, a discussion of career objectives, the use of references, and the need for establishing a record-keeping system. Now we'll briefly examine methods for job hunting on the Internet.

JOB SEARCHING ON THE INTERNET

Any discussion of written job-search strategies in today's marketplace would be incomplete without a discussion of the role of the Internet in the job search. A recent search of the keyword *"employment"* using one of the more popular search tools on the Internet resulted in over 240 million hits related to this topic! Space does not permit listing all the employment sites out there in cyberspace; readers seeking this type of information are referred to the sample list of World Wide Web sites later in this chapter. This section will suggest resources for identifying and utilizing job search sites, review some of the uses of the Internet in a job search, and provide sample sites for further exploration.

You can generally find career and job search information in one of several ways, using the Internet or other sources:

TABLE 12.7 RECORD OF EMPLOYER CONTACTS

Employment Activities & Events	Employer Contact Information: Person, Title, Telephone	XYZ Corporation Mrs. Alice Martin, Recruiter (407) 892-1944
1. Inquiry for Job Opening Sent		10/16
No Openings Available		
Job Announcement Received		10/29
2. Applied for Job		11/4
Acknowledgement Received		11/17
Interview Offer Received		11/25
3. Accepted or Rejected Interview		Accepted, 11/28
Signed up for Campus Interview		
Researched Organization & Position		11/26
Follow-up Letter Sent		11/29
4. Second Interview Accepted or Rejected		Accepted, 12/8
Follow-up Letter Sent		12/9
5. Job Offer Received		12/16
Responded by		12/19
Acceptance or Rejection Sent		Accepted, 12/19
6. Rejection Letter Received		----------------
7. Terminated Job Contract		----------------
8. Sent "I Remain Interested" Letter		----------------

- Use online indexing systems ("search engines"), such as Yahoo or Google.

- Look in publications or directories of specialty sites on the Internet.

- Ask professionals in your career area for the electronic addresses of helpful sites.

- Identify special topic Web pages that may link to useful sites.

Books with Internet information related to career planning and job-hunting on the Internet have been written since 1995, reflecting how the Internet has developed over the past decade. These resources provide detailed information about using the Internet for your job search, such as locating specific sites and services and developing helpful strategies for different career development and job-search activities. Books and/or lists of books about the Internet are usually available in career center, campus, and community libraries. Bookstores also sell current Internet titles, which can be found in the career and/or computer sections. In using any resource materials, always consider the qualifications of the authors or presenters and the date of publication. *Remember that the Internet and the job-hunt process are changing continuously*!

Here are some current titles:

- *Best Career and Education Web Sites: A Quick Guide to Online Job Search* (Wolfinger, 2007)

- *Guide to Internet Job Searching 2008–2009* (Dikel & Roehm, 2008)

- *Job Hunting on the Internet* (Bolles, 2008)

- *The Almanac of American Employers 2008: Market Research, Statistics & Trends Pertaining to the Leading Corporate Employers in America* (Plunkett, 2007)

In addition to these books, there are other information resources and tools to help you increase your Internet savvy. Relevant articles about finding jobs and other information on the Internet can usually be found in career center library files and in other libraries. Professional newsletters, daily newspapers, and popular magazines publish articles about using and finding information on the Internet. In many campus and public library settings, you will find guides or information sheets with step-by-step or generalized instructions for using and finding information on the Internet. Finally, consider attending a workshop for step-by-step instruction, in-depth assistance, and hands-on practice on the Internet. Many of these are offered on campus and through continuing education programs.

How Can I Utilize the Internet in My Job Search?

Most authorities suggest that the Internet should supplement, not replace, other information sources and job-search methods. Margaret Riley-Dikel and Frances Roehm (2008) emphasized that the Internet should only be one of the resources used in your job search! You must continue to utilize all contacts, information resources, and services available to you for the most effective and efficient search for employment." Like other job-search tasks, using the Internet requires you to use good research and critical evaluation skills.

Using the Internet for your job search lets you do the following:

- Access timely (and often free) employment resources and data both day and night.

- Locate unusual or difficult-to-find career information.

- Communicate with many people or resource groups in specialized areas.

- Research potential employers and organizations.

- Identify position openings by occupation and state.

- Post your resume and apply online on various networks.

Some drawbacks of using the Internet for your job search include:

- Vast, unwieldy amounts of career and job search information (sometimes it's like looking for a needle in a haystack).

- Privacy issues related to posting your resume online.

- Over-utilizing the Internet while under-utilizing traditional job hunting resources (print, people, etc.)

- Disappearance or relocation of useful sites without notice.

- Dated or inaccurate information found on some Web sites.

Despite these drawbacks, the Internet can still have an important role to play as one tool in your job-search kit. Through various Web sites you can locate job openings in different parts of the country or the world, find and copy files of employer literature, exchange electronic messages with professionals in different fields, and share ideas and information with specialty user groups online. Employers increasingly use the Internet as a recruiting tool, and a 2006 employer survey indicated that almost half require completion of an online application (National Association of Colleges & Employers, 2006). Obtaining an electronic mail (e-mail) account is essential in your job campaign, and for security reasons (e.g., Internet broadcasting) it might be different from the one you use for other purposes. Many job-search services and resources on the Internet are free to job seekers, but some are not. Three job search activities—(1) networking, (2) researching employers, and (3) identifying job openings—particularly take advantage of the Internet's capabilities.

Social Networking Sites

Facebook, Friendster, and Myspace have been in the news with respect to an emerging issue in the employment campaign. "Digital dirt," which includes one's rants and raves, photos, hobbies, and other unflattering personal information drifting around the Internet on blogs and social networking sites, has become a frequent discussion topic. It has reportedly doomed some job searches before they got started because employers checked out these sites about prospective hires (Johnson, 2006). Flesher (2006) reported that 75 percent of recruiters in one survey use search engines to uncover information about candidates, and 26 percent have eliminated candidates because of information found online. In contrast, Collins (2006) noted that while 40 percent of recruiters surveyed by the National Association of Colleges and Employers were considering visiting social networking sites in making hiring decisions, only 10 percent actually used this practice in the 2006-2007 recruiting season.

Melber (2008) reported that 80 percent of college students are registered with Facebook, and more than 60 percent have posted political views, relationship status, interests, photos, and an address. It should be noted that everything posted on Facebook is automatically licensed to this private company for its perpetual and transferable use, distribution, or public display (Melber, 2008). Given this situation, it is important for students to use privacy settings to limit access to sites such as a Facebook profile, to closely monitor their online material (do some "narcisurfing" to Google yourself or use dogpile.com to see what's out there), and contact a webmaster if something needs to be changed. Flesher (2006) and Lavallee (2007) provided additional ideas for cleaning up online reputations.

In spite of these problems, Cullen (2007) reported that Jobster, an online job board, is teaming with Facebook to launch a site featuring video resumes. Other companies, e.g., YouTube, HireVue, Resumevideo, are reportedly engaged in similar ventures. Some claim that it is only a matter of time before the paper resume is outdated. However, as noted earlier in this chapter, employers are hesitant to adopt these new schemes because of lawsuits that might claim discrimination based on sex, race, or other things as a result of using such media materials in recruiting.

Gather Networking Resources

The Internet can be a great way to network with professionals in different fields and organizations, even though you do not generally interact face-to-face. In fact, a great deal of your networking communications will be written e-mails or postings, and should follow good "netiquette" (an appropriate level of formality). Developing relationships, building up your contacts, sharing information, getting advice, and establishing a credible presence in your field can be done with mailing lists, professional association Web sites, chat rooms, and Usenet newsgroups. Association Web sites, in addition to providing career information and education resources, may offer online mentoring programs, sponsor chat rooms and/or provide access to membership directories. An example of an association Web site for public relations majors is http://www.prssa.org/. Another is the American Society for Association Executives which provides directories to people in various professional groups (http://www.asaecenter.org). Mailing lists (sometimes called "listservs") allow members to send and automatically receive messages via e-mail; thus, professionals use mailing lists for their particular career area to discuss significant industry topics and post an occasional job opening. Usenet newsgroups (sometimes called discussion forums) can provide you with current job openings in your field and/or professional networking opportunities, as users ask and answer questions of interest to the newsgroup, and post job openings, career fair announcements, and resumes.

While e-mail is so common and flexible, it is important to remember that in a job campaign your messages communicate an image of you as a professional. Besides being detailed and concise, here are some other pointers: (1) use spell check; (2) provide an informative title in the subject line; (3) never use "hey" as a greeting instead of Mr., Ms., or Dr.; (4) reply in a timely fashion; (5) sign off courteously; and (6) don't use a graphical business card in your signature because it may be blocked by the recipient's computer (Primm, 2004).

Access Employer Information

Using effective online research strategies, you can locate specific, detailed industrial and employer data on the Internet. The more you develop skills in keyword and advanced searching techniques, the more effectively you can communicate your research objectives and obtain the information you need. Directory Web sites maintain databases of public and private enterprises, where you can identify employers by location, industry, occupation or employer name. For example, you can locate the chamber of commerce directory for many towns in the U.S. at http://www.chamberofcommerce.com if your job target is in a particular city. Another useful Web site, http://www.learnwebskills.com/company/index.html, provides a way for you to search for companies online. Don't forget that your college (campus) library may have other tools to help you research employers. Articles from newspapers, magazines, and other media sources, available through online databases, can give you the history of an employer, its current position in the industry, new products or services, majors competitors, and general financial status. Employer Web sites often contain their mission statements, annual reports, employee benefits information, and press releases. Information on employer sites typically favors the employer, so you may want to use other resources in your research to get a complete picture.

Identify Job Opening Resources

Current, unique, and abundant employment sites can make the Internet a productive place for you to find job openings. Job database services contain job listings that may be searched by criteria such as location, industry, occupation, salary level, position, etc. The more you know about the type, level and location of the job you want, the more efficient your search will be. Specialty sites focus on certain geographic regions (local, state or international), type of work (industry or occupation), or populations (minorities, persons with disabilities or career changers), and usually include both job openings and career information. In addition to some of the Web sites listed below, don't forget to check newspapers in towns where you are seeking employment, e.g., http://www.orlandosentinel.com, or specialty sites, e.g., http://www.overseasjobs.com. At times an employer may ask you to send your resume electronically. For some job hunters, particularly those with technical training, this is a way to demonstrate your skills with the latest technology. However, many organizations want you to do things the "old-fashioned way" and send your resume and related application materials through the (snail) mail. Read the instructions carefully when following up on any job listing to see which communication methods the employer prefers.

World Wide Web Sites

As noted at the beginning of this chapter, entire books contain lists of specific job search sites. Space does not permit us to give widespread coverage to these sites, but following is a sampling of Web pages related to job searching. Neither the authors nor the publisher take responsibility for any information contained in these sites. Also, please note that addresses may have changed since the publication of this text.

Occupational Information—useful to review prior to researching specific job titles and employers.

- **Occupational Outlook Handbook (OOH)** <http://www.bls.gov/oco/>
- **O*NET** <http://online.onetcenter.org/>
- **State Occupational Projections** <http://www.projectionscentral.com/>

Employer Research—needed to identify possible employers and do research prior to interviews

- **SEC Edgar** Company Filings Search <http://www.sec.gov/>
- **GuideStar** National Database of Non-Profit Organizations <http://www.guidestar.org>
- **Researching Companies Online** <http://www.learnwebskills.com/company/>

Job Openings—post open positions; often offer applicant resume database services

- **America's Job Bank** Ceased operations in July, 2007
- **Career One Stop** <http://www.careeronestop.org>
- **Careerbuilder** <http://www.careerbuilder.com>
- **Monster** <http://www.monster.com>
- **Yahoo Hot Jobs** <http://hotjobs.yahoo.com/>

Government Employment/Jobs—focus on openings at federal, state, or local levels

- **State Government Jobs** <http://www.50statejobs.com/gov.html>
- **Federal government jobs** <http://www.usajobs.gov>

Job Search Process—contain articles, guides, lists of resources, etc. to guide the job seeker

- **America's Career InfoNet** … links to state job banks <http://www.jobbankinfo.org/>
- **CareerJournal.com** … executive career site <http://www.careerjournal.com/>
- **JobWeb** … advice for new college graduates <http://www.jobweb.com>
- **The Riley Guide** … career and employment information <http://www.rileyguide.com>

Salary and Relocation—helpful for salary negotiations and making decisions on job offers

- **Bureau of Labor Statistics Wage Estimates** <http://stats.bls.gov/oes/2000/oessrcma.htm>
- **Homefair.com** <http://www.homefair.com/>
- **Salary.com** <http://www.salary.com>

University Career Center—check the Web sites provided by your campus career center

- **Florida State University Career Center Library** <http://www.career.fsu.edu/library/links.html>

This is a brief introduction to using the Internet as part of your written job search strategy—to locate job listings, research employers, network with professionals, and learn about specific job search topics such as salary negotiation, interviewing or starting your first job. Understanding how to use the Internet effectively may give you an edge in your job campaign. As can be seen from all the activities described above, job searching involves considerable information processing, storage and retrieval. This is part of the reason why we believe a Cognitive Information Processing (CIP) approach to career problem solving and decision making is appropriate.

A CIP PERSPECTIVE

We have discussed written communications associated with a job campaign, including letters and resumes. Now we'll review what we have learned about this topic from a CIP perspective.

Self-Knowledge

In developing various forms of written communication in the job-search process, your self-knowledge is extremely important. Both the cover letter and the resume are marketing tools that communicate to prospective employers how you see yourself and what you have to offer. Using the results of your self-assessment, you can better describe the skills you want to use, the types of interests you want to incorporate into your work, and what's important to you about the type of work you do. If your self-knowledge is vague or disorganized, it makes it hard to focus your job search and communicate to employers what it is you want to do for them and with them.

Option Knowledge

Being effective in written communication in your job campaign means knowing enough about prospective employers, job targets, and industries to express effectively why you want to be considered for a particular position and why your qualifications make you a good candidate for the position. There's an old saying in the job-hunting process: "You can't go looking until you know what you're searching for." A job campaign means knowing "what's out there," and that involves learning about the various environments where you might find employment.

Decision Making

The information gathered in the Analysis phase of the CASVE Cycle helps you move to the Synthesis phase, where you may expand your thinking about job search options and then narrow that list to those three to five options with the most potential for you. When you move into the Execution phase and begin writing resumes and cover letters, these tasks become a little easier when you're working with accurate and well-focused information about what your want in a job and which employers have the potential to meet your objective.

Targeting employers and implementing a plan to reach them through various forms of written communication require you to give attention to each aspect of the CASVE Cycle. Most experts agree that a job hunter who goes right to the Execution phase, sending out dozens of resumes, applying for anything, anywhere, is doomed to failure, either because that person will fail to turn up any serious offers or will accept a position that is a poor fit with his or her longer-term personal requirements. In developing your PCT for solving employment problems, you will want to avoid this trap.

Executive Processing

Some job hunters sabotage themselves early on in a job campaign with the poor quality meta-cognitions embedded in their Personal Career Theory. For example, we often hear job hunters saying things such as "I don't have anything to put on a resume." "What employer would be interested in me?" "I don't have any work experience in my field." These job hunters allow themselves to be intimidated by thoughts of rejection, and they engage in negative thinking when they put themselves on paper or the Internet. They only have vague notions of what they want to communicate, and their lack of confidence comes through in their job-search documents.

If you don't think you're someone worth hiring, employers probably won't either. We suggest that you use the techniques described earlier in this text to learn how to think more positively about what you have to offer, and make sure this is clearly communicated in all your written correspondence with prospective employers.

SUMMARY

This chapter has highlighted and contrasted basic forms of written communication used in the employment campaign. Despite many advances in electronic communication, much of the job-search process still relies on standard forms of written and verbal communication. In fact, you may see employers noting in their position announcements "Do not send e-mails." Demonstrating effective written communication skills can greatly increase your chances of gaining access to employers and achieving the ultimate goal of a job offer that matches your personal goals and preferences. We concluded this chapter with an analysis of how CIP concepts can help you think through the information you need to communicate in written forms to prospective employers and avoid the tendency to let negative thinking interfere with your ability to successfully present your paper "credentials." The goal was to enable you to improve the quality of your PCT related to written communications and the employment process.

REFERENCES

Bolles, R. (2008). *Job hunting on the Internet.* Berkeley, CA: Ten Speed Press.

Collins, M. (2006, December). College recruiting and hiring: What to watch in 2007. *NACE Journal, 67,* 14–16

Cullen, L. T. (2007, February 22). It's a wrap: You're hired! *Time.* Retrieved March 5, 2007, from http://www.time.com/time/printout/0,8816,1592860,00.html.

Dikel, M., & Roehm, F. (2008). *The guide to Internet job searching 2008–2009.* Columbus, OH: McGraw-Hill.

Farr, J. M. (2004). *The very quick job search.* (2nd ed.) Indianapolis, IN: JIST Works, Inc.

Flesher, J. (2006, January 12). How to clean up your digital dirt before it trashes your job search. *CareerJournal.com.* Retrieved March 3, 2008, from http://executiverecruitment.com/jobhunting/usingnet/20060112-flesher.html.

Johnson, T. (2006, March 16). Tory Johnson: Dusting your digital dirt. *AC News Internet Ventures.* Retrieved March 3, 2008, from http//abcnews.go.com/print?id=1729525.

LaVallee, A. (2007, June 13). Firms tidy up clients' bad online reputations. Retrieved June 14, 2007, from http://online.wsj.com/public/article_print/SB118169502070033315.html.

Melber, A. (2008, January 7/14). About Facebook. *Nation,* pp. 22–24.

National Association of Colleges & Employers (1996). One-page resumes rate high. *Spotlight, 18*(21), 1.

Plunkett, J. W. (Ed.) (2007). *The almanac of American employers 2008: Market research, statistics & trends pertaining to the leading corporate employers in America.* Houston, TX: Plunkett Research.

Primm, C. (2004). E-mail etiquette. *KForce professional staffing.* Retrieved May 3, 2005, from http://www.kfroce.com/kforce/corporate/me.get?WEB.entities.show&Kforce_00548.

Wolfinger, A. (2007). *Best career and education web sites: A quick guide to online job search.* Indianapolis, IN: JIST Works.

INTERPERSONAL COMMUNICATIONS IN JOB HUNTING

I n addition to the written communications presented in Chapter 12, job hunters also need skills in verbal and interpersonal communication. A person might get a job offer without submitting a resume, or without filling out an application, but it is almost inconceivable that a person would get a job offer without being interviewed. Job hunting is basically a social process that involves meeting and talking with different people. There is no way to escape this reality.

The interpersonal communication skills needed in job hunting take many different forms, including information interviews, networking, initial interviews, and second interviews or site visits. Mastering the skills associated with these different kinds of interview situations can greatly increase your potential for success as a job hunter. There are entire books, Web sites and seminars devoted to helping job hunters improve their skills in these forms of verbal communication, and this chapter will provide a basic overview. We will include distinctions between the terms listed above and suggest strategies for effectively using these communication techniques in the job-search process. (*Note*: Although our focus is on job hunting, effective interpersonal communication is also associated with applications for job-training programs, internships, co-op positions, and graduate school.)

As you read about how verbal communications are used in a job campaign, think about how your Personal Career Theory (PCT) and strategic career thinking can be improved by this information. How will this information affect the kind of job campaign activities you will pursue, how will you go about preparing and improving your *interviewing skills, and how much time will you devote to these activities? How and when will you begin preparing for the interpersonal aspects of a job campaign? Our goal in this chapter is to help you improve your PCT and the interpersonal skills needed for solving employment problems.*

INFORMATION INTERVIEWS

One way to research a potential employer or career field is through "informal" sources of information. Information interviews involve direct meetings set up with selected people to obtain "insider" information about an industry, occupation, organization, or training program, which may provide answers to your questions that print or electronic resources do not cover. An information interview can help you learn about special problems or needs associated with a work area and how you might fit into a job situation.

Information interviews can often be arranged regardless of an existing job vacancy. In contrast, an employer may not grant a job interview because vacancies do not exist. Unlike job interviews, information interviews require you to initiate contact with an employer and schedule the appointment. If you already have a referral through friends, family, former employers, or associates, you can call or e-mail the interviewee directly to set up an appointment at his or her convenience. If you don't have a referral, you may seek contacts from career services staff at your school, faculty or other university personnel, members of professional organizations and trade associations, or local newspapers and magazines, or you can call the employer and ask the receptionist for suggestions. In setting up an information interview, a possible lead-in might be to explain that you are conducting *personal research* on occupations in areas of interest to you.

Preparing for the information interview and knowing how to conduct yourself during the appointment are very important, and these are somewhat different from a job interview. You must truly desire to obtain information from the interviewee and have well-prepared questions related to the occupation or work area you're trying to learn more about.

Information interviews should not be used in a dishonest way to obtain a job interview with an employer. For example, don't pretend to need information about a position or organization as an excuse for an interview when you already have the information. People who do this have given information interviewing a bad name in some places, and organizations have adopted policies prohibiting staff from participating in information interviews.

Information interviews should *not* be used to obtain information that is readily available somewhere else, such as in employer literature, videotapes, CDs, or Web sites. Also, do your homework on the field you're seeking to enter by reading career literature *before* you call to setup an information interview. You can then use the information interview to verify your impressions from the print material.

Preparing for the Information Interview

Here are some possible questions you might want to ask in an information interview. Remember, you are using this technique in *personal research* related to your career options, and you want to select questions that will provide information to help you move through the CASVE Cycle.

1. *Background.* Tell me how you got started in this field. What was your education? What educational background or related experience might be helpful in entering this field?

2. *Work environment.* What are the daily duties of the job? What are the working conditions? What skills/abilities are utilized in this work?

3. *Problems.* What are the toughest problems you deal with? What problem does the organization as a whole have? What is being done to solve these problems?

4. *Lifestyle.* What, if any, work obligations do you have outside the workweek? How much flexibility do you have in terms of dress? Work hours? Vacations?

5. *Rewards.* What do you find most rewarding about this work?

6. *Salary.* What are starting salaries for people entering this field? What are some typical fringe benefits? What are other forms of compensation (bonuses, commissions, securities)?

7. *Potential.* Where do you see yourself going in a few years? What are your short- and long-term goals?

8. *Promotional.* What are the opportunities for advancement in this organization? How does one move from position to position? What happened to the person(s) who last held this position? How many people have held this job in the last five years? How are employees evaluated? What types of training are typically available to help employees maintain and diversify their skills?

9. *Industry.* What trends do you see for this industry in the next three to five years? What kind of future do you see for this organization? How much of your business is tied to the economy, government spending, weather, supplies, global marketplace conditions, and so forth.

10. *Demand.* What types of employers hire people in this line of work? Where are they located? What other career areas are related to this type of work?

11. *Networking.* Whom might you contact to obtain further useful information? Which employers are likely to have job openings in this field? What are the names and phone numbers of contact people at these organizations?

Answers to these and related questions should provide you with supplemental information beyond what is available in library resources, on Web sites, and in recruiting materials.

Arranging an Information Interview

To arrange an information interview, e-mail, phone, or write people you wish to interview and request a brief meeting (20 to 30 minutes) at their convenience. "Since no one truly owes you the courtesy of their time and information, your approach to them will determine to some extent the speed at which you are successful" (Stoodley, 1990, p. 11). It's preferable if you can introduce yourself by using a personal referral, for example, "Ms. Jones in the Human Services department suggested I get in touch with you to get more information on opportunities in the field of gerontology." If the person you contact is busy, ask when would be a better time in the future to speak to you, or ask if he or she could suggest someone else in the organization that might be able to answer your questions.

Be prepared to encounter receptionists who may not let you through. Be persistent. Be aware that, having been abused by other job hunters, some employers may be suspicious, and they may question you rather directly about your motives and purpose in seeking to meet with them. Be ready to answer questions from people you call about *why* you want the meeting. Some people only hear the word "interview" and immediately try to put you off by saying, "we don't have openings" or something similar. You need to be clear in your purpose—that you're seeking some "real world" information about a field or industry you're interested in, information not available through print sources. Anticipate these types of questions by employers so that you're not intimidated or flustered, and politely but firmly explain your purpose in seeking a face-to-face meeting with them.

Sometimes when you make your phone call to set up the interview, the person will say, "I have some time now—what would you like to know?" Be prepared for this! This means you that you will need to have designed your interview before you call and have the questions in front of you, so you will not be thrown by the interviewee's willingness to talk on the spur of the moment.

The following are more tips for handling an information interview:

- Practice with a friend who can help you become comfortable asking questions if information interviewing is a new skill for you.

- Dress as if it were an actual job interview. First impressions are always important, and it is possible that the interviewee might be impressed with the way you conduct the interview and offer you an internship or an opportunity to interview for a job later.

- Get to your appointment a few minutes early, and *be courteous* to everyone that you meet—secretary, receptionist, security personnel, etc.

- Take the initiative in conducting the interview. You ask the questions; you interview the person. Ask open-ended questions that promote a discussion and cannot be answered with one-word responses. Make it a conversation—ask follow-up questions about things that interest you.

- Once inside the organization, look around. What kind of work environment do you find? What are the dress styles? The communication patterns? The office arrangements? The organizational culture? Is this a place you would want to be trained or work?

- Do not exceed your requested time for the interview, but be prepared to stay longer in case the interviewee is willing to continue the conversation beyond the allotted time.

After the Interview

After the information interview, do some follow-up. Immediately send a note thanking the person for taking the time to meet with you. This can be done via e-mail, but remember, as noted in Chapter 12, to communicate in a professional manner regardless of the method. If, as a result of the meeting, you want to pursue further employment with the organization, you may follow up later with a cover letter, resume, or application. Record the information you obtained in the interview, e.g., names, comments, new referrals. Make appointments to conduct follow-up interviews with the referrals you were given. Every information interview contact will hopefully produce the names of additional individuals to add to your networking circle.

Evaluate your experience. Were you pleased with how the process went? Did you get the information you sought? What information do you still lack? What do you need to do next? Sometimes people come away from information interviews saying, "That was a waste of my time. They didn't have any openings." That kind of statement reflects a lack of understanding of the many uses of the information interview. While it would be ideal if every information interview uncovered "hidden" openings, you need to go in with the understanding that in most cases all you will be getting is a unique source of information to help you in exploring options and employers, and possibly referrals to other useful contacts. Any information about specific openings is simply "gravy"—a bonus. *Getting job leads should not be the primary goal in conducting information interviews.*

Information interviews have the potential to make you a more informed job hunter and enable you to make better decisions about your future options, including internships, training programs, and organizational preferences. Many job-hunting books (e.g., Bolles, 2008) have additional tips devoted to information interviewing. If you're unsure about how to best use information interviews in your job search process, or are hesitant about getting started, read additional information about this technique in these books or talk with a career advisor about how you can incorporate this useful tool into your job-hunting kit.

SOCIAL NETWORKING

Much like information interviews, social networking can be a valuable asset in the job-search process. It is another example of the interpersonal processes of job hunting. Networking can provide the following information:

- Information about job opportunities, especially the "hidden" job market

- Means for making valuable contacts in the job-search process

- Ways to gain general information about career fields and industry trends

Studies have consistently shown that networking is a very effective job-hunting strategy (Eby & Buch, 1994; Lin, Ensel & Vaughn, 1981; Silliker, 1993). Much useful information about occupations, job openings, what's happening in organizations, and industry trends can be learned by researching more than print materials. The people contacts in your network are just as important (and sometimes more important) as print-based resources, especially given the rapidly changing nature of the workplace. People sources are more likely to have up-to-the-minute information about what's happening in a particular field or organization, as well as to provide direct access to the people making hiring decisions.

The power of networking was apparent at one professional meeting several years ago. A workshop leader asked 75 participants if anyone needed help in their job campaign. A woman raised her hand and indicated that she was being transferred and that her spouse was looking for a job in the private security field in the Seattle area. By asking a series of questions of the group, such as did anyone have a family member or friend working in the investigative and security fields or did anyone know people working in that career field in the northwestern United States, the leader quickly found three people whom the woman could talk to about jobs for her spouse in Seattle. In two minutes, the woman went from zero potential job contacts to several, and more were probably reported to her after the session ended.

There are several important factors related to networking that are useful to keep in mind:

- Networking *is* a transferable skill that can be learned and polished.

- Join a professional group (even as a student member) and volunteer to serve on a committee or in a leadership role.

- Network with alumni from your school who majored in your field; many career centers have Web-based resources for this purpose.

Although networking may seem like a simple and familiar term, there are several factors to consider when including this as part of your job-search strategy. First, networking is an activity that draws upon your self-knowledge. Whom you choose to network with may be based on your ideas about people who share your interests or values or work in organizations that reflect your interests or the skills you would like to use. For example, do you enjoy being outdoors (interest) and believe it's important to protect the environment (value)?

Second, this self-knowledge can be used to narrow the list of organizations or employers that you will focus on in your research. In the case of the person who likes the outdoors, he or she might seek employment with environmental nonprofit organizations and might find it helpful to network with members of the Sierra Club or Audubon Society. This knowledge about yourself and the options you're considering can help guide your networking activity.

Third, networking is like a web of interconnected persons and can be the basis of lifelong relationships (Watson, 2002). A network is not something to be used for short-term gain and discarded.

JOB INTERVIEWS

The ultimate aim in a job-search strategy is a *job offer*. However, the gateway to offers is generally through the face-to-face interviewing process. The initial job interview may occur in a college or university setting (often called "on-campus interviews"), at conventions, on location at the work setting, or even in hotel rooms. As with other forms of interpersonal communication used in the job search process, job interviewing is a skill that can be learned and polished. At this point, we discuss what must happen before the initial job interview, what to expect during the job interview, and how to follow up after an interview.

Preparing for the Interview

When an appointment is made for an interview, it is imperative that you be fully prepared for it. There are two critical areas of knowledge that come into play in this process: self-knowledge and employer knowledge. Your knowledge in each of these two areas is an important part of your pre-interview preparation.

Know yourself. You need to know many facts about the employer, and the interviewer needs to know many facts about you in order to make a fair evaluation. Both of you are looking for a good match of interests, skills, and values. Before an interview, it's important to know what you have to offer a potential employer. Evaluate yourself in terms of your strengths and how you could translate these strengths into skills your prospective employer can use. It is also helpful to know your weaknesses, because no one is perfect. If you state a weakness, do not elaborate on it. Instead, try to turn it around into a potential strength for the organization.

Think about how your interests, skills, and values fit with the type of organization and position for which you are being interviewed. You may have to prioritize these in some fashion. For example, if one of your values is to make money, will this be more important than other work values you've rated highly, such as job security, having leisure time, helping others? Review the list of values in Chapter 2. Think about these in relation to each interview situation.

Be ready to talk about your career objectives, your long- and short-range goals, and your interests. Study your resume and be familiar with your educational and work background. Practice illustrating how your extracurricular activities are examples of skills in leadership and responsibility. The most important point to remember when preparing for an interview is that the prospective employer is primarily concerned with hiring someone who will make a valuable contribution to the organization.

In Chapter 9, we described jobs as being "gaps" between what the employer wants and the present situation. You as an employee are a potential "gap remover." Be prepared to present five key points that summarize your skills related to the job, and prepare questions to ask the employer about the position (Paulsen, 2001). With many applicants for the same job, it will be up to *you* to convince the interviewer that of all those interviewed, you are the best choice. To help prepare, study the sample questions in Table 13.1.

Bolles (2008) suggests that an employer wants to know five things about you, and your self-knowledge provides the basis for responding to these questions: (1) Why are you here? (2) What can you do for us? (3) What kind of person are you? (4) What distinguishes you from the others? (5) Can we afford you?

Know your employer. Once you've done the research on yourself, you need to use your best research skills in understanding your potential employer. You may research employers in a number of different ways using a variety of different schema, such as by geographic region, a specific industry, an association, a specific position, a specific organization, or all of these.

- If you know where you want to work, such as San Francisco, you may research employers by location.

- If you want to work in an industry, like health care, you can research employers this way as well.

- If you want to work in a specific setting, such as nursing homes, you can research employers by associations and professional groups that serve the elderly.

- If you are interested in an occupation or position, such as nursing, you can also research employers by positions available.

- Finally, when you have identified the organization(s) you want to work for, you can begin to search for information by the employer's name.

TABLE 13.1   SAMPLE INTERVIEW QUESTIONS

1. What are your long- and short-range career goals and objectives, when and why did you establish them, and how are you preparing yourself to achieve them?

2. What specific goals (other than occupation) do you have for the next 10 years?

3. What do you see yourself doing five years from now?

4. What do you really want to do in life?

5. How do you plan to achieve your career goals?

6. What are the most important rewards you expect in your career?

7. What do you expect to be earning in five years?

8. Why did you choose the career for which you are preparing?

9. What do you consider to be your greatest strengths and weaknesses?

10. How would you describe yourself?

11. How do you think a friend or professor who knows you well would describe you?

12. What motivates you to put forth your greatest effort?

13. How has your college experience prepared you for your chosen career?

14. Why should I hire you?

15. What qualifications do you have that make you think that you will be successful in this field?

16. How do you determine or evaluate success?

17. What do you think it takes to be successful in an organization like ours?

18. In what ways do you think you can make a contribution to our organization?

19. What qualities should a successful manager possess?

20. Describe the relationship that should exist between a supervisor and supervisees.

21. What two or three accomplishments have given you the most satisfaction? Why?

22. Describe your most rewarding college experience.

23. If you were hiring a graduate for this position, what qualities would you look for?

24. Why did you select your college or university?

25. What led you to choose your field of major study?

26. What college subjects did you like the best? The least? Why?

27. If you could do so, how would you plan your academic study differently? Why?

28. What changes would you make in your college or university? Why?

29. Do you have plans for continued study? An advanced degree?

30. Do you think that your grades are a good indication of your academic achievement?

31. What have you learned from participation in extracurricular activities?

32. What have you learned from your previous jobs?

33. In what kind of work environment are you most comfortable?

34. How do you work under pressure?

35. In what part-time or summer jobs have you been most interested? Why?

36. How would you describe the ideal job for you following graduation?

37. Why did you decide to seek a position with this organization?

38. What do you know about our organization?

39. What two or three things are most important to you in your job?

40. Are you seeking employment in an organization of a certain size? Why?

41. What criteria are you using to evaluate the organization for which you hope to work?

42. Do you have a geographical preference? Why?

TABLE	
13.1	**SAMPLE INTERVIEW QUESTIONS (CONTINUED)**

43. Will you relocate? Does relocation bother you?
44. Are you willing to travel?
45. Are you willing to spend at least six months as a trainee?
46. Why do you think you might like to live in the community in which our organization is located?
47. What have you done that shows initiative?
48. What major problem have you encountered and how did you deal with it?
49. What have you learned from your mistakes?
50. Describe an example where you worked as part of a team.

Although researching employers is a process that should be continuous throughout one's job hunt, it becomes even more important prior to the actual interview. Researching potential employers can be useful for a number of reasons.

1. Employers are looking for someone with a real interest in their organization, and your personal research reflects your interest, thoroughness, and enthusiasm. This is your first opportunity to show how you prepare for completing important tasks.

2. When you know something about an organization, you can describe in more relevant terms how you could work within that culture or how your skills could help the organization be successful. Being familiar with an organization can also help you answer questions such as "Why are you interested in our organization?" "Will my personality fit in this environment?" "Do my goals correspond to the promotional structure?"

3. There is more to many organizations than meets the eye. When you assume that you know enough about a potential employer without researching it, you could be overlooking important information. For example, most of us know that Purina makes pet food, but did you know that Purina also makes cereal and owns a major tuna fish company? You may be talking with a subsidiary of a much larger organization and not realize it.

4. Researching employers and asking informed questions will strengthen your position and help you make a positive first impression in an interview. Targeted questions resulting from research will also provide you with answers that can help you decide whether to accept an offer of employment.

Your task in the interview is to discover what kinds of workers employers need and are looking for (Farr, 2003). It is important for you to find out as much as you can about the organizational history and culture where you are interviewing. Areas you may want to focus on in your research include knowledge of the industry, specific employer, occupation, and position. Ask yourself the following questions:

1. What does the organization make, or what type of service does it provide?

2. What is the size of the organization? What is its organizational structure? How much potential for advancement is there within this structure?

3. Who are the organization's officers, administrators, and leaders? What about their background, recent achievements?

4. What are the employer's personnel policies? What employee benefits are typically provided?

In your research, try to find out how a position of interest to you is structured in relation to the whole organization. Review the contents of Chapter 8 on organizational culture and

Chapter 9 on ways of working to obtain ideas about things to investigate. Try to pinpoint some problems, policies, or philosophies of the organization, and plan to focus on these during the interview.

You can find some of this information on the Internet, in your career center library, college library, or at the local public library. It is essential to start early when researching a specific employer. You may find a lot of information that you will need to sort through to find the important facts. On the other hand, you may not find any printed information and need to make phone calls or set up information interviews for answers. Specific resources in a career center library that might be helpful are employer literature files, *Job Choices Guides*, *Guide to Employer Directories*, and *Almanac of American Employers*.

Table 13.2 provides a checklist that may be used as a guide for gathering data on potential employers. The earlier you start researching, the more categories you will be able to cover. Remember, not all facts may be relevant; it depends on the type of organization you are researching.

Your research on prospective employers will not only increase your self-confidence, but it will also impress interviewers. They will regard you as a person who has sincere interest in the organization because you took the time to find out something about it. However, simply being informed about an employer does not guarantee a successful interview unless you use that information effectively. Knowledge of products and opportunities is only helpful if you know how to tactfully weave that knowledge into the interview. Spouting out facts or prefacing a question with a lot of memorized details will not convince the employer of your interest and/or knowledge. In a later section, we will discuss how to use your research in developing questions to ask the employer during the interview. Although your personal and employer research are critical aspects of pre-interview preparation, the key to using this knowledge well is to practice what you'll say *before* the real thing.

Practice, Practice, Practice

The best way to improve your communication skills in this area is to practice role-playing before the interview. Ask a friend, your spouse, or roommate to help simulate an interview using the sample questions in Table 13.1 as a guide. Make sure you are critiqued on the strength of your voice, posture, and eye contact.

Another suggestion for role-playing might be to get together with people who are also preparing for interviews. You could learn a lot by critiquing different approaches, and this might also be a good way to boost each other's morale. If you have access to video or audiotape equipment, consider taping the practice interview and reviewing the results with someone whose opinion you respect and trust. Many career centers offer mock interview training programs, which can be a great way to improve your interview skills.

A critical point to remember while practicing is to avoid memorizing what you want to say. Whether you are talking about yourself or the organization with which you are interviewing, let it be a natural flow of words. If you come across like you have a speech prepared, your interview will be less effective. Job interviews are, in essence, social interactions, so try to make the interview a positive social experience. Bolles (2008) suggests a 50-50 rule and a 20 second-2 minute rule. With the former, try to share "air time" equally with the interviewer. With the latter, keep your responses to questions between 20 seconds and no more than 2 minutes.

You probably will be nervous during the interview. Concentrate on what is being asked and respond appropriately. Sometimes people make their voices more monotone in order to sound professional. It is better to use your normal tone. Don't speak too softly.

Dress

Although there are a number of things you can't control in the interview process, it is important to use to your best advantage the things over which you do have control. One of

TABLE 13.2   CHECKLIST OF EMPLOYER FACTS TO KNOW

Basic Facts

- Name, address, telephone of organization
- Complete product line or services provided
- Number of plants, stores, outlets, divisions, branches, and employees
- Geographical locations
- Location of corporate headquarters
- Parent or subsidiary company information

Employer History/Image

- Position of organization in the industry (leader, newcomer?)
- Organization's national and local reputation, awards, other recognition
- Associations in which the employer is an active member
- Major competitors (How can you help the employer gain a competitive edge?)
- Stock prices and history (if relevant)

Financial Information

- Size of organization and industry
- Potential growth
- Annual sales and budget growth for past five years

Philosophy/Goals

- Mission statement—should reflect current strategies and long-term goals
- Biographical information on top executives—salaries, age, education, history
- Political, research or social interests and financial support

Professional/Work Environment Concerns

- Organizational structure and processes, including teamwork
- Position descriptions, including part-time and permanent
- Types and quality of training programs
- Salary and benefits
- Typical career paths
- Employer's review or evaluation process of workers
- Background of entry-level positions and managers

these is the impression you make on employers with your attire. If you are seeking a professional position, you must look like a professional. A good guideline to follow is to dress as others do in the position. For some organizations, you can often take your cues from the organization's literature. Observe how staff members are portrayed in the photos included in this literature.

Remember: Employers are evaluating you as soon as you walk in the door, and clothes make a critical first impression. Make sure it's a positive one! Yate (2004) suggested that the safest look for both men and women at interviews is traditional and conservative. Although certain workplaces may tolerate more relaxed styles of dress, don't dress the part until you have the part. Here are some other general guidelines:

Women. Wear a simple tailored pants suit or skirt suit. Wear conservative nail polish and lipstick. Have a neat hairdo. Keep accessories to a bare minimum, e.g., small watch and maybe small ear rings. Make sure the bag or briefcase is not large (Colista, 2002). Be especially moderate in use of perfume and makeup.

Men. Wear a clean, pressed, conservative suit with a nonflashy shirt and tie. Have your shoes shined and wear plain socks. Have your hair neat and trimmed. Long hair and extremely long sideburns are out. Clean and trim your nails. Avoid flashy jewelry. Limit the use of fragrances. Neatly trimmed facial hair may or may not be OK, but it is probably best to cover tattoos until you have a better sense of the organizational culture.

Puente (2004) noted there are conflicting opinions about appropriate dress at work. It all ultimately depends on the organizational culture of the employer. One safe rule might be to dress like your prospective boss.

Kara Swisher (1994) found evidence of employment discrimination based on appearance and indicated that federal laws don't protect short, heavy, and unattractive people from "looks discrimination." Besides the common negative stereotypes for the overweight—slovenly, lazy, poor physical condition—overweight people report more employment discrimination and problems with coworkers. This is more true for women than men. Swisher also cited research that people who are considered good looking are paid on average about 10 percent more than those considered unattractive. Engemann and Owyang (2005) reached similar conclusions—it helps to be tall, slender, and attractive. However, it was unclear to the authors if this means that people who are short, fat, and plain are victims of discrimination or just have less self-confidence. The bottom line for us in reports like these underscores the importance of good dress and appearance in job hunting and employment.

Being on Time

It is better to be a few minutes early than even one minute late for your interview. Interviewers have a busy schedule, and if you are late, it will cut down the amount of time allotted to you. Most important, if you are late, you will make a bad impression. As the saying goes: "You don't get a second chance to make a first impression." If your interview is in an unfamiliar location, make sure you allow enough time for any problems with traffic or for locating the specific building or office. It is a good idea to make a test drive to the interview location at the time of day you will actually be interviewing so you can account for traffic. Ask about the best place to park. Check your appearance in the restroom beforehand.

The Initial Interview

Interviews can take many different forms. They can vary from a one-to-one contact between you and an employee of the organization, such as a human resource specialist, campus recruiter, or department manager, to a panel composed of several different employees representing various levels, functions, or teams. The situation also can vary from a single interview with an organization representative to a sequence of several interviews on a given day. It is somewhat hazardous to be very definitive and concrete about what happens in job interviews.

For example, Camille DeBell and Timothy Dinger (1997) pointed out that even though much has been written about on-campus recruiting interviews, research on what actually happens in interviews is limited. In a series of studies, they found that most recruiter questions were in four areas: (1) the candidate's college experience, (2) work experience, (3) strengths and weaknesses, and (4) biographical background. They also found differences in types of questions depending on the type of company and the gender of the recruiter. A complete summary of their study and the questions actually asked by the recruiters was published in the *Journal of Career Planning and Employment* (DeBell & Dinger, 1995).

DeBell and Dinger concluded that many of the suggestions about how to prepare for interviews are not completely consistent with their findings. "Applicants might be better prepared if they know that the process of some screening interviews might be loosely structured; the recruiter might talk a great deal, and the questions might not be as clear-cut as the trade press's lists of questions suggest" (1997, p. 563).

With this caution in mind, we will proceed to discuss what various authorities have indicated might happen in initial recruiting interviews and other employment interactions. Our goal is to inform you about this process and help you more effectively plan your job campaign.

On-campus Interview. Bill Beebe (1996) described a typical on-campus initial interview lasting 30 minutes:

- *Prework*, 2 minutes—review job requirements and candidate's resume.

- *Getting started*, 3 minutes—small talk to put candidate at ease and explain the interview structure.

- *Gathering and evaluating data*, 14 minutes—questions/answers, determining a possible match.

- *Giving information*, 6 minutes—explain company, job environment, answer questions.

- *Closing*, 2 minutes—summarize, explain possible next steps.

- *Postwork*, 3 minutes—complete evaluation add supporting comments.

Telephone Interviews. Although face-to-face interviews continue to be the most common method used in hiring, some organizations are increasingly using telephone interviews as their initial screening method. When you're actively engaged in a job hunt, you should be prepared at any time to pick up the phone and converse with an employer who might be calling. Telephone interviews are just as important as face-to-face interviews.

This leads us to make a point about a related issue: When you're expecting calls from employers, don't have cute, weird, or long and drawn-out messages on your phone. At best, some employers will question whether you're really a candidate they want; at worse, they'll be so put off that they'll hang up and move on to the next candidate on their list.

In any case, most formal telephone interviews are set up by employers in advance. They will arrange a day and time to call you. It is probably best to take the call on a "land-line" phone rather than your cell phone to reduce the possibility of a disconnection. They should also tell you the format for the call, such as how long the interview will last, what other staff will be sitting in, whether they will call you or whether you are to call them at a set time. Like other types of interviews, phone interviews require you to do your homework on both yourself and the organization.

One advantage of telephone interviews is that you can have some "cheat sheets" or note cards spread out in front of you to help you in responding to questions. You can also more easily take notes because you don't have to worry about maintaining eye contact. However, don't let your note taking distract you from listening carefully to what is said. Some job hunters have reported that they dress for the phone interview and remember to smile because it helps them be both professional and relaxed during the interview (Donlin, 2004).

Make sure you understand who's sitting in on the call, if there is more than one person present, and what their position is in the organization. You may want to sketch out a little diagram or chart of the participants in the group. If you take the call at home or in an office setting, make sure there are no distractions—hang out your "Do Not Disturb" sign. If the telephone interview goes well, you should expect a face-to-face interview at some point and certainly before a job offer is extended.

Videoconference Interviews. Under special circumstances, e.g., all interviewers are not in the same location as the candidate, a videoconference may be set up to conduct the interview. Interviewees need to remember to speak slowly and clearly because there might be a delay in the sound transmission. It is also important to look at the camera and not the monitor so your face will be visible on the interviewer's monitor. Ideally, a technician will be available to help with the transmission.

Behavioral Interviews. These types of interviews have become popular. "Behavioral interviewing is a structured process which is used to facilitate the selection of individuals based on prior demonstration of job specific skills" (Wilson, 1996, p. 18). Employers using this form of interviewing seek to predict future behavior by examining past behavior. Questions tend to focus on success experiences in your past and specific behaviors you engaged in to achieve that success.

Beebe (1996) noted that the basic premise of behavior-based interviewing is that past behavior is the best predictor of future behavior, that more recent behavior is a better predictor than older behavior, and long-standing patterns are more predictive than isolated events. What skills are targeted for probing by interviewers? Damir Stimac (1995) identified 19:

1. Alertness
2. Assertiveness
3. Clarification
4. Commitment to task
5. Coping
6. Corporate policies and procedures
7. Creativity and imagination
8. Dealing with ambiguity
9. Decision making
10. Focus
11. Goal setting/achieving
12. Leadership
13. Listening
14. Management
15. Oral communication
16. Organization and planning
17. Perception
18. Problem solving and analysis
19. Team building

Students can prepare for behavior interviews by becoming proactive in preparing "stories" that specifically illustrate what they can do to solve a job problem related to the 19 items shown above (Fulk, 1997). The stories should draw attention to specific job skills by explaining a problem and the candidate's solution. The stories should also provide quantitative measures, such as percentages, and candidates should be prepared to explain unexpected results or provide more details in response to interviewer questions.

A good way to prepare for a behavior based interview is to use the four steps in the STAR technique: Situation (S), Task (T), Action (A), and Result (R) or outcome. For example, you might recall a situation (S) when communication in a group had broken down. To resolve the problem (T), you organized informal meetings at lunch and other times (A) where members discussed issues related to the situation. As a result of these meetings and discussions, communication improved and productivity increased (R).

Beebe indicated that 30 percent of employers are using such behavioral interviews, and more appear to be moving in this direction for both on-campus and second interviews. Additional information about behavioral interviews and the STAR technique is available in Stimac (1995).

Stress Interviews. Although some job hunters consider all interviews to be stress interviews, there really is a more high-pressure type of interview beyond the ordinary. According to one author (Yate, 2004), this type of interview is widespread in the professional world. These may be characterized by a barrage of unusual questions (e.g., what animal would you be if you could be any type? Why?), and the questions may be flung by many different people in a rapid-fire manner. What may seem like a simple question posed by the interviewer initially may be immediately followed by a series of why, when, who, what, how, and where questions. In this type of interview, the interviewer(s) may be intentionally trying to upset you or see how you react under pressure. Often the key to handling this type of interview is to refuse to be intimidated, keep your emotions in check, and rely on your pre-interview preparation. Don't be afraid to ask for time to think about a question or ask for clarification. If you have a really bad experience with this type of interview, you may ask yourself whether you really want to work for a place that screens prospective employees in this way.

Trick Questions. Students sometimes worry about "trick questions" being used in a job interview. While there is no evidence that these are used often, there is some indication that puzzles and riddles may be posed by interviewers in an effort to gauge the intelligence, resourcefulness, or "outside-the-box" thinking of applicants. Pachter (2003) offers several examples: "If you could remove any of the 50 states which would it be?" "Why are beer cans tapered on the ends?" "How long would it take to move Mt. Fuji?" "Why does a mirror reverse right and left instead of up and down?" If you are applying for positions in an industry where such questions are more possible, the book by William Poundstone (2004) might help you prepare for these kinds of questions.

Performance, or In-Basket, Interviewing. In this type of interview you will be asked to perform tasks associated with a job in a limited amount of time. Mistakes are expected; the employer is looking for the way you handle yourself. In some cases, you will be given a particular organizational problem or situation to analyze, and you will be allowed to go into another room and formulate a response or plan for dealing with the problem. You may be given access to a computer to write your response, or you may be asked to make an oral presentation.

Finally, a study by Katz (2007) provided some insights into what actually happens in job interviews. She found that while behavioral interviews were often cited as common practice, in reality they were not. Employers were actually using more traditional interview questions designed to elicit information about the applicants traits and abilities in the areas of initiative, judgment, motivational fit, presentation, teamwork, information, and negotiation. Katz suggested that applicants should prepare for seven general questions: (1) What do you know about us? (2) What do I need to know about you? (3) How do you work with others? (4) What are your skills relevant to this position? (5) What are your personal goals? (6) How much do you know about your area of specialization? (7) How have you handled specific situations? (The latter is a behavioral question.)

Although we have presented some general guidelines related to preparing for interviews and what to expect, it is important to remember that interviews are often unpredictable and no two interviews are alike. A lot depends on the interviewer, who has control and will take the lead in conducting the interview. Try and pick up cues from the interviewer regarding when and how to respond.

Salary

One question you should be ready to answer is about the expected salary. You should *not* mention salary on your resume. You can leave it blank or put "negotiable" on your application form. In an interview, however, you might be asked to state a figure. Know what others with your general qualifications are being offered as starting salaries in positions similar to the one for which you are interviewing. An extensive discussion of salary issues in interviewing and negotiating job offers is presented in Chapter 14.

Candidates whose rates are too high might price themselves right out of a job offer. If you are too low, the interviewer might not consider you an ambitious person, and there is a chance you will be removed from further consideration for employment. Another possibility is that they might hire you at a lower rate, and then there will be no chance for negotiating a higher salary figure. One way to handle salary questions is to give a salary range. Be prepared to back up your salary request with specific information about your education and experience, as well as the research you have conducted on this question that informs your response.

Other "Sticky" Interview Topics

Despite the progress that's been made in the area of equal employment opportunity and the efforts that have been made to eliminate discrimination in the workplace, there are still interview situations where *improper questions* are asked. It might be noted that a discriminatory question differentiates people on a basis other than merit, while illegal questions vary among cities, counties, and states. However, employers can be held liable for discriminatory questions even if the questions were not meant to intentionally discriminate against an applicant.

In certain situations, employers may appropriately ask questions in these areas if they are asked of all candidates, if the information is clearly relevant to success on the job, and if the information obtained does not lead to employment discrimination on the basis of age, sex, gender, ethnic heritage, race, national origin, marital status, religion, or disability. For example, some government agencies or contractors are required by law to hire only U.S. citizens. Religious organizations are permitted to discriminate on the basis of religion when hiring. Some position advertisements can legitimately request gender-specific applicants, for example, for acting roles or modeling jobs.

Here are some examples of "illegal" questions:

- Are you a U.S. citizen?

- How old are you?

- What is your marital status?

- What social organizations do you belong to?

- Do you have any disabilities?

- Have you ever been arrested?

There is no one right answer regarding how to deal with these types of situations or so-called "problem" interview questions. Conrad and Salgado (2007), writing in the *NACE Journal* (National Association of Colleges and Employers), noted that you have several options:

1. *Answer the question.* While you are free to do this, remember that you are answering a question that is not related to the job, and if you do not answer it satisfactorily it could hurt your chances of getting an offer.

2. *Refuse to answer the question.* Depending on how your frame the answer you might be perceived as challenging or abrupt. This probably would not make you an ideal candidate for receiving an offer.

3. *Examine the intent of the question in relation to the job and respond accordingly.* For example, if the interviewer asks, "Do you plan to get married?" You might answer, "I can meet the travel and work schedule required for this job."

Most sources suggest you try to understand interviewers' motives in asking these types of questions. Do they want to know about your commitment to the job? Your ability to travel? Your willingness to relocate or work long hours? Getting angry or offended at the employer is unlikely to win you any points, so it is best to avoid this reaction, no matter how much you are put off by the questions. In a positive nondefensive manner, reassure the employer about your interest in the job and why you believe the position is a good fit with your skills and qualifications.

Conrad and Salgado (2007) provide numerous examples of improper and proper questions in relation to all of the sensitive topics listed at the outset, e.g., race, gender, as well as some others.

Criminal history or arrest record can be especially problematic. While some states have laws regulating criminal history information in the context of hiring, others do not. Even in the case of a conviction, employers must show that criminal history is related to the job. Off-the-job conduct, e.g., smoking, is another legal grey area, and employers must demonstrate that such inquiries are job related. Employers may obtain an applicant's credit report.

If you experience this type of questioning in the interview, you may decide that this is not the organization for you. However, don't always assume that the interviewer is completely representative of the organization. This person may only do preliminary screening, and your supervisor may be totally different. Don't prematurely remove yourself from the job application process until you are completely sure that the organization is not a good fit, based on contact with several individuals, particularly those who would be your colleagues or team members.

During the interview, the most important thing to remember is to *be honest*. Interviewers will not be able to evaluate you fairly if you attempt to mislead them. Telling interviewers what you think they want to hear is not the purpose of the interview. If you try to con interviewers, and they catch on to your game, the chance of being invited for a second interview is slim.

Your Turn to Ask Questions

Following the interviewer's questions, you should be given an opportunity to ask some questions of your own. If you have done your pre-interview research, then you should have prepared some important questions in advance. As one author noted: "The goal is to show yourself at your best to land the job you want. That means asking questions because you care about the job and the organization, not because you want to look good" (Quinn-Szcesuil, 1997, p. 10).

Ask questions that encourage the employer to expand on information from the literature you have reviewed. Some examples of topics you could ask the interviewer to address include (1) corporate policy regarding government regulations (rather than a local environmental scandal), (2) future marketing strategies for specific products (rather than a recent drop in stock prices), or (3) descriptions of the organizational structure and culture.

Some additional questions you might ask include the following:

1. What kind of training do you provide? How long is the training period?

2. Where does this position fit in the organizational structure?

3. What is the normal progression of a trainee over the first few years?

4. How much travel is involved in this position?

5. Do you encourage continuing education in the local colleges on a tuition reimbursement basis?

6. What options do I have in selecting (or accepting) assignments?

7. Will I have the opportunity to work on special projects?

8. What staff development programs are available after the initial training?

9. What qualities do you see as essential for someone seeking to fill this position?

10. Is this a new position? If not a new position, what happened to the last person who held this position?

Never ask about vacation time or retirement. These are not work-related activities. You must talk opportunity, not security. However, you could ask for more information regarding all fringe benefits. It will also be helpful to prepare questions concerning the organization's markets, methods, mission, and strategic plans. Don't just ask these types of questions to find out what's in it for *you*, but show that you'd like to know more about the organization. Interviewers will be impressed by your interest and preparation.

Closing

During the interview, be sensitive to signals that the interview is coming to a close. Campus interviews are usually scheduled for twenty or thirty minutes. Interviews end in different ways. Some interviewers might look at their watch, which is a cue for you that the interview is nearing an end; other interviewers are blunt—they stand up, hold out their hand, and thank you for coming in. Most employer representatives, however, expect you to sense the proper time to leave on the basis of subtle indications that your time is up.

When the interview is over, thank the interviewer for taking time to talk with you. Ask the interviewer for his or her business card. You can use this information for writing your follow-up letters. Re-emphasize your interest in the position (e.g., you want the job) and your appreciation for being considered. This is important, since many candidates mistakenly assume that interviewers sense their interest. Employers don't want to be rejected either, and believing that you are genuinely interested gives them confidence in making a job offer to you.

If the interviewer does not definitely offer you a job (this is very rarely done in the initial interview) or indicate when you will hear from him/her, ask for an estimate of a date when a decision might be made about making a job offer.

After the Interview

Following-up after an interview is a critical part of the whole interviewing process and one that is often overlooked by job hunters. It is important to send the interviewer a thank you letter after the interview. Bolles (2008) described not sending a thank you note right after the interview as—the most overlooked step in the entire job-hunting process. You can use post-interview follow-up letters in several ways. Tell the interviewer that you are still interested in the position, and go over some of your qualifications discussed in the interview so that the interviewer's memory will be refreshed. You might include in your note a couple of pertinent questions that you did not ask in the interview.

It is important for you to be tenacious in this process, to "sell" yourself. Keep the communication going without harassing the employer. Some employers have noted that those receiving an offer have most likely asked for it. It shows initiative and commitment.

If the interviewer answers you quickly, this might be an indication that you are still under active consideration for an offer. If you decide on the basis of the interview that you would not accept the position if it were offered, use the letter-writing guidelines presented in Chapter 12 to halt the selection process. For most interview situations, these letters are considered business correspondence. They should be typed and can be printed on the same paper that you used for your cover letters. For further hints, see the section in Chapter 12 on "Thank You Letters."

As soon as possible after the interview, write down what you have learned. Ask yourself these questions:

- What points did I make that seemed to interest the employer?

- Did I present my qualifications well?

- Did I talk too much? Too little?

- Was I too tense? Was I too aggressive? Not aggressive enough?

- What questions gave me a tough time? How can I improve my answers?

By reviewing your performance, you can make plans to improve your skills. You may want to discuss your experience with someone whose opinion you respect and trust. Remember, the more you interview, the sharper your skills become and the sooner you will receive an offer! A next step before the offer, however, is often the second interview or site visit. We will now look at how these might differ from the initial interview.

Second Interviews/Site Visits

The second or on-site interview, also called the "plant visit," is usually the final step in obtaining a job offer. You probably have a 50 percent chance of receiving an offer at this point, although this probability varies according to industries and organizations. Both the employer and you as the interviewee should have specific goals during the second interview. What might some of these be? In initial interviews, employers typically focus on many general qualities that are important in their organization. In the second interview, employers are more likely to be trying to determine if you have the specific qualities they are seeking in a new employee. Employers also want to see how others in the organization respond to you and if you fit into the organizational culture.

As an interviewee, this is an additional opportunity to decide if this is the organization from which you would accept an offer. It is important to remember that the second interview allows you the opportunity to view the facilities, get answers to questions not addressed in the first interview, meet other employees of the organization besides the initial interviewer, possibly tour the local community, and generally determine whether or not this organization is a good fit for you.

Second interviews can take several different forms. Two broad categories used to describe them are *structured* and *unstructured* interviews. A second interview is considered structured if each interviewer has specific criteria they use to assess you. For example, one person may ask questions to determine your work ethic or your sales ability. Another person may only ask you about your educational background or your work experience. The key to doing well in this type of interview is identifying the specific quality being assessed and then directing all your answers to information about that area.

In the case of unstructured interviews, interviewers are making a broad evaluation. You may get similar questions from all the interviewers. Treat each interviewer with equal importance. Answering the same question over and over again can become boring, but try not to let it show. Indeed, it is important that each interviewer gets the same message from you, otherwise your truthfulness and trustworthiness may be questioned. Remember, interviewers often compare notes about an applicant.

Preparing for Second Interviews

If possible, obtain an itinerary and interview schedule in advance. It is important to know the schedule of the day's activities, including names and titles of the interviewers. Knowing who will be interviewing you can help you anticipate the questions they may ask, because these may be tied in with their particular area of responsibility. For example, you may be interviewing for an advertising position, but the person from budget and finance may want to see if you understand the economic realities of putting together an ad campaign. Can you produce a budget? Manage the funds allotted to a project?

You will want to continue your employer research in preparing for the second interview. Ask the first-round interviewer to send you any additional information that you should know about the job, the organization, the department, or team you would work in, or anything else they think is important to review before your visit. Check periodicals and the Internet for timely articles or information about the organization or industry.

Interviewees who are prepared for the upcoming schedule, who understand what to expect and have knowledge of the workings of the organization and its related industry, stand a greater chance of success than candidates who do not care enough to do the necessary research.

Prior to the second interview, you should understand from your contact person how the costs for travel, lodging, car rental, and other expenses will be handled. You may be asked to make your own arrangements, or the organization will handle them for you. Ask your contact person what expenses will be prepaid and what expenses you will need to request reimbursement for (pay attention to the receipts you will need to collect while traveling). With some organizations, you may be asked to pay all the travel expenses, while others will reimburse you only if they extend a job offer and you accept.

As with other types of interviews discussed earlier, it is also important to send a follow-up letter or letters after the second interview. You may want to thank the person who coordinated your visit and/or the person who chaired the search committee or other key people who were involved in the interview process. These letters can be used to once again restate your interest in the position and why you think you're the best candidate for the job.

Other Sources

The literature on job hunting includes scores of books on interviewing. The Web site at http://www.amazon.com, an online bookstore, has over 866 titles listed for job interview. Major bookstores have many of these books in the careers or business section. Several helpful books on the topic are *Job Interviews for Dummies* (Kennedy, 2008), *101 Smart Questions to Ask on Your Interview* (Fry, 2006), and *Interview for Success* (Krannich & Krannich, 2008).

A CIP PERSPECTIVE

In this chapter, we learned about the social interactions associated with job interviewing, including information interviews, networking, initial interviews, and second interviews or site visits. Now we'll review what we have learned from a CIP perspective.

Self-Knowledge

This chapter has focused on the interpersonal relationship aspects of the job campaign, particularly social networking and interviewing. With respect to self-knowledge, it is important to note that job interview skills can be learned. We emphasized that through drill and practice of standard interview questions included in Table 13.1 you can improve your interviewing performance.

We also determined that good interview behavior requires knowledge of personal interests, skills, and values, because these are a focal point of interest in job interviews. Employers want to know about your self-knowledge in these three areas. In addition, a thorough understanding of your priorities—geographic location, job title, salary, and training opportunities—will enable you to respond to interviewer questions with confidence and consistency. You will not have to worry about what you told one interviewer in one situation when speaking with another interviewer, because your answers will be consistent and based on your self-knowledge. Self-knowledge, we believe, is the cornerstone of your PCT and strategic career planning, and it will be reflected in your interpersonal communications related to employment.

It is interesting to note that Holland's RIASEC theory is applicable in the following way. The theory predicts that ease in job hunting will follow the following code order: SEIACR (Holland, 1997). You'll remember from Chapter 2 that the Social and Enterprising types are the most people-oriented of the six types, and it is these two types that should have relatively more ease in job hunting, especially in the interpersonal communication aspects.

Option Knowledge

We learned that information interviews and social networks provide an important way for us to go beyond printed materials and get "insider" information about an industry, training program, occupation, organization, or position. Table 13.2 provided examples of the kinds of information that would help us in researching an employer. Interpersonal communications, both formal and informal, are powerful tools for improving the facts and data in the knowledge domain about options. With better knowledge in this area, we can make better decisions about employment and job offers.

Decision Making

The social interactions inherent in interview behavior can impact each phase of the CASVE Cycle. Through social interactions, such as information interviewing and networking, you can develop information useful in the Analysis phase to fine-tune matches between your preferences and an employer's needs. Social interactions enable you to make judgments about the organizational culture or the personal characteristics of team members with whom you might be working. Regarding the Valuing phase, conversations with your possible supervisor or coworkers can provide the information that can help you prioritize your employment options and to think more concretely about whether you would accept an offer. Finally, social interactions are essential in the Execution phase of decision making because this is where you develop the information that will enable you to take the next steps to start a new job.

Executive Processing

Throughout this chapter, we have repeatedly noted the importance of positive self-talk, self-awareness, and control and monitoring. When seeking employment, you must build these metacognitions into your PCT. Initiating information interviews and creating social networks in your job campaign will not happen if your self-talk is negative. We have often encountered job hunters that don't make good use of these tools because they allow themselves to be derailed by negative thinking. They say things such as "What if I can't think of what to say?" "Won't employers think I'm bothering them if I call?" "The employer didn't return my phone call; she must be trying to avoid me."

Effective interpersonal communication in the job search requires you to be aware of the tendency for this type of negative thinking to "creep in" and to use appropriate reframing techniques such as those described in Chapter 5 to learn how to think differently. Successful face-to-face interviewing depends on your ability to effectively and quickly process information coming from an interviewer about your behavior. Positive self-talk is also associated with handling the stress of rejections following poor interviews.

As we stressed throughout this chapter, these job-search communication skills can be learned and improved upon over time. If you find yourself trapped in a cycle of negative thinking based on your interpersonal interactions during the job search, talk with a career services professional or a trusted friend about how to frame these experiences in a different and more positive light.

SUMMARY

This chapter has reviewed various forms of interpersonal communication that are important in the job-search process. In the early stages of job hunting, job seekers can use information interviews and networking skills to make valuable contacts and gain useful information about positions, employers, and organizations. This information continues to be useful in the job interview process, both in preparation for the interview and for communicating with employers during the actual interview. By successfully negotiating initial interviews, one will hopefully have the opportunity for second interviews or site visits with prospective employers.

We concluded with an analysis of how CIP concepts can help you think about what you need to communicate with prospective employers, as well as avoiding the tendency to let negative thinking interfere with your ability to effectively present your credentials in an interview. The goal was to enable you to improve the quality of your PCT related to interpersonal communications and employment processes.

REFERENCES

Beebe, B. (1996, Winter). The process called "behavior-based interviewing." *Journal of Career Planning & Employment*, pp. 41–45.

Bolles, R. N. (2008). *What color is your parachute?* Berkeley, CA: Ten Speed Press.

Colista, C. (2002). Dressed for interview success. *Graduating Engineer & Computer Careers*, pp. 48–51.

Conrad, N., & Salgado, T. (2007, December). Legal Q & A. *NACE Journal*, pp. 8-13.

DeBell, C., & Dinger, T. J. (1995, Summer). Actual questions recruiters actually ask. *Journal of Career Planning and Employment*, pp. 28-31, 51–53.

DeBell, C., & Dinger, T. J. (1997). Campus interviews: Some challenges to conventional wisdom. *Journal of College Student Development, 38*, 353–364.

Donlin, K. (2004). How to ace a telephone job interview. *CollegeRecruiter.com*. Retrieved August, 23, 2004 from www.collegerecruiter.com/pages/articles/article248.htm.

Eby, L., & Buch, K. (1994). The effects of job search method, sex, activity level, and emotional acceptance on new job characteristics: Implications for counseling unemployment professionals. *Journal of Employment Counseling, 31*, 69–82.

Engemann, K. M., & Owyang, M. T. (2005, April). So much for that merit raise: The link between wages and appearance. *The Regional Economist*. Retrieved April 9, 2005, from http://stlouisfed.org/publications/re/2005/b/pages/appearances.html.

Farr, J. M. (2003). *The very quick job search: Get a better job in half the time.* Indianapolis, IN: JIST Works, Inc.

Fry, R. (2006). *101 smart questions to ask on your interview* (2nd ed.). Manassas Park, VA: Impact Publications.

Fulk, S. S. (1997, September 14). Technique puts twist on interviewing. *Richmond Times-Dispatch*, p. S12.

Holland, J. L. (1997). *Making vocational choices.* Odessa, FL: Psychological Assessment Resources, Inc.

Katz, S. M. (2007, October). The job interview: Is career services giving students a realistic picture of what to expect. *NACE Journal*, pp. 38-44.

Kennedy, J. L. (2008). *Job interviews for dummies.* New York: John Wiley.

Krannich, C. R., & Krannich, R. L. (2008). *Interview for success* (8th ed.). Manassas Park, VA: Impact Publications.

Lin, N., Ensel, W. M., & Vaughn, J. C. (1981). Social resources and strength of ties: Structure factors in occupational status attainment. *American Sociological Review, 46,* 393, 405.

Pachter, R. (2003, May 12). Author explains perverse logic behind trick questions. *The Herald,* p. 5D.

Paulsen, K. (2001). Checklist for interview success. *Careers and the engineer, 12*(1), 39.

Poundstone, W. (2004). *How would you move Mount Fuji?: Microsoft's cult of the puzzle.* New York: Little, Brown, & Co.

Puente, M. (2004, December 1). How not to dress for work. *USA Today,* pp. D1-D2.

Quinn-Szcesuil, J. (1997). Ask and ye shall be hired. *EEO Bimonthly, 28*(4), 10–13.

Silliker, S. A. (1993). The role of social contact in the successful job search. *Journal of Employment Counseling, 30,* 25–34.

Stimac, D. J. (1995). *Winning career strategies for today's competitive job market.* Lawrence, KS: Seaton Corp.

Stoodley, M. (1990). *Information interviewing: What it is and how to use it in your career.* Garrett Park, MD: Garrett Park Press.

Swisher, K. (1994, February 2). Employees claiming discrimination on the basis of weight, appearance. *Tallahassee Democrat,* p. 15D.

Watson, M. (2002). Cultivating networks make your opportunities bloom. *Planning job choices: 2002.* Bethlehem, PA: NACE.

Wilson, S. (1996, January). The interview. *Collegiate Recruiter,* pp. 18–20.

Yate, M. (2004). *Knock 'em dead 2005: The ultimate job-seeker's guide* (6th ed.). Holbrook, MA: Adams Media Corporation.

NEGOTIATING AND
EVALUATING JOB OFFERS

The job-search activities we have discussed in Part Three are designed to help you obtain job offers from prospective employers. Offers mean opportunities! We must understand, however, that opportunities really don't mean much until a deal is closed, until agreements are finalized, until negotiations have occurred. As we will learn in this chapter, job offers are not the end of an employment campaign. There is more important work to be done after the job hunter receives the offer.

Many college students fail to successfully negotiate an offer or to accept the best job. It is like running a good race and then crossing the wrong finish line or shooting a great round of golf but failing to sign the score card. How does this happen? After doing everything right, how does a person mess up at the end? To find some answers, let's look at the case of Anna.

Anna had completed a bachelor's degree in childhood education, and she had received two job offers. She was very happy and relieved to receive the offers because she believed that there was little demand for someone with her degree and skills. She was afraid to ask many questions about the two offers because she feared the employers might take this in a negative way. In other words, there were many aspects about the actual jobs that she did not really understand due to her failure to learn more about the positions.

Both jobs would have enabled her to stay in the same town as the university from which she had graduated. One position involved teaching at a local elementary school, and the other involved working for a child welfare agency to investigate child abuse cases. The second position paid about $4,000 more than the first, but the teaching job provided two months of summer break. Anna's friends and her mother told her to "go for the money," so she accepted the second job in child welfare.

What happened? Anna quit her new job after six weeks, and she was very unhappy about the stress and disappointment she got from the job. Why? She never fully understood that the second job required almost two weeks of travel per month, that she might be out of town three to five days at a time, and that she would be returning from most trips after dark. Anna had pets that needed care when she was away, she did not like to travel, and she disliked returning to her apartment after dark. Anna's lack of skill in negotiating her job offers, together with her failure to act on the basis of her values and personal preferences, led her to make a poor employment decision. Even worse, after all this she found herself unemployed again.

The concepts in this book and particularly in this chapter, can help you avoid an experience like Anna's. The process of evaluating and negotiating job offers is an activity that draws upon many of the ideas discussed in previous chapters. It is an activity that requires you to process information about yourself (see Chapters 2 and 5), prospective employers (see Chapter 3 and Part Two), and it requires application of the CASVE decision-making skills discussed in Chapter 4.

This chapter will discuss the following:

- The importance of negotiating job offers

- The skills needed to negotiate effectively

- A process you can use in evaluating offers

- The proper steps to follow in accepting and declining job offers

Finally, we will conclude with a CIP perspective on negotiating and accepting job offers.

Before we begin, it might be useful to reflect on this part of the job campaign in CIP terms and to explore several important metacognitions. First, if you are not very confident of your job skills, it is probably difficult to imagine how you could be strong and confident enough to tell an employer what you want in a job. This lack of self-confidence is a gap that needs to be removed in order to be successful in an employment campaign. We talked about this in Chapters 5 and 11.

Second, if you are not very sure of your goals and values—what you want to obtain from a job—it is almost impossible to imagine how you could evaluate two or more offers and choose the best one for yourself. Therefore, in order for you to fully understand and appreciate the material in this chapter, it is essential that you be confident of your value to an employer and for you to be clear about what is important to you in a job. These are essential metacognitions in negotiating, evaluating, and accepting offers.

THE CONTEXT FOR NEGOTIATING

Employers and job hunters enter the recruiting and employment process with different needs. First, we'll look at employers' needs.

The National Association of Colleges and Employers (NACE; 1997, November 17) conducted a national study of 1,529 employers, and 421 respondents reported the 10 top *personal characteristics* sought in job candidates:

1. Honesty/integrity

2. Motivation/initiative

3. Communication skills

4. Self-confidence

5. Flexibility

6. Interpersonal skills

7. Strong work ethic

8. Teamwork skills

9. Leadership skills

10. Enthusiasm

In another question, these employers reported the most highly rated *skills* sought in job candidates using a scale of 1 = not important to 5 = extremely important. The ratings are shown in parentheses after each item.

1. Interpersonal skills (4.67)

2. Teamwork skills (4.65)

3. Analytical skills (4.56)

4. Oral communication skills (4.53)

5. Flexibility (4.52)

6. Computer skills (4.32)

7. Written communication skills (4.12)

8. Leadership skills (4.08)

9. Work experience (4.05)

10. Internship experience (3.77)

11. Co-op experience (3.37)

Based on these data, students can begin to assess their personal qualities and skills and how they might be used in applying for jobs and negotiating offers. The more effectively students can communicate their personal characteristics and document their skills, the more likely it is that employers will evaluate their employment applications positively. As we noted in Chapter 2, a portfolio can be very useful in this process.

In Chapter 13, we said that it is almost impossible to imagine a situation where you could obtain a job without being interviewed, without talking to the person who will make the hiring decision. This can also be said about negotiating. From the very beginning of the first interview, it is important to realize that you have begun to negotiate an employment offer. A recent survey by NACE revealed that employers extend jobs, on average, to almost 40 percent of new college graduates they interview, and about 66 percent accept these offers. On average, employers take about 24 days after the interview to extend an offer or notify candidates they are no longer being considered (National Association of Colleges & Employers, 2007).

What exactly do we mean by *negotiating*? *Merriam-Webster's Online Dictionary* (http://www.merriam-webster.com/) defines it as "to confer with another so as to arrive at the settlement of some matter." In this chapter, negotiating refers to an interpersonal process that involves reaching an agreement about employment. Think of negotiating as a way of reaching a common goal: your agreement to work for the employer. Both you and the employer should end up "winning." If one person wins and the other person loses, the agreement is not likely to last, either the employee will be dissatisfied and quit or the employer will be dissatisfied and will either not promote or fire the employee.

Whether you realize it or not, you already have a lifetime of experience in negotiating. Most of this has been done with your family, but it has probably also involved roommates, coworkers, teachers, and friends. Many of our daily social interactions involve negotiations. As we saw in Chapter 10, negotiations in dual-career situations involving child care and relocation are very important in career success.

Think about your negotiating experience thus far. Are you a skilled negotiator? Do you like the negotiating process? Do you feel really good about successful outcomes that you have negotiated? Have you ever negotiated a lower price for an item, such as a car, insurance, or monthly rent? Some of us have probably had better experiences than others in negotiating, but many of us could probably benefit from improving our skills in this area.

SOCIAL POWER IN NEGOTIATING JOB OFFERS

Negotiating is a social process between two or more people—you and the employer (the person in the organization with hiring authority for your position). As in any social relationship, the idea of social power or influence applies to this situation. Social power comes from perceptions of leadership, expertise, ability, integrity, desirability, authority, and so forth. In employment negotiations, the social power changes over time (see Figure 14.1). In Figure 14.1, the applicant is represented by the solid line and the employer by the dotted line.

At the time of the initial interview, the employer has the most social power. However, as the process moves along, the applicant gains more power in the relationship. As Figure 14.1 shows, the best time for the applicant to negotiate is after the job is offered and before it is accepted. That is when the job hunter is at the highest level of social power in negotiating. *Once you have received a job offer, you immediately have more "power" than at any other time in the interviewing and negotiating process.* As Martin Yate (2007), the author of one job-search guidebook noted, the crucial period after the applicant has received a formal offer and before he or she accepts it is probably the one point in the relationship with the employer when the job hunter has "the upper hand."

Before the offer and after the offer has been accepted, the employer is relatively higher in power. This is true because as the interview process moves along, the employer is making more and more commitments to the applicant, showing an interest, and spending money to recruit the applicant for the position. Recruiting is an expensive process. The success of an organization depends greatly on getting the right people into the right positions. The stakes are really higher for an employer than many applicants realize.

When an empoyer makes an offer, there is a public indication that the applicant is the one wanted for the position. In effect, the employer is saying, "Forget about the rest. We want you." At this point, employers have usually invested considerable financial and emotional energy in recruiting and picking the best people to work in their organization, and they don't want to lose them. Bringing new workers into the organization once they have been selected is very important to the managers in most organizations. It is a matter of successfully finishing the recruiting process at this point—egos are on the line. So contrary to what you might be thinking as a recent graduate, you do have some negotiating power once an offer is made. A NACE (2007) survey of over 13 thousand graduating college students revealed that 80 percent received at least one job offer with an average of 2.24 offers for all applicants. Don't accept the first offer pitched and then realize later that you should have done more negotiating (Dittmann, 2005).

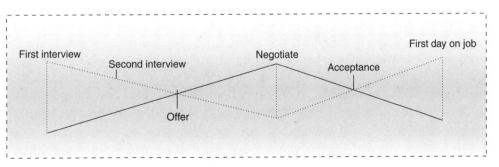

FIGURE 14.1

Social Power in Employment Negotiation

MAXIMIZING YOUR BARGAINING POWER

Job hunters can increase their bargaining power in negotiating job offers by paying attention to the eight items listed below. If you happen to be six months or more away from launching your employment campaign, this list might help you focus your efforts on building your resume or taking other actions that will increase your negotiating power later.

1. *Knowledge increases power*. The research that you do on the industry, organization, and job will provide information that will be invaluable in negotiating. The more you know about the job and organization, the less likely you will be "sold" a position that you will not like, will not be qualified for, or will not perform well in. Be prepared to explain why you are better than other candidates. Knowing the average salaries for positions such as the one you seek, the cost of living in different areas, or new types of training associated with jobs can strengthen your negotiating position with an employer.

2. *Solid recommendations*. Your reputation and prior work record, including internships, volunteer work, part-time employment, summer jobs, and campus activities, can provide you with documented references that increase your bargaining power. Make it a point to get letters from former supervisors and professors that can provide recommendations based on your personal work habits and work standards. Never underestimate the value of any letter that speaks to your leadership, team spirit, commitment to group goals, punctuality, and consideration of others.

3. *Poise and confidence*. Your negotiating style can be very helpful in increasing your success in obtaining desired employment outcomes. Negotiating provides the employer an opportunity to learn more about you. It is important for you to be clear about your goals, be respectful of the other people involved in the negotiating process, and avoid becoming intimidated by the social power of the interviewers (don't be rushed into making decisions). Remember, negotiating is a social process, where friendliness, listening and speaking clearly, and personal presentation (e.g., dressing appropriately) are very important. As we explained in Chapter 10, be aware that the employer might assume you are a Generation Y type person with expectations that are out-of-whack (Hira, 2007). Emphasize that you're not trying to skip steps or be impatient and that you value the learning process and the experience of those proceeding you. If you handle the employment negotiating process in a highly professional manner, the employer is able to learn more about how you might handle other delicate work situations that involve negotiating.

4. *Inside recommendations*. If you have some contact with a person already working in the organization, this can increase your negotiating power. In effect, this is a special kind of recommendation, focusing on how and why you should become a member of the organizational team. Unlike other recommendations that vouch for your skills and background, this one focuses on you as a potential high-quality new member of the "organizational family." It is a recommendation that says you'd be a good fit within the culture of the employing organization.

5. *Supply and demand*. If the job, industry, or organization is currently "hot" and there is a shortage of qualified workers in this field, your bargaining power increases. Your research should provide you with information about the current labor market demand relative to this job or the particular skills needed for a position. For example, there is a critical need for counselors who have computer skills because relatively few counselors have them and computers are increasingly used in career services. A low unemployment rate in the surrounding area will similarly work in your favor.

6. *Other offers*. If you are already considering other job offers, then your bargaining power is increased. If employers know that someone else wants you, that may raise their competitive

fires to want to beat the competition. However, you need to be careful and honest with this information, because misleading someone (not bargaining in good faith) can seriously damage your reputation among many employers. It is unwise to assume that different employers will not communicate with each other about your "offer" after you become employed.

7. *Persuasion*. Give the employer reasons to negotiate a better offer to you. Explain your qualifications clearly. List your accomplishments related to the job, explain how it matches your goals, and compare and contrast yourself with others who may have held this position. Your goal at this stage is to *demonstrate your potential value* to an employer, how your contributions could exceed the employer's expectations for the typical person in the position. One technique for doing this is to summarize your understanding of the duties and responsibilities of the position: "I understand that I would be responsible for a budget of $1 million, would cover a three-state territory, would report to the regional manager, and would head a staff of five." Again, good employer research can strengthen your position.

8. *Silent on salary*. Your bargaining power in negotiating can be enhanced if you can successfully sell your credentials and yourself to an employer without having to discuss the topic of salary. By keeping the focus of the employment communications on your goals, the organization's mission, the high quality of the match between you and the organization/job, you are reassuring the employer that you are interested in more than money. If you are asked about salary early in the interview process, try to buy time by indicating "open" or "willing to negotiate." We'll say much more about salary later in this chapter.

These eight factors can strengthen your position in negotiating a job offer. However, if you are unable to negotiate from a position of strength and power, don't try to "fake" it. The employer probably has more experience in negotiating job offers than you do, so you don't want to lie about other offers, your recommendations, your prior experience, or the results of your research regarding the supply and demand of workers for position.

RECEIVING A JOB OFFER

Several matters are important to consider upon receiving a job offer. These include timing of offers, personal impressions, clarifying the offer, and deciding when to make a decision.

Timing of an Offer

Job hunters often wonder, "When can I expect to receive an offer?" Generally, an offer can arrive anywhere from one day to six weeks after your second or third interview. Occasionally employers will give you the offer at their final interview.

Impressions Still Count

Don't assume you can "let your hair down" once you have an offer in hand. You will want to continue to make a good impression when the offer arrives; the employer is still collecting data about you. This requires a delicate balancing act. It is important to let employers know you are pleased to receive an offer, but do not let them hear you announce to your roommate or significant other, "Yahoo! I got the job!" On the other hand, you do not want to make a negative impression with employers by telling them how sought after you are and how many other offers you have already received.

While we are focusing mostly on the impression you are making on the employer, remember that you are also still in a position to collect data on the employer. If you feel that the employer is not respecting you in the negotiating process, not listening to your concerns, or not treating you in an adult way, then think about what it might be like if you accept the offer and the employer still has such an attitude. Remember, you are in your relatively strongest position in the relationship after the employer has extended an offer.

Clarify the Offer

In the excitement of receiving an offer, job hunters may overlook certain details that are important to clarify with the employer before they sign on the dotted line or verbally agree to an offer. Be clear on all the factors that make up the offer. These include position title, general responsibilities, salary, location, reporting date, travel or relocation expenses, signing bonus, and deadline for an answer. Other information is important when deciding on your acceptance of an offer, and this will be discussed later in this chapter.

Negotiate Time of Decision

Do not accept the job offer on the spot. Although you may have already been considering the possibility of an offer, you need time to evaluate all the factors in this decision. Have a date in mind when you can give the employer your decision *prior* to receiving an offer—this will help you negotiate more effectively. Remember not to be "starstruck" by the excitement of the offer. Be prepared to negotiate when you can give the employer your decision about an offer. Employers should not be surprised that you are interviewing with other organizations, and they will appreciate your being honest and careful about your decision. Employers give candidates 16 days on average to accept or reject offers (National Association of Colleges & Employers, 2007).

Now we'll take a look at some of the things that might be negotiated by a new college graduate.

THINGS THAT MAY BE NEGOTIATED

Remember you have nothing to negotiate until you have an offer. However, once you receive an offer it is important that you consider all the possible factors that could be negotiated. In this section, we review 15 things that might be negotiated, depending on the policies of the organization and your employment needs. If you have done careful research about the organization and have been clear and consistent about your employment needs, you'll have less difficulty figuring out what areas you might want to negotiate. Barkley and Sandburg (1995) and Burt (2007) suggested that these things be negotiated in approximately the order that we have presented them here. They believe that salary and compensation issues should be agreed upon first, because other items in the list may be directly connected to these, for example, benefit package as a percentage of base salary.

1. Salary

The offered salary may or may not be negotiable; it may or may not be a fair offer. You should research salaries offered in your field by geographic locations, experience, degree level, major, and previous offers prior to negotiating this factor. You will often find that the salary an employee receives varies greatly from job to job, employer to employer, and from one region of the country to another. Some consultants suggest that you come up with three figures: (1) your minimum or bottom-line figure, (2) a realistic midpoint desired salary, and (3) a "dream salary" (Yate, 2007).

It is much easier to negotiate down from your upper range than it is to negotiate up from your bottom-line figure. You do not want to give a figure that is too low because you will undervalue

TABLE 14.1	POSSIBLE FACTORS FOR NEGOTIATING AN EMPLOYMENT OFFER

Benefit package	Location of the job (cost of living adjustment)
Bonuses	Long-term disability insurance
Car	Mentoring systems
Cellular phone or PDA	Mileage
Child-care expenses	Office furnishings
Club memberships	Overtime work
Company recreation facilities	Pension plans
Consumer product discounts	Professional training and conferences
Division, department, title, or classification of position	Profit sharing
Educational expenses (tuition reimbursement)	Relocation expenses
Expense account	Reporting date
Fitness center	Salary
Flextime	Sales commissions percentage
Frequent flyer or travel clubs	Severance pay
Fuel allowance	Stock options
Fulfillment and fun	Supervisor
Health insurance	Supplemental life insurance
Home or personal computer	Support staff
Home-based work	Termination agreement
Job duties	Timing of appraisal reviews
Job title	Vacations

yourself and give the employer a reason to think less of you. L. M. Sixel (1997) suggested that the salary you ask for should be within 20 percent of the average. Here are several resources that are useful in researching salary. The first one is available in most college career center libraries.

- National Association of Colleges and Employers (NACE) Salary Survey

- *Occupational Outlook Handbook* (also available at http://www.bls.gov/oco/)

- Online job notices from newspapers

- www.homefair.com/calc/salcalc.html (a Web site that helps you compare salary levels in different geographic locations)

In negotiating salary, try to avoid mentioning a specific salary—talk about ranges. Indicate that you want to be flexible and consider options. If you have researched the organization and job carefully, then you have some ideas about an appropriate salary. Ask for the top of the range, for more than what you expect the employer to offer.

2. Timing of Appraisal Reviews

Some employers may give bonuses for the quality of job performance. Often these salary increases are attached to your appraisal reviews. If the organization uses this type of appraisal system, it might be possible to ask for an earlier review to increase your earnings sooner than normal. Sometimes you might consider accepting a lower salary with the understanding that your first salary review will be sooner than originally stipulated. If the first review typically takes place at six months and involves a 15 percent salary increase, you might want to negotiate an earlier three or four months review (Barkley & Sandburg, 1995).

3. Signing Bonus

The relocation package may also be in the form of a signing bonus, which is simply an agreed upon amount of money given to you at the time of your acceptance of the offer. If an employer does not offer a signing bonus or a relocation package, you might want to consider negotiating for one. Allen (1998) reported that 36 percent of employers indicated offering signing bonuses, especially to technical graduates. The amount of the signing bonus may also be contingent on how quickly you accept the offer.

4. Sales Commissions, Profit Sharing, Stock Options

If the job is in the private sector, the employer might offer you a package of base salary and other financial incentives. These might be based on sales and meeting quotas. Your research into the field will help you know what kind of salary package is typically offered in the industry, and then you can evaluate what might be good for you.

5. Location of the Job

There are many differences between working in one city or another. Take the time to check out the geographic area of your new position. Here are some possible questions to consider:

- Does the community offer the lifestyle you are looking for?

- Are there sufficient cultural, sports, recreational opportunities available in the community?

- What other community factors are important to you, for example, family, schools, churches, and so forth?

- Would you feel comfortable living there?

- What is the cost of living compared to where you live now?

- How long a commute would you likely have?

- Can you choose the location of the job?

The location of the job directly impacts the cost of living. A standard reference often used to measure this factor is the *ACCRA Cost of Living Index*, which is available in most libraries or from the association (AACRA; http://www.coli.org/). Using the Internet, you can find information on salaries and other job matters at www.salary.com. We suggest you do the "salary wizard" first and then check different locations to see how your net worth will change if you live in one place or another. Another site sponsored by the National Association of Colleges and Employers, http://www.jobweb.com/, has a salary and negotiation program that might be helpful in relocation.

6. Insurance, Pension Plans, and Other Benefits

An organization's benefit package might be as much as 30+ percent of the salary offer. It is important to convert the benefit package into salary or expense dollars so you have a more complete measure of the financial terms of an offer. For example, if the employer provides complete health coverage, what is the equivalent in premium costs if you had to go into the market and purchase all or part of this yourself?

Organizations vary in terms of exactly what is included in employment benefits, the flexibility of building a benefit package to meet your special needs, tax liabilities of benefits, who can be covered by the benefits, and the transferability of the benefit programs. Items included in an optional benefits package could include incentive savings, 401(k) plan, maternity/paternity leave, dental/optical insurance, frequent flyer/travel clubs, disability insurance, sick leave, life insurance, assistance with interest on loans, tuition reimbursement, wellness program, and child-care expenses. These may be points of negotiation for you.

7. Relocation Expenses

Many employers provide relocation benefits to help you move to the community where the job is located. A survey of employers by the National Association of Colleges and Employers (2007) revealed that 80 percent planned to offer relocation assistance to hires from the class of 2007. This may include travel to the community to look for a place to live, mortgage assistance, cost of moving your possessions or car, and living expenses until you are settled. Other compensations might include the cost of temporary lodging, moving expenses, home mortgage rate differential, closing costs, and real estate broker fees. You might want to negotiate for a short-term interest-free loan to help you cover the costs for relocating to the new job. These costs associated with your relocation to the work site may be negotiable.

8. Expense Account, Car, Mileage, Fuel Allowance

Another part of a financial package offered by an employer could include reimbursement or advances for expenses associated with the job. These items might include a mobile phone or pager, a public transportation reimbursement, expenses for commuting or parking. You might be able to negotiate for a better or larger car if that was important to you. There may be tax advantages to having this income as a business expense, or perhaps you want it as a benefit. Your research can help you become informed about how to evaluate and negotiate these matters with the employer.

9. Club Memberships

If the job involves entertaining customers, or if it is a stress-producing situation, you might want to negotiate paid memberships at a private club, tennis club, or fitness center. Does the employer have a recreational facility that you can use? Can any fees be waived or reduced? Your prior research into the organization and position can help you learn whether these memberships are part of the base offer for the position.

10. Consumer Product Discounts

Your organization may have options for employees to participate in discount buying programs of various kinds. You might be able to negotiate your participation in such programs.

11. Office Furnishings

Another aspect of "location" that you might want to negotiate involves the location of your work space or the physical arrangements of your office. Do you want to work from a home office? What kinds of arrangements would need to be made for you to do this? What types of communication and office equipment might you need in a home office that the employer might provide? Do you have a disability that requires reasonable accommodations? If having an office with a window is going to affect the quality of your work, negotiate for it. Perhaps new office furniture, a new computer, or a notebook computer might be tied to improving the location of your work. Remember, if these things are important to you, the time to negotiate is *before* you accept an offer.

12. Reporting Date

Depending on the organization and the job, some employers might be able to offer a flexible starting date. If you have ever dreamed of backpacking or cycling through Europe, now may be the time, or maybe you just want to take some time off to relax. Remember, it's probably too late to negotiate the reporting date after you accept the offer.

13. Vacations

Vacation time may vary in terms of the actual amount (days, hours), whether it is paid, and when it can be taken. If taking time off at a particular season or time of year is important to you and will make you a happier, more satisfied employee, then it might be something you want to negotiate.

14. Division, Department, Title, or Classification of Position

In general, not all jobs are created equal within an organization. Find out as much as possible about your options before you accept an offer. If you decide that certain divisions or departments appeal to you more than others, let it be known before you sign. The division or department responsible for your specific work assignment might be a factor that can be negotiated. Related to this, you might be able to negotiate a different title or classification for your job, which might place you in a better salary pool or offer other advantages.

15. Fulfillment and Fun

For some new workers entering the job market, the sky is often the limit in what can be negotiated. "Gold-collar" workers who are in very high demand expect to be well paid and fed, but they also seek a job that's fun and offers fulfillment. As Monk (1998) observed several years ago:

> When many of the most desirable employees out there are twenty-somethings, it is no surprise that adolescence, with its eternal quest for romance, now reaches beyond college and into every nook and cranny of corporate America. Some companies resist this trend, fearful that once the precedent has been set there's no going back. But in a labor market as tight as this one, if your competitor lets employees keep a birdbath in the office, you may have no choice but to follow suit. (p. 66)

Monk noted that if the corporate goal is to hire and retain the most talented people on the block, "the best way to do that, it seems, is let them do whatever the hell they want" (p. 74).

In contrast to Monk's views, Mimi Collins (1998) reported a survey of 2,120 college seniors who made it very clear that they were looking for security in their benefits, not "out there" perks. Their most desired benefits in order were medical insurance, retirement plans, annual salary increase, dental insurance, life insurance, tuition reimbursement, stock options, family-friendly benefits, two plus week's vacation, and flextime.

Not all of these factors will be negotiable in your situation, but it is prudent and reasonable to explore them if they are important to you and will impact your ability to be a successful and satisfied employee in the organization.

SOME ADDITIONAL WORDS ABOUT SALARY

The matter of salary is especially important and critical in negotiating job offers, and we should say a few more words about it. The basic strategy in salary negotiation is to know what a job pays and what you're worth, and to wait until it's clear the employer wants only you. Later we will offer some ideas about how to research information that helps you determine your worth.

In negotiating salary, as well as other aspects of an offer, you should assume that the employer is seeking to take steps to make you a happy, satisfied employee. As a result, *you* must be clear with the employer about what will make you a happy, satisfied employee. Indeed, you can even use this kind of language as you discuss the details of an offer.

In discussing salary, employers sometimes talk about salary in terms of rates of time, hour, week, month, or year. Do your homework, and be prepared to think about salary in these terms. Employers may also talk about percentage increases, never using actual dollar amounts, so be prepared to know what these percentages really mean. If you are unsure, ask for time, clarification, or assistance in understanding all aspects of an offer before you begin negotiating. Most employers have had much more experience than you in discussing and thinking about these matters, so take the necessary steps to keep the negotiating field somewhat equal among all parties involved in the process.

The salary for your first professional position is of special importance. In some organizations, you cannot negotiate the beginning salary offer. Nevertheless, this salary is important because your future positions will probably be based in part on what you were making in your last job. Your next employer will typically offer you at least 10 to 15 percent more, so your starting salary is important for this reason. In addition, salary increments are usually based on a percentage of your current salary, for example, a 10 percent New Year's bonus. Future salary negotiations often are based on a percentage of your current or base salary. Benefits may also be calculated in terms of the base salary.

Salaries are typically set for positions in the organization, not the people who will fill the positions. Because of this, it is to your advantage to explain what added value you can bring to the position if you have the job. This means that any special qualities you bring to the position, such as international experience, language skills, leadership, community service, or technical expertise, can increase the salary you might receive. These matters can become the substance of negotiating.

What if an employer asks, "What are your salary needs?" What should you answer? Rather than blurt out some numbers, you could ask, "What is the typical range of pay in your organization for this position?" This puts the ball back into the employer's court. Let's say the employer cites a pay range of $28,000 to $30,000 for a position. You could respond that you are glad to hear those numbers because you were hoping to earn $29,500. Krannich and Krannich (2002) suggested that you place the bottom of your range in the top of the employer's range. If the employer declines to name a figure, then you can cite the results of your research. You might say, "I've learned that the market rate for the job is $31,000. I would consider that a fair offer." In this regard, you should be aware that the NACE survey of 2007 college graduates (National Association of Colleges and Employers, July 2007) revealed that average starting salaries were about $5,000 higher than anticipated by applicants.

Never accept a job until you know the salary and are sure that it is acceptable to you. Once you have accepted, be certain to get a letter detailing all aspects of the offer. *Never, never leave a job for another one unless you have a written offer in hand.* Write a formal letter of acceptance expressing appreciation for the time and energy of those involved in the recruiting process and reiterating all details of the offer, including position title, starting date and place, starting salary, and special arrangements. Remember, the person you are negotiating with might not be there when you arrive later, so it is important to have everything in writing.

THE PROCESS OF NEGOTIATING

In closing this section, we want to mention several matters that are important in successfully negotiating of job offers. These have to do with using your positive metacognitions to guide the process.

Decide Your Conditions

It is important to determine what you want from the offer, but it is also important to know the minimum you will take from an offer. Create a plan that will allow flexibility. You want to be consistent in communicating to the employer what is important to you in a job. Typically, there will not be many surprises in negotiations. However, if you ask for more salary, but the organization cannot offer more money, would you be willing to take a signing bonus instead? Remember, you only have one opportunity to get the most from this offer, so thoroughly plan prior to any negotiation.

Remain Positive

The person you are negotiating with may be your future supervisor or at the very least your colleague. If you are truly interested in the job, don't put the employer on the defensive when negotiating. The key ingredient is to stay positive about the other person, the offer, and the organization. Restate that you are really interested in working for the organization and say, "Is there some way we can work this out?" or "I really want to try and make this happen."

Make a Decision

Be prepared to make a decision once the organization has stated their final offer. Know when to stop negotiating and either accept or decline an offer. Try not to focus too much on the salary in the offer; consider all aspects of the offer in making a decision. It might be possible to convert some of these factors into dollars or a percentage of your salary. After negotiations are completed, the next task is to evaluate the outcomes and make the best employment choice available to you. Now we will examine the sometimes difficult process of evaluating offers.

Be Honest with Employers

Negotiating is not really a "game," where deceit or lack of integrity work very well. Indeed, it is in your interest to be as honest and forthright in negotiations with employers as possible. Capell (1997, p. 22) quotes Ellen Glazerman, a national director of campus recruiting for Ernst & Young, which hires 1,000 to 2,000 college graduates annually: "If they're interested in the job and have other offers, just give the information to the recruiter. If they tell us what's on their minds and what their true concerns are, that's very different from playing the negotiating game." At the same time, it is important to note that employers may not always be as forthcoming as they should regarding the amount of flexibility they have to negotiate salary and other aspects of a job offer.

EVALUATING OFFERS: MAKING THE BEST CHOICE

We presented the story of Anna and her difficulties in successfully negotiating and evaluating two job offers at the beginning of this chapter. Now we will examine in more detail the matter of deciding between, or among, offers. Let's look at some other scenarios, as reported by Gordon (1998).

> Ling Cheng, majoring in Chinese and management information systems, had 30 interviews in the fall semester and expected multiple offers. Her biggest challenge was organizing her priorities to make the right choice. Her priorities were a challenging work environment and room to advance, and she wasn't planning to stick around if the first employer did not measure up.
>
> Chris Epple left his job after eight weeks. The graduate of a state university, he wanted a position that emphasized teamwork and training, and would pay enough to finance a graduate degree. Feeling pressure from the employer to decide, he accepted a sales position in advertising with a small firm. After joining the firm, he quickly learned that the culture was not what he had expected. The company atmosphere was competitive, impersonal, and unfriendly, and in spite of an impressive salary, he quit and found himself unemployed.

What does all of this mean for a college student launching an employment campaign? Gordon (p. 5) quoted Jack Rayman, the director of career development and placement at Penn State University: "Students should understand they're in demand. If they have the skills and a background that makes them attractive to one company, others also will be fond of them." This means that students need to take an active approach. As a job hunter you should be very clear about your goals and take specific steps to develop information that will enable you to make wise employment decisions.

Waiting on Other Offers

Evaluating two or more offers and deciding which one to accept is likely to involve a host of factors. It is entirely appropriate to tell Employer A that you need more time because you are waiting to hear from Employer B and Employer C. There is nothing wrong in talking with several organizations at the same time about your employment situation. Indeed, it probably increases your value. Employers are each trying to hire the best persons for the job, and knowing that you are being considered elsewhere makes you more attractive to all three organizations.

The Sales Pitch

Remember that the recruiter's job is to bring you into the organization, to get you to say "Yes." During the negotiating process, you may be "wined and dined" by organizations—provided first-rate meals, lodging, and entertainment. You may be told about many perquisites ("perks") that the organization offers new employees. However, you have to gauge all of this information and experience during the recruiting and negotiating process against your values—what you *really* want and need in a job.

Ethical Dilemmas: Would You Renege on an Accepted Offer?

Once you have negotiated with a prospective employer, several scenarios are possible. In the event that you only have one offer, once you have negotiated your best deal, you must decide whether to take the employer's offer or decline and continue searching. You may put yourself in a very awkward position if you have been demanding with the employer during the negotiations, the employer has met all your demands, and then you turn down the offer. If you decline the offer, you should have very legitimate reasons for doing so. Otherwise, the employer may not believe that you were negotiating in good faith, and this can come back to haunt you in the future. Remember, you are building a reputation among members of a professional or industry group.

You may also encounter intense pressure from an employer to make a decision about an offer. If you have been unable to negotiate more time to evaluate other offers or to consider acceptance of the offer, there are some things to reflect upon. The pressure you feel from your employer may give you an idea of how you will be treated as an employee. If this is how you are made to feel at a time when you have some social power in the relationship, imagine what you can expect from the employer after you accept and your power decreases.

Another situation involves turning down a job *after* accepting it. When an employer offers a job and the candidate accepts it, a contract for employment has been created. Today, however, with massive corporate layoffs and the demise of the old employment contract, the ethical codes are less clear for some people. Leaving a job after only a few weeks or months can be taken as a sign of impulsiveness or impatience. In reality, it may take longer than a few weeks or months for you to adequately assess whether a job is a good fit for you.

Students are expected to accept offers in good faith; however, there may be circumstances that force one to renege, such as an unexpected family responsibility—a critically ill parent that prohibits a person from taking a job in a distant location. If a new hire must renege, he or she should immediately notify the employer and withdraw the acceptance. Any signing bonus should be returned (Kaplan, 1999).

How do employers and new college graduates view this matter of reneging on accepted offers? According to Allen (1998), employers reported that only 3.7 percent of new college graduates reneged on their acceptances of offers, so it is not something that happens frequently. The most common scenario involves a technical graduate with multiple offers who does not want to relocate. On the other hand, 62 percent of students said they would renege on an acceptance if a better offer came along, and 9 percent indicated they would continue to interview for a better position after acceptance (Collins, 1998). There seems to be a discrepancy between what students say they would do and what actually happens.

Being Sure About the Job

In helping you think about an offer, we have drawn upon an article by Humphrey, Nahrgang, and Morgenson (2007) who used a meta-analytic research procedure to examine factors contributing to good working situations. Here are some factors they identified that you might use in deciding whether or not to accept an offer:

1. Autonomy – the freedom to carry out tasks and activities of the job.

2. Skill variety – the extent to which different skills are used in performing the job.

3. Task identity – the extent to which one can complete a whole project.

4. Task significance – the extent to which the job impacts the lives of others.

5. Feedback from the job – the extent to which the job provides information about your work performance.

6. Social support – the extent to which the job provides opportunities for getting assistance and advice from supervisors or coworkers. Considering that you may spend 25 percent of your week at work, make sure it is a place where you are comfortable and can grow.

7. Outside interactions – the extent you can connect with others and gain insight and feedback on specific job tasks.

8. Compensation – the extent to which the job provides satisfactory monetary rewards.

9. Meaningfulness – the extent to which cherished goals can be pursued in work.

In addition to these nine factors, Koc (2007) identified a tenth factor that may be important to you.

10. Location – the extent to which the job is close to home. Koc analyzed 2007 NACE survey results which indicated that current college graduates prefer employers close to home when looking for a first full-time job. Location might also involve the commuting time, which could involve transportation costs and stress. Just a 25-minute commute each way means 200 hours per year.

Bottom line? The feeling you have when you ask yourself: "Do I really want to work here?" Consideration of these factors may help you verify what you know what is important about the job you have been offered and are trying to make a decision about accepting.

FINAL STEPS BEFORE YOU START

Once you have accepted an offer, the next step is reporting on the first day, right? Well, not quite. There are several other important things that will probably happen before you actually start to work. Your contract or signed appointment papers will probably hinge on the employer obtaining some final pieces of information. These might include a physical, a drug test, civil and criminal background checks, loyalty oath, nondisclosure agreement, and even checks of your references. Depending on the type of organization, it may take weeks for this information to be obtained and for you to be appointed.

Regarding the *drug test*, most organizations test employees and job applicants for drug use. However, this testing has dropped from 81 percent in 1996 to 62 percent in 2004 (Cadrain, 2006). The reason? Employers in some industries are finding that drug testing shows no return on investment and, as a result, they want to streamline the hiring process. So, before you are given a reporting date for your first professional job, you may need to move past this final screening procedure.

USING CIP TO NEGOTIATE AND DECIDE ON AN OFFER

In this chapter, we have been discussing the process of negotiating and deciding on employment offers. Now we'll review what we have learned about these topics from a CIP perspective. Our goal is to help you improve key elements in your Personal Career Theory (PCT) for solving employment problems.

Self-Knowledge

Just as self-knowledge is important in exploring occupational and educational alternatives, it also has a role to play in helping you evaluate job offers and selecting the best one. Clear knowledge of what you seek in a job will give you a "yardstick" by which to measure the opportunities that come your way.

Some questions related to self-knowledge that might help you evaluate offers include the following:

- In day-to-day work, how much is done independently or with a team? How intense is it? What skills are used?

- How much of the work will involve skills I don't yet have? How will I obtain those skills? What time and effort will be required?

- How much independence do I have? Who gives me work? What needs approval?

- How well does this job match my most important interests, skills, and values?

In Chapter 2, we emphasized the importance of values in solving career problems and making career decisions. Values are very evident in making decisions about offers. Gordon (1998, p. 5) urged students to make the right employment decision the first time "by determining what you want. That way you'll recognize a good job when you see it. To make sure a position fits, list the criteria you're seeking in a first employer before you start interviewing. List job factors that are important to you,...then rank them in order of importance. Evaluate every job you consider against this list."

The employment decision-making exercise in *Appendix L* includes a list of factors that you can use to determine your job priorities. This values-clarification process also might involve reviewing the self-assessment information included in Chapter 2 and reviewing the information in Chapter 4 on "Career Decision Making."

Knowledge of Options

In researching occupational alternatives, you have learned something about what you want in a job you might hold now or in the future. Knowledge about options includes knowledge about specific positions with various employing organizations. To effectively evaluate competing offers you must be fully informed about what each employer is offering. Many job hunters create problems for themselves by accepting positions where their knowledge about the specific job was incomplete, as in the case of Anna. What else do you need to know to effectively evaluate the offer? What gaps are there in your knowledge about the position?

Some questions related to option knowledge that might help you in deciding about offers include the following:

- Are the work activities related to what you are looking for in a job?

- Is the training program attractive and comprehensive?

- Does the organization provide advancement and mentoring opportunities?

- Are the pay and benefits consistent with your needs and goals? How does the benefit package compare to those of other employers?

- How will I be evaluated? By whom? Are criteria different across the groups to which I might be assigned?

- What are the formal and informal hours of work? How important is "face time" in the office? How many hours per week do people in this office really work?

- Are the surroundings and people pleasant?

- Is the geographic location conducive to you and your family's hobbies, community activities, and social support groups?

Applying the CASVE Model

We suggest that you evaluate each offer based on the same set of factors. The CASVE Cycle model presented in Chapter 4 can be applied to the problem-solving and decision-making process associated with evaluating job offers.

Communication. An employer extending a job offer is an example of an external event that would cause you to begin the career problem-solving and decision-making process. Your own emotions are likely to be at work during this time as well. You may be excited at having received an offer, but at the same time anxious about committing to a particular employer or turning down an offer that is not an ideal fit with your preferences. In CIP terms, the gap is not simply getting a job offer or becoming employed, it is negotiating the best possible terms of employment related to each offer and then accepting the offer that comes closest to best satisfying your employment goals.

Analysis. Having accurate and complete knowledge about yourself and your options is a critical aspect of choosing among offers. In analyzing a job offer, you will want to determine the extent to which the offer meets the skills, values, interests, and goals you have identified as important in meeting your employment needs. These personal characteristics are examined in terms of the trends in the industry, the way jobs are changing, the culture of the organization, and other environmental matters.

Synthesis. With respect to evaluating job offers, the Synthesis phase of the CASVE Cycle involves both Elaborating and Crystallizing offers. In Elaboration, you try to negotiate more features into the job being offered that meet some of the important factors and issues identified in Analysis. Table 14.1 identified some of the factors that might be used in negotiating, or Synthesis Elaboration in CIP terms.

The process of evaluating offers is more likely to be focused on narrowing one's options, or Synthesis Crystallization. The number of job offers you may have to consider at any one time is likely to be small. Eliminating some options may be relatively easy—for example the pay is way below your acceptable range, the geographic location is too remote. However, when the offers are equally attractive or they satisfy different sets of criteria you've identified in the Analysis phase, the process of deciding may be much harder.

Working through the Valuing phase of the CASVE Cycle may help you prioritize your choices. You may also find that a structured exercise that helps you weigh various factors would be helpful, and an example of one of these is in *Appendix L*.

Valuing. As noted previously, this phase of the CASVE Cycle includes considering the costs and benefits of each option, not only to yourself but also to significant others, your cultural group, community, and society, now and in the future.

- Does this job accommodate your needs and lifestyle preference with regard to your family (Would I accept a job offer that means working a considerable distance from my family?)? Would you accept a job offer that makes it more difficult for your spouse to find appropriate employment?

- What about issues that may relate to your cultural group (Has this employer typically discriminated against members of my cultural group?) or community (Would I work for a chemical company that has been cited for polluting the drinking water in my neighborhood?), and society (What is the employer's reputation across the country?)?

- Remember only you can decide what factors are important to you. What is important to one person isn't necessarily important to someone else. The "Employment Decision-Making Exercise" in *Appendix L* is one method that you can use to compare and evaluate offers by weighting factors that you rank more highly both personally and in a job. *Appendix L* includes a list of factors that might be important considerations in negotiating and evaluating job offers.

- Finally, if you were considering more than one offer, the outcome of this process would be a ranking of your offers. You would identify the employer that is your first choice, followed by your other priority rankings. In general, you would not want to eliminate any options until you had accepted an offer, received written confirmation, and signed an agreement letter.

Execution. Once you have made a decision, there are several key steps related to the Execution phase of the CASVE Cycle. The first of those is communicating with the employers who have extended offers. Once you have decided to accept an offer, it is extremely important to communicate with other prospective employers who extended offers to you. This includes declining both verbally and in writing to those employers whose offers you did not accept. This is an important step because you may have contact with these employers at a later time—so never burn your bridges.

After you have made a verbal commitment to an employer who has extended you an offer, the next step is to confirm your acceptance in writing. Acceptance letters are extremely important in restating your understanding of the offer. Remember to include the position title, salary, starting date and time, location, any perks or signing bonuses that were negotiated, and any other factors that you feel were vague or were not included in the offer.

Table 14.2 includes a sample acceptance letter.

Executive Processing

Your ability to think strategically and effectively is a critical aspect of the process of negotiating and evaluating offers. In addition, you're required to consider a great deal of information about yourself and your options at a time of great pressure. There may also be significant others involved who are providing their input.

Negative thinking is likely to occur when you only have one offer on the table. There may be a tendency to jump at the first offer that comes along. You hear yourself saying, "I'd better take a sure thing." "What if I don't get another offer?" "This is a very good opportunity—I'd be stupid to turn it down." You are the only person who can decide the level of risk you are willing to take in turning down offers in hopes that something better will come along. Challenging your thinking in this area might involve saying, "If one employer thought I was good enough to extend an offer to me, chances

---

TABLE 14.2   SAMPLE OFFER ACCEPTANCE LETTER

P.O. Box 334
State University
Anywhere, FL 32301–4708
March 28, 2008

Ms. Alice Murphy
Recruiting Coordinator
Information Systems Technologies, Inc.
Denver, CO 80207

Dear Ms. Murphy:

Thank you very much for your letter dated March 17, 2008. I am pleased to accept your offer for the position of account executive within the Customer Support division. I understand that my initial assignment will be working with Mr. Bruce Allen in the Network Support group at a salary of $35,000 per year.

As we agreed, I will start work on Monday, June 2, 2008, and I will report to Personnel that morning at 8:00 a.m. to complete the necessary paperwork. As you noted in the offer letter, I will be reimbursed for my moving expenses up to, but not exceeding, $2,500.

I appreciate all your efforts on my behalf. If additional information related to my appointment is needed prior to June 2, please let me know. I look forward to joining the team at Information Systems Technologies, Inc.

Sincerely,

Joan Roberts

are another employer will as well." Negotiating job offers is a process that requires your highest levels of self-confidence and positive self-talk.

As we noted, it is important to be aware of the quality of the information you have throughout this process. Being completely informed about a particular job opportunity may help you avoid disappointment at a later date when you realize the job you accepted does not meet your expectations. This is an all too common experience among job hunters.

SUMMARY

This chapter has reviewed the factors associated with negotiating job offers, including what items you may wish to negotiate and the steps to follow in the negotiation process. The Pyramid of Information-Processing Domains and the CASVE Cycle were used to demonstrate the steps that job hunters might follow in evaluating offers. We noted that metacognitions, the quality of one's thinking, can influence the process of negotiating and evaluating offers. The goal was to enable you to improve the quality of your PCT for negotiating job offers.

REFERENCES

Allen, C. (1998, Spring). NACE employer benchmark survey. *Journal of Career Planning & Employment, 58*(3), 25–30.

Barkley, N., & Sandburg, E. (1995). *The Crystal-Barkley guide to taking charge of your career.* New York: Workman.

Burt, E. (2007, April 19). How to choose the right job. Retrieved from http://www.kiplinger.com/columns/starting/archive/2007/st0418.htm.

Cadrain, D. (2006, June). Drug testing falls out of employers' favor. *HR Magazine, 51*(2), 38–39.

Collins, M. (1998, Spring). Great expectations. *Journal of Career Planning and Employment, 58*(3), 41–47.

Dittmann, M. (2005, January). Getting what you're worth. *GradPSYCH*, pp. 34–36.

Gordon, J. (1998, Spring/Summer). Choices, choices: Multiple job offers are raising a bevy of ethical dilemmas. *Managing Your Career*, pp. 4–5, 18.

Hira, N. A. (2007, December 17). Getting paid. *The gig.* Retrieved from http://thegig.blogs.fortune.cnn.com/2007/12/17/getting-paid/.

Humphrey, S. E., Nahrang, J. D., & Morgenson, F. P. (2007). Integrating motivational, social, and contextual work design features: A meta-analytic summary and theoretical extension of the work design literature. *Journal of Applied Psychology, 92*, 1332–1356.

Kaplan, R. (1999, May 3). A legal look at job offers, acceptances. *Spotlight*, retrieved April 28, 2005, from http://www.naceweb.org/pubs/spotlight/s050399leg.htm.

Koc, E. W. (2007, December). Attracting the recent college graduate: The question of location. *NACE Journal*, pp. 17–20.

Krannich, C. R., & Krannich, R. L. (2002). *Interview for success* (6th ed.). Manassas Park, VA: Impact Publications.

Krantz, L. (2002). *Jobs rated almanac: The best and worst jobs.* Fort Lee, NJ: Barricade Books, Inc.

Mish, F. C. (Ed.) (1997). *Merriam-Webster's collegiate dictionary* (10th ed.). Springfield, MA: Merriam-Webster.

Monk, N. (1998, March 16). The new organization man. *Fortune*, pp. 63–74.

National Association of Colleges and Employers. (2007, July). *Moving on: Student approaches and attitudes toward the job market for the college class of 2007 (executive summary).* Bethlehem, PA: Author.

National Association of Colleges and Employers. (2007, June). *NACE 2007 recruiting benchmarks survey: A report on key measures for college recruiting & experiential education (executive summary)*. Bethlehem, PA: Author.

NACE (1997, November 17). Job outlook '98. *Spotlight, 20*(8), pp. 1–8.

Sixel, L. M. (1997, February 26). Know what a job pays and what you're worth. *Tallahassee Democrat*, p. 20D.

Wright, J. W. (2000). *The American almanac of jobs and salaries 2000–2001 (Serial)*. New York: HarperCollins.

Yate, M. (2007). *Knock 'em dead 2008: The ultimate job-search guide*. Holbrook, MA: Adams Media Corporation.

THE FIRST JOB AND EARLY CAREER MOVES

Many career books do not include a chapter like this one because they focus on career preparation and job hunting rather than on the job itself. Ironically, employment is viewed as something separate from career development and planning. A national survey in late 2007 by the American Psychological Association (Anderson, 2008) revealed that 74 percent of respondents feel "work" is the number one source of stress in their lives. Such data lead us to take a different view—we actually think that this last chapter might serve equally well as the first chapter in this text. Therefore, it is appropriate for us to end this book with the job hunter on the job and anticipating his or her first year at work, which can be stressful.

One recent college graduate shared her story about her job campaign and her first day on the job. Traci was a management information systems major who had put together an excellent job campaign, had been recruited by a dozen organizations, had successfully negotiated an outstanding offer, and reported for her first day on the job. Upon arriving, she was surprised to learn that the person with whom she had negotiated the offer, and had expected would be her supervisor, had left the company. Things were rather disorganized; indeed, it seemed like they weren't expecting her at all. The appointment papers were not ready, nor was her office. She wondered if she had made a mistake. Fortunately, people at the work site quickly rallied, and Traci was soon feeling better about her career situation. While this is not a typical first day on the job, the story illustrates the unexpected things that can happen in a new job and why it is important to be prepared.

This chapter is about transitions. Dr. Ed Holton (1999) noted that first year employees are no longer college students but they are not really professionals yet either. They are in a unique transition period. Some hang on to their student attitudes and behaviors acquired over 17 years for too long, and they fail to realize that it takes time to earn the rights of a full-fledged professional. There is a different set of rules to follow during this break-in stage, and those are the focus of this chapter.

This chapter includes the following:

- Transition problems between college and work

- A discussion some of the economic realities of contemporary workplaces

- Strategies for adjusting to professional work life

- Strategies for job success in the first year

- Ideas to help you decide whether to leave or stay

- Ways to shift your thinking from career planning to career management

Along the way we will provide concrete suggestions for helping you develop appropriate metacognitions for effectively solving career problems and making career decisions during this first year. Finally, we will offer a CIP perspective on starting a new job. As we said in Chapter 1, "career" is a process where solving one career problem leads to subsequent problems and career decisions. This will become evident as we proceed through Chapter 15.

As you read this chapter about moving from the world of college to the world of employment, consider how your PCT and strategic career thinking can be improved by this information. How will this information affect the way you approach the job, *your boss, and your coworkers? What goals will you set for the first year of professional employment? What new metacognitions are needed to help you solve career problems and make career decisions at this point in your career?*

TRANSITION PROBLEMS BETWEEN COLLEGE AND WORK

In writing about college graduates and employment, Philip Gardner and Wen-Ying Liu (1997) reported that employers view college students as poorly prepared for the new and changing workplace. "The problems new graduates struggle with are more likely to be relational and personal competencies—skills not directly taught in the classroom" (p. 54).

Gardner and Liu went on to provide examples of problem areas that both technical (e.g., engineering, computer science, accounting) and nontechnical (e.g., general business, social sciences, communications) graduates had in their first jobs.

Technical graduates had these problems:

- Making group presentations
- Writing in a business context
- Applying academic knowledge to real-world situations
- Leading a group
- Integrating learning and business operations
- Teamworking skills

Nontechnical graduates fell short in applied problem solving and in relational and personal management skills, such as the following:

- Goal setting
- Time management and setting priorities
- Understanding workplace values and ethics
- Negotiating the system
- Handling conflict and criticism
- Drafting a project proposal

Elsewhere, Gardner (1998) reported that poor attendance, failure to follow instructions, and lack of initiative were the most common reasons why new college graduates were fired from their jobs.

These same metacognitions and behaviors are often evident in the classroom. It is important for some students to overcome these weaknesses in their career behavior.

It appears that lack of self-management and poor relationship skills are at the heart of the problem. Some of these problems may be traced to deficiencies in all sectors of the Pyramid of Information-Processing Domains, including lack of self- and occupational knowledge, poor interpersonal problem-solving skills (CASVE Cycle), and inadequate metacognitions in the executive processing area, such as negative self-talk, lack of self-awareness in the job situation, and inadequate control and monitoring of feedback and personal experience in the job situation. These concepts were introduced in Part One of this text and will be elaborated throughout this chapter.

What are some of the issues associated with the transition from college to fulltime professional employment? There will be many changes in lifestyle and routine, but what particular areas might be most troublesome? How will your student lifestyle change as a new hire? What kinds of new relationships can you expect? What kinds of things can you do as a college student completing your degree that will help you prepare for the first day on the job? These are some of the topics we will explore in this section.

The Reality of the New Job

In another study, Philip Gardner and Stephen Lambert (1993) reported on the results of a survey of 2,000 college graduates who were now on the job. In a nutshell, they noted that things would have been easier if the students had realized how hard it was going to be in the new job situation. Among their findings were the following:

- Students used only a small portion of the available information to find out about jobs before they accepted employment. As a result, they accepted the first job offered and/or experienced some difficult adjustments for which they were unprepared. *The material you have learned in Part Three of this text, especially Chapters 13 and 14, will help you avoid these kinds of problems.*

- Students correctly anticipated their beginning salaries but underestimated the time they would spend on the job during the first six months, about 45 hours per week. *Rereading Chapters 8 and 9 might be helpful here.*

- Students grossly overestimated the amount of feedback they would get from supervisors and the frequency of performance appraisals. Self-appraisal became an important element in judging work performance. *This issue is related to schema development, which we discussed in Chapter 5.*

- Most students expected to be with their first employer for three years, but fewer than 50 percent were actually still there after the first two years. Indeed, firings and layoffs occurred in spite of good work performance (last hired, first fired). *We'll address this topic more in this chapter.*

- Students had difficulty adjusting to the politics and culture of the work organization, correctly decoding the indirect messages regarding work standards and job performance from colleagues and supervisors. *Chapter 8 can help with this problem, and there is material in this chapter that provides additional information about organizational culture.*

- More than 30 percent of the respondents (all but two were women) reported experiencing harassment or discrimination in the workplace. The students were quite unprepared for this. *Much of the material in Chapters 8 and 10 is relevant to this issue.*

Gardner and Lambert (1993) provided one of the few studies of the actual employment experiences of new college graduates.

College and Work Compared

One of the best papers on this topic was written by Daniel Feldman (1987), a professor of management at the University of Florida. He shared some of his observations about the "entry shock" of college students into new jobs. He advised a group of graduating college students that the world they were about to enter was very different from the one they were leaving. Table 15.1 elaborates upon these views. It shows some points of comparison between (1) the college and job cultures, (2) the attitudes and behavior of your professor and your boss, and (3) the nature of the learning process at college and on the job. Reviewing and thinking about these differences might help you develop metacognitions that will be more useful in the employment setting.

Table 15.1 pointedly illustrates why some college graduates may have problems adjusting to their first job. The issues center around use of time, ambiguous structure, organizational culture, sustained effort, and more complex interpersonal relationships. In the following sections, we'll focus on these topics in more detail and make suggestions to ease your transition into the professional workplace. Let's first examine more "bottom-line" realities of the workplace.

TABLE 15.1   COLLEGE VS. WORK ENVIRONMENTS

Job Culture	College Culture
1. More rigid time schedule	1. Flexible time schedule
2. You can't skip work	2. You can skip class
3. Feedback is irregular and infrequent	3. Feedback more regular and specific
4. No summer vacations and few holiday breaks	4. Long vacations and liberal holiday breaks
5. Very few right answers to problems	5. There are correct answers to problems
6. Assignments may be vague, unclear	6. Syllabus provides clear assignments
7. Team performance is evaluated	7. Individual competition for grades
8. Longer work cycles lasting for months or years	8. Short cycle work periods: class meets one to three times weekly, 17-week semester
9. Rewards based more on subjective criteria and personal judgments	9. Rewards based on objective criteria and merit

Your Boss	Your Professor
1. Not often interested in discussion	1. Encourages discussions
2. Assigns rush jobs with short lead time	2. Schedules lead time for completion of assignments
3. Is sometimes arbitrary; not always fair	3. Is expected to be fair
4. Is outcome (profit) oriented	4. Is knowledge oriented

The Learning Process	The Learning Process
1. Concrete problem solving and decision making	1. Abstract, theoretical principles
2. Based on incidents happening on the job; concrete, real life	2. Formal, instructional, symbolic learning
3. Socialized, shared learning	3. Individualized learning

ECONOMIC REALITIES

Gardner and Lambert (1993) titled their article "It's a Hard, Hard, Hard, Hard, Hard, Hard World." Dr. Lawrence Jones (1996) used a similar title, "A Harsh and Challenging World of Work: Implications for Counselors." Even though most of you are not counselors, Jones's ideas are pertinent to the concepts in this book.

In a nutshell, Jones reminded career counselors that harsh threats to health and economic security face many workers in contemporary America. Jones reported that about 200 people die each day in the United States from work-related injuries or illness, and 9 million people are injured on the job each year. Many of these problems are the result of violations of safety regulations. The leading occupational illness is repetitive motion sickness, and others include chemical reactions, noise-induced hearing loss, skin disorders, reproductive disorders, and psychological disorders. In addition, we have already noted the lack of job security with the passing of the old social contract discussed in Chapter 8. Jones summarized the matter this way:

> Millions of workers today are beset with challenges that threaten their economic, physical, and mental health. Many (a) die or are injured as a result of their work, (b) are unemployed, or will be, (c) will lose their health insurance, (d) are unprotected against the unscrupulous employer, and (e) are becoming less and less able to financially support themselves and their families. (p. 455)

What do these "harsh and challenging realities" mean for college graduates? Jones suggested that individuals must learn *that work is fundamentally an economic exchange—labor for pay*. Workers are employed to produce goods and services for the benefit of the organization. To fully understand this fact, college students entering the job market need to learn three things:

1. Students need to know the market value of their skills and how to communicate this information to employers. They also need to know which skills they like to use, how they can improve their skills, and how skills transfer to other jobs.

2. Students need to know how to look out for their own self-interests. This might mean recognizing how the organization is engaging in illegal or unethical practices in order to increase its profits or protect its image. It could mean paying attention to technological or global trends that will affect the economic health of the employing organization. It could mean leaving an employer.

3. Students need to limit their emotional involvement with an employer. They need to remember that it is their economic value, not their personal value, that ties them to an employer.

Finally, Jones (1996) suggested that workers see themselves as "free agents," or self-employed. This is a concept familiar to those who follow professional sports. The motto of the free-agent worker might be something like the following:

> Seek those assignments that look best on your resume and avoid those that detract from your marketability, cultivate networks, protect yourself psychologically and financially, be ready to move and take advantage of new opportunities, and look at changing jobs as a challenge. (p. 456)

Dan Pink (2001) further examined this idea and suggested that tens of millions of Americans have taken on this role.

Thus, with these admonitions from Larry Jones in mind, the following section will examine some additional, specific suggestions for adjusting to the first job.

ADJUSTING TO PROFESSIONAL WORKLIFE

Dr. Robert Greenberg, the former director of Career Services at the University of Tennessee, wrote a booklet in 1991 for graduating seniors that was designed to help them make the adjustment from college to employment. He identified three areas of adjustment that we call (1) the job culture, (2) personal life after graduation, (3) first-year financial management, and (4) assessing the culture. In the next section, we will elaborate on his ideas.

Organizational Culture

Some of Greenberg's suggestions for adjusting to the culture of the work organization include skills in managing the clock, your boss, and your coworkers, as well as skills in handling supervisor feedback in a positive way.

Clock and Calendar Management. Greenberg observed that consistent punctuality is one of the easiest ways to make a good initial impression at the job. Moreover, it is essential to be alert and ready to start early each day. Good clock-management skills might also require some evening and weekend hours to get projects completed. In addition, make it a point to be early or on time, and do not leave every day exactly at the closing hour.

As a professional, you are expected to be more committed to your job than hourly employees might be. This could mean staying a little longer to finish a project on some days. Make sure that your supervisor and office assistants know where you are during the day and when you travel. Calendar management involves not asking for holidays or vacations until you have been on the job six months, unless you successfully negotiated otherwise before you accepted the job offer. These areas might be the most critical ones in the new job.

Richardson and Tulgan (1997) noted the importance of taking control of your own schedule on the job. You should try to set clear goals for every project. Specify exactly who is responsible for what. Clarify what is to be done next and who will do it. Set timelines for when activities need to be completed that will move the project along to conclusion. Develop a written plan for the project, and make sure everyone involved gets a copy. Keep everyone informed about the current state of the project. Get feedback from those affected by the project as the work progresses. If you have not had special training on project development, management, and evaluation, seek it out early at your first job, even if you have to learn it on your own and in your free time. One study found that 35 percent of management graduates reported planning and executing a project as one of their first assignments in a new job, without benefit of written guidelines, samples, or mentoring (Schindler, 1997).

Finally, your new job may require you to focus on more than one task at a time, multitasking. For those of us who like to concentrate on just one thing, this can be a real challenge. Balancing multiple responsibilities and opportunities requires some new metacognitions involving self and time. You may have heard of or read Stephen Covey's (2004) best-seller, *The 7 Habits of Highly Effective People*. He distinguished between things that are "urgent" and "important." Urgent things often involve matters that are in front of us—on our desk, the phone ringing, calendar, or computer screen—and they are often unimportant. Important things, on the other hand, have to do with results, and they contribute to our long-term mission, values, and high priority goals. Successful people find ways to connect various projects and activities into a whole that is more than just a series of separate parts. We sometimes call this "synergy," or the combined effects of two or more actions. Creating synergy in our work helps us become better at multitasking.

Impression Management. Greenberg also noted that image is very important on the job, much more important than in college. Most college students will have to make an initial investment in clothing and grooming that will be evident from their first day on the job. Impression management begins on the first day, and it is too important in most organizations to risk an initial bad impression.

Besides dress, it is important to make sure that you do not use the phone or office supplies for personal or social reasons. Make sure you're clear on policies regarding use of office e-mail. Managers can quickly pick up on this kind of new employee behavior, and it is guaranteed to create a negative impression. It may seem petty, but make sure you know how others in the office want to be addressed, both in private or public. Clarify their titles. It might also be wise to go slow in decorating your office or work area. Observe how others at your level have done this. Also, you probably want to be sensitive about the display of religious or political symbols, and be careful about posters and cartoons that might be offensive to coworkers or customers.

Impression management, however, also includes your work performance. On work products, form most often precedes substance in the workplace. Coworkers will sometimes not read what you write unless it is in the proper form—attractively formatted, no typos or spelling errors. Sloppy work is generally not tolerated in the workplace, even though your colleagues may say otherwise.

If you act like a college student rather than a new professional, you'll be labeled "green" or "wet behind the ears." Accept the fact that you are in a kind of fishbowl where much of what you do will be observed, and supervisors and coworkers will be evaluating your potential to succeed. The fact that you have no track record tends to magnify what you do. Holton (1995) suggested avoiding any behavior that reminds coworkers of college student behavior. Remember that what is appropriate for more experienced people may not be appropriate for you, and do the little things that demonstrate a positive attitude.

One final point on this topic: Be aware that your private behavior (drinking, drugs) can become part of a public record and affect your job evaluations or continued employment. Having the reputation as someone who "parties hard" might have been acceptable in college, but in the work organization it could be considered a lack of maturity and limit your potential for promotions.

Managing Your Boss. From the very beginning, you want your boss to become an ally in your career development. As you get settled in on the first day, ask your boss to name particular people who might help with procedures, policies, or materials. Then use his or her name when you follow up with coworkers and ask for assistance.

To make your boss look good, you will need to complete projects of high quality on time, act like a professional, and maintain a positive attitude. Indeed, Holton indicated that employers' *number one complaint about new hires is their negative attitude.* A positive attitude will be evident in your readiness to learn and change, in the tolerance you have for the "imperfect" organization, and your willingness to go the extra mile when needed.

You'll want to cultivate a reputation as one who knows how to maintain confidential information and who is honest. If you make a mistake, it is better to inform your boss immediately and take the necessary steps to learn from the error and avoid it in the future. Typically, your boss will be more upset about being surprised and caught off guard or learning about the mistake from someone else.

Making the boss look good could mean sacrificing personal weekend time during your first year to complete unscheduled, emergency projects that your boss needs to have done. This kind of flexibility, cooperation, and willingness to sacrifice for the organization usually earns "career advancement points" from higher management in the organization. Holton (1995) called these "followership" skills as opposed to "leadership" skills.

Sometimes you will encounter a supervisor who is unfair, overly demanding, or even deceitful. Greenberg (1991) cautioned against quitting a job if you have an unreasonable, extremely difficult boss. Rather, it is better to try to get promoted or transferred away from such a boss. Above all, don't let such a boss create a negative work attitude (metacognitions) or weak performance on your part.

Relationships with Coworkers. Developing peer, coworker relationships is another critical area of adjustment. On the one hand, you will likely be asked to collaborate with colleagues in completing projects as a team. On the other hand, you will probably be competing with these colleagues for recognition and advancement. Greenberg advises students to go slowly in forming relationships. People with negative attitudes and gripes about the organization may befriend you at first—keep your distance, they are usually going nowhere. Take your time in developing permanent lunchtime associates. Be friendly to everyone initially, and when you have determined who is positive about themselves and the organization and is doing his or her job well, go ahead and form friendships with those people.

Greenberg cautions against using coworkers as confidants because over time you might develop supervisor/supervisee relationships or other kinds of dual relationships with these people, and this might create ethical problems. However, as we noted in Chapter 10 when discussing the Amerco case study, employees tend to form very close relationships with coworkers. This is a difficult area that requires your good judgment over an extended period of time.

Holton (1995) noted that you will be an outsider until you prove otherwise to your colleagues. You'll want to demonstrate that you are part of this new organization by *not trying to change it* at the outset. In other words, learn the business and understand the culture (before you try to change it). As we noted earlier, learn all you can about your new work organization by reading its history, learning how the different departments interact, talking with workers in many different areas, and studying about industry trends and organizational behavior. For example, find out what shift workers in production are doing and how that affects marketing. As a faculty colleague once remarked, "You never really understand how an organization works until you try to change it."

As a new professional, you may find yourself doing many of the same tasks as hourly employees, those who are not salaried (Greenberg, 1991). You may also have supervisory responsibility over several such employees, such as office assistants, salespeople, or production workers. From your first day on the job, it is important for you to treat these lower-level coworkers with respect. Indeed, although many of them may not have bachelor's degrees, they may have worked in the organization for many years, have earned considerable good will from other managers in the organization, and have seen other novice professionals move into your position. The key is to treat these workers with respect and learn from them about how the organization functions.

Don't complain about doing low-level tasks. Given that most people don't start at the top, you might find yourself beginning as a "go-for" doing "grunt work." This can include getting coffee and lunch, running errands, stuffing envelopes, and the like. Such activities might be especially important if you start your work through a temporary staffing company or you do not have technical skills needed for the job. It is essential that you not complain about these errands but use them as an opportunity to learn about the organization and the other people who work there. Almost every job has some duties that are boring or apparently pointless.

Glicken (1997) told the story of John, a junior accountant, who received his first performance evaluation after six months on the job. This is standard practice during the first year, after which evaluations are typically done every 12 months. John was shocked to learn that in almost every respect, his work was below the organization's expectations. Why did this happen? Glicken suggests several strategies to avoid this problem.

1. Pay attention to sometimes subtle, even nonverbal, cues about the quality of your work; it's late, it's inaccurate, it doesn't follow policy, it's messy.

2. Read your job description very carefully and clarify what you don't understand; preview the rating form that will be used in your evaluation. Make sure that your supervisors know about your activities in the categories of information used in the personnel rating form.

3. Ask your supervisor and coworkers whom you trust for frequent feedback on your work.

4. Read the organization's personnel policies regarding tardiness, ethics, drugs, dress, deadlines, absence, and other matters. Don't allow your behavior to break policy because of ignorance on your part.

5. Realize that the evaluation will be made in the context of a social relationship. The evaluation may say more about your boss's evaluation of you as a person than your job performance. Pay attention to the human factor every day in your interpersonal relationships at work.

Glicken concludes with the reassurance that a negative first evaluation is not the end of the world. Because organizations do not want to spend the money and time to hire and replace workers, you can obtain a second chance if you don't become defensive and if you let the employer know that you want to improve your performance. Remember that your performance has to be good all the time, so find out what is expected and show consideration and respect for coworkers.

Your most valued trait in your relationship with coworkers might be your ability to listen and give undivided attention to others when needed. Coworkers appreciate those who are genuinely interested in their stories and opinions. At the same time, you don't want to reinforce griping or get involved in office gossip.

A final point regarding coworkers pertains to harassment. You may recall that Gardner and Lambert (1993) found that more than 30 percent of recent graduates reported experiencing harassment or discrimination in the workplace. In essence, this refers to sexual conduct that is unwelcome and sufficiently severe or pervasive to create a hostile or offensive workplace. Many complaints arise out of genuine misunderstandings, and there is sometimes confusion about what is personal dislike and harassment and what is genuinely obnoxious behavior and harassment. The U.S. Equal Employment Opportunity Commission Web site at http://www.eeoc.gov/types/sexual_harassment.html provides helpful information. If you find that you are having a problem in this area, investigate the harassment policy of the organization and follow the procedures provided for filing a complaint.

Your Evaluations. Your performance evaluations are likely to be informal, continuous, ambiguous, critical, and very important. Your boss is usually your principal evaluator, and the evaluation may include some negative comments about your work. Greenberg (1991) advised new employees to avoid becoming defensive and to take the feedback as a challenge to improve job performance. It is important to recognize that even informal comments (e.g., "That phone call was long" or "This report is very short at the beginning") point to behaviors that need to be corrected. Such observations and feedback are often shared among supervisors, and their cumulative memories are long, so it is important to avoid a reputation as one who does not respond positively to supervisory feedback.

Personal Life

If you are married or living with a significant other, some of this section might be less relevant. This section is written with the assumption that you are still single as you begin your first job. In this regard, Greenberg (1991) noted that some students fail to establish a personal life apart from their job.

Finding social relationships away from work is sometimes difficult. Unlike college, people in your new surroundings may be more varied in age, background, social status, interests, and affiliations. However, while situations in college change every semester or year, life in the workplace and elsewhere may operate on a longer calendar. Greenberg advised students to look for friends in places away from work, including the apartment or neighborhood, sports and fitness activities, religious groups, volunteer activities, alumni groups, continuing education courses, service organizations, and professional associations.

Related to personal life issues, Pratt (1996) noted that the first six months in a new job can be very stressful. There is a high probability that you will be on probation, will make mistakes, will have much to learn, and will be physically tired. In this situation, you will want to learn as much as you can about stress-reduction activities and developing a healthy lifestyle. For some, this will be one of the most significant areas of adjustment.

There is one other sensitive area of personal life, which actually is directly related to the job culture. This area has to do with *office romances*. With so many men and women working closely together in organizations, in constant contact and often on their best behavior, more than 47 percent of employees reported being involved with a coworker in an office romance in 2007 (Vault.com, 2007). Other findings from this survey revealed that 33 percent of employees knew of a married co-worker having an affair with someone at the office, and 36 percent knew of an office romance currently taking place at the organization. Carol Hymowitz (1998) noted that next to downsizing and mergers, office romances are the biggest activity disrupters in a work site. The blurring of boundaries between personal life and job by a couple can lead to gossip among coworkers and awkward moments in the office. Even more problematic are relationships between supervisors and supervisees and between employees and clients or customers. In the former situation, coworkers may believe that their colleague is getting favored treatment and special information from the boss. In the latter situation, the boss may question the loyalty of the employee.

These romantic relationships can threaten your job or lead to a transfer. It is important to check out company policies in this area and to inform your supervisor about such matters if they come to affect other employees in the organization. In the Vault.com (2007) survey, 41 percent of respondents did not know if their company had a policy on office romances, while 16 percent reported that it did.

Managing Finances

This section is also written with the assumption that you are single and living alone. We would focus on things a little differently with the assumption that you are married or jointly managing your finances with another person.

Greenberg (1991) reported that some college graduates find that managing finances during the first year on the job is a challenging area of adjustment. He noted that a major problem stems from overestimating the spending power of the new salary in relation to the start-up costs of beginning a new job in a new community. Taking a similar view, Clements (1998) urged college graduates to live *beneath* their means and stressed the importance of saving.

Greenberg reported that an informal survey of recent college graduates revealed a large majority of them had to borrow money from their parents or borrow additional money during the first year to make ends meet. What areas might be included in a first-year budget? We categorize them in terms of living arrangements, wardrobe development, transportation, food, and loans, credit, and savings.

Living Arrangements. If you have been living in an apartment, you already know something about the deposits and advances that are required in renting. Chances are, however, that you will be shouldering many of these costs alone as a new professional. In addition, you will need furniture and a good bed, as well as kitchen items and home entertainment items. Greenberg noted that one problem faced by many new job holders involves spending too much money on furniture and home entertainment while skimping on a good bed and food. Chances are that you'll be working harder, longer hours than in college, and you don't want to cheat on items that will affect your health. Another possible adjustment difficulty has to do with maintaining a pet, especially if your job requires even a small amount of travel.

Wardrobe Development. Depending on the culture of the organization in which you are working, you might find that you will need to spend several thousand dollars on an appropriate wardrobe. Although you may need to make some purchases immediately, it may be wise to take some time in buying most of these new clothes. Consult with people who have worked in the organization successfully for awhile regarding a priority list of items to purchase; buy good-quality durable items that will last; and consult with knowledgeable salespeople about wardrobe trends as you make purchases.

Transportation. Greenberg advised students to be cautious in purchasing an expensive automobile until all the other budget items have been settled. His view was that safe, reliable transportation might be sufficient for the first year. It is also important to remember that insurance, fuel, parking, and tolls will need to be factored into transportation costs. If public transportation will be used, then fares will need to be included in your budget.

Food. It is likely that you will be eating and drinking differently as an employed professional than as a college student. Chances are that it will be common for a group of employees to have lunch together. These lunches might involve eating out more than you did as a student; they will also have a budget impact because they could easily add $60 a week to your expenses. If you do any entertaining, this will affect your budget situation, too. Of course, if you are able to cover these items with an expense account, that will help out. In general, however, you will probably be spending more of your money on better-quality food and in the preparation and care of that food now that you are employed.

Loans, Credit, and Savings. Finally, financial management adjustments in your first job will involve issues surrounding loans, credit, and savings. Chances are good that you will be making more money in this first job than you have ever made before. This can be a heady experience. However, there can be some nasty realities to consider. Let's say you are making $30,000 a year, or $2,500 a month. With taxes and other payroll deductions, your actual take-home pay may be less than $1,500 per month. Payroll deductions for life insurance, long-term disability insurance, health insurance, annuities, stock options, and savings plans are often valuable, but they further limit your take-home pay. When signing all the appointment papers for your new job, be sure and clarify exactly what your take-home pay will be each month.

There are two other financial pitfalls. Johnson (2007) noted that college graduates are entering the job market owing an average of $20,000, of which $3,200 is credit card debt. With an average starting salary of $30,000, this level of debt affects home purchases, vacations, starting a business, and credit ratings. In addition to credit cards, penalties for late payments on bills, rent, utilities, checking overdrafts, and so forth can also sap your financial resources.

You will probably need some start-up funds to pay deposits and buy clothes. If family members cannot provide assistance, then look for a loan through your employer's credit union, or use some mechanism that will pay back the loan through payroll deductions.

Finally, it is absolutely essential to save something out of each paycheck. Think of it as "paying yourself first." Putting some money into an interest-bearing equity account will provide the funds you need for "big ticket" purchases in the future, such as a house. Clements (1998) advised that you initially invest in a taxable account, so the funds will be readily available if you need them. He pointed out that $2,000 invested each year in a portfolio earning 9 percent annual total return will yield $676,000 after 40 years. If you delay starting just five years, you will have $431,000, or 36 percent less.

Sizing Up the Culture

Throughout this chapter, we have referred to the culture of the organization and how important it is to learn about it during the first year on the job. As we noted in Chapter 8, organizational culture is much like the personality of an individual; it captures what is unique, memorable, persistent, and noteworthy about the organization. In general, organizations want new employees embrace their culture, to "fit" in, to understand "how things are done around here." How do you do this as a new hire?

Holton (1995) reported that employers sometimes worry more about a new hire's ability to adjust to the nontask aspects of the job than to the position requirements. He suggested that outstanding performance on the basic tasks will not result in an outstanding rating, because this is reserved for employees who have a positive attitude, get along well with coworkers, and have learned the culture of the organization, or "fit in." Perhaps the most critical skills in learning an organization's culture have to do with listening to and watching more experienced members of the organization. Read about the founders of the organization, and ask for information about how and why they started the organization. Observe what items of information are highlighted on the organization's Web site. Watch for evidence of the work ethic in the organization in the behavior of experienced and successful colleagues; observe how they spend their time. What schedules do they keep? How do they address others? How do they dress?

In learning about the culture of an organization, you must realize that *politics* is not a dirty word. Holton (1995) suggested that you consider the political aspects of everything you do as a member of an organization and that you use the first year to develop your organizational political skills. However, he cautioned against playing politics until you have more experience.

Holton further noted that organizations, or at least important people in an organization, are sometimes illogical, unfair, slow, resistant to change, not fun, make wrong decisions, and don't like newcomers. In other words, they are not perfect. This fact is related to the unrealistic expectations that new hires carry into the job.

In Chapter 8, we described Schein's (1985) six practical ways to observe organizational culture, including its regular behaviors, norms, dominant values, philosophy, rules, and feeling or climate. We also identified some common ways organizational culture impacts individual career development and behavior. As you prepare to begin a new job in a new organization, we think it might be especially useful to reread Chapter 8 to help you prepare for this new life situation.

In summarizing this section on culture and adjusting to the new job, we are reminded of Holland's (1997) RIASEC theory, which we introduced in Chapters 1 and 2. You will recall that Holland identified six kinds of occupational personalities and six corresponding work environments: Realistic, Investigative, Artistic, Social, Enterprising, and Conventional. We believe that these six types provide a useful framework for you in thinking about your personality and the expectations and rewards of a particular work environment. The differences in culture among RIASEC types are often significant and help us understand the culture of an organization or work group.

DEVELOPING A CAREER STRATEGY FOR THE FIRST YEAR

Here are some thoughts on strategies college graduates might adopt to increase the likelihood of positive evaluations at the end of their first year on the job. These were offered by management experts and young workers.

In-service Training

The American Society for Training and Development (ASTD; 2004) found that a national sample of 344 organizations spent $820 on training in 2003. Training via learning technologies increased from 15.4 percent in 2002 to 23.6 percent in 2004. These organizations provided 26 hours of formal learning per employee in 2003. As a college graduate, you might think that your education and training will be over when you enter the workforce. Nothing could be further from the truth.

Besides what the organization offers in training, you can join professional associations or trade groups in order to keep abreast of changes in the field, maintain contacts, and receive job offers. Association directories, available online and in most libraries and career centers, can be invaluable in this regard. (Review Chapter 12 for details.)

You can also get beyond networking. Richardson and Tulgan (1997) suggested that you invest in long-term relationships with individuals who are creating value in an organization. This could include a mentoring relationship. It might mean developing a proposal that will add more productivity to the work of a person that you admire. As we noted in Chapter 9, organizations typically create new jobs when individuals get behind in their work (i.e., the demand for their work outputs increases beyond their capacity to deliver), and you can use this understanding of how jobs are created to connect yourself with productive workers to improve your own career situation.

As a new employee at your first job, these data suggest that it would be very important for you to expect to spend considerable time in training. Indeed, you should embrace these training opportunities with a positive attitude and enthusiasm. Some authorities suggest that the only thing workers might reasonably expect from an organization is ongoing training to enable the worker to become more productive and competitive in the marketplace.

Communications Skills

Pratt (1996) suggested that improving your communications skills is especially important in the first six months on the job. He thought it especially important to develop presentation skills and suggested taking special speech courses or joining organizations like Toastmasters International. His point was that your ability to present your ideas in face-to-face discussions, staff meetings, or large group presentations will depend on your ability to make effective presentations.

Pratt targeted a second area for communications skills improvement—the telephone. Although you have probably spent a great deal of time on the phone, it was probably not for professional purposes. Pratt suggested using a preplanned agenda to help make calls as brief and productive as possible, to create an outline and take notes on important information or decisions made during the call, and to use a clock to time your calls. We might add that it is very important for you to seek training to learn how to use all the features of the telecommunications system in your office, such as parking calls, call waiting, conference calls, messages, remote use, "office netiquette," and so forth.

Be Your Own PR Machine

Doing good work is essential, but if it isn't noticed, it will not be rewarded. Asher (1998) suggested trading free time for face time. Let people know what you are doing. Keep others informed of your progress with projects. Share interesting articles with colleagues. Volunteer to make presentations about your work. Share your ideas on listservs and through e-mail as appropriate. Directories for mailing lists and newsgroups are at http://www.lsoft.com/catalist.html and http://groups.google.com. Keep your resume updated, especially after you obtain new certificates, complete important projects, or gain new skills. Maintain and update your personal Web page or portfolio.

QUITTING

Given conditions in today's workplace, 20-somethings change jobs every 18 months and 75 percent of workers indicate they are looking for a new job (Loeb, 2007). In this section, we'll briefly comment on your decision to remain with the first employer, and some of the factors that appear to be relevant to this issue.

The 2007 NACE survey of college recruiting revealed that respondents retained an average 91 percent of their new hires within the first year of employment. The percentage retained after five years dropped to 67 percent. This means that about two out of three new employees were retained after five years.

The general consensus of the literature on this topic indicated the importance of negotiating a solution to job problems rather than quitting. Hal Lancaster (1995), for example, suggested negotiating with your boss for better circumstances in your current position. He framed the matter in terms of taking care of yourself, of taking the initiative in negotiating your future with your boss. Lancaster cautioned against discussing your plan during a performance review or a job evaluation meeting because the boss's agenda is most important in this situation. As we explained in Chapter 14, negotiating is a matter of reaching an agreement, and you need to be fully prepared before engaging in this process.

L. M. Sixel (1995), a columnist with the *Houston Chronicle*, reported that discussing your decision to quit with your boss is directly related to the quality of your relationship with your boss and the boss's management style. Some bosses are supportive of career changes, and others aren't. If you do not have a good relationship with your current boss, Sixel advised against saying anything about quitting until you have a firm, written offer from your next employer. Your current employer might suggest that you leave immediately, because quitting is seen as a sign of disloyalty, and the manager doesn't want a "rotten apple spoiling the barrel." If your relationship is good and supportive, then let your boss know that you have offers, and ask for assistance in completing your current projects and setting priorities. In general, the poorer the relationship, the longer you wait to say anything.

Some companies such as Deloitte & Touche (Coster, 2007) have gone so far as to hire career coaches as independent contractors to help employees explore career opportunities within the organization rather than going outside. This company claims that 23 percent of its employees (9,700 persons) have been through this process.

In any case, your departure will probably place your employer in a bind. Cho (2006) reported that it costs a company twice the annual salary to replace the person leaving. It typically takes weeks or months to fill a position and involves many hours of work by the remaining employees.

Loeb (2007) offered these suggestions: (1) give at least two-week notice and more if a high level position or the employer handbook specifies a specific time; (2) write a resignation letter; (3) finish outstanding projects and leave directions for completing the others; (4) offer to help in filling the position; (5) know what severance benefits you have; (6) don't criticize your former employer; (7) stay in contact with your former boss and colleagues; and (8) say thank you to your former associates in writing and highlight the positive aspects of your job.

The bottom line: Don't burn any bridges, especially if you plan to remain in the same field, because your reputation will follow you into other work organizations in the future and you may become colleagues again with your former associates.

FROM CAREER PLANNING TO CAREER MANAGEMENT

In your new job situation, career planning will shift slightly in focus because you now have supervisors and managers who can help you develop and manage your career journey. As we noted in Chapter 8, an organizational career development program could include such things as individual and group career counseling, assessment, job vacancy postings, training and development, organizational career planning, and special programs for targeted groups, e.g., outplaced, younger workers, preretirees. One of your early tasks will be to study the career program offered by your employer and find one or more *mentors* who can advise you about managing the career process in this new organizational context. This is an important issue, so take some time and make it an effective part of your ongoing career development.

USING CIP FOR GUIDANCE IN YOUR NEW JOB

In this chapter, we have been learning about the process of beginning a new professional job and working through the first year. In this next section, we'll review what we have learned about *these topics from a CIP perspective. We want to focus on the new metacognitions that have been created and added to your PCT and strategic career thinking.*

Self-Knowledge

In Chapter 2, we emphasized the importance of interests and values in solving career problems and making career decisions. These are also very evident in helping you set your priorities and preferences in the way you will perform in the new job. This new job will provide opportunities for you to clarify your interests and values and to validate your job skills. Self-knowledge will help you determine how you are adjusting to your new job because it will provide the criteria that you will use to determine whether or not you are satisfied and happy in the job.

Knowledge of Options

Knowledge about options includes knowledge about occupations, specific positions, and the culture of an employing organization. To effectively assess a new job situation, you need to learn everything possible about the organization, your boss and coworkers, and how you will be evaluated in your first performance review. This is essential in order to make an optimum adjustment to your new job and to make progress during the first year.

Applying the CASVE Model

We suggest that you evaluate your new job and the first year based on the same set of factors that we have used throughout this text, the CASVE Cycle.

Communication. In a new job situation, you might find yourself feeling alone, lost, uncertain, or overwhelmed. Some of the difficulties might stem from the differences between the culture in college and the workplace. These kinds of feelings may signal that a career problem exists or that decisions need to be made.

On the other hand, you may be excited at all of the opportunities available to you in your new position but unsure of how to choose from among them. A focal point of your feelings about the new job will come from the quality of the relationship with your new boss, and/or the coworkers with whom you spend most of your time. In either case, it is essential to properly frame the "gap."

Your ability to think strategically and effectively is a critical aspect of the process of adjusting to a new job and moving ahead during the first year of professional employment. This task requires you to take a "metaview" of the organization. It means recognizing the dominant culture of the organization as well as the subcultures within departments and divisions. The process becomes more complex over time as you acquire more life roles and adult responsibilities. There may also be significant others involved who are providing input about what they view as your most appropriate career strategies.

In CIP terms, the gap is not simply surviving the first few days or weeks, it is developing an ongoing awareness of yourself in your work environment, your feelings, your impressions, your comfort with work and colleague relations. If discomfort arises, don't deny it or think it will go away. Stay attuned to what it might signal in the way of a gap.

Analysis. As noted in the previous section, having accurate and complete knowledge about yourself and your new job and organizational culture is a critical part in adjusting to the new work situation. Many of the cultural behaviors and values acquired and used in college will be counterproductive in employment. In analyzing a gap, you will want to determine the extent to which the job meets the skills, values, interests, and goals you have identified as important in your employment. These personal characteristics are examined in terms of the relationship with your boss and coworkers, the organizational culture, the results of your first performance evaluation, trends in the industry, the way jobs are changing, and other environmental matters.

Analysis also involves having a complete knowledge and understanding of the position you are in and all the policies and rules that apply to it in the organization. Other key aspects of Analysis would be understanding how you can best accommodate yourself to your supervisor's expectations, deciding when to ask for help, and developing a strategic plan for your advancement in the job, organization, or industry.

If you find yourself having difficulty trying to analyze a gap related to adjustments in your first job, find a trusted friend to serve as a confidant for exploring causes of a gap. This would probably not be a colleague, but may be a mentor. The outcome of the Analysis phase is in forming a mental model of the problem and its causes.

Synthesis. With respect to evaluating your options in the new job, the Synthesis phase of the CASVE Cycle involves both Elaborating and Crystallizing offers inside and outside your organization. In Synthesis Elaboration, you try to generate more options for ways you can work in the job or in the organization to increase the quality of your career, including the possibility of leaving.

The process of evaluating your adjustment in your new job is more likely to be focused on narrowing your options, or Synthesis Crystallization. This might involve decreasing your expectations, concentrating on the most important parts of your job, and meeting the expectations of your supervisor.

After you master your first position in the organization, your knowledge of options may expand to include how you can advance in the organization or what types of lateral transfers would provide some level of job enrichment or career development for you. You may also find that a structured exercise that helps you weigh various factors would be helpful, and an example of one of these is provided in *Appendix L.*

Valuing. This phase of the CASVE Cycle includes considering the costs and benefits of each job adjustment option, not only to yourself but also to significant others, your cultural group, community, and society, now and in the future.

- Does this job accommodate your needs and lifestyle preference?

- How does your decision impact your significant other and family?

- What about issues that may relate to your cultural group or community and society?

You are the only one who can decide whether to adjust to the organizational culture. What is important to one person isn't necessarily important to someone else. The "Employment-Decision Making Exercise" in *Appendix L* is one method that you can use to compare and evaluate options by weighting factors that you rank more highly both personally and in a job.

Execution. Once you make the decision to stay at your job, there are several key steps related to the Execution phase of the CASVE Cycle. The first of those is communicating to your boss that you are committed to the organization and that you want to improve your performance in the organization. The second involves improving your personal performance, such as clock management, impression management, personal financial management. The third pertains to developing effective, collaborative relationships with coworkers within the context of the organizational culture. This will lead to your success in managing projects and providing leadership on the job.

If you choose to leave the job, cut your ties and don't look back. Have no regrets or second thoughts about your choice. You are already on the way to the next place in your career path.

Executive Processing

Executive processing is thinking about how you identify problems and how you solve problems. Awareness of yourself as a problem solver regulates how you approach work problems. Your goal is to think about yourself as a problem solver, not only of work tasks but life and career tasks as well.

Negative thinking is most likely to occur when you enter a new job and the realities of life in the organization impact your expectations. You are the only person who can decide if you are happy and satisfied enough to remain in the job until something better is created or appears. Challenging your thinking in this area might involve saying, "If one employer thought I was good enough to extend an offer to me, chances are another employer will as well. I can make something positive happen in this job situation." This process requires your highest levels of self-confidence and positive self-talk.

Adjusting to the new job means taking responsibility for yourself and your future—for taking action to create situations and environments that will foster your career development. You are not a passive observer in this process, but an active designer and creator of your career within the jobs that you hold in the organization. Finally, your career metacognitions at the executive-processing level will enable you to set standards for your work ethics and values, for establishing an effective balance between the job in relation to your other life roles and the level of excellence that you will seek to achieve in your life and work.

SUMMARY

This chapter has examined the topics relevant to beginning a new professional position and setting goals for the first year on the job. The chapter included research findings regarding new college graduates and job adjustments, fundamental differences between college and work environments, economic realities of contemporary work life, strategies for adjusting to a new professional job and the first year, thoughts about quitting or staying at the first job, and moving from career planning to career management. The chapter concluded with a CIP perspective of issues associated with starting a new job and moving through the first year of professional employment. The goal was to provide information to help you improve the quality of your PCT and strategic career thinking as you begin your employment. The ideas in this chapter are intended to help you learn from your early experiences as a new professional. We might add that a particularly relevant Web site regarding career development and career management can be found at http://careers.wsj.com/. This site includes materials from the *Wall Street Journal Interactive Edition* and the *National Business Employment Weekly*.

REFERENCES

Allen, C. (1998, Spring). NACE employer benchmark survey. *Journal of Career Planning & Employment*, 58(3), 25–30.

American Society for Training & Development (2004, December 1). *ASTD 2004 state of the industry report: Executive summary*. Alexandria, VA: Author.

Anderson, N. B. (2008, February). Toward reducing work stress. *Monitor on Psychology*, p. 9.

Asher, D. (1998). How to earn a promotion in 12 months or less. *National Business Employment Weekly* [On-line], 1–5. Available: http://public.wsj.com/careers/resources/documents/980106asher-promotion.htm.

Cho, H. F. (2006, May 10). The squeeze for talent. *Baltimore Sun* [online], retrieved March 6, 2008, from http://www.baltimoresun.com/business/careers/bal-wk.hire10may10,0,3036681.story?col=bal-business-headlines.

Clements, J. (1998). How to build a nest egg as a recent graduate. *Wall Street Journal Interactive Edition* [On-line], 1–2. Available: http://public.wsj.com/careers/resources/documents/19980528-clements.htm.

Coster, H. (2007, October 15). Baby please don't go. *Forbes*, pp. 86–87.

Covey, S. (2004). *The 7 habits of highly effective people: Powerful lessons in personal change* (15th ed.) New York: Free Press.

Feldman, D. C. (1987, November). *Critical choices in early career planning.* Unpublished paper read at the Beta Gamma Sigma Initiation, University of Florida, Gainesville.

Gardner, P. D. (1998). Are college seniors prepared to work? In J. N. Gardner, G. Van der Veer, & Associates (Eds.), *The senior year experience* (pp. 60–78). San Francisco: Jossey-Bass.

Gardner, P., & Lambert, S. (1993, Winter). It's a hard, hard, hard, hard, hard, hard world. *Journal of Career Planning & Employment*, pp. 41–49.

Gardner, P., & Liu, W. (1997, Spring). Prepared to perform? Employers rate work force readiness of new grads. *Journal of Career Planning & Employment*, pp. 32–35, 52–56.

Glicken M. D. (1997, Winter/Spring). Earning good grades at your first job. *Managing Your Career*, pp. 10–11.

Greenberg, R. M. (1991). *Enjoying career start-up: Surviving the transition from college to career.* Knoxville, TN: Career Services, University of Tennessee.

Grossman, L. (2005, January 24). Grow up? Not so fast. *Time*, pp. 42–54.

Gurchiek, K. (2007, December). Career development gets failing grade from many workers. *HRMagazine*, p. 49–50.

Holland, J. (1997). *Making vocational choices* (3rd ed.). Odessa, FL: Psychological Assessment Resources.

Holton, E. (1995, Fall). How to earn an "outstanding" rating while new on the job. *Journal of Career Planning & Employment*, pp. 51–52.

Holton, E. (1999, Spring). Managing the transition to work. *NACE Journal*, pp. 28–31, 49–56.

Hymowitz, C. (1998, May 3–9). Office affairs. *National Business Employment Weekly*, pp. 37–38.

Inkson, K., & Arthur, M. B. (2002). Career development: Extending the "organizational careers" framework. In S. G. Niles (Ed.), *Adult career development: Concepts, issues, and practices* (3rd ed., pp. 285–304). Tulsa, OK: National Career Development Association.

Johnson, D. (2007, September 28). College student debt. Retrieved March 10, 2008, from http://www.creditsolutions.com/learning-center/drews-corner-student-debt/.

Jones, L. K. (1996). A harsh and challenging world of work: Implications for counselors. *Journal of Counseling & Development, 74,* 453–459.

Lancaster, H. (1995, February 15). Try negotiating a solution instead of jumping ship. *Tallahassee Democrat,* p. 17D.

Loeb, M. (2007). How to make a graceful job exit. *MarketWatch,* [online], retrieved April, 27, 2007, from http://www.cbsnews.com/stories,2007/04/25/business/printable2724936.shtml.

National Association of Colleges and Employers (NACE; 1995) Recruiting. *Spotlight, 1*(18), 1–2.

Pink, D. H. (2001). *Free agent nation: The future of working for yourself.* New York: Warner Books.

Pratt, H. J. (1996). Getting in high gear. *Equal Opportunity, 29,* 22–23.

Richardson, B., & Tulgan, B. (1997, Fall). The 1997 career survival guide. *Tools for Life, 2*(1), 11–27.

Schein, E. (1985). *Organizational culture and leadership.* San Francisco: Jossey-Bass.

Schindler, P. (1997, Winter). Demonstrating competence: The portfolio interview for management positions. *Journal of Career Planning & Employment*, pp. 40–46.

Sixel, L. M. (1995, January 18). Should you tell your boss you're in the job market? *Tallahassee Democrat,* p. 9D.

Vault.com. (2007, February 5). Vault office romance 2007 survey: More employees caught canoodling. Retrieved March 18, 2008 from http://www.vault.com/nr/printable.jsp?ch_id=420&article_id=28739469&print=1.

GLOSSARY

Analysis. A phase of the career problem solving and decision making (CASVE cycle) marked by career thoughts associated with identifying the causes and relationships among components of a career problem; a period of reflection to more fully understand all aspects of the problem.

Career. The time extended working out of a purposeful life pattern through work undertaken by the person. The combination of a person's multiple life roles, including worker, student, parent, child, spouse/partner, citizen, and retiree. Occupation is an important part of one's life and career, as well as educational field of study, leisure pursuits, and family roles.

Career Development. The total constellation of economic, sociological, psychological, educational, physical, and chance factors that combine to shape one's career.

Career Problem. A gap between an existing state of career indecision and a more desired state of decidedness; may be multifaceted in nature involving feelings, beliefs, behavior, family, community, leisure and spiritual dimensions.

Career Thought. An outcome of one's mental activity (thinking) about behaviors, beliefs, feelings, plans, and/or strategies related to career problem solving and decision making.

CASVE Cycle (pronounced Ca SA, Veh). A career problem-solving and decision-making process using a series of logical, rational steps to enhance decision making that also recognizes the role that feelings and behavior play in this process. The simplest way to think about the CASVE cycle is as the means by which clients recognize and solve a career problem–they need to resolve the "gap" between where they are now and where they'd like to be. The CASVE cycle includes the phases of Communication, Analysis, Synthesis, Valuing, and Execution.

Code (also Holland or SDS Code). One to three RIASEC letters that indicate which types a person, occupation, field of study, or leisure area most resembles.

Cognition. The memory and thought process that a person engages in to perform a task or attain a goal; it is the thinking process.

Commitment Anxiety. The inability to make a commitment to a specific career choice, accompanied by generalized anxiety about the outcome of the decision making process, with anxiety perpetuating the indecision; a scale on the CTI.

Communication. A phase of career problem solving and decision making (CASVE cycle) marked by career thoughts related to becoming fully "in touch" with all aspects of a career problem, or the gap between the present and an ideal career situation. Cues about a gap may come from external sources, e.g., a parent's remark, or internal sources, e.g., negative emotions, avoidance behavior.

The awareness of a gap motivates one to seek a solution to the career problem.

Congruence. The degree of matches between *two* codes, e.g., a person and an occupation, in the Holland RIASEC model; e.g., a Realistic person in a Realistic occupation is very congruent, whereas a Realistic person in a Social occupation is incongruent.

Consistency. The degree of consistency in an SDS code is determined by the distance between the first two code letters on the Holland hexagon: High, first two letters are adjacent on the hexagon (e.g., RI); Average, first two letters are alternate on the hexagon (e.g., RA); Low, first two letters are opposite on the hexagon (e.g., RS).

Contingent Work. Employment that is uncertain, unplanned, somewhat accidental, dependent on changing conditions and the employer's immediate needs; work that is not permanent and is time limited.

Control and Monitoring. Control alludes to regulation of thought process, whereas monitoring refers to observing one's self in the act of problem solving. Control and monitoring allows one to know when to move forward in the CASVE cycle and when to stop and get more information.

Decision Making. It includes the four steps in the problem solving cycle (CASV), but it adds the development of a plan or strategy for implementing the chosen solution and the adoption of a risk-taking attitude and commitment to carry the plan to completion (E). Decision making, then, adds our feelings and behaviors to the problem solving process, and includes the *implementation* of a choice.

Decision-Making Confusion. The inability to initiate or sustain the career decision making process as a result of disabling emotions and/ or a lack of understanding about the decision making process itself; a scale in the CTI.

Decision-Making Skills Domain. Middle-level region in the Pyramid of Information Processing that Includes the five elements of the CASVE cycle, comprised of

Communication, Analysis, Synthesis, Valuing, and Execution.

Diamond-Shaped Organization. An organizational structure where the top of the diamond is reserved for the top executives and managers (5–10 percent of the workers); the bottom portion of the diamond has 15–40 percent of the workers that might be employed as contract workers or temporary employees; the remaining middle portion of core workers (50–80 percent of the organization's workforce) are involved in leading teams, supervising coworkers, monitoring quality control; these workers may enjoy higher earnings and more job security because of their contributions to the success of the organization.

Differentiation. The level of definition or distinctness of a personality profile. A person is highly differentiated who demonstrates a profile with large differences between scales, whereas a person who is undifferentiated demonstrates a "flat" profile with small differences between scales.

Dual-Career Family. Usually reserved for families in which both partners hold professional, managerial, or technical jobs and are seeking to manage both careers and family relationships concurrently.

Enterprise Web. High-value business enterprises that are very complex, flexible work organizations, which also may be very temporary; may be best understood in terms of a spider's web where each connecting point is a place where information is exchanged by the workers.

Execution. A phase in career problem solving and decision making (CASVE cycle) marked by career thoughts that involve the planning and implementation of steps to carry out the solution to a career problem; may involve a tryout or reality testing of a first choice solution to a gap.

Executive Processing Domain. The cognitions associated with the apex of the Pyramid of Information Processing. The cognitions associated with monitoring, controlling, regulating, and evaluating lower-order information processing, including an awareness of one's self as a career problem solver via self-talk, with the complimentary cognitions about one's ability to solve career problems.

External Conflict. The inability to balance the importance of one's own self-perceptions with the importance of input from significant others, resulting in a reluctance to assume responsibility for decision making; a scale on the CTI.

Hexagon. A six-sided figure showing the order and symmetry of the RIASEC types according to Holland's theory; can also be used to show the degree of agreement between a person's type and alternative occupational environments; persons can use a Personal Career Theory to think about careers in terms of personal typologies and matching jobs, e.g., "Where is she on the hexagon?"

Independent Contractors. Self-employed workers who obtain customers on their own to provide a product or service; also consider themselves to be consultants or free-lance workers.

Job. A paid position held by one or more persons requiring some similar attributes in a specific organization; *Persons* lose or gain jobs; *organizations* lose or gain positions.

Job Campaign (or employment campaign). Involves thinking and planning about the many aspects of a job search, including identifying goals and objectives, finding resources for identifying potential employers, specifying employers and/or job targets, considering alternative work settings and ways of working, preparing letters and resume(s), contacting employers, interviewing with employers, making on-site visits, maintaining a record-keeping system, and choosing from among job offers.

Knowledge Workers. Those who know how to acquire and use knowledge and information to produce marketable goods and services; they produce something of intrinsic value; see also symbolic analysts.

Leisure. Relatively self-determined non-paid activities and experiences that are available due to discretionary income, time, and social behavior; the activity may be physical, intellectual, volunteer, creative, or some combination of all four.

Mailing Lists/Listservs. Topical discussion groups that allow one subscriber to e-mail messages to all other subscribers; it may or may not be moderated.

Metacognitions or Metacognitive Skills. The skills that govern *how* we think about career problem solving and decision making, that is "thinking about thinking." The prefix "meta" simply means "beyond" or "higher," such as "higher order thinking skills."

Netiquette (Internet etiquette). Preferred conduct for communicating with professionals and employers via discussion groups, e-mails, and chat sessions on the Internet; use the appropriate level of formality for various types of communications such as thank you letters, requests for information, or online forums.

Newsgroups. Topical discussion groups that post messages to a central location for readers to access; read the FAQ section before participating in a newsgroup.

New Social Contract. Based on the employee's opportunities for training and development in an organization; loyalty may be more to the occupational group or profession than the organization.

Occupation. A group of similar positions found in different industries or organizations.

Occupational Level. The relative prestige, status, education required, usual income, or substantive complexity of an occupation compared to other occupations.

Occupational Knowledge. One of the knowledge domains in the lower tier of the Pyramid of Information Processing; includes cognitions related to the acquisition, storage and retrieval of information about individual occupations, fields of study, training programs, and the structure of the world of work.

Office Work. Part of the services industry; employs large numbers of all workers, pays the highest salaries, is growing the fastest, employs over half of college graduates, and captures about half of all earnings; includes accountants, managers, sales representatives, and brokers.

Old Social Contract. Now generally outdated tradeoff that if workers were loyal to the organization and dedicated their working lives to producing its products and services, then the organization would maintain the worker as an employee and pay them benefits in retirement.

Organization. Special-purpose institution that concentrates on one task and functions best when it has a clear purpose and the persons working in the organization know exactly how to align themselves with this larger purpose.

Organizational Culture. Characteristic of a stable social group, that has a history, and where members have shared important experiences in solving group problems; these common experiences have led the group members to have a shared view of the world and their place in it; this shared view has worked successfully long enough as to be taken for granted by the group, and has now dropped out of member's awareness; they take this shared view for granted as members of the group; "culture" may be viewed as a learned product of group experience, and it is found in a group or organization with a significant history.

Permutation. Alternative orderings of letters in a 3-point Holland code: RIE, IRE, IER, etc.

Personal Career Theory (PCT). Personal views and ideas about careers and work, which may include a typology of work personalities and environments, as well as a variety of career thoughts about educational and career decision making, job hunting, and life roles. A weak PCT may lead to career problems. PCTs may be related to the hexagon and the pyramid.

Personality Pattern. The profile of scores unique to individuals earned on interest and personality inventories; the SDS, MBTI, and CTI are all instruments that provide profiles.

Position. A group of tasks performed by one person in an organization; a unit of work with a recurring or continuous set of tasks; a task is a unit of job behavior with a beginning point and an ending point performed in a matter of hours rather than days.

Problem Solving. Thinking or processing information that will lead to a course of action to remove the gap between a state of indecision and decidedness. In other words, problem solving is "gap removal," and it can occur with respect to any aspect of our lives. This thinking process involves (1) recognizing the gap, (2) analyzing its causes, (3) coming up with different ways to remove the gap, and (4) *choosing* one of these ways to remove the gap. Thus, problem solving involves arriving at a *choice* among plausible alternative courses of action.

Profile. A pattern of scores earned on interest and personality inventories or other tests.

Pyramid of Information Processing. Based on cognitive information processing theory, a figure showing the three domains of knowledge (self and occupational) at the base, decision skills in the middle (CASVE cycle), and executive processing at the top. Career thoughts operate at all three levels to inform, guide, and control career decision making. A person's career situation can be understood in terms of the quality and content of his/her status within the domains of the pyramid, e.g., "Where is she in the CASVE cycle?" "How well developed is her occupational knowledge?"

Reframing. The process of changing or restating a metacognition or thought as it is reflected in a sentence or statement; for example, one might reframe a negative thought into a more positive one by rewriting a sentence or statement that alters a negative thought into one that is more positive in nature.

Self-Awareness. A state of self-detachment that enables an individual to perceive one's self as a doer of a task; a state of self-consciousness.

Self-Knowledge. One of the knowledge domains at the bottom tier of the Pyramid of Information Processing. It includes cognitions related to the acquisition, storage, or recall of information about one's personal characteristics, e.g., interests, skills, and values.

Self-Talk. The verbalization one uses to talk to one's self as if from the perspective of an observer. Self-talk may be kind or punitive. For example, you can make a positive statement about yourself, such as "I am a good decision maker" or "I could never trust myself to make good decisions that are best for me."

Services Industry. Occupations that provide or assist individuals in having certain experiences or in acquiring certain kinds of information, e.g., an airplane ride or telephone call; includes low paid burger flippers and floor sweepers, as well as highly paid brain surgeons, defense lawyers, movie stars, and accountants.

Social Economy. See Third Sector.

Strategic Career Thinking. Planning your career according to a vision or mission by setting your career direction in light of the internal forces, e.g., your interests, values, and skills, in relation to the external forces existing in society, e.g., global economy, new ways of working.

Subtype. The second or third letter in a 3-part Holland code. For example, saying that a person is identified with the RI subtype means that the person resembles the R type most, followed by the I type.

Success. With respect to career, it is a personal standard of achievement and satisfaction; an individual matter that has much to do with life satisfaction; is based more in internal factors and one's state of mind rather than external factors over which one may have little control; involves trade-offs among personal values.

Synthesis. A phase of career problem solving and decision making (CASVE cycle) marked by career thoughts related to the formulation of a plausible set of alternatives for resolving a career problem; synthesis *Elaboration* involves brainstorming a wide variety of possible solutions, and synthesis *Crystallization* involves narrowing the potential solutions to the best 3-5 options to bring forward into the valuing phase of the CASVE cycle.

Temporary Work. Individuals employed as contingent workers ("temps") who do not expect to stay with their current employer more than a year or the job has a specified ending date; however if one has continuing employment with a temporary services company, then the work is permanent, not temporary or contingent; this means that one can have permanent employment with a temp agency.

Third Sector or Social Economy. Known as the independent or volunteer sector, in contrast to the Public Sector (government) and the Market Sector (business); includes volunteer and community organizations that feed the poor, protect the environment, teach reading, and build churches.

Type. Holland's theory makes use of six personality types, e.g., RIASEC, and six environmental models in explaining behavior in environments; no person or environment is a true, perfect type, but the intent to which one resembles a type helps in describing the person or environment.

Usenet. Network of discussion forums or newsgroups; currently run by Google (explanation at http://groups.google.com/googlegroups/basics.html).

Valuing. A phase of career problem solving and decision making (CASVE cycle) marked by career thoughts related to the prioritizing of possible solutions in terms of what is best for the individual, significant others, community, and society; a tentative best choice emerges from this phase of decision making.

Vocational Aspiration. A person's desired occupational or career aim; similar terms include vocational expectation, occupational aspiration, occupational daydream, and occupational expectation; classified aspirations or expectations can be used to derive a person's Holland code; aspirations are a measure of expressed interests.

Vocational History. A work history of a person's positions, occupations, or vocational aspirations can be used to derive his/her Holland code.

Work. Activity that produces something of value for oneself or others; work, is not limited to activity for which we get paid; it can include unpaid, volunteer activity, if it produces something valuable for us or another person, e.g., coaching youth baseball, leading the church choir.

Chapter Study Guide (CSG)

Directions: This brief outline is designed to help you process the information in each chapter. The CSG is based on a cognitive information processing model, and the quality of your learning depends upon proper execution of the CSG. You can duplicate and use this form for note taking on the materials you read in the chapters.

As you read the assignment, mark key ideas that will help you complete this form. Concentrate on new words and concepts. Focus on (a) what you already know and (b) what you're unsure about.

1. *Definitions of terms/concepts.* List all the terms that were new or difficult. Define new terms in your own words. Do you agree with the definitions being used. Do you understand the meanings of terms.

_____
_____
_____
_____
_____
_____
_____

2. *Author's message.* Briefly summarize the author's major ideas.

_____
_____
_____
_____
_____
_____

3. *Analysis of major ideas.* Do you understand the author's major themes, methods, arguments, and sources. Are they important now and in the future? Headings and subheadings in the reading are cues to finding the author's major ideas.

_____
_____
_____
_____
_____
_____

4. *Connecting other knowledge.* How useful are these ideas in relation to other things you know and have experienced? Have the ideas been covered in any of your other classes? Have you seen these ideas expressed on TV or in other things you have read? Do these ideas or concepts differ from or support other things you know?

_____

_____

_____

_____

_____

_____

_____

5. *Applying the information.* How do these ideas affect you personally? Are there implications for your educational and career planning? Do the ideas affect the way you will function in your community, family, or other social group?

_____

_____

_____

_____

_____

_____

_____

_____

6. *Evaluating the author's ideas.* Are these ideas likely to be useful to you in the future? Were there particular points in the reading that were more interesting or useful? If you disagree with the author's ideas, how would you refute them?

_____

_____

_____

_____

_____

_____

_____

_____

7. *Write down in your notebook one important learning you will take away from this chapter.*

_____

_____

_____

_____

_____

A GUIDE TO WRITING YOUR AUTOBIOGRAPHY

Imagine you are preparing for an interview about a job or graduate school application. You can be sure the interviewer will ask you about your background, and how it has influenced your goals. The purpose of this assignment is to help you prepare for the interviewer's questions. The time you spend on this assignment will probably payoff in numerous ways in the future.

Directions

In reviewing your history, concentrate on three areas of your life that have influenced your present life/career goals. Your autobiography will include 4 sections:

1. Family Experience,

2. Educational Experience,

3. Work Experience, and

4. Current Life/Career Goals.

Each section will include about 250-300 words, and begin with a left margin subhead. Use your best writing skills in producing this paper. Try not to simply report activities in each section, but *analyze or review* your experiences to uncover deeper meanings affecting your life/career. It might help to think about how a special person or event impacted your life in each section.

Only your instructor will read the information in your autobiography. This paper and all other course materials can be reclaimed at the end of the course. Completed autobiographies may range from 4-6 pages in length (printed, double-spaced, 1-inch margins, 12 point font).

Sections:

1. *Family Experience.* Consider experiences and activities from childhood and how they have affected your life/career choices. How have work roles of your family members influenced your thinking about career? You might want to focus on where you lived, immediate and extended family member relationships, ethnic heritage, your gender, and family activities.

2. *Educational Experience.* You might want to focus on favorite subjects or activities in school from kindergarten through 12th grade, as well as important teachers, organizations, and achievements that have impacted your life/career.

3. *Work Experience.* Recall aspects of your working experiences that have had the most impact on you. Remember that the definition of "work" includes unpaid, volunteer experiences. You

might want to focus on relationships with supervisors or peers, the nature of the work organization, the work activities (what you did and did not like about them), or trends in your work experiences. Are you seeking new work experiences?

4. *Current Life/Career Goals.* Write 3 of your current life/career goals or aspirations. Explain how your family, education, and work experiences are related to each of your goals. If your goals about education and occupation are presently uncertain, try to project 5-10 years into the future and focus on what you will have accomplished.

Riasec Hexagon

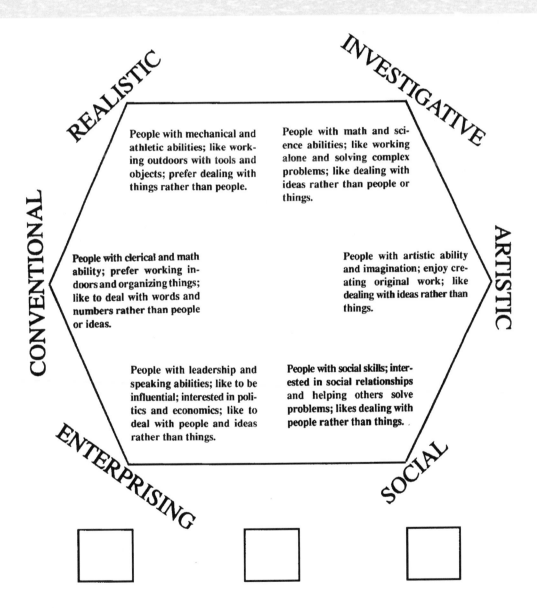

REALISTIC

INVESTIGATIVE

CONVENTIONAL

ARTISTIC

ENTERPRISING

SOCIAL

People with mechanical and athletic abilities; like working outdoors with tools and objects; prefer dealing with things rather than people.

People with math and science abilities; like working alone and solving complex problems; like dealing with ideas rather than people or things.

People with clerical and math ability; prefer working indoors and organizing things; like to deal with words and numbers rather than people or ideas.

People with artistic ability and imagination; enjoy creating original work; like dealing with ideas rather than things.

People with leadership and speaking abilities; like to be influential; interested in politics and economics; like to deal with people and ideas rather than things.

People with social skills; interested in social relationships and helping others solve problems; likes dealing with people rather than things.

Reproduced by special permission of the Publisher, Psychological Assessment Resources, Inc., from *Making Vocational Choices*, copyright 1973, 1985, 1992, 1997 by Psychological Assessment Resources, Inc. All rights reserved.

CAREER FIELD ANALYSIS (CFA)

Purpose

This project is designed to help you learn about sources for occupational and educational information, and to give you an opportunity to either explore several alternatives in occupations or majors or conduct more in-depth research on one occupation.

Objectives

1a. Become more informed about 1 occupation in-depth by researching information across 16 categories using at least **5** of the 12 different kinds of information sources shown below, **or**

1b. Become more informed about 3 occupations or majors by researching information across 6 categories using at least **3** of the 12 different kinds of information sources shown below for *each* of the 3 occupations/majors you select.

2. Write a research paper, including proper **intext** and **end reference citations**, in order to improve and demonstrate personal research skills. (*Note: A personal, subjective writing style is not appropriate for this assignment.*)

3. Learn how to more effectively use career information resources in the Career Center Library, the Internet, or other resource settings.

4. Demonstrate project management skills in executing a work assignment effectively and on-time.

Procedures

1. Confer with your instructor and decide if it will be most helpful for you to study one occupation or three occupations/majors, objective 1a or 1b.

2. Decide on the name(s) of the occupations/majors you will study.

3. Learn how to use the various *types of information sources* including the 12 numbered items shown below and on the following page:

   1. books published on occupations, career fields, or majors

   2. information interviews, e.g., resource persons, networking;

   3. employer literature, e.g., annual reports, employer Web sites;

4. computer-assisted career guidance systems, e.g., Choices™ Planner, e-Discover®, SIGI³

5. university or college-produced publications

6. government documents, e.g., U.S. Dept. of Labor publications, *Occupational Outlook Handbook*;

7. professional association materials, e.g., reports, newsletters, pamphlets, or Web sites; or bulletins;

8. news reports, e.g., newspapers, news magazines, *Black Collegian, Job Choices*;

9. occupational briefs, e.g., Chronicle Guidance Publications;

10. multimedia materials, e.g., videos, CDs, DVDs;

11. directory information, e.g., Chamber of Commerce Directory;

12. job announcements in print/electronic forms

4. Select the *types* of information sources you will use to research the occupation(s) and/or major(s) in your report, using *at least* **5** different *types* of 12 sources for objective 1a, and **3** different *types* of 12 sources for *each* occupation/major in 1b. Examples of 12 types of information sources are shown in the numbered items above.

5. Prepare a 6–8 page (*excluding* references, table of contents, etc.) narrative, typed, double-spaced research report using the topics described below to format your paper. Staple the pages in the upper left corner, do not use a binder, and number each page. *Each topic used will be a left margin subheading in your paper.*

6. Use proper reference citation procedures for *all* facts and data included in your paper. Except for the introduction and conclusion, all topics in the paper should have a *minimum* of one in-text reference citation. An example of the preferred American Psychological Association (APA) style for reference citation is shown below. *APA style is used in your text*–look there for examples of referencing.

7. The research paper will be evaluated using the CFA Evaluation Form shown at the end of this document, with 25 percent of the points allocated for the technical aspects of the assignment and 75 percent allocated for the substantive aspects.

8. Attach the Evaluation Form to your paper when it is turned in.

9. Both CFA options 1a and 1b should include the 3 elements listed below:

- *Title Page*, including your name, your instructor's name, title of research paper, and date;

- *Table of Contents*, including *page numbers* of each topic used in the paper; see the topic lists for options 1a and 1b in the next section below;

- *References*, including proper in-text references for those sources used in your paper *and* a reference list at the end; only sources cited in the paper should be included in the references.

Option 1a: Use a 16 Topic Format for Researching One Occupation (report on one occupation using 16 topic subheadings)

1. *Introduction*. Provide a brief, basic description of the occupation, such as typical work settings and kind of work done, etc.

2. *Typical Career Path*. Describe the typical career path for someone in this occupation from entry to the highest level position.

3. *Trends.* Describe how technology, new organizational structures, diversified training, and other management or economic trends are affecting the occupation.

4. *Salary Information.* Provide salary range information for different types of positions in this occupation; indicate differences for entry level and experienced workers, and if there are geographic differences in salary.

5. *Skills Used.* Describe the skills or abilities typically used by persons in this occupation.

6. *Employing Organizations.* Explain what kinds of organizations hire persons in this occupation; what industries are involved; are persons self-employed in this occupation?

7. *Women and Minorities.* Explain if a particular gender or ethnic group dominates employment in the occupation.

8. *Becoming Employed.* Describe how persons find employment in this occupation; are internships, volunteering, job fairs, faculty referrals, Web sites, and other means used?

9. *Typical Job Notices.* Review and describe a typical job notice in this occupation that is of personal interest to you.

10. *Work Conditions.* Describe the physical environment, stress level, type of supervision, customer/client contact, hours, work-related travel, etc.

11. *Education/Training.* Describe the majors or fields of study related to preparation for working in the occupation.

12. *Certificate/License.* Identify any licenses or certificates required in the occupation, if any; are there requirements for ongoing training; does this vary across states? what are the requirements in states where you plan to reside?

13. *Affiliations.* Specify professional or organizational memberships typically held by persons in this occupation; are the organizations international, national, regional, state, local?

14. *Outlook.* Describe the current and projected job openings in the occupation, regional influences, industry changes, etc.

15. *Lifestyle Impact.* Discuss how working in this occupation affects family roles and relationships, leisure options, vacations.

16. *Conclusion.* Write a brief summary or review of your general findings and conclusions as a result of your research.

Option 1b: Use a 6 Topic Format for Researching 3 Occupations and/or Majors (report on 3 occupations/majors using 6 topic subheadings for each)

1. *Introduction.* Provide a brief, basic description of the occupation or major field of study, such as the kind of work done or courses taken, typical settings for work or learning, typical career or educational path (e.g., entry level position, first promotion, how you enter the major, field experience required, etc.).

2. *Interests/Skills Used.* Describe the interests, skills, or abilities typically used or needed by persons in this occupation or field of study.

3. *Work or Learning Conditions.* Describe the physical environment of work or classes; stress level; type of supervision or instruction; nature of customer/client/instructor contact; hours worked in class or in study; relationships with colleagues; nature of work or learning activities, e.g., labs, research, writing, equipment used, etc.

4. *Training/Education//Licenses.* Describe the ways in which one prepares for this occupation or field of study, e.g., on-the-job training; majors or fields of study related to the occupation; courses taken in the major, including prerequisites; identify licenses or certificates required; specify organizational memberships typically held by workers or students.

5. *Outlook/Salary.* Describe the current and projected job openings in a occupation or those related to a field of study; current and future salaries; regional influences impacting outlook for the occupation or major; demand for workers or students with this training; anticipated changes in training or curriculum, etc.

6. *Conclusion.* Write a brief summary or review of your general findings and conclusions as a result of your research about **each** occupation and/or field of study.

Suggestions for Referencing

Avoid *academic dishonesty* and *plagiarism* in writing research papers for this class. Consult with your instructor if you have any questions about proper referencing of materials used in your paper.

APA Style

The preferred writing style for the CFA is found in the *Publication Manual of the American Psychological Association* (APA, 2001). This style was, in fact, developed for the preparation of manuscripts for publication in journals in the areas of social sciences and education. It presents an easy–almost shorthand–way of citing references within the CFA; long, complicated citations in the form of footnotes and endnotes are avoided. Therefore, it is also useful for academic and research projects other than this CFA.

What to Cite/Document

Your sources and how well you use them allow the reader to evaluate the quality of your research. You are, therefore, expected to document **within** your paper any and all of the following:

1. Direct quotations

2. Statistics, Tables, Figures

3. Words, ideas from sources other than yourself

4. Paraphrases and restatements of facts, ideas from sources other than yourself

If you are unsure whether or not you should acknowledge a source, document it!

How to Cite Material in the Text of the CFA

APA style simply acknowledges a source within the text of the CFA, giving the reader only enough information to find that source in the alphabetical reference list (bibliography) at the end of the document. This information usually consists of:

1. *The last name(s) of the author(s)* (if author's name unavailable, use the first words given for the document/source in reference list)

2. *Year of publication* (or interview)

3. *Page number(s)* (if available) *for all direct quotations.*

This information may be "worked-into" the words of your paper or set within parentheses. **The text uses APA style–examine it for examples of how to reference your work for this paper.** Some other examples follow in the next section. These are only intended as examples. Use the exact information from your data source in creating your reference citations.

1. *Quotations in the CFA narrative text.*

   a. all reference information is within the parentheses for a direct quote:
      "The profession of law is becoming popular among women" (Jones, 2005, p. 7).

   b. partial information within the narrative:
      In considering this phenomenon, Jones (2005) writes "the profession of law is becoming popular among women" (p. 7).

   c. long quotations (more than 40 words) in the CFA are indented block style, and double spaced (note–no quotation marks are used):
      Jones (2005) writes:
      The profession of law is becoming popular among women. For the past ten years law schools have admitted more women each year; in a few law schools, women now outnumber men. Likewise, increasing numbers of women are being admitted to the bar in every state. (pp. 7–8)

2. *Citing paraphrased material that is not a direct quote, and the author's name **is** available.*
   In citing the source of information not directly quoted from the original, cite the author(s) and year; page references are not necessary.

   a. reference information is within the parentheses:
      Women are beginning to enter law in greater numbers (Jones, 2005).

   b. more than one author:
      Women are beginning to enter law in greater numbers (Smith & Smith, 2005).

   c. Reference information is out of the parentheses:
      Jones (2005) tells us that women are entering law in greater numbers.
      or
      In 2005, Jones found more women were entering law.

   d. more than one source says the same thing:
      Women are beginning to enter law in greater numbers (Jones, 2005; Smith & Smith, 2005).

3. *Author's name **is not** available.*
   When an author's name is not available, you simply use in the text narrative the first word or words found in the alphabetical reference list so that the reader can locate the full reference. This could also be used with references from the *Occupational Outlook Handbook* or computer guidance systems. If you have several sources with the same first word, make sure you use enough of the title to distinguish one source from other sources with the same first word in the title. [Note: If 2 or more sources begin with the same name or words, e.g., Biologist or Smith, use letters, e.g., a, b, c, after the date to distinguish between or among them.]

Women are beginning to enter law in greater numbers (Women, 2005b).
In the reference section at the end of the paper, list as:
Women and Law. (2005b, December). *Working Women*, pp. 43–45.

4. *Citing an Interview.*
   To cite an information interview in the text, simply enter the person's last name and the date of the interview as in no. 2 above.

How to Cite References at the End of the CFA Paper

The following are examples of specific references. They are shown in bold print. Items on the Reference list should be in *alphabetical* order, *not* in the order they appear in the paper.

1. ***Books, pamphlets, brochures (specific).***

   a. Author known, whole book:
      Stair, L., & Stair, L. (2005). *Careers in business* (5th ed.). Lincolnwood, IL: McGraw-Hill.

   b. Author unknown, whole book:
      Medical school admissions requirements, 2008–2009: United States and Canada (2007). Washington, DC: Assoc. of American Medical Colleges.

   c. Book in a numbered series (an unusual type of reference, but there are often several sources like this in a library):
      Administration, business and office (Career Information Center Series, No. 1). (2005). Encino, CA: Glencoe.

   d. Pamphlet/brochure (note: corporate author; author is publisher):
      National Association of Social Workers. (undated). The point is helping people. Washington, DC: Author.

2. ***Books reference type.***

   a. *Occupational Outlook Handbook* (referencing a specific occupation).
      Securities and financial services sales workers. (2007). *In Occupational outlook handbook* (2007–2008 ed.) (pp. 263-265). Washington, DC: U.S. Government Printing Office.

   b. *Encyclopedia of Careers* (this is a multivolume, edited work):
      . . .author of section known (Vol. I):
      Bogart, L. (2007). Chemical and drug industries. In W. E. Hopke (Ed.), *The encyclopedia of careers and vocational guidance* (14th ed.): Vol. I. Reviewing career fields (pp. 193-197). Chicago: J. G. Ferguson.

      . . .author of selection unknown (Vol. II):
      Flight Attendants. (2007). In W. E. Hopke (Ed.), *The encyclopedia of careers and vocational guidance* (14th ed.): Vol. II. Selecting a career (pp. 407-470). Chicago: J. G. Ferguson.

3. ***Periodicals (magazines, newspapers, newsletters, journals).***

   a. Magazine:
      Thompson, P. A., & Dalton, G. W. (2008, February). Balancing your expectations. *Business Week Careers*, pp. 32-35.

   b. Newspaper:
      Snelling, R. O., Sr., & Snelling, A. M. (2008, April 21). New era in marketing creates greater need for professionals. *The Atlanta Journal and Constitution*, pp. 28–30.

c. Newsletter (author unknown):
   Entrepreneurs–who are they? (2008, April). *Career Planning & Adult Development News-letter*, p. 5.

d. Journal:
   Blustein, D. L. (2005). Decision-making styles and vocational maturity: An alternative perspective. *Journal of Vocational Behavior, 30,* 61–71.

4. *Occupational Briefs/Biographies*
   Purchasing agents (Occupational Brief 167). (2007). Moravia, NY: Chronicle Guidance. Funeral director (Career Summary S-14). (2007). Largo, FL: Careers, Inc.
   Bank loan officer (Vocational Biography L, 6, 19). (2007). Saulk Center, MN: Vocational Biographies.

5. *Computer Guidance Systems*

   a. Specific occupational information:
      Pediatrician. (2007). CHOICES Planner [Computer software]. Oroville, WA: Bridges Transitions, Inc.
      Market research analyst. (2007). SIGI^3 [Computer software]. Tucson, AZ: Valpar International Corporation.
      Sales manager. (2007). e-DISCOVER [Computer software]. Ames, IA: American College Testing Program.

6. *Electronic Media*
   Electronic media change rapidly creating a need for frequently updated referencing style. Such updated information can be found at www.apastyle.org/elecref.html. However, as with other references, the goal is to credit the author and enable the reader to find the material. Electronic correspondence, i.e., E-mail messages are cited as personal (see Information Interview note below).

   a. Elements of references to on-line information
      American Dental Association. (2008). *Careers in dentistry.* [On-line]. Retrieved March 21, 2008, from http://www.ada.org/public/careers/index.asp.

7. *Others*

   a. Report:
      National Association of Colleges and Employers. (2008, March). *NACE salary survey: A study of 2006-2007 beginning offers.* Bethlehem, PA: Author.

   b. Information Interview (by you):
      H. P. Jones (personal communication, February 10, 2008)

8. *Missing Information/ strange sources.*
   Career resource libraries often attempt to provide as much information as possible about each career field. Sometimes this means that there will be "clippings" in the files with incomplete referencing information. Don't hesitate to use these if the information is pertinent; just do the best you can with the reference. Example:
   Glut of lawyers. (no date available). (Clipping found in a Career Center vertical file II B 211 "Lawyer".)

Career Field Analysis Project Evaluation Point Distribution

Instructors will use the Career Field Analysis Evaluation Form to guide their evaluation of your paper. The final evaluation of the CFA is based on an evaluation of both the Content (75 percent) and Format (25 percent) of the paper. The points assigned to the CFA by letter grade are shown in the table below. Information about the *APA Style Manual* can be found at http://www.apastyle.org/pubmanual.html.

Letter Grade	Content Points	Format Points	Total Points
A+	74-75	25	98-100
A	70-73	24	93-97
A-	68-69	23	90-92
B+	66-67	22	88-89
B	62-65	21	83-87
B-	60-61	20	80-82
C+	58-59	19	78-79
C	55-57	18	73-77
C-	53-54	17	70-72
D+	51-52	16	68-69
D	47-50	15	63-67
D-	45-46	14	60-62

References

American Psychological Association. (2001). *Publication Manual* (5th ed.). Washington, DC: Author.

Name: ———————————————— Date Due: ————————————————

CFA (Career Field Analysis) WORKSHEET

Objective 1a: One Occupation/Major Field Researched

Name of occupation/major field to be studied:————————————————

Indicate at least **5 types** of information resources to be used:

1. ————————————————————————————————

2. ————————————————————————————————

3. ————————————————————————————————

4. ————————————————————————————————

5. ————————————————————————————————

Other possible sources for information:

1. ————————————————————————————————

2. ————————————————————————————————

3. ————————————————————————————————

4. ————————————————————————————————

5. ————————————————————————————————

6. ————————————————————————————————

Name: —————————————————Date Due: —————————————————

CFA (Career Field Analysis) WORKSHEET

Objective 1b: One Occupations/Major Fields Researched

Name of **first** occupation/major field to be studied: —————————————

Indicate at least **3 types** of information resources:

1. ——————————————————————————————————

2. ——————————————————————————————————

3. ——————————————————————————————————

4. ——————————————————————————————————

Name of **second** occupation/major field to be studied: —————————————

Indicate at least **3 types** of information resources:

1. ——————————————————————————————————

2. ——————————————————————————————————

3. ——————————————————————————————————

4. ——————————————————————————————————

Name of **third** occupation/major field to be studied: —————————————

Indicate at least **3 types** of information resources:

1. ——————————————————————————————————

2. ——————————————————————————————————

3. ——————————————————————————————————

4. ——————————————————————————————————

Other possible sources for information:

——————————————————————————————————

Student Name: ————————————— Due Date: —————————————

Points: ————————————— Grade: —————————————

Career Field Analysis Evaluation Form

Technical Aspects (25%) ————————————————————————

• Table of Contents included ————————————————————

• Conclusion Section ——————————————————————————

• Reference Page ———————————————————————————

• Paper properly bound, pages numbered———————————————

• Grammar, spelling, punctuation, typos ——————————————

• On-time delivery ———————————————————————————

• Evaluation form attached ————————————————————

Substantive Aspects (75%)

• Correct number of different reference types used ————————

• Correct number of topics used ——————————————————

• All contents properly referenced —————————————————

• Depth of coverage———————————————————————

• Narrative shows integration of content ——————————————

• Quality of content (currency, appropriateness, etc.) ————————

Instructor Comments:————————————————————————

————————————————————————————————————

————————————————————————————————————

————————————————————————————————————

GUIDE TO GOOD DECISION MAKING (GGDM)

Note: The CASVE cycle (see Figure 4.2) can be used to show the steps in making a career choice

Knowing I Need to Make a Choice

Events - things that happen to me
"I need to choose a major by next semester."

Comments from my friends and relatives
"My roommate said that I'll have problems if I don't make a decision soon."

The way I feel
"I'm scared about committing myself."

Avoiding my problems
"I'll get started next week."

Physical problems
"I'm so upset about this, I can't eat."

Understanding Myself and My Options

Understanding myself, such as:
My values. My interests. My skills.

Understanding occupations, programs of study, or jobs
Understanding specific occupations, programs of study, or jobs
Understanding how specific occupations, programs of study, or jobs are organized

Understanding how I make important decisions; Understanding how I think about my decisions
Self-talk
Self-awareness
Being aware of and controlling my self-talk

Expanding and Narrowing My List of Occupations, Programs of Study, or Jobs

Identify occupations, programs of study, or jobs that fit my values, interests, and skills

Pick the 3 to 5 best occupations, programs of study, or jobs using what I learned from
"Understanding Myself and My Options"

Choosing an Occupation, Program of Study, or Job

Costs and benefits of each occupation, program of study, or job to:

Myself? My family? My cultural group? My community or society?

Rank occupations, programs of study, or jobs

Make a choice

Make back-up choice(s) in case I have a problem with my choice

Implementing My Choice

Plan—Make a plan for getting education or training

Try Out—Get work experience (full time, part-time, volunteer) and take courses or get training to test my choice

Apply—Apply for and get a job

Knowing I Made a Good Choice

Have events changed? How did my friends and relatives react to my choice? How do I feel now? Am I avoiding doing what needs to be done?

Instructions For Completing Your Individual Action Plan (IAP)

Instructions:

Breaking your decisions into small concrete steps makes the process of career choice more manageable. Your small group leader can help in developing your action plan. Refer to the sample IAP for "Jeff" on the following page to help you draft your own IAP. Complete in pencil the blank IAP form to prepare for your Instructor Conference. Follow these steps:

1. Write your name and the date at the top of the IAP Form.
2. Write down your decision-making goal in the space provided. Examples include:
   - choose a college major, or
   - get a job related to my education.
3. In the first column, list any activities that you can think of that will help you reach your goal. Examples include:
   - learn about entry requirements for physical therapists,
   - talk with professionals in my field, or
   - locate possible job openings.
4. In the second column, identify any people or information resources that you will need to complete each activity. Examples include:
   - occupational descriptions of physical therapists, or
   - identify people who can help me locate possible job openings.
5. Review the activities you have written down and then show in the third column which activities you will do first, second, third, etc. The information you get in one activity may be needed in a following activity. For example, you will need to know where job openings may be, before you can fill out a job application or send a resume and cover letter.
6. In the fourth column, write the date that you plan to complete the activity. This step makes your action plan more concrete.
7. As you complete each activity in the plan, place a check mark in the fifth column. This will give you feedback on your progress.

Adapted and reproduced by special permission of the Publisher, Psychological Assessment Resources, Inc., 16204 N. Fl. Ave., Lutz, FFL 33549, from the Career Thoughts Inventory by Sampson, Peterson, Lenz, Reardon, and Saunders, Copyright 1994, 1996 by PAR, Inc. Further reproduction is prohibited without permission from PAR, Inc.

SAMPLE INDIVIDUAL ACTION PLAN (IAP)

Name ___Jeff_____ Date __6/02/08_____

Goal ____Choose a college major where I can get good grades and then get a good job__

_____

Activities to Help Me Reach My Goal	People or Information Resources Needed	Activity Order	Date	Activity Complete (✓)
Talk with counselor	Marilyn Abbey	1	June July	
Finish workbook	CTI Workbook	2	7/2	✓
Learn how to make better decisions	Marilyn Abbey	3	July	✓
Identify possible majors	Computer Guidance System	5	7/8	✓
Identify majors	Educational Opportunities Finder	4	7/3	✓
Learn about possible majors	Dept. info in Career Library/Bulletin	7	7/10	✓
Learn about occupations	Career Guidance System & Career Library Resources	6	7/8	✓
Talk with people in occupations	Career Center Online Network	8	7/15-7/19	✓
Learn about majors— Talk with advisors	Dr. Ortez Dr. Chu	9 10	7/22 7/29	✓
Complete change of major forms	Undergraduate Studies Office	11	by 8/26	

Adapted and reproduced by special permission of the Publisher, Psychological Assessment Resources, Inc., 16204 N. Fl. Ave., Lutz, FL 33549, from the Career Thoughts Inventory by Sampson, Peterson, Lenz, Reardon, and Sounders, Copyright 1994, 1996 by PAR, Inc. Further reproduction is prohibited without permission from PAR, Inc.

Individual Action Plan (IAP)

Name _____ Date _____

Goal _____

Activities to Help me Reach my Goal	People or Information Resources Needed Complete	Activity Order	Date	Activity Complete (✓)

EXERCISE FOR IMPROVING YOUR CAREER THOUGHTS

Directions:

The following page shows an example of four negative career thoughts taken from the Career Thoughts Inventory (CTI) and corresponding new thoughts that have been reframed into more positive statements.

Examine your results on the Career Thoughts Inventory (CTI) and note the items you marked "Agree" or "Strongly Agree." Rewrite one of these items in the column marked "*Old* Career Thought." You might want to add some detail that makes it even more relevant and personal, e.g., use names of persons involved.

Examine your "old" career thought in light of each of the following questions.

1. What is the evidence for this thought? Looking objectively at all of your experience, what is the evidence that this is true?

2. Does this belief invariably or always hold true for you?

3. Does this belief look at the whole picture? Does it take into account both positive and negative ramifications?

4. Does this belief promote your well-being and/or piece of mind?

5. Did you choose this belief on your own or did it develop out of your experience of growing up in your family?

Does the old thought still make sense? Does the old thought help you make a good decision? If you **now** think the old thought does not help you engage in effective career problem solving or decision making, then rewrite the thought into a more positive statement in the column headed "*New* Career Thought."

You might find it useful to use the remaining spaces on the exercise worksheet to reframe other negative career thoughts that interfere with your effective career planning.

The Career Thoughts Inventory Workbook provides extensive materials to help you reframe many thoughts important in career problem solving and decision making. Your instructor can help you use the *CTI Workbook* if that might be a useful activity for you to pursue in the process of becoming a more effective career decision maker.

EXERCISE FOR IMPROVING YOUR
CAREER THOUGHTS WORKSHEET: AN EXAMPLE

Item No.	Old Career Thought	New Career Thought
6	The views of my parents make it harder to	I know my parents want me to be a success. I
	choose a new major.	will talk this over with them, but I need to think
		it through and make a good choice.

Item No.	Old Career Thought	New Career Thought
8	I get so worried when I have to make	It's OK to be worried about an important
	decisions that I can hardly think.	decision like this. Instead of getting stuck,
		I need to use the help available to make a
		good choice.

Item No.	Old Career Thought	New Career Thought
16	I've tried to find a good major three times	I can learn to make better choices, Thinking
	before, but I can't make good choices.	I'm a failure only keeps me stuck. Waiting
		until it's too late won't help either. Help is
		available.

Item No.	Old Career Thought	New Career Thought
19	If I change my major again, I will feel like a	I can change my mind if I make my choice on
	failure again.	good information. I've made some bad choices,
		but I'm NOT a bad person!

Adapted and reproduced by special permission of the Publisher, Psychological Assessment Resources, Inc., 16204 N. Fl. Ave., Lutz, FL 33549, from the Career Thoughts Inventory by Sampson, Peterson, Lenz, Reardon, and Saunders, Copyright 1994, 1996 by PAR, Inc. Futher reproduction is prohibited without permission from PAR, Inc.

EXERCISE FOR IMPROVING
YOUR CAREER THOUGHTS WORKSHEET

Item No.	*Old* Career Thought	*New* Career Thought

Item No.	*Old* Career Thought	*New* Career Thought

Item No.	*Old* Career Thought	*New* Career Thought

Item No.	*Old* Career Thought	*New* Career Thought

Adapted and reproduced by special permission of the Publisher, Psychological Assessment Resources, Inc., 16204 N. Fl. Ave., Lutz, FL 33549, from the Career Thoughts Inventory by Sampson, Peterson, Lenz, Reardon, and Saunders, Copyright 1994, 1996 by PAR, Inc. Futher reproduction is prohibited without permission from PAR, Inc.

INFORMATION INTERVIEWS ASSIGNMENT

Directions:

This assignment involves conducting two (2) information interviews with persons who have special knowledge that can help you in your educational and career planning. Review the section on Information Interviews in Chapter 13 and the notes below before beginning this assignment.

Some organizations have policies that limit staff participation in information interviews. You may find it helpful in gaining access to interviewees if you mention that this is part of a class assignment. Some tips for arranging and conducting information interviews include:

- Use friends, family, former employers, and career center staff to identify contacts

- Research the career field or industry where your contacts are employed

- Prepare a list of questions (use the sample questions in Chapter 13 as a starting point)

- Make arrangements by phone or e-mail for a time to interview the person

- Dress appropriately and be respectful of the person's time

- Ask the person for names of additional people who might be good information interview contacts

- Follow-up with a thank-you note, and if appropriate, a cover letter and a copy of your resume

- Think about how the information gained can be used to shape and improve your PCT

Many employers view information interviews as a professional contact. Some well-prepared students have been sufficiently impressive in information interviews that interviewees have invited them to submit applications later for internships or jobs. You are encouraged to think about this activity as more than simply a class assignment.

In completing this assignment for the class, prepare a brief typed report for *each* interview that includes the following information:

1. Name of interviewee

2. Position title

3. Type of employing organization

4. Date of interview

5. Brief summary of interview content (1 paragraph)

6. Your personal reactions to the interview (1 paragraph; e.g., What new information did you obtain? Were you surprised by anything you heard or saw?)

STRATEGIC ACADEMIC/ CAREER PLANNING PROJECT

Directions:

This project is the culminating activity of the course. It is designed to help you pull together all that you learned in the course. You should use *all* of the papers and reports you have produced to prepare this paper. Think of this project as the "open-book, take-home, cumulative final exam" for the course. There are 100 possible points available for this project.

Specific Requirements:

1. Use the stages of the CASVE cycle (see following pages) as section headings to structure your paper. You may also choose to use additional subheadings if you feel they would make your presentation clearer. Use the questions in each section to stimulate your discussion. Read the material in each of the six sections below before you begin to write and refer to them again while preparing your paper.

2. If you are still unsure of your academic and/or career plans, discuss this situation with your instructor, advisor, or counselor and specify the processes and resources you plan to use to make your academic/career decisions. Use the CASVE model.

3. This is a formal paper and should follow appropriate academic style. It should be **typed** with a **cover page** and a table of contents. If you make reference to specific sources of information, that must be properly cited and a reference list included. **Staple** the pages together in the upper left corner, DO NOT USE A BINDER OR COVER. If you adequately cover the categories outlined, your paper will be at least **six typed pages**.

Summary:

Remember that the purposes of this project are to help you pull together what you have learned about yourself and the academic and career options available to you and to use that information to develop a plan for yourself. This paper should represent your highest level of academic work and career thinking. If you have any questions–or get stuck–work with your instructor.

Outline of Strategic Academic/Career Planning Project:

Cover Page
Table of Contents

Contents:

1. Communication

2. Analysis

3. Synthesis

4. Valuing

5. Execution

6. Communication

Evaluation Form

You paper and table of contents should include the following 6 sections:

1. **Communication**

   a. *What was the concern that prompted you to begin the academic/career problem-solving and decision-making process at the beginning of the class?* What was the gap between your situation at that time and the situation you wanted to be in? (Example: "I began this class not having any idea about a major beyond that it should have no additional math requirements." OR "Ever since I was a small child I wanted to be a doctor, but since taking biology and chemistry courses I know that I cannot do well enough in those courses to get into medical school. I wanted to know what careers might better suit me.").

   b. *What internal (feelings, emotions, hunches) and external (parents, the university, news reports, grades, letter saying you had to declare a major) cues did you experience that alerted you to this need to reduce the gap between your situation and the desired state ?* (Examples: "I had just begun to realize that I will graduate in the spring and really have no idea about what I will do when school is over. My dad keeps asking me about my plans and I am seeing my friends getting jobs and moving away. This made me nervous and anxious. It was time to 'get a clue.")

   c. *What did you want to learn from this class?* (Examples: "I wanted to find out about careers that I might enjoy." OR "I wanted to decide on a major."). What were your learning goals?

2. **Analysis**

   a. *What have you learned about yourself in this class that is important in making your academic and/or career decisions?* Examine your values, interests, skills, and experiences. Refer to assignments from the first part of the class (SDS, autobiography, computer printout, skills exercise, etc.) in addressing the "Analysis" topic.

   b. *What have you learned about "the world of work" that will influence your decisions?* In a broad sense, what kinds of occupations/majors seem most attractive? What types of organizations? What kind of activities? What scheme did you learn about for organizing options?

   c. *What have you learned about your decision-making processes that will relate to this?* In general, which phase or phases of the CASVE Cycle are you in? What evidence can you provide to support your thinking about this? Do findings from the CTI apply regarding decision-making confusion? Commitment anxiety? External conflict?

3. **Synthesis**

   a. *What have you done (or plan to do) to generate educational and/or occupational alternatives for yourself?* This might include getting suggestions from others, the media, and using resources in the Career Center (computers, inventories, books). *Be specific about resources and learning activities.*

   b. *Identify three to five educational and/or career alternatives that you have, are, or plan to consider.* What have you eliminated in the process of reducing this number to 3-5?

4. **Valuing**

   a. *What factors were/are/will be important to you in making this decision?* What will make this decision a good decision or a bad decision? This might include factors internal to yourself (interests, values), practical factors (you can enter the field/major from your current preparation), or factors that relate to others (my parents would pay for that major, my fiancée will be working in Denver and I want to work near her).

   b. *What are the costs and benefits of* each *alternative to yourself, your significant others, and society?* How would the effort and expense (costs) of each alternative compare to the potential benefits to yourself and others?

   c. *Based on these questions and your answers to them, prioritize (rank) the alternatives identified in your synthesis section.*

5. **Execution**

   a. *What would you need to do to implement your first choice?* Be as specific as you can; lay your plan out step-by-step (it is okay to number the steps). Who will you talk with? Where will you go? What new behavior will you undertake? What resources will you use? How will you implement your valued options? This is your strategic plan. It may involve both educational, occupational, and employment activities. It should include a time frame for accomplishing each step.

   b. *How much effort do you think it will take to implement this alternative?*

6. **Communication**

   a. *Where are you now in your educational and/or career decision making and where do you want to be in a year?* By thinking about the difference between where you are now and where you would like to be in the near or far future you can better anticipate and plan for the next decision that may have to be addressed.

   b. *How do you feel about your current academic and/or career situation?* What are your internal and/or external cues telling you about your current situation? Are you satisfied or not?

   c. *What are the next questions or issues that you will need to address?* If you are currently satisfied, what do you think might be the next issue that you will need to address ("I'm happy with my major, now it is time to find some experiences related to possible careers."). If you are not currently satisfied, what do you need to focus on now?

Note: Remember to attach the Evaluation Form on the following page to your paper.

Strategic Academic/Career Plan Project Evaluation Form

Name: ——————————————————— Due: —————————————————

Points: ——————————————————— Grade: —————————————————

Technical Aspects (25%):

On time: ————————————————————————————————

Reference page (if needed): ——————————————————————

Grammar, spelling, punctuation: ———————————————————

Readability (neatness, format): ————————————————————

Cover page, table of contents: ————————————————————

Used CASVE headings:————————————————————————

Appropriate length: ——————————————————————————

Properly bound, pages numbered: ———————————————————

Evaluation form attached:————————————————————————

Substantive Aspects (75%):

Paper demonstrates understanding of the CASVE cycle: ————————

Paper demonstrates ability to apply CASVE in student's situation: ———

Narrative highlights use of class activities/Career Center resources: ——

Narrative addresses stimulus questions: ————————————————

Narrative demonstrates integration of course content: ————————

General Comments: ——————————————————————

————————————————————————————————————

————————————————————————————————————

RESUME CRITIQUE WORKSHEET

CRITERIA	COMMENTS

1. *Heading*: Is the name, address, & phone number located at top of first page? Is name on subsequent pages? Temporary address? For how long? E-mail (optional)

2. *Objective*: Does career objective appear immediately under identification? Emphasize area in which employment is sought? Indicate general level of job they wanted? Clearly stated? Focused?

3. *Overall Appearance*: Does the resume look professional? Do you want to read it? Easy to follow? Correct spelling, grammar, & punctuation?

4. *Layout*: Do key sales points stand out? Uncluttered? Uses margins, white-space, headlines, bold type, capital letters, underlining, etc.

5. *Organization*: Is key information presented to accentuate skills, abilities, and accomplishments? Appropriate categories emphasized? Specifics stand out? Avoids unnecessary captions, strongest to weakest order? Consistent format?

---

6. *Action-oriented*: Do sentences begin with positive action verbs? Avoids introductory phrases? Results-oriented? No exaggerations or lush adjectives?

---

7. *Concise*: Uses short, clearly written phrases and paragraphs; avoids complete sentences; summary statements? Lists of accomplishments?

---

8. *Relevance*: Has extraneous material been eliminated? Focuses on specific information about experience? Provides facts? Avoids generalities?

---

9. *Controversial*: Does the resume raise more questions than it answers? Avoids mentioning controversial activities? values?

---

10. *Bottom Line*: How well does the resume present a positive picture of the applicant's qualifications for obtaining an interview?

---

11. *Additional items*:

EMPLOYMENT DECISION-MAKING CASE STUDY

A Profile of Suzy

Suzy is a 22 year old college senior who is about to graduate with her bachelor's degree from State U. She majored in psychology and minored in business management. She was raised in a small town in a rural part of the state. She chose State U. because of the school's reputation in psychology and because it is located near her home.

Suzy has shown an interest in helping people. Since her sophomore year, she has been a volunteer telephone crisis counselor. In her senior year, she interned at the local community mental health half-way house for adults who were recovering from alcohol dependency. Suzy received a great deal of satisfaction when she helped one of her clients through a difficult period. She enjoyed the opportunity to help others learn new skills. She liked the constant variety and challenge presented to her by her clients. Once she demonstrated her ability to help others she was given the freedom to work independently, which she valued. Suzy enjoyed the family atmosphere between the staff members.

During her summers, she worked as an administrative assistant to the supervisor of a small publishing company. She liked the fast pace of the business world and the excellent salary she received. Suzy hoped to find a job that would provide her the opportunity to help others, to manage the work of others, and to make a good salary that would allow her to enjoy some of the finer things in life. Suzy has been offered two positions described below. Which job should she choose?

Suzy has identified the following eight factors for consideration in her employment decision-making. How important would you rate each of these factors in Suzy's thinking, e.g., (1) Somewhat important, (2) Important, (3) Very Important?

1. Independence

2. Opportunities to help others

3. Variety

4. Advancement opportunities

5. Compatibility with employer

6. Work-related travel required

7. Closeness to home

8. Salary/Income (present)

Job Offer #1

Suzy has been offered a full-time, live-in job at the half-way house where she interned. A dorm-type room and meals are provided. Her job title: Mental Health Technician. Starting salary: $28,000 with a raise to $30,000 after one year. Tuition reimbursement and release time is available if she pursues her master's degree. She will be a member of a five-person para-professional support team. Turnover in house staff is frequent due to morale problems which stem from long hours and low pay. With hard work, Suzy could be promoted to the position of House Director within two or three years. Some of her friends and instructors in psychology have told her that this is an excellent entry-level opportunity to gain a wide range of skills and experiences in the mental health field.

Job Offer #2

Suzy has also received an offer to work as a New Employee Trainer within the Training and Development section of the Human Resources Office of a new telecommunications firm in Jacksonville. Personnel work has always sounded exciting to Suzy. She has been offered a starting salary of $38,000. She would be required to do research on how to teach others new skills, and to develop written and multimedia materials to aid in training. Her supervisor expects all decisions to be cleared by him. The job would require her to evaluate the progress of new trainees and to recommend the termination of those who failed to meet the minimum job standards. During slow periods, she would be expected to help the clerical staff with the paperwork. One of her friends works for the organization. She told Suzy that the benefits were good but there was very little turnover and the opportunities for advancement were slim. However, after two years, she would be eligible for admission to the management training program at the firm. Suzy has heard that women are being actively recruited into this program.

Criteria for Evaluating Offers

The table below has four sets of 47 factors that can be considered in evaluating job offers. Each factor can be weighted both in terms of its importance and the degree to which a job offer satisfies it. A form for evaluating offers is included at the end of this exercise.

Factors to Consider in Evaluating Job Offers

Suzy looked at these 47 factors in evaluating her job offers. Consider her self-knowledge and her knowledge about the employment options as you determine which job she should take.

1. Lifestyle

   - Flexible benefit package
   - Community size
   - Further formal education required
   - Geographic location
   - Flextime available
   - Impact on your spouse and/or child
   - Social expectations outside working hours
   - Shift work required
   - Work-related travel required
   - Closeness to home
   - Cultural and recreational opportunities

2. Nature of the Employer or Job

   - Reputation
   - Product/service offered
   - Advancement opportunities
   - Compatibility with fellow workers
   - Compatibility with supervisor
   - Organization size
   - Pleasant surroundings at work
   - Job security

- Job duties
- Job title
- Stability of the organization
- Support staff

3. Pay and Benefits

- Cost of living (taxes, housing, transportation, food)
- Education assistance
- Professional development opportunities
- Salary/income (present)
- Salary/income (potential)
- Moving expenses

4. Work Activities

- Creativity
- Independence
- Intellectual stimulation
- Opportunities to help others

- System for performance evaluation
- Type and amount of on-the-job training
- Opportunities for mentorship

- Home computer, telecommunications
- Association memberships
- Vacation
- Insurance programs
- Health club
- Child care

- Opportunities for leadership
- Prestige
- Variety
- Work in your field

EMPLOYMENT DECISION-MAKING EXERCISE

<u>Directions</u>: Write the names of Suzy's relevant job factors in the blank spaces in the left column. Write the names of potential employers at the top of the other columns.

Using the numbers below, weight how important you think each FACTOR is to Suzy ( ) in the left column below (FACTORS & weights): **1** – Somewhat Important **2** – Important **3** – Very Important	Using the numbers below, rate ( ) how well you think each EMPLOYER meets Suzy's factors in the remaining columns: **0** – Not at All **1** – Poor Match **2** – Close Match **3** – Exact Match

Multiply the weight for each factor times the rating for each employer in meeting that factor, and then total the scores for each employer in the last row below. Which job should Suzy take?

FACTORS & (weights)	EMPLOYER 1 ( )	EMPLOYER 2 ( )	EMPLOYER 3 ( )
( )	x ( ) =	x ( ) =	x ( ) =
( )	x ( ) =	x ( ) =	x ( ) =
( )	x ( ) =	x ( ) =	x ( ) =
( )	x ( ) =	x ( ) =	x ( ) =
( )	x ( ) =	x ( ) =	x ( ) =
( )	x ( ) =	x ( ) =	x ( ) =
( )	x ( ) =	x ( ) =	x ( ) =
( )	x ( ) =	x ( ) =	x ( ) =
TOTAL			

COMPUTER/WEB SITE SYSTEMS FEEDBACK FORMS

Directions: Use the two forms, Nos. 1 and 2, in this Appendix to provide evaluative comments and feedback on the computer systems used, e.g., SIGI^3, eDiscover, Choices Planner, or Web sites used to obtain information in the self-knowledge and options knowledge domains related to your Personal Career Theory.

COMPUTER/WEB SITE SYSTEM FEEDBACK FORM <u>No. 1</u>

NAME: —————————————————— DATE: ——————————————————

SYSTEM USED: ————————————— DATE(S) USED: —————————————

How useful/helpful did you find this system?

What did you like about this system?

What did you dislike?

What occupations/career fields were suggested which you would like to investigate further?

Are the system's suggestions consistent with your own ideas about yourself and occupations? Why/why not?

What is the most important thing you learned from using this system?

COMPUTER/WEB SITE SYSTEM FEEDBACK FORM <u>No. 2</u>

NAME: ——————————————— DATE: ———————————————

SYSTEM USED: ————————— DATE(S) USED: ——————————

How useful/helpful did you find this system?

What did you like about this system?

What did you dislike?

What occupations/career fields were suggested which you would like to investigate further?

Are the system's suggestions consistent with your own ideas about yourself and occupations? Why/why not?

What is the most important thing you learned from using this system?

Name Index

SUBJECT INDEX